HANDBOOK OF
DENOMINATIONS

HANDBOOK OF
DENOMINATIONS

IN THE UNITED STATES

New Sixth Edition

Frank S. Mead

Abingdon Press

NASHVILLE • NEW YORK

Library of Congress Cataloging in Publication Data

Mead, Frank Spencer, 1898–
  Handbook of denominations in the United States.
  Bibliography: p.
  Includes index.
  1. Sects—United States. I. Title.
BR516.5.M38 1975   200′.973   75-2363

ISBN 0-687-16569-5

MANUFACTURED BY THE PARTHENON PRESS AT
NASHVILLE, TENNESSEE, UNITED STATES OF AMERICA

TO THOSE

... bishops and brethren, prelates and patriarchs, and plain people, moderators, clerks (stated and without state), superintendents, overseers, secretaries (general, corresponding, recording, executive, and board), statisticians, correspondents, historians, editors (in-chief, associate, and managing), canons, elders, chairmen and vice-chairmen of this or that, directors of public relations and offices of information, guardians of records in farm kitchens on RFD 1 and on Riverside Drive

... critics, lay and clerical, official or just interested, caustic and charitable, who read previous editions and suggested changes in this one

... who accepted our plea to distinguish between plain truth and propaganda and who were content to give us the facts and leave the writing to us

We gratefully dedicate
this book
on its 20th birthday

CONTENTS

CONTENTS

CONTENTS

ADVENTISTS

Adventism in general is a Christian faith based upon the conviction that the second advent of Christ is the sole hope of the world. It holds that man's nature is fallen because of sin and that on the basis of neglect or rejection of God's plan of salvation those rebellious against the government of God will be ultimately destroyed, while believers, by God's grace, will be saved. After this cataclysmic event Jesus Christ will reign in triumph through the thousand-year period, or millennium, of Rev. 20:1-6. The whole Adventist thesis rests heavily upon the prophetic and apocalyptic texts of Daniel and Revelation.

As a religious movement it began with a widespread "awakening" on the question of the advent, which developed spontaneously in the Old World and in the New in the early decades of the nineteenth century. It became strongest and most clearly defined in the United States, at first under the leadership of William Miller (1782-1849) of Low Hampton, New York, a veteran of the War of 1812 and a man respected as a diligent student of the Bible even though he did not have formal college or seminary training.

The movement under Miller was at first an interchurch (or more accurately, *intra*church) development, with many Methodists, Christians, Baptists, Presbyterians, and Congregationalists among its adherents. It was thus a movement within the existing churches, and in the days of its beginnings there was no intention or attempt to organize a separate denomination.

So influential was William Miller that for years his followers were known as Millerites. Miller himself became a Baptist in 1816. He began at once a careful study of the Scriptures, concentrating on the prophecies of Daniel and Revelation. Using only the Bible, its marginal references, and Cruden's *Concordance* as his sources, he came to the conclusion that many Old and New World biblical scholars had already reached—namely, that the symbolic "day" of Bible prophecy represents a year. He also concluded that the 2,300 "days" of Dan. 8:14 started concurrently with the 70 weeks of years of Dan. 9, or from 457 B.C., the year of the command to rebuild and restore Jerusalem; and he believed that the longer of the two periods would end in or about the year 1843 as calculated by Jewish reckoning. Miller thought that the "sanctuary" mentioned in Dan. 8:14 was the earth (or the church) which would be cleansed by fire at the second advent. He came to believe that this cleansing would occur sometime between March 21, 1843 and March 21, 1844.

When the advent expectation failed to materialize by the spring of 1844, many left the movement. Miller's associates, on the basis of meticulous study of Old Testament types, set a second date, October 22, 1844, as the great antitypical Day of Atonement, confident that the "day of the Lord is near, even at the door." By 1844 there were between fifty thousand and one hundred thousand Adventists in North America. Many disposed of their property as the day of expectation approached, gave away their goods, settled all their accounts, and waited prayerfully for the Lord to come. October 22 came and passed with no second coming. Now vast numbers lost all interest in Adventism and went back to their former churches or abandoned the Christian faith altogether.

Those who continued as Adventists formed several smaller bodies. At first a loosely-knit Adventist organization came into being at a conference in Albany, New York, in 1845. This group held generally to Miller's positions and theology, emphasizing the personal and premillennial character of the second advent of Christ, the resurrection of the dead—the faithful to be raised at Christ's coming, the rest a thousand years later—and the renewal of the earth as the eternal abode of the redeemed. Known at first as the American Millennial Association, a portion of them later came to be called Evangelical Adventists, a church which has dwindled with the passing of the years to the point of obscurity. Another and larger group in 1861 became known as the Advent Christian Church.

While the general expectation of the advent had united the disparate groups, the disappointment brought all differences to light again. Nearly all Adventists were, at first, agreed that the second advent of Christ will be premillennial—that is, that his return will *precede* the thousand-year period foretold in Rev. 20. Today, however, many of them, including the Advent Christian group, hold the amillennial position.

In other areas there was wide difference of viewpoint also. Just what is the state of the dead—conscious or unconscious—as they await the resurrection? Who are to arise—the righteous *and* the wicked or only the righteous? Is there to be eternal punishment for the wicked or ultimate annihilation? What is the nature of immortality? Does the cleansing of the sanctuary of Dan. 8 refer to a sanctuary in heaven or on earth? When should the sabbath be celebrated—on the first day or on the seventh, on Sunday or on Saturday? Over these questions the Adventists, as organized bodies, became divided into the four major groups in which we find them today.

18

Seventh-day Adventists

By far the largest single Adventist body in point of numbers, both in the United States and particularly throughout the world, is the Seventh-day Adventist Church, which traces its beginnings back to the 1840s. It traces its convictions on the Sabbath back to the earlier Seventh Day Baptists of New England and the Old World.

The first major point of disagreement between Seventh-day Adventists and the other Adventist groups was not over the Sabbath question, but the question of the "sanctuary" in Dan. 8:14 and the interpretation of that passage. A small group of Adventists became convinced that the sanctuary was in heaven and not on earth and that there would be work of "investigative judgment" in the heavenly sanctuary prior to the second advent. Other Adventist bodies of the period still held that the sanctuary was on earth.

Coupled with this divergence came another, concerning the time of the second advent. The Seventh-day group claimed that the historical and prophetic evidence pointing to October 22, 1844, was correct, but that the error lay in a mistaken interpretation of Dan. 8:13-14—that Christ was not at that time to come out of, but was to *enter into*, the Most Holy Place in heaven to complete the second phase of his high priestly ministry before coming to this earth. The group holding these views also came to advocate the observance of the seventh day.

As early as 1844 a small group of these Adventists near Washington, New Hampshire, had begun observing the Sabbath on the seventh day. A pamphlet written by Joseph Bates in 1846 gave the question wide publicity and created great interest. Shortly after this, Bates, together with James White, Ellen Harmon (later Mrs. James White, whose writings Seventh-day Adventists hold "in highest esteem . . . [they] accept them as inspired counsels from the Lord"), Hiram Edson, Frederick Wheeler, and S. W. Rhodes, set out with the aid of regular publications to champion the seventh-day Sabbath, along with the imminence of the advent. Hence their name—Seventh-day Adventists.

The growth of the group around these leaders was slow at first, owing to the general derision in which Adventists were held and to their economic limitations and social handicaps. By 1855, however, they were prosperous and numerically strong enough to set up headquarters at Battle Creek, Michigan, with a publishing house called the Review and Herald Publishing Association. In 1860 they officially adopted the name Seventh-day Adventists, and in 1903 they moved their headquarters to its present location in Washington, D. C.

Doctrinally the Seventh-day Adventists are evangelical conservatives with a sound Protestant recognition of the authoritative nature of God's revelation of himself through the inspired writings encompassed in the entire Bible. Their standard statement of belief, ap-

19

pearing annually in their *Yearbook*, reveals that they believe in the transcendent, personal, communicating God as revealed in the Father, the Son, and the Holy Spirit, each equally and uniquely divine, personal, and eternal. They believe in creation by divine fiat and recognize the fall of man. Man is by nature mortal, but may receive immortality through divine grace and the redemption offered through the total atoning work of Jesus Christ.

They hold the Ten Commandments to be a transcript of the character of God, as exemplified in the life of Jesus Christ, and thus the standard of righteousness for men of all ages. They base their observance of the seventh day as the Sabbath on the fourth commandment —"Six days shalt thou labour, . . . But the seventh day is the sabbath of the Lord thy God." The tithing of incomes provides the entire support of the ministry of the church. Beyond the tithe they give generously toward missions, local church expenses, and other church enterprises. In 1971 their total per capita giving was $420.51 in North America and $117.73 in the world field.

They believe in the gift of prophecy in the church; that the dead awaiting the resurrection are in an unconscious state; that the whole person will be resurrected in the last day with immortality for the righteous and destruction by fire for the wicked. They seek religious liberty for all and advocate the complete separation of church and state. They consider the body of man to be the temple of the Holy Spirit and, in consequence, rigidly abstain from the use of alcoholic beverages, tobacco, and the promiscuous use of drugs. Likewise, they advocate sound principles of healthful living through diet, exercise, and helpful outlook. They believe in the premillennial, personal, visible return of Christ "at a time unknown but close at hand" and in a new earth to be created out of the ruins of the old as the final abode of the redeemed. They practice immersion as the biblical form of baptism and foot washing as a preparatory service for Communion.

The overall administrative body of the church is the executive committee of their General Conference, which is chosen by delegates from the various church groups in the quadrennial sessions of the General Conference of Seventh-day Adventists. Working under this General Conference are three lesser governmental units: (1) the 12 "division" organizations, administering church affairs in different continents; (2) 76 "union conferences" making up the divisional organizations; and (3) 371 "local conferences" or missions, the smallest administrative units.

Each unit has a large amount of autonomy. Local congregations elect lay elders, deacons, and other officers; the local conference office supervises all local pastoral and evangelistic work and pays all pastors and other workers in its territory from a central fund. Theirs is a highly representative form of government.

Evangelism, publishing, educational, health and welfare work are outstanding and highly successful among Seventh-day Adventists.

20

Regarding themselves not as just another church, but as a movement established in the fulfillment of Bible prophecy to prepare mankind for the second advent and to revive and restore neglected truths of the Reformation and of the Apostolic church, they carry forward their work in 557 languages and dialects—167 with publications and 390 orally. They have 48 publishing houses distributed over the world, with 5 in the United States.

In North America they have 10 liberal arts colleges, 2 universities, a theological seminary, and medical, dental, and physical therapy schools. In the United States and abroad they support 341 medical units and 37 nurses' training schools, 452 colleges and secondary schools, 3,934 elementary schools. Their welfare work operates from 1,422 metropolitan centers. There are 4,181 weekly radiobroadcasts in 55 languages—2,527 in North America and 1,654 abroad; 10,449,898 students are enrolled in Bible correspondence schools. An international broadcast, "The Voice of Prophecy," goes out over 2,156 stations in 91 countries. "Faith for Today," a weekly TV program, is viewed on 311 outlets, and "It Is Written" is seen on 114 outlets weekly.

Inasmuch as they practice adult (age of accountability) baptism, no infants or small children are reported in their membership, which is listed at 2,145,061 in 16,726 churches, and it is limited to those who uphold their church standards, including abstention from liquor and tobacco. There are 454,096 Seventh-day Adventists in the United States and Canada, organized into 3,423 churches, as of 1971.

Advent Christian Church

While William Miller was never active in the founding of the Advent Christian Church, which later became the Advent Christian General Conference of Advent Christian Churches, and finally the Advent Christian Church, his teachings concerning the imminent return of Christ were strongly influential. More important were the teachings, concerning the nature and mortality of man, of such men as Professor Charles F. Hudson and George Storrs. Dissatisfied with what they felt was a purely Platonic doctrine of the immortality of the human soul, they rejected it completely and sought a more biblical emphasis, preaching a new doctrine of "conditional immortality," which declared the unconscious state of all the dead until the resurrection at Christ's return, the establishment of a divine tribunal for the determination of rewards and punishments, the ultimate extinction of all evil, and the inauguration of the everlasting kingdom of God upon this earth as a restored paradise.

The first Advent Christian Association was established at Salem, Massachusetts, in 1860, and its members—still Adventists, though cut off in their new doctrine from other Adventist churches—publicly disclaimed any intent to form a separate denominational group. They founded two colleges—Aurora College at Aurora, Illinois, and the Boston Bible School (now Berkshire Christian College at Lenox, Masssachusetts). Missionary work began in 1891; today there are mission stations in Mexico, Malaysia, Japan, India, and the Philippines. The church maintains 2 homes for the aged, an orphanage, and a publishing department, which issues 7 denominational periodicals.

Congregational in polity, 30,713 members in 402 local churches are grouped in 5 regional districts of the United States and Canada. These conferences, together with various institutions and cooperating societies, are associated under the Advent Christian General Conference of America, which meets in biennial session. The only creedal statement is a declaration of principles adopted by the General Conference of 1900, with revisions in 1934 and 1964. Two sacraments are observed —baptism by immersion and the Lord's Supper. Worship is held on the first day of the week.

In 1964, this church merged with the Life and Advent Union, an Adventist group with 3 churches and 300 members, organized by John T. Walsh in 1848.

Church of God (General Conference)

This church is the outgrowth of several independent local groups of similar faith; some of them were in existence as early as 1800, and others date their beginnings with the arrival of British immigrants in this country around 1847. Many of them organized originally under the name of Church of God in Christ Jesus. The corporate name, today, is the Church of God General Conference, Oregon, Ill.

State and district conferences of these groups were formed as an expression of mutual cooperation. A national organization, instituted at Philadelphia in 1888, met again in 1889; however, because of strong convictions on questions of congregational rights and authority, it ceased to function until 1921, when the present general conference was formed at Waterloo, Iowa.

The Bible is accepted here as the supreme standard of faith. Adventist in viewpoint, the second (premillennial) coming of Christ is strongly emphasized. The church teaches that the kingdom of God will be literal, beginning at Jerusalem at the time of the return of Christ and extending to all nations. It believes in the restoration of Israel, the times of restitution, the mortality of man (a sleep in death until the resurrection), the literal resurrection of the dead, the reward of the righteous on earth, and the complete destruction of the wicked in second death. Membership is dependent upon acceptance of doctrinal faith, repentance, and baptism (for the remission of sins) by immersion.

Delegates from each church meet each year to determine church plans and policies and to elect officers who serve as a board of directors. A general conference operates Oregon Bible College for the training of ministers; the printing and publishing of church literature; the Berean Youth Fellowship; the Department of Missions; and the Sunday School Department. The work of the general conference is carried on under the direction of the board of directors, which meets as necessary throughout the year. The executive officer is an executive secretary who administers the work as a whole. The conference is incorporated as the Church of God, General Conference. Because of the congregational nature of the church's government the general conference exists primarily as a means of mutual cooperation and for the development of yearly projects and enterprises. There are 7,500 members in 121 churches, divided into 10 state and district conferences. The church periodical, *The Restitution Herald*, is published monthly. Mission stations are located in India, Mexico, and the Philippine Islands, Lebanon, Nigeria, and Ghana.

Primitive Advent Christian Church

This is a splinter group from the Advent Christian Church, with 578 members in 10 churches, all of them in West Virginia. As the name implies, it represents an attempt to reemphasize the principles and teachings of earliest Adventism. The groups holds a strong pacifist position.

THE AFRICAN ORTHODOX CHURCH

Believing that Negro Episcopalians should have churches of their own, a Protestant Episcopal rector, the Rev. George Alexander Mc-Guire, withdrew from that church in 1919 to establish independent Negro churches in the United States, Cuba, and Canada. He called them Independent Episcopal churches, but in 1921 the first general synod of the new body changed the name to The African Orthodox Church and elected McGuire as its first bishop. He was consecrated by Archbishop Vilatte, who took his episcopal orders from the West Syrian Church of Antioch; this put McGuire in the traditional apostolic succession, which he valued highly.

The church lays strong emphasis upon the apostolic succession and upon the historic sacraments and rituals. It has the original 7 sacraments of the Roman Catholic Church; its worship is a blending of Western and Eastern liturgy, creeds, and symbols. The liturgy is usually Western, a mingling of Anglican, Greek, and Roman patterns. Three creeds—Apostles', Nicene, and Athanasian—are used.

The denomination maintains the position that no priest may remarry the guilty party to a divorce, and innocent parties are remarried only after special permission by a bishop. The government is of course episcopal; bishops are in charge of dioceses or jurisdictions, and groups of dioceses form a province, each led by an archbishop and a primate, who in turn presides over the provincial synod. At the head stands a primate archbishop metropolitan, who is general overseer of all the work of the church, which now extends over the United States, Canada, Latin America, and the Union of South Africa. Membership, as in the Roman Catholic Church, is counted not by communicants but by the number of persons baptized; in the United States there were 24 churches and 6,000 members in 1957.

AMANA CHURCH SOCIETY

Officially named the Amana Church Society (which from the Aramaic means "to remain faithful"), this group stems from the Pietistic movement in early eighteenth-century Germany. In 1714 a small company under the leadership of Johann Friedrich Rock and Eberhardt Ludwig Gruber stirred the German people with their preaching that the days of true and direct inspiration from God had not ended. Both these leaders and others had the divine gift of inspiration. They established new churches in the Province of Hessen, Germany, but were persecuted until 1842, when they came to America, settling near Buffalo, New York. There were approximately 800 of them, and they organized a Christian communal group called the Ebenezer Society.

All property was held and shared collectively; each person did the work for which he was fitted and shared equally in the rewards. Each of the six Ebenezer villages had a common school, meetinghouse, and store, and they farmed the land round and about them which had been purchased through an American land syndicate, which had purchased the area from the Seneca Indians. In 1854 and subsequently they removed to Iowa, where the villages of Amana, (East, South, Middle, High, West,) and Homestead were established. Here they became incorporated under the laws of Iowa as a nonprofit, religious corporation, taking the name "Amana Society."

In 1932 many communal practices were abandoned, and the Amana business society with its own board of directors and the Amana Church Society with a separate board of 13 trustees were organized, the Amana Church Society remaining nonprofit and the Amana business society operating under a cooperative plan as a pecuniary corporation. The business society conducts 28 different businesses and farms 25,000 acres of land, with stockholders voting for the directors in that $10,000,000 corporation.

The Amana Church Society is still pacifistic in its views, and the traditional garb for church going is still used by the women. People who work for the Amana business society on the other hand are paid salaries and/or wages.

24

The purpose of the Amana Church Society is purely religious; it is based upon the salvation of souls in the service of God. They believe that God can now, as well as of old, inspire men, but none have been inspired since the old historic leaders and the two early American leaders, Christian Metz and Barbara Landmann, died in the latter part of the nineteenth century. The Amana Church Society accepts the teachings of a holy universal church, the remission of sins, the communion of saints, the resurrection of the body, the punishment of the wicked, and life everlasting. It acknowledges baptism by fire and the Holy Spirit. Young members are confirmed and admitted to the church at age 18; the children attend both church-sponsored Sunday schools and the public schools regulated by the State Department of Public Instruction of Iowa. There is no ordained ministry in the church; the services consist of hymn singing, prayer, readings from the testimonies of Rock, Gruber, Metz, and Landmann, and sermons preached by the elders. The church is separated from the temporal affairs of the community but is still a dominant influence. There are four village German congregations (serving all seven villages) and one English service is conducted for all seven villages. There are 735 members in 7 churches.

AMERICAN ETHICAL UNION

The Ethical Movement in the United States builds its thought and program upon moral philosophy and the ethical traditions of the great religions of mankind; its main emphasis is upon ethics, rather than upon creed or ceremony; members include both theists and non-theists. A statement of principles declares that

the search for ethical values and their progressive realization are inherently a religious enterprise. . . . All human beings, however different in their abilities or backgrounds, have an equal right to such fulfillment as encourages the fulfillment of their fellowmen. Such a goal requires diversity in beliefs and practices, and therefore freedom of conscience, thought, and expression. . . . Our attitude toward that which is beyond present knowledge, including questions about cosmic matters, is one of free and cooperative exploration, and respect for individual experience.

Stress is laid upon the development of conscience and a sense of responsibility as great creative forces among men.

There are 25 active Ethical Culture societies in the Ethical Union, the first of which was founded by Felix Adler in 1876. The Union is a founding member of the International Humanist and Ethical Union with organizations in some 30 countries around the world. Meetings of the societies feature inspirational music, meditation, readings from scripture or other inspired poetry or prose, and an address upon some social, political, philosophic, religious, or ethical subject. Ethical Culture leaders serve as counselors, officiate at weddings and funerals, name children, and perform in general the functions of the minister. There are Sunday schools, young people's groups, and study groups; very effective work is done in educational, philanthropic, and social efforts and projects. The New York Society must be given credit for the starting of settlement work in the cities of this country; at the present time societies in New York, Chicago, and Philadelphia sponsor such programs. Free kindergartens, visiting nurses, the Child Study Movement, the abolition of child labor and capital punishment, model tenements, the inauguration of free public legal aid societies, civil liberties, and interracial adoption practices— all constitute Ethical Culture drives.

Outstanding Ethical Culture schools have been developed at Central Park and Riverdale in New York City, and in Brooklyn, attracting many who are not otherwise identified with the movement. There are approximately 5,000 members.

AMERICAN EVANGELICAL CHRISTIAN CHURCHES

Launched in 1944, and first incorporated in Illinois, the A.E.C.C. is described as "an ecclesiastical body or denomination of interdoctrinal character." It seeks to compromise the difference between Calvinistic and Arminian beliefs. Local churches established under its charter are known as American Evangelical Churches and often as American Bible Churches or simply as Community Churches. Each church is sovereign in its management, but is obliged to cooperate with the national headquarters if it is to retain membership in the body.

Ministerial applicants must subscribe to seven articles of faith: (1) the Bible as the written Word of God; (2) the Virgin Birth; (3) the deity of Jesus Christ; (4) salvation through the atonement of Christ; (5) the guidance of life through prayer; (6) the return of Christ; (7) the establishment of the kingdom of God on earth. Upon completion of training, ministerial students are granted licenses enabling them to perform all the functions and offices of the ministry with the exception of officiating in marriages. Full ordination is withheld until the licentiate has become pastor of a regular congregation, or is engaged in full-time evangelistic or missionary work.

All ordinations must be performed under the supervision of either regional or national officers; five regional offices in the United States and one in Canada supervise the work of the organization. A training school and missionary home are operated in Pineland, Florida, and an American Bible School in Chicago specializes in home study

26

courses. There are 35 churches operating in the British Isles.

The present ministerial membership is reported at 500, of whom about fifty percent are engaged as full-time pastors. No further statistics are available.

AMERICAN MINISTERIAL ASSOCIATION

This association was organized in 1929 by a small group of independent ministers seeking fellowship and conferences in the ministry. The alliance was first known as the American Conference of Undenominational Ministers. It was reorganized in 1944, and the name was changed to the American Ministerial Association. Incorporated in several states, it gives churches and ministers standing equivalent to that of a denomination. Men and women are admitted to the ministry and are ordained on the approval of national headquarters. The membership represents all parts of the United States and Canada and some foreign fields, showing a continual increase.

The association is unique in the fact that it is not a branch of, or a split from, any denomination, but rather a coming together of members from many denominations. It is described as

not a "come out" movement, but a "coming together" movement, recognizing all members of the One True Church, the Body of Christ; the membership is embracive, not exclusive; its ministry is not restricted by tradition, knowing that dogmas and creeds have held sway for centuries, but that truth is a divine revelation.

The association prefers to be known not as a denomination but rather as an evangelistic and missionary movement; yet it has a familiar denominational organization with home and foreign mission boards, a department of education, and a publishing commission.

Dr. Grant T. Billett heads the group as president, and a limited ecclesiastical authority is vested in the national headquarters office, which guides the associational work in business, education, and benevolence. Its main work lies in the establishing of independent, nonsectarian local churches and missions. Regional offices are maintained throughout the United States and Canada, and the ministers meet for mutual consultations and inspiration in conferences. A college and seminary are maintained at Springfield, Illinois.

Doctrine and teaching here might be described as middle-of-the-road, embracing the customary Christian position, "yet allowing its ministers to live the religious life unhampered by creedal obligations." The cosmopolitan complexion of its ministers and membership, including as it does representatives of many different schools of religious thought, would naturally produce such an emphasis. Approximately 550 ministers are in affiliation with this body. Statistical records on membership of the associated churches are unavailable because of the autonomous nature of the local churches.

AMERICAN RESCUE WORKERS

Incoporated in 1896 and with a name amended to the organizational charter in 1913, the American Rescue Workers engage in a typical rescue mission work in offering emergency aid (lodgings, clothing, food), half-way houses and rehabilitation centers for alcoholics and drug addicts, workshops and industrial programs for the socially and physically handicapped, and evangelism, yet have the status of a full-fledged nonsectarian church. The rites of baptism and Communion are administered by the officers and ministers in charge of local corps, and regular church and Sunday schools services are held in their chapels and mission halls. Ministers are ordained at annual councils.

Their articles of religion include subscription to the Trinity, the inspiration of the Scriptures and their use as the divine rule of faith and practice, the fall of man, redemption through the atoning sacrifice of Christ, restoration through repentance and belief in Christ, regeneration through the work of the Holy Spirit, and the immortality of the soul.

Government is by a board of managers elected by the members of the corporation. Organization is on a military pattern, with William H. Schafer as commander in chief and with territorial commanders in charge. A periodical, *The Rescue Herald,* is published in Philadelphia. There are 2,500 members in 25 churches.

ANGLICAN ORTHODOX CHURCH

Rev. James Parker Dees resigned in 1963 from the priesthood of the Protestant Episcopal Church in protest to what he believed to be "its failure to proclaim firmly the Biblical doctrine, and on account of its emphasis on the social gospel and pro-communist program." With a group of former members of the Episcopal Church, he organized the Anglican Orthodox Church to preserve the traditional tenets of Anglicanism—belief in the fundamental (King James) Bible truths and morality, the (1928) Book of Common Prayer, the thirty-nine Articles of Religion, the Homilies, the doctrines of the Anglican Reformers and the basic Anglican traditions and church government. Dr. Dees was consecrated bishop by Bishop Wasyl Sawyna of the

Holy Ukranian Autocephalic Orthodox Church and by Bishop Orlando J. Woodward of the Old Catholic succession.

The fundamentalist doctrines of the Virgin birth, the atoning sacrifice of the Cross, the Trinity, the Resurrection, the Second Coming, salvation by faith alone, and the divinity of Christ are emphasized. There are 2,630 members in 37 established churches and 5 missions in the United States and missionary congregations in Canada, Europe, and Asia. The ministers of the Church are trained at Cranmer Seminary, in Statesville, North Carolina.

APOSTOLIC CHRISTIAN CHURCH
(Nazarean)

The Apostolic Christian Church (Nazarean) began in this country with the arrival of a Swiss, S. H. Froelich, about the year 1850. Froelich went to work immediately among Swiss and German immigrants, founding a number of small churches among those nationalities in the Midwest.

The theology here is conservative; the Church consists of members who have been converted to Christ, reborn, and baptized, and who strive for sanctification, "and of such friends of the truth who sincerely and earnestly strive to attain adoption to sonship in Christ." They are required to live "according to the Gospel of Christ, subject to the authorities, strive to be at peace with their fellow men, and fulfil their obligations as good citizens." They do, however, refuse to take up arms, since this denies the biblical command to love one's enemies; they will engage in noncombatant service, but they will not kill.

The local churches are independent in polity but united in loose, fundamental organization. Each church is served by elders who are also authorized to baptize, lay on hands, serve the Lord's Supper, and conduct meetings for the exercising of church discipline.

Nearly half the membership is found in Illinois and Ohio; small bodies are located in nearly all the northern states from New England to the West Coast and Canada. With 54 churches and 3,771 members, there are missionaries in Brazil, Argentina, and Guinea. There is also a nonprofit service organization at work, known as the Apostolic Christian Church Foundation.

APOSTOLIC CHRISTIAN CHURCH
OF AMERICA

The Apostolic Christian Church of America began with the labors of Benedict Weyeneth, a Swiss who came to America about 1847 and organized a number of Swiss-German churches. Its doctrine is based largely on the teaching of entire sanctification, aiming "solely at the saving of souls, a change of heart through regeneration, and a life of godliness guided and directed by the Holy Spirit." Members are noted for their pacifism, but will engage in any service in support of the government "which is compatible with the teachings of Christ and the Apostles." Willful disobedience of church doctrine is punished by expulsion, but membership can be restored. There are no educational institutions and the ministers are not paid, nor are they expected to study or prepare their sermons but to depend entirely upon the inspiration and revelation of the Holy Spirit. There are more than 10,000 members and 78 congregations, 4 in Japan, 1 in Canada.

APOSTOLIC FAITH

Organized in Portland, Oregon, in 1907, by Rev. Mrs. Florence L. Crawford "not to promote any new doctrine but rather to reestablish, maintain, and teach all the doctrines as taught by Christ and by his Apostles in the days of the early church," the Apostolic Faith is "Trinitarian, Fundamental and Evangelistic." Arminian in theology, it presents the usual doctrines of fundamentalism, stressing especially justification by faith (as taught by Luther), entire sanctification (as taught by Wesley), and the Baptism of the Holy Ghost, as evidenced at Pentecost. There are 43 churches and 5,000 members in the United States (mostly in the South and West), and churches abroad.

Shunning "the swelling of numbers," there are baptismal records but no membership reports; a "born again" experience and subscription to the doctrines of the group are required for membership. It is "a church without a collection plate" (no offering is taken during services); worldly amusements (dancing, theater, card playing, drinking, smoking) are banned; women may not use facial makeup nor bob their hair, and both men and women are required to dress conservatively. There is no marriage with unbelievers.

Governing bodies consist of a board of 5 trustees, of which the general overseer of the denomination is chairman, and a board of 24 elders. It was incorporated as "the Apostolic Faith Mission of Portland, Oregon, U.S.A." A headquarters church, a tabernacle, and a publishing house, circulating evangelical literature in more than 70 languages and dialects, are also located in Portland.

APOSTOLIC OVERCOMING HOLY CHURCH OF GOD

Bishop W. T. Phillips, founder and senior officer of this church and a former member of The Methodist Church, became deeply concerned with the teaching of the doctrine of holiness and in 1916, after four years of study and preaching on the doctrine, organized the Ethiopian Overcoming Holy Church of God. The word "Ethiopian" was later changed to "Apostolic."

Active in 14 states and with missions in the West Indies and Africa, the ministers of the body are supported by tithe payments of the membership; the clergy are also required to tithe. Worship includes foot washing and divine healing. Services generally are free, emotional affairs, with the participants speaking in tongues and engaging in ecstatic dances.

It is claimed that this church existed "even from the days of Enos," when Christianity was known to be in existence in Abyssinia. Marriage to unsaved men and women, the use of snuff, foolish talking, jesting, and the use of slang are forbidden.

In doctrine, sanctification and holiness are stressed, with the tenet of the deity of Christ receiving major emphasis. The church has a publishing house in Mobile, Alabama, and an Old Folks Rescue Home. Bishop Phillips is the senior of nine bishops supervising the work of a church claiming 100,000 members, more than 900 ministers and missionaries, and 350 local churches.

ARMENIAN CHURCHES

Armenia claims to be the first Christian nation. The apostles Thaddeus and Bartholomew were believed to be there during the time of Paul, and Christianity was adopted as the state religion in A.D. 301. St. Gregory the Illuminator, preaching in Armenia at that time, became the first head of this national church, with the title of Catholicos.

The story of the Christian Church in Armenia is written in blood; it suffered both in the inevitable conflict between the Byzantine Empire and Persia and in numerous persecutions by the Turks. Thousands escaped to America before and after World War I, and here they functioned under the jurisdiction of the Etchmiadzin See from 1887 to 1933, when a dispute arose over the domination of the Church in Soviet Armenia insofar as it affects the American diocese. A split occurred, in which one group organized independently, and remained so until 1957, known as the Armenian Apostolic Church of America; they went under the jurisdiction of the Holy See of Cilicia. Those who remained are known as the Armenian Church of North America and are under the See of Etchmiadzin.

Today, in spite of the division into two dioceses, and still facing the question of loyalty to one or the other jurisdiction, the Armenian churches work in harmony where dogma and liturgy are concerned. Both elect their own primates. Deacons, priests, bishops, and archbishops are ordained and elevated by the hierarchical authorities of their respective jurisdictions. Both the Armenian Church of North America (including the diocese of California) and the Armenian Apostolic Church of America claim to be the true American branch of the Ancient Church of Armenia. The former group has a membership of 372,000 in 58 churches, working under the jurisdiction of the Etchmiadzin See; the latter has 125,000 members in 29 churches and is under the jurisdiction of the Holy See of Cilicia, Antelias-Lebanon.

In government, both churches are democratic in that they elect their own officials. Every province and diocese in this country, and indeed in the world, has a constitution adapted to its particular needs, but which must be approved by the Catholicos of its respective jurisdiction.

Doctrine is based on the historic writings and declarations of the early Church Fathers. The saints and the Virgin Mary are venerated; the Assumption of the Virgin is celebrated but not accepted as a dogma. A translation of the Scriptures by St. Sahak and St. Mesrob and of their students is accepted as the only authoritative Armenian Version of the Bible. There are seven sacraments: Baptism by immersion eight days after birth, Confirmation immediately following Baptism, Holy Communion even for infants, Penance, Marriage, Ordination, and Extreme Unction. The principal service is the Holy Sacrifice of the Divine Liturgy; various orders of "Hour" services and celebrations of feasts are observed. The Bible is read in Armenian at these services. Language schools, Sunday schools, cultural programs, and libraries help to keep the native tongue alive.

ASSEMBLIES OF GOD
(GENERAL COUNCIL OF)

The largest of the Pentecostal bodies, with 1,099,606 members and 8,871 churches, the General Council of the Assemblies of God is actually an aggregation of Pentecostal churches and assemblies accomplished at Hot Springs, Arkansas, in 1914. The founders were former ministers and pastors of evangelical persuasion who wished to unite into one body in the interests of a more effective preaching and an enlarged missionary crusade.

Ardently fundamentalist, its theology is Arminian; there is strong belief in the infallibility and inspiration of the Bible, the fall and redemption of man, baptism in the Holy Ghost, entire sanctification, a life of holiness and separation from the world, divine healing, the second advent of Jesus and his millennial reign, eternal punishment for the wicked and eternal bliss for believers. Two ordinances, baptism and the Lord's Supper, are practiced. Members stand officially opposed to war, but large numbers of their youth accepted noncombatant and even combatant service in World War II. They are especially insistent that baptism in the Holy Spirit is evidenced by speaking in tongues. The Assemblies of God believe that all the gifts of the Spirit should be in operation in the normal New Testament church.

The government of the assemblies is an unusual mixture of Presbyterian and Congregational systems. Local churches are left quite independent in polity and in the conduct of local affairs. District officers have a pastoral ministry to all the churches and are responsible for the promotion of home missions. Work is divided into 54 districts in the United States, most of which follow state lines, each with a distinct presbytery which examines, licenses, and ordains pastors. In addition to these there are 7 foreign-language branches. The General Council consists of all ordained (not licensed) ministers, and local churches are represented by one lay delegate each. This council elects all general officers, sets the doctrinal standards, and provides for church expansion and development. Missionary work is conducted under the guidance of a central missionary committee; there are 1,063 foreign missionaries at work on a total missionary budget of $15,000,000—unusually high among Protestant churches. The Sunday schools of the group have an enrollment of 1,078,332. A weekly periodical, *The Pentecostal Evangel,* has a circulation of approximately 220,000; and a prosperous church press produces books, tracts, and other religious literature. There are 8 Bible institutes and one liberal arts college. The latest school to be established is a graduate school of theology located in Springfield, Missouri. There are 95 Bible institutes abroad, and there is an international broadcast, *Revivaltime,* on 630 stations.

BAHA'I

The Bahá'í Faith aims at the universal brotherhood of man, the unity of all religions, and peace for the whole world. Its founder, Bahá'u'lláh, said, "The religion of God is for the sake of love and union; make it not the cause of enmity and conflict." His followers see in his teachings the same universal spirit that spoke in Moses and Jesus, Krishna and Buddha, Zoroaster and Muhammad; to them he is the "return" of all previous prophets, religious leaders, "Manifestations of God," and "The Promised One" of the world's great religions.

Actually, the Bahá'í Faith originated with the teachings of Mírzá 'Ali Muhammad, called the Báb (Arabic for "gate" or "door"), who suffered persecution and was martyred in 1850. It is estimated that 20,000 followers of the faith, then known as Babism, were slain during this persecution. His successor was Mírzá Husayn 'Ali, who was given the title of Bahá'u'lláh ("The Glory of God"), and who died in 1892. He left a vast accumulation of writings which are still treasured as the sacred scriptures of Bahá'í belief. His mantle fell upon his eldest son, 'Abbás Effendi, later known as 'Abdu'l-Bahá. The son spent some 40 years in captivity; released in 1908 at the time of the revolution of the Young Turks, he toured Egypt, Europe, and the United States. In 1912, at Wilmette, a suburb of Chicago, he laid the cornerstone of the first Bahá'í house of worship in the Occident. This is now the seat of Bahá'í national administrative offices in the United States.

The Wilmette temple is a unique religious structure, in which the numeral 9, the symbol of unity in Baha'i, is repeatedly emphasized. There are 9 concrete piers, 9 pillars or pylons, and 9 arches; it is set in a park with 9 sides, 9 avenues, gateways, and fountains. The building was dedicated in 1953 to "the unity of God, the unity of his prophets, the unity of mankind." Services of worship are conducted weekly in the auditorium with *a capella* music and readings from the sacred scriptures of the world's religions. A Bahá'í home for the aged was built in Wilmette in 1958.

Coordination and direction of international Bahá'í activities is now vested in the Bahá'í Universal House of Justice, a body of 9 members in residence at the World Center in Haifa, Israel, elected for a term of 5 years. In addition to administrative and judicial functions for the Bahá'í faith at large, this body legislates on matters not expressly revealed in the Bahá'í writings. To direct the teaching activities, another international institution, known as the Hands of the Cause, functions with auxiliary boards assigned to each continent. Local groups are organized as local Spiritual Assemblies, which in turn are supervised by a National Spiritual Assembly which consists of 9 members. Since 1963 there has been a marked growth in membership; there are more than 14,000 local assemblies, and 113 National Assemblies. Followers of the Faith now reside in 6,200 localities in the United States and 60,591 worldwide; within this world fellowship we find men, women, and children of all races and creeds—black, yellow, brown, and white, Europeans, Asiatics, Africans, Americans, former Moslems, Hindus, Christians, and Jews. It is perfect integration, in recognition of the truth of their founder's statement, "Ye are the fruits of one tree and the leaves of one Branch."

There are central Bahá'í temples at Frankfurt, Germany; Sydney, Australia; Kampala in (Uganda), Africa; Wilmette, Illinois, in the United States, and Panama City, Panama. Publishing trusts have been established at Wilmette, London, Buenos Aires, Rio de Janeiro, New Delhi, Teheran, Kampala, Frankfurt, and in Belgium. The writings of the Bahá'í Faith have been translated into 415 languages.

There is no ritual, no clergy in Bahá'í. Traditional rites and sacraments practiced by the religions of the world are ruled out, in the belief that each seeker may receive truth and the Spirit without ecclesiastical mediation. Unpaid teachers and "pioneers" give assistance to students. Marriage and funeral services are simple and flexible. Meetings vary from public lectures, study classes, and discussion groups for inquirers to meetings for the Bahá'í community, assembly meetings, conventions, and summer and winter schools and institutes. Summer schools are located in Maine, California, and Michigan. Events within their communities are scheduled by a special calendar of 19 months of 19 days each, with the New Year at the vernal equinox. The Bahá'í day starts and ends at sunset.

The chief purpose of Bahá'í is to unite the world in one religion and in one social order; hence, its chief principle is "the oneness and the wholeness of the human race." Among other dominant principles are the following:

1. Independent investigation of the truth.
2. The essential harmony of science and religion.
3. Recognition of the divine foundation of all religions.
4. Universal compulsory education.
5. The equality of all men and women.
6. The spiritual solution of economic problems.
7. The need for a universal auxiliary language.
8. Universal peace based upon a world federation of nations.
9. The elimination of all prejudice.
10. Recognition of the essential unity of mankind.

Beyond this, in its effort to develop the spiritual qualities of character, Bahá'í prescribes monogamy, discourages divorce, emphasizes strict obedience to one's government, condemns idleness, exalts any work performed in the spirit of service to the rank of worship, prohibits slavery, asceticism, and monasticism, the use of alcohol and narcotics except for medicinal purposes, and insists upon prayer and fasting as means of elevating the soul.

BAPTISTS

Baptists constitute one of the major Protestant forces in the United States. Twenty-seven Baptist denominations reported an approximate membership of 27,527,471 in 1971; there are approximately 94,508 local Baptist churches, each one independent of the others, with members also completely independent of one another yet bound together by an amazingly strong "rope of sand" in a great common allegiance to certain principles and doctrines based generally upon the competency of each individual in matters of faith.

It is often heard among them that they have no founder but Christ and that Baptists have been preaching and practicing from the days of John the Baptist. That is true in a limited sense; there were certainly men and women holding what have come to be considered distinctly Baptist principles all across the years. But as a church, or as organized churches, they began in Holland and England.

When the Reformation came early in the sixteenth century, scattered groups appeared advocating the convictions of faith which are today the warp and woof of Baptist theology and ideology. We find the name Baptist in various forms in Germany and Switzerland: Pedobaptists, among whom, however, there were no "Baptists in the modern sense," inasmuch as they baptized infants and children; Anti-Pedobaptists, who opposed infant baptism; and Anabaptists, who rebaptized adults once baptized as children. The Anabaptists were the left wing of the Reformation and held to a literal application of the word of God in social matters; they were communistic and pacifistic, opposing capital punishment, oaths in court, the holding of public office, and payment of taxes and interest. They rejected infant baptism as unscriptural, insisted upon the separation of church and state, and defended this belief heroically and to the point of fanaticism and martyrdom. Under persecution they spread all over Europe. Some fled to Norway, others to Italy, Poland, Holland, and England.

In Holland a group of Mennonites, or followers of the former Anabaptist leader Menno Simons (see Mennonites, p. 177), taught Anabaptist principles: that the Scriptures were the sole authority for man's faith and practice, that baptism was a believer's privilege, that church and state should be completely and forever separated, and that church discipline should be rigidly enforced in business, family, and personal affairs. These Mennonites met and perhaps deeply influenced a little group of British Separatists who had taken refuge in Amsterdam from the religious persecutions under James I; many of them lived in Mennonite homes, and one of their leaders, John Smyth, was completely captured by the Mennonite argument. He rebaptized himself and his followers in the Anabaptist, or Baptist, faith and with them organized the first English Baptist Church in 1609. When he tried to make Mennonites of them, however, he went too far; Baptist they would be, but not Mennonite, for that meant a threat to their British heritage, and they were still good Englishmen and proposed to remain so. Smyth was excommunicated, and he died in 1612, leaving behind him, in a "confession," his convictions that

the magistrate, by virtue of his office, is not to meddle with religion, or matters of conscience, nor to compel men to this or that form of religion or doctrine, but to leave the Christian religion to the free conscience of every one, and to meddle only with political matters.

So died John Smyth, Baptist to the last. His people drifted back across the Channel and, with persecution waning, established yet another Baptist church in London.

These first 2 churches were General Baptist churches, believing in a general atonement for all men. In the course of time there arose a Particular Baptist Church, holding to the predestinarian teachings of John Calvin and preaching a limited atonement. The first Particular (British) Church dates back to 1638. Three years after their founding, a third body, known as Immersion Baptists, broke away and in 1644 wrote a confession of faith which is still held by many modern Baptists. It was this confession that stamped these people popularly for the first time as Baptists.

These early British Baptists wielded a tremendous influence in their time and upon the future; it is claimed for them that "more than any king or Parliament, they set the heart and mind of England free." John Smyth's teaching that "the magistrate . . . is not to meddle with religion, or in matters of conscience" has become one of mankind's great spiritual principles. They sent William Carey to India in 1793, and Carey became the pioneer of modern missions. More than a century earlier, in 1631, Roger Williams had come to America; he was to be the first great champion of freedom for faith and conscience on this side of the Atlantic.

Williams was not a Baptist but a Separatist minister when he arrived. His story is well known: preaching "new and dangerous opinions against the authority of magistrates," he organized a Baptist church at Providence, Rhode Island. John Clarke established another Baptist church at Newport, Rhode Island, at about the same time. The Baptists are still arguing as to which church came first; many scholars put the Providence church in 1639, the Newport church in 1641.

These were Particular, or Calvinistic, Baptist churches. Their strength was challenged by the rise of interest in Arminian theology during the preaching of George Whitefield, but their Calvinism prevailed; it is the theological standard of many, if not most, Baptists in this country today. Their progress was slow; a bitter persecution of their church ennobled them and left one of the darkest blots on colonial history.

Following the tour of Whitefield through the colonies, a dispute arose among the Baptists, dividing them into Old Lights, or Regulars, who distrusted revivals and emotionalism, and New Lights, or Separates, who demanded a reborn membership in their churches. Separate Baptists were outstanding in the fight for religious freedom in the new land. The friction died down with the signing of the Constitution, however, and a new unity was found in a foreign missions crusade. The first Protestant missionary board in America was the American Board, made up of Baptists, Reformed, Congregational, and Presbyterian churchmen. In 1814 the Baptists organized their own separate General Missionary Convention of the Baptist Denomination in the United States of America for Foreign Missions.

This convention, representing a national Baptist fellowship, marked the first real denominational consciousness of American Baptists. It was followed eventually by other organizations which welded them firmly together: a general Baptist convention; a general tract society —later called the American Baptist Publication Society; various missionary societies for work at home and abroad; an education society; and the Baptist Young People's Union.

These organizations were on a national scale. Their unity was disrupted first by a feeling that home missions agencies within the body had failed to evangelize southern territory, and later by the question of slavery and the Civil War. The great division over slavery came in 1845, when the Southerners "seceded" to form their own Southern Baptist Convention in order to carry on more effectively the work of the Southern Baptist churches. From this point forward there were to be Northern and Southern Baptist conventions.

Various other Baptist groups, following to the logical end their love of independence, established themselves from East to West. While they differ in certain minor details, they are generally agreed upon the following principles of faith: the inspiration and trustworthiness of the Bible as the sole rule of life; the lordship of Jesus Christ; the inherent freedom of the individual to approach God for himself; the granting of salvation through faith by way of grace and contact with the Holy Spirit; 2 ordinances—the Lord's Supper and baptism of believers by immersion; the independence of the local church; the church as a group of regenerated believers baptized upon confession of faith; infant baptism as unscriptural and not to be practiced; complete separation of church and state; the immortality of the soul; the brotherhood of man; the royal law of God; the need of redemption from sin; and the ultimate triumph of God's kingdom.

These overall doctrines have never been written by the Baptists into any official Baptist creed for all their churches, but they have been incorporated in 2 important confessions of faith for the denomination. The Baptist churches of London wrote a Philadelphia Confession in the year 1689, and this confession was enlarged by the Philadelphia Association in 1742. The New Hampshire State Baptist Convention drew up another confession in 1832. The older Philadelphia Confession is strongly Calvinistic in statement; the New Hampshire Confession, only moderately so.

Baptists have insisted upon freedom of thought and expression in pulpit and pew. This has made them one of the most democratic religious bodies in America—and one in which liberal and conservative doctrine is preached freely. They have insisted, too, upon the absolute autonomy of the local congregation; each church arranges its own worship, examines and baptizes its own members. There is no age limit set on membership, but the candidate is usually of such an age that he can understand and accept the teachings of Christ. Candidates for the ministry are licensed by local churches and ordained upon recommendation of a group of sister churches.

Baptist churches are commonly found grouped into associations, local and state, for purposes of fellowship. National conventions are established among many of them to carry on educational and missionary work and to make pension plans. Most state conventions meet annually, with delegates representing all Baptist churches in the given area. They receive reports and make recommendations, but they have no authority to enforce their decisions.

In Washington, D.C., there is a Baptist Joint Committee on Public Affairs for both American and Southern conventions and other Baptist groups; this committee serves mainly to spread the Baptist conviction on public morals and to safeguard their principle of separation of church and state. Finally, there is the growing Baptist World Alliance, organized in 1905 and now including over 31,432,130 Baptists all over the globe. The alliance meets every 5 years and is a purely advisory body, discussing the great themes and problems common to all Baptists. Headquarters of the Alliance are now located in Washington, D.C.

American Baptist Churches in the U.S.A.

Up to the time of the Revolutionary War, Baptist work in the northern states was in the hands of the local churches, some few of which formed themselves into associations such as the Philadelphia Association or the Warren Association of Rhode Island. Beyond these associations, which were limited to Virginia, New Jersey, Pennsylvania, and Rhode Island, there was no central administrative body to bind the churches together. The association did well, building churches, colleges, schools, and libraries; by the time of the split with the Southern Baptists about 1845, plans for a national coordinating body were under way.

In the early years of the nineteenth century there were 3 Baptist organizations in the North mutually maintained: the American Baptist Home Mission Society; the American Baptist Missionary Union, later known as the American Baptist Foreign Mission Society; and the American Baptist Publication Society. The defection of the Southern Baptists served to intensify the efforts of these 3 bodies; they were separate corporations, but they often called annual meetings at the same time and place.

The women of the northern churches formed their own home and foreign missionary societies in the 1870's. Separate appeals for funds to support all these competing societies created confusion and dissatisfaction, and led eventually to the formation of the Northern Baptist Convention in 1907. This convention, actually a corporation with restricted powers in conducting religious work, receiving and expanding money, and affiliating itself with other bodies, changed its name in 1950 to the American Baptist Convention. In 1955 the two women's missionary societies joined administratively with their counterparts, the older foreign and home mission societies. Consequently, the two foreign societies and the two home societies, respectively, function now under identical officers, boards of managers, and administrative staffs, though each of the societies maintains its own corporate identity. In 1968 the Women's Foreign Society was legally merged into the American Foreign Missionary Society. These societies, with the American Baptist Historical Society, the Ministers and Missionaries Benefit Board, and the American Baptist Board of Education and Publication, were known as cooperating organizations of the convention.

State conventions and city mission societies were drawn into closer unity by grouping them into affiliated organizations through which they raised and distributed funds under a cooperative plan with a unified budget. The Division of World Mission Support supervised the collection of money for this unified budget. Numerous other councils and committees carried on the work of the convention under the supervision of the General Council, which functioned between the annual gatherings of the convention. In 1950, for the first time, a general secretary was elected.

In 1972, the Convention adopted its third and present name, American Baptist Churches in the U.S.A. and restructured to strengthen the representational principle and to develop a much fuller integration of the national program agencies into the structure of the American Baptist Convention. A larger (200-member) general board, representative of election districts, is the policy-making body. A national staff council of executives of national program boards and regional, state, and city units, serves to coordinate the corporate affairs of the denomination under the leadership of the general secretary.

The local church, however, is still the basic and independent unit of American Baptist government and administration. There are 6,029 churches and 1,562,740 members, 27 regional and state conventions, and 9 Baptist city societies. The church is at work in 14 children's homes, 48 homes for the aged, 7 hospitals, 10 theological seminaries, 6 academies, 27 senior colleges and universities, 4 junior colleges, and 1 school for nursing education. The Board of National Ministries has workers in 35 states; it supports Bacone College for Indians in Oklahoma and carries on a widespread work among Negroes, Indians, and Orientals resident in the United States. The Board of International Ministries supports missionaries in Burma, Assam, India, Bengal, Thailand, Japan, Okinawa, Hong Kong, the Philippines, and Central America, and maintains a cooperative relationship in 10 European countries. American Baptists also support the work of the Burma Baptist Convention, financially.

In matters of faith, every Baptist church speaks for itself, but there are certain Baptist doctrines held in common. The Bible is the foundation of their belief; the individual conscience, the interpreter of the Bible. There is the usual Baptist insistence upon the inspiration and validity of the Scriptures, the lordship of Christ, immortality and the future life, the brotherhood of man, and the need of man's redemption from sin. The ordinances of baptism and the Lord's Supper are considered more as aids than as necessities to the living of the Christian life and are called ordinances.

Generally it may be said that Northern Baptists represented in the American Baptist Churches in the U.S.A. are less conservative in thought and theology than those in the Southern Baptist Convention, but this doctrinal difference is no longer the major cause of the continuing separation of the two groups. Divergent views on the questions of race, open Communion, and especially of the Protestant trend toward ecumenicity are now the major hurdles, with the latter predominant. American Baptists are represented in the National Council of the Churches of Christ in the U.S.A. and in the World Council of Churches; Southern Baptists are represented in neither. American Baptists have made gestures toward union with the General Baptists, the Southern Baptists, the National Baptist Convention, the Seventh Day Baptists, the Disciples of Christ, and the Church of the Brethren, and have welcomed the Free Baptists into full fellowship. Unless and until these varying attitudes are changed or reconciled, there does not seem to be any real possibility of the reunion of the two larger Baptist bodies in the United States.

Southern Baptist Convention

It was inevitable that Northern and Southern Baptists should split over the slavery question, even before the outbreak of the Civil War. The friction between the two sections began a quarter of a century before Bull Run. The acting board of foreign missions of the Baptists in the country had its headquarters in Boston. Being located there, it was naturally strongly influenced by the abolition movement. There was bitter debate among the board members, and in the early 1840's it became evident that this board would not accept slaveholders as missionaries. This question of missionaries and of missionary money was the immediate cause of the split. The "brethren of the North" first suggested separation; a month later, in May of 1845, the Southern Baptist Convention was organized, establishing at once its own boards for foreign and home missions.

Southern historians now recognize that in addition to the slavery issue there was a long-standing disagreement between Baptists in the North and Baptists in the South over the nature of denominational organization. Certainly the slave issue precipitated the break, but there was a very significant consequence to it. Baptists in the United States under northern leadership heretofore had no central denominational organization. Instead there were separate and independent organizations (usually designated as "societies") for various phases of cooperative effort, such as foreign and home missions and publication. Southerners had desired instead to have one organization controlling these varied activities. From the beginning the Southern Baptist Convention was such an organization. Northern Baptists, on the other hand, waited until 1907 to form a convention uniting their societies. This cohesion of centralized organization and cooperative societies has had much to do, Southern Baptists believe, with their growth.

In Maryland, Virginia, North Carolina, South Carolina, Georgia, Louisiana, Kentucky, and Alabama, 300 churches entered the new organization. Up to the outbreak of the Civil War this convention met biennially; since 1869 it has met annually.

A hard struggle for existence lay immediately ahead. The new convention suffered badly in point of churches, membership, and finances during the war. Homes, schools, churches, the livelihood of citizens, and the very pattern of southern society was destroyed, with devastating effects among all the churches; an anti-missionary movement decimated their ranks, and membership—not finances and leadership—was affected when Negro Baptists withdrew to form their own convention. The recovery of the Southern Baptist Convention was amazing, however. In 1845 there were 351,951 members in the Convention, of whom 130,000 were Negroes; by 1890 there were 1,235,908 members, all of them white; in 1972 there were 12,067,284 members in 34,534 churches, including Negro churches related to the Convention.

As previously noted, Southern Baptists generally hold to a more conservative theology than their northern brothers, but the basic items of belief are quite the same. The Southern Baptist faith is more definitely Calvinistic, and it is one of the ironies of Baptist history that the Southern Baptist Convention adheres more firmly to the New Hampshire Confession of Faith than do the American Baptists. Church polity and government are the same in both Conventions; both membership and ministry are exchanged in harmony and understanding.

Twenty denominational agencies work with 33 state conventions in home and foreign missions, Sunday schools, educational institutions, and ministerial retirement. The Home Mission Board, with 64 members, works throughout the United States, Panama, and the Panama Canal Zone, with more than 2,200 missionaries active in the field. It cooperates with Negro Baptists, works among migrants in the South and Indians in the West and Southwest, among several language groups and the deaf, and provides loans for the erection of new church buildings.

Foreign missionaries are at work in 75 countries and on 4 continents; yet in comparison with their huge membership Southern Baptists rank second among Protestant denominations in the number of missionaries sent overseas—with over 12,000,000 members in 34,512 churches; they have 2,526 active missionaries abroad. There are 661 schools supported by foreign missions programs, 6,045 churches and 6,463 chapels, 20 hospitals, and 151 clinics and dispensaries.

The Sunday School Board provides the literature for and supervises the work of 7,177,651 students in 33,549 Sunday schools. The first chair of Sunday school pedagogy was established in 1915 at the Southwestern Seminary in Fort Worth, Texas. There are 7 theological seminaries in the Southern Baptist Convention with 5,574 students, 44 senior colleges and universities, 12 junior colleges, 8 academies, and 4 Bible schools.

The publishing work of the Convention is one of the most prolific in Protestantism—circulation of its publications reached a figure of more than 109,000,000 in 1972. A chain of 53 bookstores distributes this material across the nation.

Southern Baptists are said to be the fastest-growing religious group in the United States; new churches are being established not only in southern but in northern, eastern, and western states as well. Their annual convention is being held increasingly in northern and western cities, and two reasons are given for this: one is that there are few southern cities with hotel accommodations adequate to care for the ever-increasing numbers of delegates attending conventions; the other is that there are so many Southern Baptists living in northern territory that northern cities from sheer force of numbers are entitled to national conventions within their own states. State and territorial lines are being crossed, and it is more and more evident that the word "Southern" in their name is a misnomer. This is fast becoming a national Baptist body in every meaning of the word.

Negro Baptists

The first Negro Baptist church in America was organized at Silver Bluff across the Savannah River from Augusta, Georgia, in 1773; other churches followed in Petersburg, Virginia, in 1776; Richmond, Virginia, in 1780; Williamsburg, Virginia, in 1785; Savannah, Georgia, in 1785; and Lexington, Kentucky, in 1790. It is interesting that Andrew Bryan, a slave, was the first pastor of the First African Baptist Church of Savannah, Georgia, and that its organization came about through the efforts of the Rev. Abraham Marshall (white) and the Rev. Jesse Peter (Negro).

As early as 1700, white slaveholders in the South were providing religious teaching and places of worship for their slaves; at least most of them did little to prevent it. Usually, however, the Negro slave sat in the gallery of the white church, identified with the faith of his owner. White ministers, sometimes assisted by Negro helpers, moved from one plantation to another holding services more or less regularly; occasionally a Negro minister was liberated to give full time to religious work among his people. These ministers had great influence; they were consulted by the whites as the respected leaders of their people and were a real power up to the time of the slave rebellion of 1831 led by Nat Turner. For a period following this disturbance it was illegal in some sections of the South for Negroes to become Christians or to build meeting houses.

The great majority of Negroes in pre-Civil War days were either Baptists or Methodists. When Bull Run was fought in 1861, there were 200,000 Negro members of the Methodist Episcopal Church, South, and 150,000 Negro Baptists. In 1793 there were 73,471 Baptists in the United States, and one fourth of them were Negroes; in 1806 one third of the Baptists of North Carolina were Negroes. The lack of formality in the Baptist churches, together with the absence of ritual and the freedom and democracy of the local congregation, appealed to the Negro more than the episcopal structure of the Methodists. This was accented at the end of the Civil War; a revival spirit swept the Negroes, creating thousands of new churches. Aided by the Freedman's Aid Society and various Baptist organizations, nearly 1,000,000 Negro Baptists worshiped in their own churches within 15 years.

The first Negro Baptist association, the Providence Baptist Association of Ohio, was formed in 1836; the first attempt at national organization came in 1880 with the creation of the Foreign Mission Baptist Convention at Montgomery, Alabama. In 1886 the American National Baptist Convention was organized at St. Louis, and in 1893 the Baptist National Educational Convention was organized in the District of Columbia. All three conventions were merged into the National Baptist Convention of America at Atlanta in 1895. In 1915 a division arose in this convention over the adoption of a charter and the ownership of a publishing house. The group rejecting the charter continued to function as the National Baptist Convention of America, while the group accepting the charter became known as the National Baptist Convention of the U.S.A., Incorporated (incorporated, that is, under the laws of the District of Columbia). The former is frequently referred to as the "unincorporated" and the latter as the "incorporated" convention, but both trace their beginnings to the Foreign Mission Baptist Convention of 1880.

Today, out of approximately 20,000,000 Negroes in the United States, better than 10,000,000 are in the South, and 44 percent of the total Negro population are church members. They are grouped into a large number of churches and denominations. There are more than 30 recognized and entirely different Negro denominations, some with less than 20 members, but seven eighths of our total Negro population is either Methodist or Baptist. Nearly 8,000,000 Negro Baptists are found in the two major conventions; 5,500,000 in the National Baptist Convention of the U.S.A., Incorporated, and 2,668,799 in the National Baptist Convention of America, usually called the "unincorporated" body.

Negro Baptist doctrine runs quite parallel to that of white Baptist churches; however, it is slightly more Calvinistic. The polity of the two larger white conventions prevails; local churches unite in associations, usually along state lines, for the purposes of fellowship and consultation. There are also state conventions concerned with missionary work and often extending beyond state boundaries.

Foreign missionary work is especially strong in Africa, and home missionary efforts are generally those expended in the direction of helping needy churches and schools, and in family support and relief. The National Baptist Convention, Inc., has several missionary stations in the Bahamas, and 5 colleges, 1 theological seminary, and 1 training school for women and girls. The National Baptist Convention of America has stations in Jamaica, Panama, and Africa, and gives support to 10 colleges.

The old enmities between the two conventions are disappearing, but no reunion is expected for some time to come. Moves have been made, however, toward the union of the National Baptist Convention of the U.S.A., Inc., with the American Baptist Convention.

As the outcome of a violent dispute in the National Baptist Convention of the U.S.A., Inc., over procedures in the election of convention officers, a new Progressive Baptist Convention was organized in 1961. No further information is as yet available on this body.

American Baptist Association

Sometimes called Landmarkers because of their historic adherence to the old apostolic order of church polity, the American Baptist Association members deny that those Baptists organized in conventions are faithful to Bible precedent. Maintaining that their own is the true New Testament form, they hold themselves separate from all other religious groups. They "strongly protest the trend of many Baptist groups to identify themselves with Protestantism, believing that their [Baptist] faith preceded the Protestant Reformation."

Starting in 1905 as the Baptist General Association, they organized under their present name in 1924 at Texarkana, Arkansas-Texas. Teaching that the great commission of Christ (Matt. 28:18-20) was given to a local congregation, they believe that the local congregation or church is the only unit authorized to administer the ordinances and that it is an independent and autonomous body responsible only to Christ. Thus, every church is equal "with every other like church"; they are sometimes called Church-Equality Baptists.

Their doctrine is strictly fundamentalist. Condemning "so-called modern science," they stand for the verbal inspiration of the Bible, the Triune God, the virgin birth and deity of Christ, the suffering and death of Christ as substitutionary, the bodily resurrection of Christ and all his saints. The second coming of Jesus, "physical and personal," is to be the crowning event of the "gospel age"; this second advent will be premillennial. There is eternal punishment for the wicked; salvation is solely by grace through faith and not by law or works. There must be absolute separation of church and state, and absolute religious freedom.

Government of both the local congregations and the annual messenger meetings of the association is congregational in nature. Missionary work is conducted on county, state, interstate, and foreign levels, with the program originating in the local church and the missionaries being supported by the cooperating churches. Educational work is pursued through the Sunday schools, 2 seminaries, 1 college, and 10 Baptist institutes.

The greater strength of this group is found in the South, Southwest, and Southeast, but much new work has been started in recent years in the East, North, and West. Their 1973 statistics show 3,336 churches with a total combined membership of 955,900; 3,326 Sunday schools with an enrollment of 450,000; and 3,368 ordained clergy with charges. Their membership continues to shift from rural to urban.

A comprehensive publishing program includes 14 monthly and semi-monthly periodicals, a Sunday school literature designed to cover the entire Bible in a 10-year period, and literature for young people's work and vacation Bible schools. National and state youth encampments are held annually, as well as annual pastors' and missionary conferences on a regional and national level.

Baptist Bible Fellowship, International

The Baptist Bible Fellowship is one of the "evangelical independent" groups—perhaps the largest and fastest-growing body of independent Baptists in the United States—loosely affiliated with each other in the preaching and teaching of ultra-conservative Baptist doctrine. They teach that Jesus was a Baptist in his thinking and work and was baptized by John the Baptist. They are biblical literalists, denouncing all modernists and liberals. They recognize only Baptist (immersion) baptism, participate in Communion only with members of their own church, and are adamant in opposing dancing, drinking, smoking, movies, gambling, and sex. No membership statistics are available, but their growth is phenomenal; eight of the ten largest Sunday schools in the nation are found in this Fellowship.

Baptist General Conference

The history of what is now known as the Baptist General Conference began at Rock Island, Illinois, in the summer of 1852. Gustaf Palmquist, a schoolteacher and lay preacher, had come from Sweden to Illinois the previous year to become the spiritual leader to a group of Swedish immigrants who had been influenced by the pietistic movement within the State Church (Lutheran) of Sweden. At Galesburg, Illinois, he came in contact with the Baptists and early in 1852 was baptized and ordained a Baptist minister. Visiting his countrymen at Rock Island, he won his first converts to the Baptist faith and baptized 3 in the Mississippi River on August 8, 1852. From this humble beginning has come a denomination of 11,364 members, 686 churches, and 18 state or district conferences. In 1879 a national conference—the Swedish Baptist General Conference of America—was organized.

For several decades the American Baptist Home Mission Society and the American Baptist Publication Society of the American (then the Northern) Baptist Convention aided the new work among the immigrant Swedes, but gradually the church became self-supporting. A theological seminary was founded in Chicago in 1871, and the first denominational paper was launched in the same year. From 1888 to 1944 foreign missionary activities were channeled through the American Baptist Foreign Mission Society; a separation came in 1944, caused largely by a desire to become completely independent. The Swedish Conference set up its own foreign board and today has more than 140 missionaries in India, Japan, the Philippine Islands, Ethiopia, Mexico, Argentina, and Brazil.

Following the First World War, with its intensified nationalistic conflicts, the transition from Swedish to English in church services was greatly accelerated and practically completed in three decades. In 1945 the word "Swedish" was dropped from the name of the conference; it had already been dropped largely by the local churches. With the language barrier removed, the growth of the conference has been rapid and far-reaching. Home missionaries are at work in all northern states, in some of the southern states, and Canada; one of their most effective organizations is the Evangelism Corps, made up of young lay volunteers who spend a year in concentrated home missions work.

The conference owns and controls Bethel College and Seminary at St. Paul, Minnesota (a 4-year college and a 3-year theological school with 1,500 students). Affiliated are 2 children's homes, 7 homes for the aged, a Hebrew mission, and the Vancouver Bible Institute, at Vancouver, B.C. Six periodicals, including *The Standard*, official denominational organ, are issued by the Board of Communication. Harvest Publications offers Bibles, books, and Sunday school materials.

Basically their doctrine is that of "theological conservatives, with unqualified acceptance of the Word of God," holding the usual Baptist tenets. They are a strong fellowship of churches, insistent upon the major beliefs of conservative Christianity but with respect and room for individual differences on minor points.

The conference tends to become more and more inclusive and to appeal to people of all nationalities. Actually about 50 percent of their pastors are not even of Swedish descent, and a large number of their churches contain very few Swedes. The transition has been fast because of the lack of Swedish immigrants and also because of the Swedes' quick assimilation into the American way of life.

Baptist Missionary Association of America

Organized at Little Rock, Arkansas, in May, 1950, as the North American Baptist Association and changing its name to the Baptist Missionary Association in 1968, these Baptists concentrate on fostering and encouraging missionary cooperation. It has had a startling growth, enrolling nearly 2,000 churches and 199,640 members in 25 states. They have 11 workers in the home missions field, and missionary work abroad in Mexico, Japan, Brazil, Formosa, Portugal, Cape Verde Islands, Uruguay, Guatemala, Costa Rica, Nicaragua, Senegal, Australia, Italy, and France. A strong publications department publishes literature for Sunday school and training classes, pamphlets, books, tracts, and magazines in English and Spanish. They also own and operate a printing business in Brazil, where literature is printed in Portuguese for use in Africa and Europe. A worldwide radio ministry is also maintained.

They are militant fundamentalists, claiming to hold the historic Baptist faith and placing strong emphasis upon the verbal inspiration and accuracy of the Scriptures, direct creation, the virgin birth and deity of Jesus, his blood atonement, justification by faith, salvation by grace alone, and the imminent, personal return of Christ to the earth. They brand as unscriptural open Communion, alien baptism, pulpit affiliation with heretical ministers, unionism, modernism, modern conventionism, one-church dictatorship, and "all the kindred evils arising from these practices." The Lord's Supper and baptism are accepted as ordinances; baptism is considered "alien" unless administered to believers only and by "divine authority as given to the Missionary Baptist churches."

Churches are completely autonomous in the Baptist tradition and have an equal voice in the cooperative missionary, publication, evangelical, and educational efforts of the association regardless of size or membership. Member churches must, however, conform to the doctrinal standards of the association and deny alien baptism and modernism in all its forms.

There are 3 junior colleges, maintained on a state level, and several orphans' homes. Two theological seminaries are located at Jacksonville, Texas, and Campinas, Brazil.

Bethel Ministerial Association

Founded as the Evangelistic Ministerial Alliance, at Evansville, Indiana, in May of 1934, this body was incorporated as the Bethel Baptist Assembly, under the laws of the State of Indiana, on March 16, 1960. There are 6,750 members in 22 churches, 75 ordained clergy, and 25 Sabbath schools with an enrollment of 7,500. Details on doctrine, organization, etc., are available from headquarters, at Box 5353, Evansville, Indiana 47715.

Central Baptist Association

This is an association formed in 1956; it is composed of forty Baptist churches in Virginia, Tennessee, Kentucky, Indiana, Michigan and South Carolina. Present membership is approximately 5,000. Following usual Baptist doctrine and polity, its officers have no jurisdiction over the member churches. A Tabernacle and Children's Home are located at Jasper, Virginia.

Christian Unity Baptist Association

The Christian Unity Baptist Association was organized in 1934 as the result of a dispute over the question of open and closed Communion in the Macedonia Baptist Association in North Carolina. The dissenters believed that all Christians in all denominations should be admitted to participation in the Lord's Supper. They are one of the smaller Baptist groups, numbering 345 members in 5 churches.

They believe in one God and the Trinity and in the Bible as the inspired Word of God; that all mankind is fallen and helpless to save itself, but can experience regeneration through a universal atonement; in the redemption of "the bodies of the saints," infants, and idiots; that sinners reach God by way of repentance and faith; that the only two authorized ordinances are baptism of believers and the Lord's Supper; in foot washing; in the resurrection of both the just and the unjust, "who shall endure to the end to be saved"; in the everlasting reward of the righteous and the eternal punishment of the wicked.

Government is strictly congregational; there is one association for advisory purposes only. Work centers largely in home missions, evangelism, revivals, prayer meetings, and Sunday schools.

Conservative Baptist Association of America

The Conservative Baptist Association of America is officially described as a

voluntary fellowship of sovereign, autonomous, independent and Bible-believing Baptist churches working together to extend the Baptist testimony. . . . The Association is wholly separated from all other organizations, Baptist as well as non-Baptist. The several churches are held together, not by elaborate machinery, but by a common abiding love for the work and person of Jesus Christ, and the Word of God, as well as love for and confidence in one another.

The founders of the association were active in an earlier organization known as the Fundamentalist Fellowship, which was founded in 1920 within the American (then the Northern) Baptist Convention. This was a group of conservative churchmen who opposed what they considered to be the infiltration of liberal and modernistic tendencies and teachings within that convention. The basic disagreement was doctrinal and had to do with fundamentally different views and interpretations of the Scriptures and of Baptistic theology. The dispute was aggravated by the "inclusive" policy of the American Baptist Foreign Mission Society under which missionaries of conservative and liberal theologies were sent out to home and foreign fields.

Formally organized on May 17, 1947, at Atlantic City, New Jersey, and working under a constitution adopted at Milwaukee in 1948, this is exactly what the name suggests: an *association* of local, conservative Baptist churches. As as association, it must be distinguished from the Conservative Baptist *movement* in the United States. Several conservative Baptist institutions—such as the Conservative Baptist Foreign Mission Society and the Conservative Baptist Home Mission Society, and a number of schools and colleges—function as part of the movement, but are completely separate and autonomous and in no way officially connected with or controlled by the Conservative Baptist Association of America.

The work of the association includes the building of a fellowship of churches; assisting churches in Sunday school work, evangelism, Bible teaching, missions, organization, and building projects; establishing state associations and aiding in related projects; challenging and aiding established churches in the planting of new churches; encouraging the creation of agencies and institutions; serving in pastoral placement; printing and distributing tracts, pamphlets, and books; endorsing chaplains for the United States armed forces; "presenting a positive testimony to and opposing departure from the Old and New Testaments as God's inspired Word and the historic Baptist distinctives."

Doctrinally they stand for the infallibility of the Scriptures; God as Father, perfect in holiness, infinite in wisdom, measureless in power; Christ as the eternal and only begotten Son of God, his sinlessness, virgin birh, atonement, resurrection, and ascension; the sinfulness of all men and the possibility of their regeneration, sanctification, and comfort through Christ and the Holy Spirit; the church as the living body of Christ, with him as head; the local church as free from interference by any ecclesiastical or political authority; the responsibility of every human being to God alone; and the ordinances of baptism and the Lord's Supper.

Associational and regional officers are elected at annual meetings; a Board of Directors is made up of the associational officials and 18 regional representatives, elected for 3-year terms. The membership totals 300,000 in 1,001 churches.

Duck River (and Kindred) Associations of Baptists
(Baptist Church of Christ)

Confined to 4 southern states, the Duck River Baptists originated in a protest movement within the old Elk River Association which was strongly Calvinistic. This came in 1825; in 1843 the ranks of the dissenters were broken by a dispute over the legitimacy of missions and the support of a publication society and of a denominational school. Those who withdrew became known as Missionary Baptists and in a few instances as Separate Baptists or the Baptist Churches of Christ. The division persists; there are today 2 Duck River associations.

Doctrinally they are liberally Calvinistic; they hold that "Christ tasted death for every man"; that God will save those who come to him on gospel terms; that sinners are justified by faith; that the saints will "persevere in grace." They stand for believer's baptism by immersion and celebrate the Lord's Supper and foot washing as scriptural ordinances. As they admit their close gospel ties with Regular, United, and Separate Baptists, there are growing sentiments in favor of union.

They are congregational in government, with 5 associations for fellowship only (Duck River, Mount Zion, East Union, and New Liberty in Tennessee; Mount Pleasant in Alabama, Tennessee, and Georgia), and one church (Pleasant Hill, in Kentucky). There is a "correspondence" relation with other associations in Alabama, Tennessee, Mississippi, and Georgia. Membership is by vote of local congregations; ministers are ordained by 2 or more ministers. There are 8,492 members in 81 churches.

Free Will Baptists

The rise of the Free Will Baptists can be traced to the influence of Arminian-minded Baptists who migrated to the colonies from England. The denomination organized on two fronts at almost the same time. The southern line, or Palmer movement, began in 1727 when Paul Palmer established a church at Chowan, North Carolina. The northern line, or Randall movement, began with a congregation organized by Benjamin Randall in 1780, in New Durham, New Hampshire. Both groups taught the doctrines of free grace, free salvation, and free will. The northern body extended more rapidly in the beginning into the West and Southwest. In 1910 this line of Free Will Baptists merged with the Northern Baptist denomination, taking along half of its 1,100 churches, all its denominational property, and several colleges. In 1916 representatives of the remnant churches of the Randall movement reorganized into the Cooperative General Association of Free Will Baptists.

There were gestures toward union of the northern and southern groups, but the outbreak of the Civil War prevented it. The southern churches organized into new associations and conferences and finally into a General Conference by 1921. The division continued until 1935, when the two groups merged into the National Association of Free Will Baptists.

Doctrinally, they hold that Christ gave himself as a ransom for the many, not for the few; that God calls all of us to repentence, and that we may all be saved. Baptism is by immersion; this is one of the few Baptist groups practicing open Communion; they also practice feet washing. Government is strictly congregational; there is 1 Bible college and 2 liberal arts colleges, and 203,000 members in 2,275 churches.

General Baptists

The General Baptists claim their name and origin in John Smyth and Thomas Helwys and the group of Baptists organized in England and Holland in 1611 (see general article on the Baptists, p. 35). They hold Roger Williams to be their first minister in the American colonies.

The General Baptists in the colonies along the Atlantic coast were at first overwhelmed by the influence of Calvinism (General Baptists have always been Arminian), but their work was reopened by Benoni Stinson with the establishment of the Liberty Baptist Church in what is now Evansville, Indiana, in 1823. The spread into Illinois and Kentucky, and a general association of General Baptists was organized in 1870. Since that time they have grown steadily; today they are strong in Kentucky, Tennessee, Indiana, Michigan, Illinois, Missouri, and Arkansas, and have located churches in Oklahoma, Nebraska, Kansas, Iowa, Arizona, California and Florida.

Their confession of faith is similar to that of the Free Will Baptists; it is their belief that Christ died for all men; that failure to achieve salvation lies completely with the individual; that man is depraved and fallen and unable to save himself; that regeneration is necessary for salvation except in the case of infants and idiots, who are not responsible for sin; that salvation comes by repentance and faith in Christ; that the Christian who perseveres to the end is saved; that the wicked are punished eternally. The dead, just and unjust, will be raised at the judgment; the Lord's Supper and believer's baptism by immersion only are the only authorized Christian ordinances and should be open to all believers. Some of the General Baptist churches practice foot washing.

Church polity is about the same as that found in all Baptist churches. The denomination is congregational in church government. Churches of a common area are organized into local associations, which are in turn organized into a general association. Both local and general associations are representative bodies and advisory in power. A peculiar feature of the General Baptists lies in their use of a presbytery, into which the ordained members of local associations are grouped; they examine candidates for the ministry and for deacons. Ministers and deacons are responsible to this presbytery, which exists only on the local level.

Current statistics show 850 churches with a total membership of 69,000. They maintain at Oakland City, Indiana, a liberal arts college with a theological department. A publishing house is operated at Poplar Bluff, Missouri, where their weekly paper, the *General Baptist, Messenger*, is issued together with Sunday school literature.

Foreign missionary work is supported in Guam, Saipan, Jamaica, and the Philippines. They have an active home missionary work in various states.

General Association of Regular Baptist Churches

Twenty-two Baptist churches of the American Baptist Convention left that convention in May of 1932 to found the General Association of Regular Baptist Churches. The protest was against what they considered to be modernist tendencies and teachings in the American Convention, the denial of the historic Baptist principle of the independence and autonomy of the local congregation, the inequality of representation in the assemblies of the convention, the control of missionary work by convention assessment and budget, and the whole convention principle in general.

Any Baptist church coming into this association is required to "withdraw all fellowship and cooperation from any convention or group which permits modernists or modernism within its ranks." Dual fellowship or membership is not permitted. Participation in union evangelical campaigns, union Thanksgiving services, or membership in local ministerial associations where modernists are involved or present is considered to be unscriptural.

Missionary work is conducted through 5 approved Baptist agencies completely independent of any convention and completely orthodox; a close watch is maintained upon these agencies before annual approval is granted. Likewise, only 6 schools are approved; these, too, are "guarded" against any deflection from approved practice or doctrine.

The association subscribes to the New Hampshire Confession of Faith with a premillennial interpretation of the final article of that confession. It holds to the infallibility of the Bible, the Trinity, and personality of Satan as the author of all evil, man as the creation of God, and man born in sin. There are doctrines dealing with the virgin birth and the deity of Jesus and faith in Christ as the way of salvation through grace. The saved are in everlasting felicity, and the lost are consigned to endless punishment. There is a bodily resurrection; Christ rose and ascended and will return premillennially to reign in the millennium. Civil government is by divine appointment. There are only 2 approved ordinances: baptism by immersion and the Lord's Supper.

Church government is strictly congregational. Associated churches have the privilege of sending 6 voting messengers to an annual convention; thus a church with 50 members has the same power as a church with 2,500 members. A Council of Eighteen is elected—9 each year—to serve for 2 years. It makes recommendations to the association for the furtherance of its work and implements and puts into operation all actions and policies of the association, and its authority depends completely upon the will and direction of the association.

In 1973, there were 1,495 fellowshiping churches with 214,000 members. The 6 approved schools had a total student body of over 3,600, and 1,644 missionaries were at work in the 5 missionary agencies. State and regional associations have been established across the country; these are supplied with literature published by the Regular Baptist Press, including *The Baptist Bulletin*, a monthly magazine.

General Conference of the Evangelical Baptist Church, Inc.

The Evangelical Baptists were organized among the members of several Free Will Baptist Churches in 1935; they were formerly known as the Church of the Full Gospel, Incorporated.

Their doctrine and organization are naturally similar to that of the Free Will Baptists, with whom they are still in close fellowship. They exchange pastors regularly with the Wilmington Conference of the Free Will Baptist Church. As of 1952, there were about 2,200 members in 31 churches.

General Six-Principle Baptists

There are 2 Six-Principle Baptist Associations in the United States, one in Rhode Island and the other in Pennsylvania. The former claims to have been founded by Roger Williams in 1638; the latter was founded in 1813. Both claim as their charter the 6 foundation principles laid down in Heb. 6:1-2—namely, repentance, faith, baptism, the laying on of hands (a custom evidently disappearing, at least in Rhode Island), the resurrection of the dead, and eternal judgment.

Broadly speaking, they are Arminian in doctrine and congregational in polity. The conferences they hold are primarily for fellowship, but there is an increasing interest in foreign missions. Rhode Island lists 137 members in 3 churches; Pennsylvania has 308 members in 8 churches.

Landmark Baptists

"Landmarkism" among Baptists is a position held by some concerning the nature of the church and certain details of church practice. The name originated with the writings of Dr. James Madison Pendleton and Dr. James Robinson Graves in Kentucky and Tennessee, in the latter part of the nineteenth century, though Landmarkers insist that their concepts go back to the apostolic period.

There are 4 distinguishing tenets of Landmarkism:

1. The church is only vocal and visible. The expression "the church" is used only when speaking of it as an institution. All saved people make up "the family of God," not "the church." While members of other churches may be saved, they are not members of true churches.

2. The "commission" was given to the church: consequently, all matters covered by it must be administered under church authority. Ministers of other denominations are not accepted in Landmark Baptist pulpits.

3. Baptism to be valid must be administered by the authority of a New Testament (Baptist) church. Baptisms administered by any other authority are not accepted.

4. There is a direct, historic "succession" of Baptist churches back to New Testament times; that is, Baptist churches have existed in practice in every century, though not by name.

These principles are held primarily by the churches of the American Baptist Association, though there are an estimated 1,500,000 members of different Baptist churches which hold to the Landmark position and doctrine.

National Baptist Evangelical Life and
Soul Saving Assembly of the U.S.A.

This assembly was founded in 1920 at Kansas City, Missouri, not as another denomination, but as an evangelical group working within the National Baptist Convention (Unincorporated). It had the endorsement of the parent body for 17 years, but became an independent group in 1937.

No new doctrine is set forth by this group; it has no doctrine except the "Bible doctrine as announced by the Founder of the Church, Jesus Christ." Concentration is mainly upon evangelical and relief efforts. The assembly maintains an "automatic" correspondence school, offering courses in evangelology, deaconology, missionology, pastorology, and laymanology; degrees are granted in 60, 90, and 120 days.

In 1951, 57,674 members and 264 churches were reported.

National Primitive Baptist Convention of the U.S.A.
(Formerly Colored Primitive Baptists)

The Negro population of the South all through the years of slavery and the Civil War worshiped with the white population in their various churches. This was true of Colored Primitive Baptists, who attended white Primitive Baptist churches until the time of the emancipation, when their white brethren helped them to establish their own churches, granting them letters of fellowship and character, ordaining their deacons and ministers, and helping in other ways.

Their doctrine and polity are quite the same as in the white Primitive Baptist organization, except that they are "opposed to all forms of church organization"; yet there are local associations and a national convention, organized in 1907. Each church is independent, receiving and controlling its own membership; there is no appeal from a decision of the officers of the local church.

They have a membership of 1,645,600 in 2,198 churches. Unlike the white Primitive Baptists, they have since 1900 been establishing aid societies, conventions, and Sunday schools over the opposition of the older and more orthodox members.

North American Baptist General Conference

The churches in this conference began in German Baptist churches established on our soil by German Baptist immigrants of more than a century ago. The first of them settled in New Jersey and Pennsylvania—where Penn's Quakers offered them the perfect chance at the religious freedom they sought in flight from the mother country. The scattered German Baptist churches later became the North American Baptist General Conference and organized their first local churches during 1840-51.

The prosperity of these German Baptist churches followed the rise and fall of German immigration. By 1851 they had 8 churches and 405 members, and in that year they organized their churches into an Eastern Conference for fellowship and mutual consideration of common problems.

The local conference idea was enlarged as their churches increased. As their membership moved across the nation they organized a total of 9 such conferences, following geographical lines. In 1865 they held a joint meeting of Eastern and Western Conferences and called it a General Conference. The General Conference is now their chief administrative unit.

Local conferences meet annually, elect their own officers and missionary committees, and guide their own work. The General Conference meets triennially and is made up of all churches in the 9 local conferences and has clerical and lay representation from all of them. It superintends the work in publication, education, missions, and homes for children and the aged. A general council acts for the General Conference between its sessions.

The German Baptists participated in the development of what is now Colgate-Rochester Divinity School in Rochester, New York. In 1935 they established a seminary of their own, known as the North American Baptist Seminary, which relocated from Rochester to Sioux Falls, South Dakota, in 1949. The North American Baptist College is located at Edmonton, Alberta, Canada. There are 7 homes for the aged and a publishing house, the Roger Williams Press, at

Forest Park, Illinois. Home missions are conducted among Spanish Americans in the United States; foreign missionaries are located in Nigeria and Cameroon, West Africa, Japan, and Brazil.

Theologically, there is little variance here from the usual Baptist position: North American Baptists in general follow the New Hampshire Confession, stressing the authority of the Scriptures, the revelation of God in Christ, regeneration, immersion, separation of church and state, the congregational form of government, and have a very strong emphasis on missions. There are 44,516 members in 246 churches.

Primitive Baptists

The Primitive Baptists have the reputation of being the most strictly orthodox and exclusive of all Baptists. Unique in that they have never been organized as a denomination and have no administrative bodies of any kind (they believe that each church should "govern itself according to the laws of Christ as found in the New Testament, and that no minister, association, or convention has any authority"), they represent a protest against "money-based" missions and benevolent societies and against "assessing" the churches to support missions, missionaries, and Sunday schools. The position taken was that there were no missionary societies in the days of the apostles, and therefore there should be none now. Apart from this, there was objection to the centralization of authority in these societies. Sunday schools also were unauthorized by Scripture; they believed in the religious training of children but not in Sunday schools. They stood for evangelism as a missionary effort, but on individual responsibility and at individual expense, and not under the sponsorship of a money-based society. Spearheading the protest, the Kehukee Association in North Carolina in 1827 condemned all such money-based and authoritarian societies as contrary to Christ's teachings. Within a decade, several other Baptist associations across the country made similar statements and withdrew from other Baptist churches.

The various associations adopted the custom of printing in their annual minutes a statement of their articles of faith, their constitution, and their rules of order. These statements were examined by every other association and if they were approved, there was fellowship and exchange of messengers and correspondence between them; any association not so approved was dropped from the fellowship. Added to this was the difficulty of communication in many parts of the South. The result was confusion; there was no chance under such conditions for growth as a denomination and little chance even for a fellowship or quasi unity. This is apparent in the variety of names, some friendly and some derisive, which have been applied to them, such as "Primitive," "Old School," "Regular," "Anti-mission," and "Hard Shell." In general, the term "Primitive" has been widely accepted and used.

A strong Calvinism runs through their doctrine. In general they believe that by Adam's fall all posterity became sinners; that human nature is completely corrupt; and that man cannot by his own efforts regain favor with God. God elected his own people in Christ before the world began, and none of these saints will be finally lost. The 2 biblically authorized ordinances are the Lord's Supper and baptism of believers by immersion. All church societies are the invention of men and are to be denied fellowship; Christ will come a second time to raise the dead, judge all men, punish forever the wicked and reward forever the righteous; the Old and New Testaments are verbally and infallibly inspired.

Ministers must be called of God, come under the laying on of hands, and be in fellowship with the local church of which they are members before they can administer the 2 ordinances; they are to deny to any other clergyman lacking these qualifications the right to administer such ordinances. No theological training is demanded of ministers among Primitive Baptists; while there is no opposition to such education, the position is that the Lord will call an educated man if he wants one, but that lack of education should not bar a man from the ministry. Some Primitive Baptists still practice foot washing, but not all do. In spite of their opposition to money-based missionary societies, they are intensely evangelistic, and their preachers travel widely and serve without charge, except when their hearers wish to contribute to their support.

Membership is granted only after careful examination and vote of the congregation. Membership is estimated at 72,000 in 1,000 churches, but probably the figure is larger. Factionalism, divisiveness, and politics prevent an accurate report on membership.

Separate Baptist in Christ (General Association of Separate Baptists)

The first Separate Baptists arrived in the United States in 1695 as one refugee section of the separatist movement in England. They were especially active during the days of the blazing preaching of Whitefield in the early eighteenth century and in the conflict between the Old Light and New Light sects. Separate Baptist churches of this period were marked by their milder Calvinism and by an occasional use of infant baptism.

In 1787 Separate and Regular Baptist churches merged in Virginia in the United Baptist Churches of Christ in Virginia. There were other mergers and gestures toward union in New England and other states, but a few Separate Baptist churches maintained their independence. In 1962 they had 84 churches and 7,496 members.

All creeds and confessions of faith are rejected by Separate Baptists; however, there is an annual statement of articles of belief by the several associations. These include statements of faith in the infallibility of the Scriptures and in the Trinity; 3 ordinances—baptism of

58

believers by immersion only, the Lord's Supper, and foot washing; regeneration, justification, and sanctification through faith in Christ; the appearance of Christ on Judgment Day to deal with the just and the unjust. The "election, reprobation, and fatality" of Calvinism are rejected. Separate Baptists do not claim to be Protestants: "We have never protested against what we hold to be the faith once delivered to the saints."

They are congregational in government, with associations for advisory purposes only. The associations carry on a limited home missions work; there is a full-time missionary stationed in India, and individual members support foreign mission programs of other denominations. A missionary periodical called *Christ for the World* is published at Tice, Florida, and a general magazine, *The Messenger*, is circulated from Kokomo, Indiana.

Seventh Day Baptists

Differing from other Baptists in their adherence to the seventh day as the Sabbath, Seventh Day Baptists (or Sabbatarian Baptists, as they were called in England) first organized themselves as a separate body on this side of the Atlantic in 1672 at Newport, Rhode Island. Stephen Mumford, a member of the Bell Lane Seventh Day Baptist Church in London, had come there knowing well the perils of religious nonconformity and had entered into covenant relation with those who withdrew from "Doctor John Clarke's (Baptist) Church" under the Sabbath persuasion. Other churches were organized in Philadelphia and in New Jersey. From these 3 centers Seventh Day Baptists went west with the frontier; they now have 5,284 members in 70 churches and fellowships.

Belief in salvation through faith in Christ, believer's baptism by immersion, insistence upon intellectual and civil liberty and the right of every man to interpret the Bible "for himself under God" have characterized this people. They hold baptism and the Lord's Supper only as ordinances, practice open Communion, and have fostered 1 university and 2 colleges.

Local churches enjoy complete independence, although all of them support the united benevolence of the denomination known as Our World Mission. For fellowship and service the churches are organized into 8 regional associations, and these often assist local church councils in the ordination of deacons and ministerial candidates. The highest administrative body is the General Conference, which meets annually and delegates interim responsibilities to its president, general secretary, and commissions. The conference promotes World Mission giving and channels it through mission, publishing, and educational agencies. It also accredits ministers certified to it by ordaining councils and local churches. The denomination participates in the ecumenical movement at local, regional, national, and world levels.

The Seventh Day Baptist World Federation, an organization of Seventh Day Baptist Conferences, includes conferences in Brazil, Burma, Central Africa (Malawi), England, Germany, Guyana, Jamaica, Mexico, Holland, New Zealand, and the United States.

Seventh Day Baptists (German, 1728)

The Seventh Day Baptists (German, 1728) are not to be confused with the original Seventh Day Baptist Church organized earlier in Rhode Island; this group was established by Conrad Beissel, a Palatinate German, in 1728. Beissel worked for a while with Peter Becker, the Germantown mystic who founded the German Baptist Brethren, or Dunkards. He left Becker in 1732 to set up a monastic, communistic religious community at Ephrata, Pennsylvania. Goods were held in common, and men and women lived in separate houses under a regulation requiring celibacy.

The community declined late in the nineteenth century; the church last reported only 150 members in 3 churches in 1951. Generally they hold the usual Dunker doctrines: the inspiration of the Bible; one God, the Father, and Jesus Christ, his Son, the mediator; the Ten Commandments as the sole rule of righteousness for all men; baptism by trine forward immersion—the candidate is immersed 3 times, for Father, Son, and Holy Ghost. They practice foot washing, anointing of the sick, and the blessing of infants; observe Saturday as the Sabbath; and induct ministers by personal request rather than by congregational election.

A general conference meets annually; there is a small home missions program but no educational or philanthropic work.

Two-Seed-in-the-Spirit Predestinarian Baptists

Tracing their thought back to the Waldenses, the Two-Seed-in-the-Spirit Predestinarian Baptists in this country began in the late eighteenth century with the protests of Elder Daniel Parker against missions and Sunday schools. Parker opposed the Arminian doctrine of the Methodists and based his dislike of the missionary effort and church schools on what he called his Two-Seed Doctrine. This, briefly, is the conviction that two seeds entered the life stream of humanity in the Garden of Eden. One seed was good, planted by God; the other was evil, from the devil. The two seeds have been in conflict in humanity ever since. Every baby is predestined, born with one seed or the other. Nothing can be done for him one way or another. Inasmuch as nothing can be done, missions are useless; they are, moreover, an institution which "usurps the privileges of God."

The seed is in the spirit, not the flesh; this is the cardinal point in the theology of the group. Other points include belief in the resurrection of the body of Christ, which is the Church, and salvation by grace alone. The church observes the Lord's Supper and practices foot washing. There is no paid ministry "inasmuch as Christ came to save sinners, and He finished his work." Government is congregational; there are associations for fellowship only. There are no home missions or benevolences. The membership is decreasing; there were 201 members and 16 churches in 1945.

United Baptists

The United Baptists represent a merging of several groups of Separate and Regular Baptists mainly in the states of Virginia, Kentucky, and the Carolinas. While these groups were bodies holding both Arminian and Calvinistic theologies, they maintained a perfect freedom in preaching and polity after their union. As the years passed, many of their members found their way into either the Northern or Southern Baptist Conventions; but they are still recognized as a separate denomination with 63,641 members in 568 churches. Their first organization was in Richmond, Virginia, in 1787; a second group organized in Kentucky in 1801. Two associations—Salem and Elkhorn (Regular Baptists) and South Kentucky (Separate Baptists)—joined to form the United Baptists.

Doctrinally there are still traces of both Arminianism and Calvinism. Generally they hold that salvation is by grace rather than by works and conditional upon gospel requirements. All men are in a state of general depravity and are commanded to repent; they are led either to repentance through the goodness of God or to rebellion by the devil. It is a matter of individual choice.

There are 26 associations for fellowship and counsel quite independent of one another, yet working together closely. They practice closed Communion in some associations and churches, open Communion in others. There are 3 ordinances—baptism, the Lord's Supper, and (in most churches) foot washing.

United Free Will Baptist Church

While they trace their history back to the same original sources of the white Free Will Baptist Church, the United Free Will Baptists (Colored) have been independent since their official organization in 1901. Their members are found largely in North Carolina, Georgia, Florida, Mississippi, Louisiana, and Texas.

Although in general agreement with the congregational polity of other Baptist bodies, this church grants a rather limited autonomy to the local church. There is a system of quarterly, annual, and general conferences, with graded authority. Doctrinal disputes may be carried up to the general conferences; district conferences may exclude members from fellowship.

Doctrinally they are in agreement with white churches of the same faith. There is one institution of higher learning—Kinston College at Kinston, North Carolina. There were 100,000 members in 836 churches in 1952.

BIBLE FELLOWSHIP CHURCH

This body, strongly evangelical in purpose and effort, was founded in 1858 and today consists of 43 congregations in Pennsylvania, New Jersey, and New York. Its doctrinal emphases include salvation through the death and resurrection of Christ, transformed life through new birth by the Holy Spirit, the authority and trustworthiness of the Bible as the Word of God, the culmination of history in the second coming of Jesus and "a shared-life in the church of believers, with every member-responsibility for the propagation of the Gospel by evangelism and missions."

The Fellowship Churches support missions on five continents, Pinebrook Junior College, Victory Valley Camp for children and youth, a Home for the Aging and Pinebrook-in-the-Pines, a conference and retreat center, in Pennsylvania.

BIBLE PROTESTANT CHURCH

The churches in this body represent a break in the Eastern Conference of the Methodist Protestant Church in 1939, when some 50 delegates (approximately one third of the Conference) withdrew in protest against the union of the Methodist Protestant Church with the Methodist Episcopal Church and the Methodist Episcopal Church, South, and what the withdrawing group considered to be the modernistic tendencies of those churches. While the church operated under its original charter of the Eastern Conference, the name was subsequently changed to the Bible Protestant Church.

Doctrine here is conservative; this church is a member of the fundamentalist American and International Councils of Christian Churches. Cardinal points in their belief emphasize the verbal inspiration of the Bible; the Trinity; the deity, virgin birth, resurrection, and ascension of Jesus; salvation by faith in his blood and sacrifice, death and resurrection. There is a strong faith in premillennialism with eternal punishment for the wicked and eternal joy for the righteous believer. Baptism and the Lord's Supper are practiced as divine institutions.

Their churches are confined to New Jersey, New York, Pennsylvania, Massachusetts, Connecticut, Virginia, and Michigan. Actually they are a fellowship of self-governing churches, organized in a conference which meets annually with lay and clerical representation. The chief officer is the president, who holds office for not more than 3 years. All local churches own and control their own property; all contributions to the conference are voluntary and not by assessment; and local churches call their own ministers from the conference roll of ministers or from other churches approved by the Committee on

Ministerial Qualifications; formal assignment of the pastor is by a pastoral relations committee of the conference. Candidates for ordination must be graduates of high school and an approved seminary or Bible school. Missionary work is conducted in Japan and among migrant workers in the U.S.A., and Bible Protestant missionaries are serving in Mexico and Africa under the mission boards of other churches. The church publishing house issues a monthly periodical, *The Bible Protestant Messenger*. There are 42 churches, 2,388 members.

BIBLE WAY CHURCH, WORLD WIDE

At a ministerial conference of Pentecostal ministers in September, 1957, some 70 churches withdrew from the Church of Our Lord of the Apostolic Faith to form the Bible Way Church, World Wide. Their doctrine and teaching remain quite the same as that of the parent body. A phenomenal growth is reported from the original 70 churches to 347 churches and something over 30,000 members, at home and abroad. A general conference is held annually in July; a publishing house at Washington, D.C., circulates periodicals, religious pamphlets, and recordings.

BLACK MUSLIMS

The Black Muslim movement in the United States began with the founding of a Moorish Science Temple in Newark, New Jersey, by Timothy Drew. Drew took the name Noble Drew Ali and preached that the American blacks were actually Moors whose forefathers had lived in Morocco. His followers divided into several groups when he died in 1920; one group was led by Wallace D. Fard in Detroit. Calling himself the reincarnation of Noble Drew Ali, he taught "The Religion of the Black Men of Asia and Africa," a teaching based at first on both the Bible and the Mohammedan Koran. But Fard was soon attacking the Bible and announcing himself as a tool in the hands of Allah. The black people, he said, were gods; the white man was the serpent devil and would ultimately be destroyed. He disappeared mysteriously in 1933, and soon after his death his followers were claiming that he was Allah personified— God, the Son of Man, the Savior. He was succeeded by the late Elijah Poole, known as Elijah Muhammad, who traced black ancestry back to men living on the moon 66 trillion years ago.

Elijah Mohammad continued to preach Fard's gospel of black rebellion and revolution which would rid the blacks of white domination and give them their rightful place (as an independent nation) within the United States. Building on the desperate conditions of poverty and underprivilege in the black ghetto areas, the movement spread across the country and increased a militant membership which has become of national interest at once religiously, politically, socially, and economically.

Elijah Muhammad went to prison when he advised his younger followers to resist the draft; in prison he converted Malcolm Little (better known as Malcom X) to his cause. (The Black Muslims spurn their "white-given, slave-masters names" and use the X to represent their unknown true names.) The flaming preaching of Malcolm X helped build the membership to more than 30,000, but disagreements developed between Malcom X and Elijah Muhammad, and the membership began to decline when Malcom X was murdered in New York City in 1965.

Today membership claims vary from 100,000 to 750,000; some students of the movement think it much less than 100,000. The followers—and non-registered sympathizers—are generally (nearly 80%) young male blacks between 17 and 35 years of age, living in city ghettos, ex-Christian or anti-Christian and anti-white, completely devoted to Elijah Muhammad's idea of the establishment of a separate Negro state (The Black Nation of Islam) in this country. They are not recognized as a legitimate branch of Islam by the orthodox Middle East Muslims, much as they desire that, but they adhere to Mohammedan principles and teachings in everything but their extreme racism. Allah is to them the one true God, and they use the Koran and the traditional Moslem rituals in their temple services.

Marred as it is by violence, their movement has some very definite accomplishments on the positive side. They have established a chain of industries to relieve black poverty—barber shops, supermarkets, bakeries, restaurants, cleaning establishments, and farms. Black Muslims do not gamble, smoke, drink, overeat, or buy on credit. They arrange parole for their convicts and offer postprison guidance. Their claim that they "give black men their self-respect" has at least that element of truth; they have reached many whom the church has been unable to reach, and that may account for much of their popularity among the blacks.

BRETHREN (DUNKERS)

The terms "Brethren" and "Dunkers" have been the cause of much confusion; they call for careful definition. Dunker is a direct derivation of the German word *tunken*, "to dip or immerse." It is a word to be identified with the peculiar method of immersion employed by this group of churches: trine immersion, in which the believer on his knees in the water is immersed not once but 3 times in the name of the Father, Son, and Holy Ghost. Variously through their long history the Dunkers have been called Tunkers, Taufers, or Dompelaars. They were first called Brethren when their first church organization was established at Schwarzenau, Germany, in 1708.

It might be said generally that these Dunker or Brethren bodies are former German Baptists who took their theology and much of their practice from the Pietists of the seventeenth and eighteenth centuries in Germany. The Pietists, who were mostly Lutherans, became unhappy with the formalism of worship and ritual in their state church and with the general "barrenness" of German Protestantism. They took the New Testament literally and endeavored to put its teachings into practice in the least detail of their living. They spurned the idea of apostolic succession, and at the heart of their practice they had a love feast or agape, which was the serving of the Lord's Supper preceded by a ceremony of foot washing. They saluted one another with a "kiss of peace," dressed in the plainest clothing, covered the heads of women at services, anointed their sick with oil for healing and consecration, refrained from worldly amusements, refused to take oaths, go to war, or engage in lawsuits. These doctrines and practices are held today by many Brethren with certain modifications.

From these German Pietists came the Church of the Brethren (Conservative Dunkers), the Brethren Church (Progressive Dunkers), the Old German Baptist Brethren (Old Order Dunkers), and the Church of God (New Dunkers, disbanded in August, 1962). Another Brethren group, unrelated historically to these and known as the River Brethren, also took its ideology from the German Pietists. This group includes the Brethren in Christ, the Old Order (or Yorker) Brethren, and United Zion Church (formerly United Zion's Children). A third Brethren body, known as the Plymouth Brethren, has a British rather than a German background.

The Brethren bodies beginning in Germany were known for years simply as German Baptist Brethren; that title has largely disappeared except in the case of the Old German Baptist Brethren (Old Order Dunkers).

Church of the Brethren

The Church of the Brethren began in 1708 with a church of 8 persons in Schwarzenau, Germany. Persecuted and driven from Germany into Holland and Switzerland, one group of the church in Crefeld, Germany, under the leadership of Peter Becker, came to America in 1719 to take up free lands offered them by William Penn. They settled in Germantown, near Philadelphia, where they were joined in 1729 by 59 families brought across the Atlantic by Alexander Mack. From Pennsylvania they spread across the country.

Their German speech, their opposition to war, and their insistence upon the inner Christian life as more important than church organization made them a suspect group from the start. Morally they opposed the Revolution; in the Civil War they opposed slavery. The suspicion and misunderstanding waned as time went on; today historians are generous in their praise of the contributions of the Brethren to American democracy. In our own day the work of their pacifists in World War II and their outstanding efforts in relief to Europe following that war have made them one of the most honored bodies in American Protestantism. In their early days at Germantown they printed the first German Bible in America and in 1743 circulated the first American religious magazine.

In 1728 a group under Conrad Beissel left the Church of the Brethren to found the famous Ephrata Community and the Seventh Day Baptists (German); and in 1848 another break resulted in the establishment of the Church of God (New Dunkers). In 1881 a third group withdrew to organize the Old German Baptist Brethren (Old Order Dunkers); and in 1882 came the worst split of all in the organizing of the Brethren Church (Progressive Brethren). In 1926, a smaller group of conservatives withdrew and formed the Dunkard Brethren Church. The original body is known today as the Church of the Brethren and has approximately 181,000 members in 1,036 churches in the United States. Overseas churches that were started as the result of missionary activity in Ecuador, Nigeria, and India are now identified with autonomous churches in those countries, but the Church maintains a cooperative relationship with them.

In doctrine this church follows the mainstream of Protestant theology, with considerable freedom of thought for its members and the clergy and great emphasis on practical biblical piety. Its practical teaching is summarized in the following divisions: (1) the doctrine of peace, including refusal to go to war and a positive peacemaking program which makes them more than war resisters; (2) the doctrine of temperance, under which total abstinence is practiced; (3) the doctrine of the simple life, under which unwholesome amusements and luxuries are shunned, and a practical, wholesome, temperate, clean way of personal and family life is stressed; they seek to develop a "concerned stewardship of life rather than prohibition of amusements and overindulgence in luxuries"; (4) the doctrine of brotherhood, under which all class distinctions are opposed as unchristian; and (5) the doctrine that religion means loving and willing obedience to Christ rather than obedience to creeds and cults. Christian living rather than forms is stressed. Baptism is by trine immersion; the love feast is observed, following the pattern of John 13:1-7.

Moderators, lay or clerical, men or women, either resident or nonresident, are in charge of local congregations, which enjoy a great deal of autonomy. Pastors are chosen by ballot of the local congregation. Above the local group stand the district (of which there are 27) and the annual conference (a legislative body composed of delegates from the churches and an "upper house" known as the Standing

Committee, made up of delegates from the districts). The annual conference is an overall unifying body.

A general board, composed of 25 members elected by the annual conference, supervises the general church program. The board administers the overseas church program. It represents the church in the field of social education, social action, relief and rehabilitation, and carries on a worldwide program of peace and human welfare. The program includes a volunteer service in America and abroad for hundreds of young men and women, including conscientious objectors to war. It supervises church schools, weekday religious education, and summer camps; and is loosely related to higher education in 6 colleges. The board provides leadership and education for the ministry in locating and supporting new churches and in evangelism and carries responsibility for the printing and merchandising interests of the denomination. There is 1 theological seminary.

The Church of the Brethren cooperates fully with the World Council of Churches, the National Council of the Churches of Christ in the U.S.A., and with local church councils.

Brethren Church (National Fellowship of Brethren Churches)

Born in the 1881-83 split in the original Brethren body in the United States (mentioned above), the Brethren Church is based doctrinally on a statement of faith called the Message of the Brethren Ministry adopted in 1921. The Message included declarations of belief in the infallibility of the Scriptures; the pre-existence, deity, and incarnation by virgin birth of Jesus Christ; the vicarious atonement of Christ and his resurrection; justification by personal faith in Christ; the resurrection of the dead; the judgment of the world; believer's baptism by trine immersion; the ordinances of baptism, confirmation, the Lord's Supper, Communion of the Bread and the Cup, foot washing, and anointing the sick with oil.

In 1939 a crisis in the Brethren Church divided it into what came to be known as the Ashland group and the Grace group. The latter group is commonly called the National Fellowship of Brethren Churches. Both groups still carry the name of The Brethren Church and operate under one charter, but each group has its own annual conference—the Ashland body at Ashland, Ohio, and the Grace body (usually) at Winona Lake, Indiana. Each conference has its own executives, and its own educational institutions and mission boards. The Grace group is more definitely congregational in government than the Ashland group. Both groups claim adherence to the Message of the Brethren Ministry, but it is generally true that the Grace group represents more nearly the Calvinistic viewpoint in theology and the Ashland group, the Arminian viewpoint.

Churches are grouped geographically into districts, which hold annual conferences. The Grace group numbers 33,392 in 276 churches, and the Ashland group 16,357 in 119 churches.

67

Old German Baptist Brethren (Old Order Dunkers)

While the Brethren Church (Progressive Dunkers) left the Church of the Brethren (Conservative Dunkers) because the latter body seemed too conservative, the Old German Baptist Brethren (Old Order Dunkers) left it because they considered it not conservative enough. The dissenters stood literally for the old order and traditions. The salient point in their opposition lay in their suspicion of Sunday schools, salaried ministers, missions, higher education, and church societies. They withdrew in 1881.

Their basic objections still hold, but with certain modifications. Children are not enrolled in Sunday schools, but they are encouraged to attend the regular services of the church and to join the church at an early age—anywhere from 15 to 20, the decision being left entirely to the individual. Many congregations list a majority of members between 15 and 40 years of age. The church today is not completely opposed even to higher education; a few of their youths enter high school and take training in college or professional schools for various professions.

They stand for a literal interpretation of the Scriptures in regard to the Lord's Supper and practice closed Communion, which excludes all but their own membership. While they advocate compliance with the ordinary demands of government, they oppose cooperation in war: "Any member who enters into military service will fall into the judgment of the Church." Noncooperation in political and secret societies is required; their dress is severely plain, and they frown on all worldly amusements. They follow other Brethren bodies in refusing to take oaths or engage in lawsuits, have no salaried ministers, enforce complete abstinence from alcoholic liquors, anoint the sick with oil, veil the heads of their women at worship, and refuse to perform a wedding ceremony for any divorced person. They have no Sunday schools, missions, or educational work. An annual conference is held each year at Pentecost, which rules on matters "on which the Scriptures are silent." There are 4,225 members in 54 churches.

PLYMOUTH BRETHREN

Restless under the close connection of church and state in nineteenth-century England and Ireland and opposing the stereotyped forms of worship in the Established Church, groups of Brethren began to meet together for quiet fellowship and prayer. They had no connection, in the beginning, with the Brethren sects in Germany, but took their name from the Scriptures; at one time or another they were also called Christians, Believers, or Saints. The largest meeting was held at Plymouth, England—hence the name "Plymouth Brethren."

These Plymouth Brethren set up their meetings on strictly New Testament lines. They recognized no division of clergy and laity, inasmuch as they held that they were "a priesthood of all believers." They put strong emphasis upon the imminent rapture of the church —to be expected momentarily, insisted upon the full deity and real humanity of Jesus, and denied fellowship to all who were not "fundamentally sound as to doctrine and godly in walk."

Differences arose over divergent views on the effects of unsound teaching in the Plymouth Assembly, and in 1848 there came a division into Exclusive and Open Brethren. The Open Brethren held that they should receive all persons sound in faith, even though some might come from an assembly in which error was taught—if they personally rejected the error. The Exclusive Brethren held that such reception disqualified the assemblies from participation in the Circle of Fellowship, which was, and is, a joint body of approved assemblies holding a corporate unity and responsibility made up of leaders who make decisions for all constituent assemblies.

The tendencies toward division followed them to America when they came here in the late nineteenth century. Today there are 6 active bodies of Plymouth Brethren in this country, distinguished by Roman numerals.

In doctrine the various bodies are in substantial agreement; their separation is caused mainly by differences in church discipline. Generally they acknowledge no creeds; they take the Bible as their only guide, believing it to be verbally inspired and inerrant. They are Trinitarians; they hold that Christ was begotten of the Holy Spirit and born of the Virgin Mary; that man is created in God's image; that by sin he has incurred physical and spiritual death, which is separation from God; that all men are sinners, whose salvation and justification come through faith in Christ's blood, apart from works; that Christ was resurrected and ascended into heaven to abide there as high priest and advocate for the redeemed. Christ's return will be premillennial; it is imminent, and personal, and he will return in glory with all his saints to judge and rule the world. All who receive him by faith are born again and thereby become the children of God. There is a bodily resurrection for the just and for the unjust, eternal reward for the righteous and everlasting punishment for the wicked.

Plymouth Brethren hold that the true church includes all regenerated believers. There are no specific requirements for membership, but all candidates are expected to give satisfactory evidence of the new birth. They are received as "members of Christ," and do not merely join an organization. There are no ordained or salaried ministers in the usual sense; "personal gift and spiritual power" from the Holy Spirit are sufficient evidence of a call to ministry (1 Cor. 12:4-11). In accordance with this they do recognize in certain men gifts of preaching and teaching, and those who devote their time to such work are supported by voluntary contributions. Gifted and godly men are acknowledged as elders and overseers who care for the spiritual needs of the saints.

Government among Brethren I and II is by individual assembly or congregation, under the leadership of their elders; these bodies hold that each assembly is responsible to the Lord alone as head of the church. Brethren III and IV, on the other hand, are joined in Circles of Fellowship, as already described.

The concept of the priesthood of all believers is practiced in their meeting, service, and ministry. There is no ritual. The larger assemblies own church buildings known as Bible or Gospel Chapels; smaller assemblies often start in private homes or (as formerly) in rented quarters known as Gospel Halls. Baptism and the Lord's Supper are observed as ordinances; the Supper is celebrated each Sunday, usually in the morning, and the gospel is preached at night. There are other meetings for prayer and Bible study, young people's meetings, missionary activities supported by voluntary subscription, tent meetings, and evangelistic services.

Plymouth Brethren I followed closely the teachings of John N. Darby, the leader of the original Plymouth congregation, who had far-reaching influence on all branches of the movement; strong emphasis is placed upon his teaching that "eternal life in Christ is the common blessing of all believers in every age," yet, among other branches, Plymouth Brethren I is described as "tight" because of its refusal to let anyone take Communion with them unless they have been associated with them for several months and agree with all their doctrines or bring a letter of commendation from some other "tight" assembly. This group does not accept members from other groups unless and until they renounce all affiliation with those groups. "PB-Is" do not wish to be considered a denomination. (Most of those formerly known as PB-I are now found in PB-II, PB-V, and PB-VI.)

Plymouth Brethren II is generally open, in comparison, welcoming anyone who believes in Christ and who has accepted him as Savior. They have fellowship with Christians outside their own membership and hold that "ecclesiastical position in itself does not disqualify anyone." There is actually a broad base of teaching here, some holding that an open ministry is obligatory, others that it is optional, and still others not tolerating it at all. PB-II known historically as "Open Brethren," is the only body to send men for training to graduate theological seminaries proportionately; the Open Brethren send out more missionaries than the Exclusive Brethren, and are more likely to have a higher percentage of communicants from non-Brethren family backgrounds.

Plymouth Brethren III is known as the "Continental Brethren" because of their close relationship to their European counterparts. They are now affiliated with those known as "Kelly Brethren," alone with PB-VII. (The Kelly Brethren came out of a schism in England in 1881 and was limited to England.)

Plymouth Brethren IV, which has refused to be designated by any name, seems to be disappearing from the scene. Widely known as "Raven Brethren" and later as "Taylorites" (following leaders of those names); their differences with other bodies have been largely in the areas of government and discipline.

Plymouth Brethren V follows closely the doctrine of the original British body, is ultraconservative, and probably the largest of the "Exclusive" Plymouth Brethren.

Plymouth Brethren VI is one of a number of very small Plymouth Brethren groups and is all but extinct.

Plymouth Brethren VII and VIII are comparatively new groups, both of which were part of PB-I up to 1936.

All in all, there are over 800 Open Assemblies in the United States and over 350 in Canada, with an estimated 70,000 communicants; there are probably 300 Exclusive assemblies with less than 10,000 members. The Plymouth Brethren support two Bible schools and one Missionary Training Center, an elaborate series of periodicals, and a radio broadcast, *Grand Old Gospel Hour*.

RIVER BRETHREN

A considerable number of post-Reformation Anabaptists and Pietists, fleeing Europe, settled in Lancaster County, Pennsylvania, during the eighteenth century. During the latter third of the century, in cooperation with other mainline denominations, they developed fellowship groups designated as the United Brethren in Christ. A group in a community near the Susquehanna River came into disagreement with the rest of the fellowship over requirements relative to the Christian ordinances, and as a result "The Brotherhood by the River" withdrew from the larger fellowship and formed a new denomination late in the century. The name River Brethren was associated with this body for more than a hundred years.

Other disputes in the new organization brought about the establishment of 2 smaller bodies—the Old Order, or Yorker, Brethren in 1843, and the Brinsers or United Zion's Children in 1855. These 3 churches today number about 11,000 communicant members in the United States and Canada.

Brethren in Christ (Formerly known as River Brethren)

With the outbreak of the Civil War the draft reached into the ranks of the Brethren, and it became necessary for them to obtain legal recognition as an established religious organization in order to protect their objectors. Nonresistance has always been one of their primary principles. A council meeting in Lancaster County, Pennsylvania, in 1863 adopted the name Brethren in Christ Church; it was not incorporated until 1904.

The Brethren in Christ Church pledges loyalty to the following doctrines: the inspiration of the Holy Scriptures; the self-existent, triune God—Father, Son, and Holy Spirit; the deity and virgin birth of Christ; Christ's death as atonement for our sins, and his resurrection from the dead; the Holy Spirit who convicts the sinner, regenerates the penitent, and empowers the believer; justification as forgiveness for committed sins, and sanctification as heart cleansing and empowerment by the Holy Spirit; observance of the ordinances of God's house; temperance, and modesty of apparel as taught in the Scriptures; the personal, visible, and imminent return of Christ; the resurrection of the dead, with punishment for the unbeliever and reward for the believer; the supreme duty of the church as worldwide evangelism.

While the government of this Church is largely in the hands of the local churches, there are 6 regional conferences and a general conference. There is also a board of administration; and a board of directors amenable to the board of administration has oversight of the general conference and of general church property and financial transactions.

The church has 2 institutions of learning: Messiah College, Grantham, Pennsylvania; and Niagara Christian College, Fort Erie, Ontario, Canada. Missionaries are at work in Africa, India, Japan, and Nicaragua. There are 11,016 members in 159 churches in the U.S. and Canada.

Old Order, or Yorker, Brethren

The Old Order, or Yorker, Brethren is the smallest of all River Brethren groups in the United States; they reported only 291 members and 7 churches in 1936. The primary reason for their existence as a separate body lay in their feeling that the Brethren in Christ had become lax in their enforcement of nonresistance and nonconformity to the world. They left the original body in 1843. Old Order in their name refers to their desire to keep the old traditions alive; Yorker resulted from the fact that most of them at the time of withdrawal lived in York County, Pennsylvania.

Their doctrine is no longer identical with that of Brethren in Christ Church. They refuse to build or meet in church edifices; lacking these, they meet usually in the homes of the members.

United Zion Church

Bishop Matthias Brinser was expelled from the Brethren in Christ Church in 1855, together with about 50 others, for building and holding services in a meetinghouse. They organized under the name United Zion's Children; this was changed in 1954 when the body incorporated under the name United Zion Church.

They are essentially the same in doctrine as the Brethren in Christ. They baptize by trine immersion, observe foot washing as an ordinance along with the Lord's Supper. They encourage the veiling of women and are opposed to divorce and immodest attire.

Located almost exclusively in Dauphin, Lebanon, and Lancaster counties in Pennsylvania, they list 877 members and 16 churches. Church officers are bishops, ministers, and deacons; the top administrative body is a general conference composed of a representation of the various district conferences; the basic unit of government is the district conference.

No foreign missionary work of their own is reported, but they support 2 missionaries working under the Brethren in Christ Church. One home for the aged is maintained, and a monthly magazine, *Zion's Herald*, is published.

UNITED BRETHREN

United Brethren in the United States are found in 2 churches—the Church of the United Brethren in Christ (Old Constitution) and the United Christian Church. The Evangelical United Brethren Church, now merged into The United Methodist Church, was until recently one branch of this body. Originally one group, they were the spiritual descendants of Philip William Otterbein and Martin Boehm (for their early historical background see p. 188). At a general conference of the parent body held at York, Pennsylvania, in 1889 a dispute arose over proposed changes in the church constitution concerned mainly with permitting members to join lodges and secret societies. There was a division into 2 churches: the majority group under the name of the Church of the United Brethren in Christ and the minority in the Church of the United Brethren in Christ (Old Constitution). The larger body merged in 1946 with the Evangelical Church, becoming the Evangelical United Brethren Church, now merged into The United Methodist Church.

Church of the United Brethren in Christ

This is the dissenting group which opposed constitutional changes in 1889; their dissent is still one of discipline rather than of doctrine. In common with other United Brethren they believe in the Trinity; they also believe in the deity, humanity, and atonement of Christ. Observance of strict scriptural living is required of all members, who are forbidden the use of alcoholic drinks, membership in secret societies, and participation in aggressive but not defensive war. Baptism and the Lord's Supper are observed as ordinances of the church.

Local, annual, and general conferences are held; the general conference meets quadrennially and is composed of ministers, district superintendents (presiding elders), general church officials, bishops, and lay delegates. Both men and women are eligible to the ministry and are ordained only once as elders. Missionary societies administer a work in evangelism and church aid in the United States and on foreign fields in Sierra Leone, West Africa, Jamaica, the Republic of Honduras in Central America, Hong Kong, and Nicaragua. A college and seminary are located at Huntington, Indiana, with secondary schools in Jamaica and Sierra Leone. There are 26,409 members in 284 churches. Still insisting upon loyalty to the old constitution they work in harmony with evangelical groups in other denominations.

United Christian Church

This church separated from the original body in 1862-70 "on account of conscientious convictions" dealing chiefly with questions of infant baptism, the bearing of arms in war, secret societies, and the wearing of fashionable clothes. The Rev. George W. Hoffman was one of its most influential leaders, and for years members were known as Hoffmanites.

Hesitant to create another denomination, this body had no formal organization until 1877. A confession of faith was approved that same year, and the present name was adopted one year later at Campbelltown, Pennsylvania. The confession of faith, constitution, and discipline now in use were approved in 1920.

Orthodox and evangelistic, doctrine in this church emphasizes the inspiration of the Scriptures, the Trinity, total depravity, justification, regeneration, entire sanctification, and strict Sabbath observance. Baptism (the mode of which is optional), the Lord's Supper, and foot washing are observed as ordinances. There are district, annual, and general conferences and an itinerant ministry; local preachers vote in the annual conference. Foreign missionaries are stationed in Africa and Japan; there were 422 members and 12 churches, as of 1959.

BUDDHISM

Buddhism is found in real strength in this country in Utah, Arizona, Washington, Oregon, California and Hawaii, and it represents the transplanting of the Buddhism of the East. Most of the Buddhists in the United States are Japanese or Japanese-Americans.

The faith is built upon the teaching of the founder, Buddha—Siddartha Gautama, the Enlightened One (566 B.C.)—who attained his enlightenment in India and whose teachings have spread all over the Far East. Often challenged as a system of religious faith, it remains a most complex and involved pattern of thought and action. It is divided into 2 schools—Hinayana, or Theravada, Buddhism, or the Lesser Vehicle; and Mahayana Buddhism, or the Greater Vehicle. These offer, on the one hand, a path of escape from suffering and, on the other, a thorough preparation for entry upon that path. Hinayana seems devised for those among its disciples who are satisfied with a comparatively modest attainment of Buddhist virtue, while Mahayana is for those who would practice a more exacting discipleship. Buddha himself put the essence of his system in these words: "One thing only I teach: sorrow [or pain], the cause of sorrow, the cessation of sorrow, and the path which leads to the cessation of sorrow." These are the Four Truths of Buddhism, the Fourth of which includes the actual means of arriving at these truths by way of the "noble eightfold path"—"right views, right intention, right speech, right action, right livelihood, right effort, right mindfulness, right concentration." This description of the 8 paths covers the whole training of the disciple who seeks nirvana, which means literally 'blown out" or "extinguished." He strives to extinguish in his living all desire, hatred, and ignorance, and thus attain a nobler life.

There are no theories of creation, no miracles, and no divine being in Buddhism. Supreme reality is neither affirmed nor denied; it is only said to be beyond the comprehension of the human mind. It is actually a system of self-education in the conquering, or forgetting, of pain, sorrow, and suffering. Recognizing that this is a long process, Buddha taught that man has an indefinite number of lives or reincarnations, in which to accomplish it.

The titular heard of American Buddhist churches bears the title of bishop; he is in charge of all religious activities, and he is authorized to transfer or dismiss the clergy under his jurisdiction. The first Buddhist church or temple in the United States was consecrated in San Francisco in 1905; the Buddhist Mission of North America was started in San Francisco in 1898 and incorporated in 1942 as the Buddhist Churches of America. There are 74 ministers and 60 churches and about 100,000 members. They represent the Jodo Shinshu Sect of Buddhism in this country, a faith based on "the anatman doctrine, supplemented by the idea of karma, and nirvana, the holy ease or a blissful mental state of absolute freedom from evil." Each church is autonomous, holding complete control of its own property. Weekly services are held, and Japanese language schools are maintained by many of the churches.

A movement known as Zen Buddhism has found some interest among non-Buddhists in this country; it seeks to transmit the spirit of Buddhism without demanding allegiance to all the teachings of Buddha. It makes use of a question-and-answer technique (*mondo*) to reveal truths not necessarily religious, but truths found within the seeker himself that will bring enlightenment (*bodhi*) and improvement of the condition of man. Wisdom (*prajna*) and love (*karuna*) are major emphases.

CHRISTADELPHIANS

John Thomas came to the United States from England in 1844. He joined the Disciples of Christ but later became convinced that their doctrine made them the apostate church predicted by Scripture and that many other more important Bible doctrines were being neglected. He left the Disciples to organize a number of societies which under his leadership began preaching the need of a return to primitive Christianity. Loosely organized, these societies bore no name until the outbreak of the Civil War, when their doctrine of nonresistance forced them to adopt a name, and Christadelphians (or Brethren of Christ) was the name chosen.

Christadelphians are both Unitarian and Adventist in theology. They reject the Trinity and belief in a personal devil, maintaining the Scriptures teach that Christ is not God the Son, but the Son of God; not preexistent, but born of Mary by the Holy Spirit. Man is mortal by nature with Christ as his only means of salvation. Eternal life comes only to the righteous. Strong millenarians, they believe that Christ will come shortly to reward the saints with immortality and to destroy the wicked; that he will take David's throne in Jerusalem, the faithful will be gathered, and the world will be ruled from the land of Canaan for a thousand years.

The church is congregational in polity; local organizations are known not as churches but as ecclesias. Membership is by profession of faith and immersion. There are no paid or ordained ministers in the usual sense; each ecclesia elects serving brethren, among whom are included managing brethren, presiding brethren, and lecturing brethren. Women take no part in public speech or prayer, though all vote equally. Christadelphians do not vote in civil elections or participate in war, and they refuse to accept public office. There are no associations or conventions, but there are fraternal gatherings for spiritual inspiration. Meetings are generally held in rented halls, schoolhouses, or private homes; there are few church edifices.

Home missions work is local, usually in the form of lectures and instruction in Christadelphian doctrine and righteous living. There are no foreign missions, but ecclesias are found in several countries. There is no educational work with the exception of summer Bible schools in several states. Found in 42 states from coast to coast, they reported 15,800 members in about 850 ecclesias in 1967. Larger numbers are located in Great Britain, New Zealand, Australia, Canada, and Germany.

CHRISTIAN AND MISSIONARY ALLIANCE

The Christian and Missionary Alliance, originated in 1881 under the leadership of the Rev. A. B. Simpson, a Presbyterian minister in New York City who left that church to carry on independent evangelistic work among the unchurched. It was at first divided into 2 societies, the Christian Alliance for home missions work and the International Missionary Alliance for work abroad. The 2 bodies were merged in 1897 in the present Christian and Missionary Alliance.

Strongly evangelical and fundamentalist, the Alliance stands for the literal inspiration of the Bible, the atonement wrought by Christ, the reality of supernatural religious experience, separation from the world, the premillennial return of Jesus Christ, Spirit baptism, and practical holiness. While there is no creed as such, there is a formula of belief built upon a fourfold gospel of Christ as Savior, Sanctifier, Healer, and coming Lord.

Work is carried on in 21 organized districts in the United States and Canada with 1,406 churches fully or partially organized. Each of these churches or groups is a self-administering and self-governing unit engaged in missionary and evangelical activities. There is an over-all conference, called the General Council, which meets annually in various parts of the United States and Canada.

Foreign missionary work is carried on in South America, Africa, the Near East, India, Viet Nam, Thailand, Japan, Cambodia, Laos, West Irian, among overseas Chinese, the Philippines, and Indonesia. In 34 different mission fields are found 893 missionaries from the United States and 4,794 indigenous workers, and there are 4,651 organized churches with 263,694 members.

In addition to the organized church work in North America, missionary work is carried on among Indians and Eskimos, as well as among other ethnic and minority groups. Bible training colleges are maintained at Nyack, New York; St. Paul, Minnesota; San Francisco, California; and Regina, Saskatchewan, Canada. In 1972 there were 162,738 members in North America in 1,406 churches. Thus the Alliance has a larger constituency abroad than at home.

CHRISTIAN CATHOLIC CHURCH

The Christian Catholic movement began prior to 1896, when John Alexander Dowie, a Congregational preacher educated in Scotland and ordained in Australia, gave it formal organization; Dowie also founded Zion City, Illinois (one of the few cities in this country planned in advance of its first settler), and when the city opened in 1901 it became headquarters for the new church. Businesses and industries were developed, all controlled and all governed by a theocracy of which Dowie was general overseer. He had extensive plans for educational and cultural projects; he criticized both the injustices of capitalism and the excesses of labor leaders, alcoholic beverages, tobacco, medicine and the medical profession, secret lodges, and the press. He was also a tireless advocate of racial equality and integration.

Theologically, Dowie was firmly rooted in orthodoxy, but he refused to be bound by what he felt was a cut-and-dried orthodox scholasticism; he objected strenuously to the doctrine of eternal punishment, contending that a God of love must provide an ultimate universal redemption for all men. He emphasized the healing of disease through prayer, and his success in healing led to the establishment of a tabernacle and "divine healing rooms" first in Chicago and later in Zion City. Several years after the organization of the Christian Catholic Church at Zion, he claimed to be Elijah the Restorer and maintained his leadership of the group until 1906, when he was deposed and Wilbur Glenn Voliva became his successor. Voliva died in 1942 and was succeeded by Michael J. Mintern, who was general overseer until 1959; the office is presently occupied by Carl Q. Lee.

At first an exclusively religious community with one church, Zion City has changed considerably since Dowie's day; the Christian Catholic Church is still strong, but independent businesses have been welcomed, and several other churches are at work in the city.

The Scriptures are accepted as the rule of faith and practice by the group; other doctrines call for belief in the necessity of repentance for sin and trust in Christ for salvation, trine immersion, and tithing as a practical method of Christian stewardship. The bases of belief and teaching have been broadened in recent years. The ministers are trained in Bethany, Gordon, and Fuller theological seminaries, Moody Bible Institute, New York Theological Seminary, and Garrett Theological Seminary. The Zion Conservatory of Music attracts many students unaffiliated with the church, and a Passion Play, started in 1935, annually attracts thousands of visitors. There are branches of the church in Chicago; Michigan City, Indiana; Phoenix, Arizona; and Sacramento, California. Missionary work is conducted in Japan, Australia, Palestine, the British Isles, and on the Navajo Indian Reservation in Arizona. An official quarterly publication, *Leaves of Healing*, has a worldwide circulation.

There are 3,000 members in 6 churches.

CHRISTIAN CHURCH OF NORTH AMERICA

This church represents a merger of 2 former Italian denominations: the Italian Christian Churches of North America and the General Council of the Italian Pentecostal Assemblies of God. The former group—and the larger—was founded in 1907 in Chicago as a nondenominational and nonsectarian union of independent Italian congregations. Its work spread across this country and into Italy, Brazil, and Argentina. The Pentecostal Assemblies Group was founded—also in Chicago—in 1904 by Rocco Santamaria and his father, John Santamaria; first named "the Unorganized Italian Christian Churches of North America," it dropped the word "Unorganized" in 1939 and the word "Italian" in 1942, as the use of the English language was gradually being adopted in the member churches. The church was incorporated under the name Missionary Society of the Christian Church of North America, in Pittsburgh, Pennsylvania, in 1948.

There are today some 15,000 members listed in 111 churches. Individual churches exist as separate religious corporations under various state laws. The first general council was held in Niagra Falls, New York, in 1927; since that time each church has sent delegates to an annual conference of the entire society. A Board of Overseers (a general overseer, 4 assistant overseers) and 5 presbyters (directors of departments) constitute an Executive Board. Mission stations are found in Canada, Italy, Africa, Belgium, Brazil, Argentina, Australia, India, North Europe, the Philippines, Venezuela, Uruguay, and the West Indies.

CHRISTIAN CHURCH (DISCIPLES OF CHRIST)

Among the half-dozen largest religious groups in the United States, the Christian Church (Disciples of Christ) might be called the most American; it was born on the nineteenth century American frontier out of a deep concern for Christian unity. There were four pioneers: Barton Stone, Thomas and Alexander Campbell, and Walter Scott. All of them had Presbyterian backgrounds.

Barton Stone believed that Christians could and should unite in the basis of simple faith in Christ, and that the divisive doctrines and practices of denominationalism should be abolished. His church at Cane Ridge, Kentucky, became the center of the famous Kentucky Revival, but Stone came out of that movement convinced that salvation had little to do with church affiliation and that "deeds are more important than creeds." Disciplinary action was brought against him and against his followers in the established churches; they withdrew and reorganized under the name "Christians," and spread across Kentucky, Ohio, and the central states.

Thomas Campbell served as a clergyman in the Seceder branch of the Presbyterian Church in northern Ireland; he settled in a Seceder church in Western Pennsylvania in 1807, where he advocated closer relations with all Christians, Presbyterian or otherwise, appealed from creeds to the Bible as a basis of faith, and practiced open Communion. Censured, he led in the formation of "the Christian Association of Washington County, Pa." and published a Declaration and Address which was to become the Magna Charta of the Christian Church

(Disciples of Christ). In this Declaration he argued that "schisms, or uncharitable divisions" in the church were "anti-Christian, anti-Scriptural, anti-natural" and "productive of confusion and every evil work." The church and church membership should be based solely upon the belief and practices of New Testament Christianity; the articles of faith and holiness "expressly revealed in the Word of God" were quite enough without the addition of human opinions or creedal inventions.

Thomas Campbell laid the cornerstone; his son Alexander Campbell gave the movement its formative theology. He left a Seceder church in Scotland to join his father in Pennsylvania in 1810, and enlarged on the concept that every church should be autonomous and completely independent—that creeds, clerical titles, authority, and privilege had no justification in Scripture; that the Lord's Supper should be served at every Sunday service and that baptism should be by immersion to adult believers (those adult enough to understand the meaning of the ordinance). He argued eloquently for both Christian union and freedom on individual faith, and welcomed to his Presbyterian church at Brush Run, Pennsylvania, all who came with simple faith in Christ as the Son of God and Messiah. He met the same opposition that his father had met, and with his congregation joined an association of Particular Baptists, only to be separated from that body in 1830. He worked in close fellowship with Barton Stone. Stone used the word "Christian" to designate his group, feeling that all of God's children should be known so. Campbell used the word "Disciples." In 1832 the Christians and the Disciples merged; both names are still used, but usually and officially the body is known today as The Christian Church (Disciples of Christ).

Early in the movement, Walter Scott popularized the term "restoration," by which he meant the restoration of the New Testament pattern and practice. Like Stone, Scott was suspicious of the values of the current revivalistic frenzies; he related faith more to the mind than to the emotions—it was not a matter of emotional experience but of intellectual acceptance of the truth of Christ's messiahship. He stressed the importance of such faith, together with repentance of sins and baptism by immersion.

The first national convention of the Disciples and their first missionary society (the American Christian Missionary Society) were organized in 1849; state conventions and societies had begun to meet in 1839. They grew rapidly through and following the Civil War period, especially in Ohio, Indiana, Illinois, Tennessee, and Missouri, in spite of conflict within the church over any emphasis on denominationalism or ecclesiastical organization. The differences between conservatives and progressives became acute in such matters as the organization of missionary societies and instrumental music in the churches; the Churches of Christ separated from the Disciples during this debate.

CHRISTIAN CHURCH (DISCIPLES OF CHRIST)

In matters of belief, conservative and progressive attitudes were and still are important, and the church allows for variance of opinion and stands for complete freedom in interpretation, starting from the historic conviction that there is no creed but Christ and no saving doctrines save those of the New Testament. It could be said that the Disciples are "God-centered, Christ-centered, and Bible-centered," but beyond that, faith is a matter of individual conviction; there is no central authority within the church empowered to say, "This is orthodoxy; that is heresy." The Bible, for instance, is accepted as the inspired Word of God, but in the interpretation of "inspiration" and "infallibility" there is wide divergence of opinion. Some hold that belief in the Virgin Birth is definitely necessary to a Christian's faith; others take a more liberal view, and do not consider it an essential. Some take a literal view of heaven and hell; others believe that reward and punishment should be left in the hands of a loving God.

But there are other areas of general agreement and acceptance. The Disciples are firm in their belief in immortality but do not accept the doctrine of original sin; they hold that all men are of a sinful nature until redeemed by the sacrifice of Christ; they are "trinitarian but not Trinitatian," and are not concerned with speculation about the Trinity and the nature of a triune God. They have no catechism, no set orders of worship. Faith in Christ as Lord is the only requirement.

For more than a century the Disciples were strictly congregational in polity—a loosely bound association of local churches. But, increasingly, it was felt that such an arrangement, with overlapping boards and agencies and with no representative voice to speak for all their churches, needed a restructure in the interest of efficiency and economy. Following a 7-year study and discussion, led by a 130-member Commission on Brotherhood Restructure, a whole new design of governmental organization was adopted at Kansas City in 1968. Under the new plan, the whole church works under a polity of "representative government" on 3 levels—local, regional, and general.

The local church is still the basic unit. All congregations listed in the latest Year Book are accepted as congregations; each congregation manages its own affairs, has its own charters and by-laws, owns and controls its property, calls its ministers, establishes it own budgets and financial policies, and has voting representatives in regional and national assemblies.

The churches are grouped into 37 regions organized to provide help, counsel, and pastoral care to members, ministers, and congregations. Each region organizes its own boards, departments, and committees. Within policies developed by the (national) General Assembly, the regions certify the standing of ministers, provide help and counsel to ministers and congregations in such matters as ordination, licensing, placement of ministers, the establishment of dissolution of pastoral relationships, and installation of ministers. Regions have regional ministers as their administrative leaders.

On the national level there is a General Assembly made up of voting and nonvoting representatives from the local churches and regions, plus ministers and a few ex-officio members, the chief officers of institutions and the general boards, and members of the General Board. The Assembly receives and acts upon proposed programs, policies, reports, and resolutions sent up through the General Board, elects the officers of the church and the members of the General Board and the division boards.

One half of the General Board is elected from members of the General Assembly; the other half by the 37 regions; it meets annually, processes business going to the Assembly, recommends policies, and reviews the total program of the church, elects the governing bodies of the various administrative units and the committees of the General Assembly and the members of an Administrative Committee. General Board members are laymen, laywomen, and (1/3) ministers.

The Administrative Committee of the General Board is made up of 40 members elected by the Board, 30 of whom are members of the Board; officers of the church are ex-officio members. Meeting at least three times a year, it provides for long-range planning, implements policies, and promotes the causes and agencies of the church.

Officers of the church are of two classes—voluntary (nonsalaried) officers of the General Assembly and general (salaried) officers. There is a moderator, 2 vice-moderators, a general minister or president, a secretary, and a treasurer.

There are now 1,356,914 members in 4,609 churches in the United States, and 46 congregations with 4,703 members in Canada. There are 32 colleges, seminaries, undergraduate schools of religion, and foundations; 7 homes for children, and 14 homes for the aged. The Disciples are represented in the National Council of Churches of Christ in the U.S.A., the World Council of Churches, and the Consultation on Church Union. A World Convention of Churches of Christ has its headquarters in New York City.

CHRISTIAN CHURCHES AND CHURCHES OF CHRIST

The churches and members of these independent Christian Churches make up not a denomination but a fellowship; there is no formal organization other than that in the local congregations, and there are no denominational societies, officials, or boards. This is a group of churches identified usually with the Disciples of Christ, with a few congregations of the Churches of Christ and the smaller Christian

Churches, who preach and teach a conservative, fundamentalist theology which they feel is being neglected, especially among the Disciples. Their doctrine in general agrees with that of the Disciples and the Churches of Christ, stressing the divinity of Christ, the agency of the Holy Spirit in conversion, the Bible as the inspired Word of God, future rewards and punishments, and God as a prayer-answering deity. They maintain that "all ordinances should be observed as they were in the days of the apostles" and observe the Lord's Supper in open Communion every Sunday.

No official membership survey has ever been made, due to the unusual nature of the fellowship, but various approximations have been made. These approximations are questionable in accuracy. There are said to be 1,036,460 members in 5,479 congregations. Some 2,300 of these churches withdrew their names from the yearbook of the Disciples, in protest against the recent "Restructuring" of the Disciples. The group supports at least 32 small Christian Bible colleges in different sections of the country; has over 450 missionaries at work operating dispensaries, hospitals, and Bible colleges; and circulates huge quantities of evangelical literature. Their publishing house—the Standard Publishing Foundation—is located at Cincinnati, Ohio.

CHRISTIAN CONGREGATION

The philosophy and work of the Christian Congregation, formed in Indiana in 1887, revolve about the "new commandment" of John 13:34-35. It is a fellowship of ministers, laymen, and congregations seeking a noncreedal, nondenominational basis for union. It is pacifistic and opposes all sectarian strife, insisting that according to the new commandment "the household of faith is not founded upon doctrinal agreement, creeds, church claims, names or rites," but solely upon the relationship of the individual to God. The basis of Christian fellowship is love toward one another, the actual relations of Christians to one another transcending in importance all individual belief or personal opinions. Free Bible study is encouraged.

Churches and pastorates are now located in every state in the union; they still remain strongest, however, in the areas in which Barton Stone preached and in which the original Christian Congregation groups were located—Kentucky, the Carolinas, Virginia, Pennsylvania, Ohio, Indiana, and Texas; for the greater part, the work is done in rural, mountain, and neglected areas. In many respects the work of the Christian Congregation is identical with that of the Stone movement and with his original Christian Church, although Christian Congregations were established and at work when the Christian Church was organized.

Polity is congregational. A General Superintendent presides over a Board of Trustees; relations between the Superintendent and the Board and the people are purely advisory. There are 52,585 members in 297 churches.

CHRISTIAN NATION CHURCH, U.S.A.

Originating in a band of independent evangelists called "equality evangelists," the Christian Nation Church was incorporated at Marion, Ohio, in 1895. Membership today stands at 2,000 in 16 churches.

The church teaches a fourfold gospel; justification, entire sanctification, divine healing, and the second coming of Christ. Two ordinances, baptism and the Lord's Supper, are celebrated. Needless ornaments on clothing, worldly organizations and amusements, tobacco and liquor, Sabbath breaking, the remarriage of the divorced, jesting, foolish talking, and the singing of worldly songs are forbidden; and marriage to the unsaved is discouraged. Each family is encouraged to "raise just so large a family of children as God will be pleased to give them," tithing is practiced, and love for friend and enemy is emphasized. Days of fasting and prayer are observed, the sick and needy are assisted, and camp meetings are strongly supported.

Government is by local churches, which are grouped into districts and which meet in annual conferences. The licenses of all pastors expire at the end of each conference year.

CHRISTIAN UNION

Christian Union represents an attempt to unite all Christians in a consciousness of unity, on a scriptural basis and to offer a larger unity in thought and worship. Organized in 1864 at Columbus, Ohio, its announced purpose is "to promote fellowship among God's people, to put forth every effort to proclaim God's saving grace to the lost . . . and to declare the whole counsel of God for the edification of believers."

There is no one creed binding upon members of the Union, but 7 principles are stressed: the oneness of the Church of Christ, Christ as the only head of the church, the Bible as the only rule of faith and practice, god fruits as the one condition of fellowship, Christian union without controversy, complete autonomy for the local church, and avoidance of all partisan political preaching. Men and women are ordained ministers; ordinances include baptism—preferably by immersion—and the Lord's Supper.

While church government is congregational, a series of councils meet for fellowship and to conduct such business as concerns the entire church. State councils meet once a year and a general council meets every 3 years with both lay and ministerial delegates.

Local missionary work is largely evangelistic and is carried on by state missionary boards; a general mission board administers home and foreign missionary work; 27 missionaries are located in Africa, Japan, Alaska, the Philippines, Liberia, Colombia, Algeria, and Ethiopia. There are no colleges, but a Christian Union Extension School is established at Excelsior Springs, Missouri. One periodical, *The Christian Union Witness*, is published monthly, also in Excelsior Springs. There are 130 churches in Oklahoma, Missouri, Arkansas, Iowa, Indiana, and Ohio; 124 ministers; and 5,821 members.

CHRIST'S SANCTIFIED HOLY CHURCH

This church began with the preaching of holiness and sanctification in the Colored Methodist Episcopal Church in Louisiana by a small body of white evangelists; it was organized in 1904 as the Colored Church South. Its central theme is sanctification by faith "as a distinct experience from justification by faith in Christ, which is not brought about by a growth in grace but is wrought instantaneously." There is emphasis on "one Lord, one faith, one baptism"; unequal persons, holy and unholy, should not marry; both men and women are ordained to the ministry; the strict observance of all church rules is required; no member using or selling tobacco or alcoholic liquors is acceptable; and members pledge that they will "expose all evil" to church officials.

The governing body is a 5-member Board No. 1, which ordains all deacons, deaconesses, and ministers and which supervises boards of extension, investigation, managers, ministers, and others. An annual conference meets in September, a district conference in June, a Sunday school convention in March. The church, listing 600 members in 30 churches in 1957, is too small to maintain any sizable missionary, philanthropic, or educational work. A summer Bible school, organized in 1940, meets at headquarters during the month of July.

CHURCH OF CHRIST (HOLINESS) U.S.A.

C. P. Jones, a Baptist preacher in Alabama and Mississippi, sought a new church and faith which would make him "one of wisdom's true sons" and "like Abraham, a friend of God." In 1894 he founded the Church of Christ (Holiness) U.S.A., which today reports 9,289 members in 159 churches.

Doctrinally, this church emphasizes original sin, the Holy Ghost as an indispensable gift for every believer, and Christ's atonement and second coming. There are 2 sacraments or ordinances: baptism and the Lord's Supper; washing and divine healing are employed not as sacraments but as aids to the growth of spiritual life. The church is episcopal in government, with final authority vested in a biennial convention. There are 7 dioceses, each under a bishop's charge; a district convention made up of elders, ministers, and local lay representatives meets semi-annually.

Missionary work is conducted at home and in Liberia and Nigeria; there is one college, Christ Missionary and Industrial College, at Jackson, Mississippi, and a national publishing house in Chicago.

CHURCH OF CHRIST, SCIENTIST

At Lynn, Massachusetts, in 1866 Mary Baker Eddy recovered almost instantly from a severe injury after reading in Matt. 9:1-8 the account of Christ's healing of the man sick of the palsy. Profoundly religious and a lifelong student of mental and spiritual causation, she came to attribute causation to God and to regard him as divine Mind. From these roots came Christian Science and the Church of Christ, Scientist.

Generally described as "a religious teaching and practice based on the words and works of Christ Jesus," Christian Science was regarded by Mrs. Eddy as "divine metaphysics," as "the scientific system of divine healing," and as the "law of God, the law of good, interpreting and demonstrating the divine Principle and rule of universal harmony." She believed "the Principle of all harmonious Mind-action to be God"; she wrote most of these definitions and descriptions of her faith in *Science and Health with Key to the Scriptures*, a famous volume which together with the Bible has become the twofold textbook of Christian Science.

Like many other religious leaders and pioneers, Mrs. Eddy hoped to work through existing churches. She did not plan another denomination; but organization became necessary as interest in the movement spread, and under her direction the Church of Christ, Scientist, a local church, was established at Boston in 1879. In 1892 she established the present worldwide organization, the First Church of Christ, Scientist, in Boston, Massachusetts, and its branch churches and societies. This church in Boston is frequently referred to as the Mother Church.

Applied not only to the healing of sickness but to the problems of life generally, the tenets and doctrines of Christian Science are often confusing to the non-Scientist and call for careful explanation. They start with the conviction that God is the only might or Mind; he is "All-in-all," the "divine Principle of all that really is," "the all-knowing, all-seeing, all-acting, all-wise, all-loving, and eternal; Principle; Mind; Soul; Spirit; Life, Truth; Love; all substance intelligence." The inspired word of the Bible is accepted as "sufficient guide to eternal

Life." The tenets state: "We acknowledge and adore one supreme and infinite God. We acknowledge His Son, one Christ; the Holy Ghost or divine Comforter; and man in God's image and likeness." Jesus is known to Christian Scientists as Master or Way-shower. They accept his virgin birth and his atoning Mission "as the evidence of divine, efficacious Love, unfolding man's unity with God through Christ Jesus the Way-shower." He was "endowed with the Christ, the divine spirit without measure." Man, made in the image of God, "is saved through Christ, through Truth, Life, and Love as demonstrated by the Galilean Prophet in healing the sick and overcoming sin and death." The crucifixion and resurrection of Jesus are held as serving "to uplift faith to understand eternal Life, even the allness of Soul, Spirit, and the nothingness of matter."

This "nothingness of matter" involves the basic teaching of Christian Science concerning what is real and unreal. Says Mrs. Eddy:

All reality is in God and His creation, harmonious and eternal. That which He creates is good, and He makes all that is made. Therefore the only reality of sin, sickness, or death is the awful fact that unrealities seem real to human, erring belief, until God strips off their disguise. They are not true, because they are not of God.

God forgives sin in destroying sin with "the spiritual understanding that casts out evil as unreal." The punishment for sin, however, lasts as long as the belief in sin endures.

It is a mistake to believe that the followers of Christian Science *ignore* that which they consider unreal; rather, they seek to forsake and overcome error and evil through Christian discipleship, prayer, and progressive spiritual comprehension of the reality of God's allness and goodness, and of man as his likeness. Error is "a supposition that pleasure and pain, that intelligence, substance, life, are existent in matter. . . . It is that which seemeth to be and is not." As Mrs. Eddy has stated (and this point is fundamental to Christian Science beliefs):

If we would open their prison doors for the sick, we must first learn to bind up the broken-hearted. If we would heal by the Spirit, we must not hide the talent of spiritual healing under the napkin of its form, nor bury the *morale* of Christian Science in the grave-clothes of its letter. The tender word and Christian encouragement of an invalid, pitiful patience with his fears and the removal of them, are better than hecatombs of gushing theories, stereotyped borrowed speeches and the doling of arguments, which are but so many parodies on legitimate Christian Science, aflame with divine Love.

She further wrote, "Nothing aside from the spiritualization—yea, the highest Christianization—of thought and desire, can give the true perception of God and Christian Science, that results in health, happiness and holiness."

Certain terms are important in the exposition of Christian Science. "Animal magnetism" is the specific, descriptive term for the mesmeric or hypnotic error of belief in a power apart from God; Christian Science is its antithesis. "Healing" is not miraculous, but divinely natural; disease is a mental concept dispelled by the introduction of spiritual truth. Heaven is not a locality but "harmony; the reign of Spirit; government by divine Principle; spirituality; bliss; the atmosphere of Soul." Hell is "mortal belief; error; lust; remorse; hatred; revenge; sin; sickness; death; suffering and self-destruction; self-imposed agony; effects of sin; that which 'worketh abomination or maketh a lie.' " Mortal mind is "the flesh opposed to Spirit, the human mind and evil in contradistinction to the divine Mind." Prayer is "an absolute faith that all things are possible to God—a spiritual understanding of Him, an unselfed love." Baptism is not observed as a traditional ceremony in this church, but is held to be a continuing individual spiritual experience, "a purification from all error."

All local Churches of Christ, Scientist, of which there are approximately 3,300, as branches of the Mother Church are organized under the laws of the states or countries in which they exist. They enjoy their own forms of democratic government within the general framework of bylaws laid down in the *Manual of the Mother Church* by Mrs. Eddy. Manual articles also provide for the Christian Science college organizations. Reading rooms open to the general public are maintained by all churches. The affairs of the Mother Church are administered by the Christian Science Board of Directors, which elects a president, the first and second readers, a cleark, and a treasurer. The board of directors is a self-perpetuating body electing all other officers of the church annually with the exception of the readers, who are elected by the board for a term of 3 years.

Important in the Christian Science movement are the reader, teacher, and practitioner. There are 2 readers in each church, usually a man and a woman; in all Christian Science services on Sunday and Thanksgiving Day they read alternately from the Bible and from *Science and Health;* the lesson-sermon of the Sunday service is prepared by a committee of Scientists and issued quarterly by the Christian Science Publishing Society. This system is followed by all Christian Science churches throughout the world. A midweek meeting, which is conducted by the first reader alone, features testimonies of healing from sin and sickness.

Practitioners devote their full time to healing and are authorized to practice by the board of directors. There is a board of education consisting of 3 members—a president, a vice-president, and a teacher of Christian Science. Under the supervision of this board a normal class is held once in 3 years. Teachers are duly authorized by certificates granted by the Board of Education to form classes of pupils in Christian Science. One class of not more than 30 pupils is instructed by each teacher annually.

There is a board of lectureship consisting of nearly 30 members. These members are appointed annually by the Board of Directors. At the invitation of branch churches free lectures are given by these members all over the world. A committee on publication serves as an ecumenical and informational office, representing the denomination to the press and public. The Christian Science Publishing Society is one of the most effective units within the church; it publishes very much and very well-written literature, including the *Christian Science Sentinel*, the *Christian Science Journal*, the *Christian Science Quarterly*, the *Herald of Christian Science* in 12 languages and in Braille, and the *Christian Science Monitor*. The *Monitor* is acknowledged in all journalism to be one of the finest newspapers in the world. There are 2 Christian Science Benevolent Association sanatoriums and a home for elderly Christian Scientists, which are maintained by the Christian Science Church. A number of nursing homes for Christian Scientists relying wholly on spiritual means for healing are independently maintained throughout the world.

The bylaws written by Mrs. Eddy prohibit the publishing of membership statistics; no comprehensive, accurate, or up-to-date figures are available. The government census of 1936 reported 268,915 members, but this figure has since been held inaccurate and not at all indicative of the total membership strength of the Mother Church and its branches. Actually today the figure would be much larger than this; in deference to the wishes of the officials of the church no estimate will be given here. It is enough to remark upon a strange situation, found here and probably in no other church in America: the number of people studying Christian Science and attending its services but not yet admitted to full membership exceeds the number who have been so admitted.

CHURCH OF GOD

At least 200 independent religious bodies in the United States bear the name Church of God in one form or another. Of these, 3 have their headquarters in Cleveland, Tennessee, where the name was first applied in the later years of the last century and where important developments have taken place.

The principal Cleveland body began on August 19, 1886, in Monroe County, Tennessee, as a Christian fellowship, first known as the Christian Union, with 8 members led by Richard G. Spurling. The Union was reorganized under the name of "the Holiness Church" in May of 1902, and a simple form of government was introduced. A. J. Tomlinson, an American Bible Society colporteur, joined them in 1903 and was elected general moderator in 1909; he was impeached in 1923 and withdrew to form a rival group known as the Tomlinson Church of God; this name was changed to the Church of God of

Prophecy in 1953. When Tomlinson died in 1943 his group was divided between his two sons, Milton A. Tomlinson, who remained in Cleveland as head of the Church of God of Prophecy, and Homer A. Tomlinson, who organized his followers under the name Church of God and established headquarters in Queens Village, New York (currently in Huntsville, Alabama). A small splinter group left the Church of God of Prophecy in February of 1957 under the leadership of Grady R. Kent to form the Church of God of All Nations in Cleveland.

Still another body, known as the (Original) Church of God (see p. 91), was organized in 1886 following a split among the followers of Richard G. Spurling; it claims to be the first church to use the name Church of God and has headquarters in Chattanooga.

Today, the Church of God (Cleveland, Tennessee) claims 305,836 members and 6,164 ministers in 4,203 churches in the United States and Canada; the Church of God of Prophecy reports 59,535 members in 1,711 churches, and has churches in 50 states and 45 countries; the Church of God (Huntsville, Alabama) claims 75,890 members and 2,025 ministers in 2,025 United States churches; the Kent group makes no report on membership.

In spite of the differences between these bodies, they hold in common doctrines of justification by faith, sanctification, baptism of the Holy Spirit, speaking in tongues, being born again, fruitfulness in Christian living, and a strong interest in the premillennial second coming of Christ. The Cleveland Church of God, especially, while "relying upon the Bible as a whole rightly divided rather than upon any written creed," is thoroughly Arminian, stressing Pentecostal and holiness tenets; practicing divine healing and condemning the use of alcohol, tobacco, and jewelry; opposing membership in secret societies; and accepting baptism, the Lord's Supper, and foot washing as ordinances. The Huntsville group puts strong emphasis upon the fulfillment of scripture "for the last days" and upon preparation now for the return of Christ.

The Cleveland churches elect their officers; the Alabama church appoints them. There are differences in licensing and ordaining ministers. The ministry includes 3 orders: ordained minister, licensed minister, and exhorter.

The Cleveland Church of God holds state conventions and a biennial general assembly; operates Lee College at Cleveland; maintains 3 Bible schools and 1 preparatory school plus a number of schools abroad, 3 orphanages, and a publishing house. Foreign missions are directed by a missions board, but home missions are in charge of a Home Missions and Evangelism Board and a general director.

Church of God (Apostolic)

Organized in 1896 at Danville, Kentucky, by Elder Thomas J. Cox, this body was first known as the Christian Faith Band and was incorporated under its present name in 1919. Its members believe that admission to the church must be only after repentance for sin, confession, and baptism; they teach holiness and sanctification, practice foot washing, and observe the Lord's Supper with unfermented grape juice and unleavened bread.

The general assembly is the governing body; under it serve officers known as the apostle or general overseer, the assistant overseer, district elders, pastors, evangelists, and local preachers. The church is divided into districts, each with an annual ministerial conference. There are 600 members in 22 churches.

The (Original) Church of God, Inc.

This church was organized in Tennessee in 1886 under the name the Church of God after a difference of opinion in regard to doctrine and teaching brought about a split among the followers of the Rev. Richard G. Spurling. The faction adhering to the original doctrines added the word "Original" to the name and incorporated in 1922.

The church believes in the "whole Bible, rightly divided"; in repentance, justification, and regeneration as defined by Martin Luther; in sanctification as defined by John Wesley; in divine healing; in the second coming of Christ; in eternal life for the righteous and eternal punishment for the wicked. Christian fruits alone stand as evidence of faithful Christian living; creeds that bind the conscience are considered unscriptural. They believe in the "filling with the Holy Spirit with the Bible evidence of speaking with tongues as the Spirit gives utterance." Ordinances include baptism by immersion, the Lord's tithing, free-will offerings, the Lord's Supper, and foot washing.

Local churches, following the apostolic pattern, take local names such as the Church of God at Corinth. Each local church is self-governing. The church recognizes the New Testament orders of ministers, apostles, deacons, exhorters, evangelists, bishops, and teachers, as given in Eph. 4:11-14. A general convention meets annually; there are a general office and publishing house, and denominational headquarters are at Chattanooga, Tennessee; a correspondence Bible school, chartered in Tennessee as Ridgedale Theological Seminary, grants dgrees up to Master of Theology and offers honorary degrees of Doctor of Divinity and Doctor of Sacred Literature. There are 90 churches, about 10,000 members.

Church of God (Anderson, Indiana)

The Church of God with headquarters at Anderson, Indiana, started about 1880 as a movement within existing churches. It prefers to have its name accepted in an inclusive rather than in a denominational sense and is actually a movement in the direction of Christian unity and the reestablishment of the New Testament standard of faith and life by realizing the identity of the visible and invisible church in the free fellowship of believers. The founders believed that the church at large was too much restricted and overburdened with organization and ecclesiasticism; it should be "more directly under the rule of God."

Doctrine in this church includes belief in the divine inspiration of the Scriptures; the forgiveness of sin through the atonement of Christ and repentance of the believer; the experience of holiness; the personal return of Christ, which is not connected with any millennial reign; the kingdom of God as established here and now; the final judgment; the resurrection of the dead; the reward of the righteous, and the punishment of the wicked.

Baptism is by immersion. Members of this church also practice foot washing and observe the Lord's Supper, but not as conditions of fellowship. They believe the church to be the body of Christ, made up of all Christians, and that all Christians are one in Christ. The confusion of sects and denominations, however, is an obstacle to this unity; being unscriptural it should be removed. God desires this restoration of the New Testament ideal in his church; it is a restoration based upon spiritual experience and not on creedal agreement.

There are 152,106 members reported in this church along with 95,-232 adherents in home and foreign mission stations. They are governed by a congregational system; while they preach the idea of God governing his church, they agree that human instrumentality is quite necessary. Membership is not on a formal basis, and hence no formal membership is kept. Ministers meet in voluntary state and regional conventions, which are chiefly advisory. The General Ministerial Assembly meets annually in connection with the annual convention and camp meeting held at Anderson, Indiana. With an unusually large Sunday school enrollment of 246,201, this is said to be one of the few Protestant groups in which Sunday school attendance exceeds church membership.

Church of God (Seventh Day)

There are 2 bodies bearing this name, 1 centered in Denver, Colorado, with a publishing house in Stanberry, Missouri, and the other in Salem, West Virginia. Both groups were known originally as the Church of God (Adventist). Located first in Michigan, this body established headquarters in Stanberry about 1900, having separated themselves from the Second Advent body (1863-65) during a debate in which the parent body was seeking a distinctive name for a new press they were establishing at Battle Creek, Michigan. Some wanted the name Church of God, others Seventh-day Adventist; when the majority voted for the latter name, the others left. The 2 factions eventually merged in a new body named the Church of God (Adventist). The Salem group split from this new church at Stanberry to form the Church of God (Seventh Day); the original group later set up headquarters in Denver, maintaining the press at Stanberry. Mr. A. N.

Dugger, prominent in the founding of the Salem church, is now in Jerusalem, apparently heading up still another Church of God movement; he calls Jerusalem "the World Headquarters of the Church of God."

The body in Salem traces its organization back to Old and New Testament churches; they choose their leaders by drawing names by lot, convinced that the method of democratic election is unbiblical. They have twelve Apostles "plus 7 and 70 in an Apostolic Council meeting biyearly, support their ministers by the tithe, observe the seventh day as the true Sabbath, practice foot washing, and abstain from the eating of pork in obedience to the scriptural teaching of "clean and unclean." The Denver group is quite similar in belief and practice, stressing the infallibility of the Bible, the imminent return of Christ, the earth as the eternal abode of the righteous, premillennialism, annihilation of the wicked, reward for the righteous at the final judgment, and abstinence from unclean foods, tobacco, alcohol, and narcotics. They have a General Conference meeting biennially. Salem reports 7 churches and 2,000 members, Denver 5,500 in 56 churches.

Church of God and Saints of Christ

The Church of God and Saints of Christ was founded in Lawrence, Kansas, in 1896 by William S. Crowdy, a Negro Baptist deacon who claimed visions from God, a divine commission to bring the truth of God to the world, and a prophetic endowment. He became the first bishop of the church, which today has a membership of 38,127 in 217 churches in the United States, with additional churches in Africa and the West Indies.

Sometimes called Black Jews, members of this church celebrate such Jewish holy and feast days as they feel have biblical authority and support; they observe the Sabbath on the seventh day, the Day of Atonement, and the Jewish New Year. They believe that their church is built upon the patriarchs, prophets, and apostles of the Jewish tradition, and that "Jesus the Anointed" is their chief cornerstone. They differentiate between prophetic Judaism ("which seeks to follow the living insight into the spiritual idea to its fullest implication") as opposed to legalistic Judaism. They accept the Decalogue as the standard of conduct for all mankind.

An executive bishop stands at the head of the church and the Bishops' Council; there is a Board of Presbytery, which is the law-making body, consisting of 12 men, and an Ecclesiastical Council made up of all evangelists and ministers; under these officials work general and district officers, deacons, teachers, and missionaries. Local churches are headed by overseers and divided into districts; each district has an appointed evangelist who assists the bishop of that district. The district bishop calls and presides over annual district conferences; a denominational religious convocation called Passover and a national business assembly are held annually, both under the guidance of the executive bishop.

The church maintains a home for the aged, an orphans' home, and a school for primary grades.

Church of God by Faith, Inc.

Organized in 1914 and chartered at Alachua, Florida, in 1923, this is a group of 96 churches scattered through Florida, Georgia, Alabama, South Carolina, Maryland, New Jersey, and New York. Doctrine contains items of belief in regeneration, sanctification, the baptism of the Holy Ghost and with fire, speaking in tongues, the Word of God as the communion of the blood and body of Christ, one Lord, faith and baptism, and the isolation of willful sinners from God and the church. Officers consist of a bishop, and an executive secretary. A General Assembly meets 3 times a year. A school (the Matthews-Scippio Academy) was opened in 1963 at Ocala, Florida. Inclusive membership is reported at 5,000 in 135 churches.

Church of God in Christ

C. H. Mason and C. P. Jones, rejected by Baptist groups in Arkansas for what the Baptists considered overemphasis on holiness, founded the Church of God in Christ in 1897. The name was divinely revealed to Mason, who put strong emphasis upon entire sanctification, and in a revival received the baptism of the Holy Spirit together with "signs of speaking with tongues"; his ardent preaching on these gifts and subjects aroused resentment and subsequent division among his followers.

Doctrine is Trinitarian, stressing repentance, regeneration, justification, sanctification, speaking in tongues, and the gift of healing as evidence of the baptism of the Spirit. Holiness is considered a prerequisite to salvation; ordinances include baptism by immersion, the Lord's Supper, and foot washing.

Church organization is held to have its authority in Scripture; there are presiding, assistant presiding, and state bishops, district superintendent, pastors, evangelists, deacons, and departmental presidents. Missionaries are found in South Africa, Thailand, Jamaica, Haiti, Liberia, and on the West Coast in Africa. Saints Junior College is maintained at Lexington, Mississippi; there is a department of publications and a Sunday school publishing house to supply the denomination with literature. There are 425,000 members in 4,500 churches.

Church of God in Christ (International)

Fourteen bishops of the Church of God in Christ (Memphis) withdrew from that Church to organize the Church of God in Christ (International) in Kansas City, Missouri, in 1969. Their disagreement with the parent body was not doctrinal, but one of polity and the authority of government. The theological background here is Wesleyan, but emphasizing two works of grace, full baptism by the Holy Ghost, and speaking with other tongues "as the Spirit gives utterance." Membership is reported at 501,000 in 1,401 churches.

Worldwide Church of God

Claiming direct descent from the Churches of God in England, the modern history of the Worldwide Church of God began with the arrival of Stephen Mumford in Newport, Rhode Island, in 1664 to establish the first Church of God congregation in the New World. (See Seventh Day Baptists, p. 59.) Over the next two hundred years congregations spread across the country to the West Coast. In 1927 Herbert W. Armstrong, a businessman of Quaker and brief Methodist background, became a member of the Church of God in Oregon, was later ordained by the Oregon Conference, and led in the establishment of a local congregation at Eugene; he began broadcasting a radio program in 1934. A monthly bulletin, later called *The Plain Truth*, was issued for its members in the Williamette Valley. The church was incorporated under the original name of the broadcast, "The Radio Church of God," and the broadcast became known as "The World Tomorrow."

Headquarters were eventually transferred to Pasadena, California, where the Church in 1947 founded Ambassador College (later separately incorporated). The broadcast beamed across the country and to Europe, gained a large audience, and resulted in the widening of the educational emphasis with the establishment of a second college campus at St. Albans in England and a third near Big Sandy, Texas (total current enrollment, 1200). *The Plain Truth* is published by the College and has a circulation of more than 2,800,000; there are radio and TV broadcasts from the College. The corporate name of the Church was changed in 1968 to The Worldwide Church of God, and currently claims a membership of 85,000 in 320 churches, largely concentrated in the United States. Local "churches," however, are hard to find; their meetings are usually held in rented schools or halls.

Doctrine includes belief in the deity of Jesus, his message of redemption, reconciliation ascension, and second coming; negatively, the doctrine of the Trinity and the personality of the Holy Spirit are denied. Salvation is by faith through observance of legalistic Old Testament rituals. The true Sabbath is held to be Saturday and not Sunday. Jewish feasts and dietary laws are observed; the Church believes that the ten tribes of Israel migrated to northwestern Europe and are found today primarily in England and the English-speaking world. The Anglo-Saxons of England and the United States are believed to be the descendants of Ephraim and Manasseh. In denying the Trinity, God becomes a "family", and we will all become members of God's family. Christmas and Easter are held to be pagan holidays. The Worldwide Church of God is the One True Church, and the Gospel it preaches is the only true Gospel; the historic churches have been false and apostate since A.D. 69, but the truth appears again in the advent of Dr. Armstrong and the Worldwide Church. Dr. Armstrong, who teaches that "the Bible interprets itself," is recognized as the true interpreter by his followers. No collections are taken at the Saturday services or are "otherwise solicited." The Church is supported by a three-fold tithing under which the member gives one-tenth of his annual income to the general work of the Church, a second tenth for personal religious obligations (including a requirement for members to spend eight days each summer at regional conventions), a third tenth collected every year for "widows, orphans and the destitute."

Among the doctrines of the group that have stirred recent dissent is that of denying remarriage of divorced persons. Opposition to this teaching and protest against the third tithe system brought about the recent defection of forty-five ministers of the Church, who formed a new national church called the Associated Churches of God. At the time of this writing, this Church had some 2,000 or 3,000 members. The dissenting body set forth what it felt to be corrective principles: there is here no requirement for tithing, divorced persons are permitted to remarry and remain members of the Church. The local church is autonomous.

While accurate statistics on membership are difficult to obtain, following the organization of this new Associated body, the Worldwide Church of God may have approximately 85,000 members (70,000 in the United States), and the Associated Churches upwards of 4,000.

CHURCH OF ILLUMINATION

Described as a "church at large rather than a church of congregations," this body was organized in 1908 under the inspiration of the late Rev. R. Swinburne Clymer, now succeeded by his son, Emerson W. Clymer, as Director-General of the church. Its stated purpose is to harmonize the teachings of philosophy with the truths of religion, thus offering a spiritual, esoteric, and philosophical interpretation of basic Bible teachings to those in search of spiritual truth. Membership is by written request and does not require severance of membership in any other church.

Much is made of the "priesthood of Melchizedek," which dates from "beyond the year 4255 B.C. and includes all that small body of chosen seekers initiated into the mysteries of the divine law"; this priesthood has come down from the days of Genesis through Jesus, the Gnostics, the early Egyptians, Greeks, Indians, and Persians to the present time, where it is to be found in the Church of Illumination.

The essence of religion here is found in the simple biblical statement that "whatsoever a man soweth, that shall he also reap." This is interpreted as being a matter of inevitable compensation rather than of rewards and punishments at the hands of God. Furthermore:

Religion teaches the Law—the way of Life—a way which makes man aware of the all-important truth that he is, in fact, a child of God, and that within him, buried by much debris, is a spark of the Divine. This Divine Spark is the *Christos*—the unconscious Soul—which may be awakened and brought into consciousness—a second or Rebirth. This is the "talent" entrusted to man and for which he is responsible to his Creator. Neglected, it remains just as it is—a tiny spark. Recognized, aroused, awakened and brought into consciousness, it becomes an inexhaustible source of wisdom and power, lifting man to the heights of Illumination and achievement. The process that makes all this possible is, in reality, the Second Birth. It is the process of Regeneration—mortality taking on immortality—the means whereby the son of man actually and literally becomes the Son of God.

Enlarging upon this, four great fundamentals are taught: (1) the law of action and reaction (sowing and reaping), (2) the indebtedness of man to God for his talents and his obligation to use them well, (3) the practice of the Golden Rule, and (4) the practice of the law of honesty. All this is the means to the fulfillment of man's destiny. It is also taught that we are now in a "manistic" age (*manisis*, the recognition of the equality of man and woman), which will last 2,000 years and in which Revelation will become the "unsealed book of the Bible," and that the world right now is the scene of the final battle of Armageddon. There is also some emphasis upon reincarnation, although belief in this is not required of adherents.

Yearly conferences of ministers and leaders are held in various parts of the country. Officially there are 14 established churches with 9,000 members, but the bulk of the membership is made up of those who are members only in correspondence and not members of any specific church.

CHURCH OF JESUS CHRIST OF LATTER-DAY SAINTS (MORMONS)

Better known as Mormons, the Latter-day Saints have had one of the most tempestuous histories of any church body in the United States. Attacked by mobs and once invaded by United States Army troops, they built a religious community in what was once a desert and established themselves as one of the outstanding religous groups of the nation.

Essentially a laymen's movement in its origin, their church is rooted in the visions of Joseph Smith, who organized the movement in 1830 at Fayette, New York. Smith claimed to have experienced a series of heavenly visitations beginning with the appearance of God and Jesus Christ to him in 1820, in which he was informed that all existing churches were in error, that the true gospel was yet to be restored, that it would be revealed to him, and that he was to reestablish the true church on earth. He was led by an angel to discover, buried in a hill called Cumorah near Manchester, New York, certain golden plates or tablets left there by an ancient prophet and containing the sacred records of the ancient inhabitants of America and the true word of God. According to the Mormons, America was originally settled by the Jaredites, one of the groups dispersed during the confusion of tongues at the Tower of Babel; the American Indians were direct descendants of the Hebrews who came from Jerusalem in 600 B.C. Jesus himself visited this country after his resurrection.

Smith translated the hieroglyphics on the golden tablets into the *Book of Mormon*, from which the name "Mormon" comes. Oliver Cowdery acted as his scribe. This *Book of Mormon* is considered by the saints as being equal with and "supporting but not supplanting" the Bible, and as being equal with 2 other writings of Joseph Smith, the *Book of Doctrine and Covenants* and the *Pearl of Great Price*, which contain the foundation teachings of the church. The golden plates were said to have been returned to the angel by Joseph Smith; their authenticity has been challenged by non-Mormon scholars and as ardently defended by the Mormons, who offer the names of 11 other persons beside Smith who saw them. Smith and Cowdery had the "priesthood of Aaron" conferred upon them by a heavenly messenger, John the Bapist, who instructed them to baptize each other. Later 3 other divine visitants, Peter, James, and John, bestowed upon them the "priesthood of Melchizedek" and gave them the keys of apostleship. This was in 1829, a year before the founding of the church with 6 charter members.

Opposition arose as the church gained strength, and the Mormons left New York in 1831 for Ohio, where headquarters were established at Kirtland. Another large Mormon center developed at Independence, Missouri, where they planned to build the ideal community with a temple at its heart. Friction with other settlers became so acute that the Mormons were expelled from Missouri in 1838-39; they settled at Nauvoo, Illinois. Violence followed them there and reached its peak with the murder of Joseph Smith and Hyrum Smith, the prophet and the patriarch of the church, in jail at Carthage, in 1844.

With Smith's death the Quorum of the Twelve Apostles was accepted as the presidency of the church, and Brigham Young as president of the Quorum. A group of the defeated minority, objecting that Young was not the legal successor to Smith, withdrew to form other Mormon churches. Some of them followed James T. Strang to Wisconsin to form the sect known as Strangites; others joined various other splinter groups, but the largest body of "anti-Brighamites" believed that the leadership of the church belonged to direct descendants of Joseph Smith, Jr., and in 1860 these people formed the Reorganized Church of Jesus Christ of Latter-day Saints, led by Joseph Smith III.

But Young held his office with the vote of the majority, and he had the courage and the administrative ability to save the Church from complete disruption and division.

He led the saints when they were driven out of Nauvoo in February, 1846, and began their epic march to what is now Utah, arriving in the Salt Lake Valley in July of 1847; here they built their famous tabernacle and temple at the heart of what was to become a worldwide Mormonism, creating a self-existent community in the desert. In 1850 the Territory of Utah was formed; it became the State of Utah in 1896.

Based on *The Book of Mormon* and the Bible, which is accepted "as far as it is translated correctly," the faith of the Mormons is a faith to be found in many conservative Protestant churches, plus the revelations of Joseph Smith. However, certain aspects of Latter-day Saints' theology depart from traditional orthodoxy. They believe that the three persons comprising the Godhead are the Father, the Son, and the Holy Ghost; that the Father and the Son have bodies of flesh and bones as tangible as man's, but that the Holy Ghost is a personage of Spirit; that men will be punished for their own individual sins and not for Adam's transgression. All mankind may be saved through the atonement of Christ and by obedience to the laws and ordinances of the gospel; these laws and ordinances include faith in Christ, repentance, baptism by immersion for the remission of sins, the laying on of hands for the gift of the Holy Ghost, and the observance of the Lord's Supper each Sunday. They believe in the gift of tongues and interpretation of tongues, visions, prophecy, and healing, and that Christ will return to rule the earth from his capitals in Zion and Jerusalem following the restoration of the 10 tribes of Israel. In addition, it is believed that the Latter-day Saints should adhere to the official pronouncements of the living president (prophet) of the church.

Revelation is not to be regarded as confined to either the Bible or *The Book of Mormon;* it continues today, in the living apostles, prophets, pastors, teachers, and evangelists of the modern Mormon church. Baptism is necessary to salvation, and obedience to the priesthood is of first importance. Subjection to civil laws and rules is advocated, together with an insistence upon the right of the individual to worship according to the dictates of his conscience.

Two Mormon practices, baptism for the dead and sealing in marriage or eternity, are exclusive with this Church. Baptism and salvation for the dead are based upon the conviction that those who died without a chance to hear or accept the gospel cannot possibly be condemned by a just and merciful God. The gospel must be preached to them after death; authority for this is found in 1 Peter 4:6: "For this cause was the gospel preached also to them that are dead, that they might be judged according to men in the flesh, but live according to God in the spirit." Baptism is considered as essential to the dead as to the living, though the rites will not finally save them; there must be faith and repentance for salvation. The ceremony is performed with a living person standing proxy for the dead.

Marriage in Mormonism has 2 forms: marriage for time and marriage for eternity (or celestial marriage). Mormons who are married by civil authority only still remain in good standing in the church, but marriage for time and eternity in the church's temples is regarded as a prerequisite for the highest opportunity of salvation. In connection with this, Joseph Smith informed his associates in the 1840's that plural marriage was also sanctioned and commanded by God. Some plural marriages had been secretly contracted for some time before Smith's revelation on the practice was announced publicly by Brigham Young in 1852.

Following the Civil War, the federal government mounted an increasingly intense campaign against Mormon polygamy. In 1882, the Edmunds Act provided stringent penalties for polygamists, and in 1887 the Latter-day Church was disincorporated and its properties were confiscated. In 1890 the U.S. Supreme Court ruled that it was constitutional to deny all privileges of citizenship to all members of the Church. Also in 1890, the Church president issued a manifesto which officially discontinued the contracting of new plural marriages. Some followers of Joseph Smith, Jr., deny that polygamy was ever sanctioned, but a few remaining Mormons (notably in the Reorganized Church of Latter-day Saints) believe that it will never end. These contemporary polygamists are excommunicated from the Mormon church and are known as "Mormon Fundamentalists."

Organization and government in the church differ in detail among 5 Mormon denominations but agree in essentials. They are based upon the 2 priesthoods: the higher priesthood of Melchizedek, which holds power of presidency and authority over the offices of the church and whose officers include apostles, patriarchs, high priests, seventies, and elders; and the lesser priesthood of Aaron, which guides the temporal affairs of the church through its bishops, priests, teachers and deacons.

The presiding council of the church is the First Presidency, made up of 3 high priests—the president and 2 counsellors. Its authority is final and universal in both spiritual and temporal affairs. The president of the church is "the mouthpiece of God"; through him come the laws of the church by direct revelation.

Next to the presidency, in the Utah church, stands the Council of the Twelve Apostles, chosen by revelation, to supervise under the direction of the First Presidency the whole work of the church and to ordain all ministers. The church is divided into stakes (geographical divisions) which are composed of a number of wards corresponding to local churches or parishes. High priests, assisted by elders, are in charge of the stakes. Members of the Melchizedek priesthood hold authority under the direction of the presidency to officiate in all ordinances of the gospel. Seventies work under the direction of the

First Council of Seventy (a presiding quorum of 7 men); they are organized into quorums of 70 each, with 7 presidents of equal rank presiding over each quorum. Seventies have a life-long responsibility to proselyte. The duties of the 12 apostles and the seventies carry them into all the stakes, wards, and missions throughout the entire church. The duties of the stake presidents, the ward bishops, the patriarchs, high priests, and elders are to supervise the work within the stakes and wards of the church. The Aaronic priesthood is governed by the presiding bishopric of three men, who also supervise the work done in the stakes and wards by members of the priesthood.

The church influences every phase of the living of every member; it supplies relief in illness or poverty, provides education, recreation, and employment. Such a program has inevitably resulted in deep loyalty among its members. Almost 17,000 young Mormons currently serve as full-time missionaries throughout the world without compensation; they give two years to the work of spreading the teaching of their church at home and abroad. (In fact, less than 50 persons in leadership positions in the church receive salaries.) Their missionary experience strengthens both them and their church and offers a model of church service.

Church of Jesus Christ of Latter-day Saints

The organization and doctrine of the Church of Jesus Christ of Latter-day Saints have been outlined in the preceding section; with headquarters in Salt Lake City, with 3,090,953 members and 5,394 congregations, this is by far the largest Mormon body. It follows the governmental pattern already described. A general conference is held twice a year at Salt Lake City, Utah. In addition, an area general conference is held annually in one of the foreign missions of the church. The church is supported by the tithes of the membership; each Mormon who earns money is expected to give one-tenth of his income.

The missionary effort of this church is constant and vigorous. There are some 101 mission stations throughout the world. In education, the Utah Mormons have lifted their state to a position in which it stands fourth among the states in the percentage of income designated to their schools. The death rate among Mormons is lower than that of any group of people of the same size anywhere in the world; it is held by some to be the direct result of Mormon abstinence from liquor and tobacco and of their welfare efforts. This church has 105 storehouses for community food and clothing; members maintain vegetable, seed, and wheat farms, orchards, a cotton plantation, dairies, sewing centers, fish canneries, soap factories, cattle, sheep, and hog farms, food processing plants, a vitamin pill factory, and several grain elevators. Most of the products of these industries are consumed at home, but thousands of relief packages have gone to Europe under a church-wide relief plan.

Reorganized Church of Jesus Christ of Latter-Day Saints

This church claims to be the continuation of the original church organized by Joseph Smith on April 6, 1830. It has more than 200,000 members located in 25 countries across the world. It bases its claims to be the continuation of the original Mormon church on obedience to the rule of succession in its presidency as found in *The Book of Doctrine and Covenants*. Court actions on two occasions, in Ohio in 1880 and in Missouri in 1894, are cited as naming it the legal continuation of the original church. The son of Joseph Smith, it is held, was designated by his father to succeed him when the son was 12 years old, and he became president in 1860.

The Reorganized church rejected the claims of the Mormons led by Brigham Young because of their abandonment of this rule, and also because of their adoption of the doctrine of polygamy in 1852, which is held to be contrary to the teachings of *The Book of Mormon* and *The Book of Doctrine and Covenants* endorsed by the original organization in 1835. It also differs from the Utah church on the doctrine of the Godhead.

At the death of Joseph Smith in 1844, the church entered a period of confusion due to several claims to leadership. Those holding to the principle of "succession" eventually reorganized, the first collective expression of this movement coming at a conference in Beloit, Wisconsin, in 1852. Joseph Smith III was chosen president in 1860 at Amboy, Illinois. His successors have all been descendants of the founder.

Basic beliefs of the Reorganized Church include faith in the universality of God the Eternal Father, Jesus Christ the only Begotten Son of the Father, and of the Holy Spirit; the worth and dignity of man; faith in God; repentance from sin; baptism by immersion; the laying on of hands by the priesthood for the gift of the Holy Spirit; the resurrection of the dead; the open canon of Scripture and the continuity of revelation; the doctrine of stewardship and the principle of the accountability of all men to God.

The work of the church is supported by tithes and free-will offerings. This is regarded as a divine principle, and the tithe is calculated upon a tenth of each member's annual increase over and above his needs and just wants.

The church has adherents on every continent of the world, and in the islands of the Caribbean and South Pacific. It maintains a 4-year accredited college at Lamoni, Iowa (Graceland College), and a leadership and ministerial seminary at Independence, Missouri (School of the Restoration). It operates a hospital and a home for the aged, also in Independence.

The administration of the church is by a First Presidency of 3 high priests, a Quorum of Twelve Apostles who represent the presidency in the field, and a pastoral arm under the high priests and elders. Bishops provide for the financial needs of the church. Church doctrines, policies, and matters of legislation must have the approval and action of a delegate conference held biennially at the Saints Auditorium in Independence.

Church of Christ (Temple Lot)

Claiming status as a remnant of the church founded by Joseph Smith in 1830, this church has some 2,800 members in 32 local congregations. After the death of Smith in 1844, and following the western trek of the Mormons, a number of those who remained in the midwest became convinced that the church leaders were advocating new teachings quite at variance with the original doctrines, and by 1852 there were two protesting groups, one known as the New Organization and the other, centered in Crow Creek, Illinois, functioning under the original name of the Church of Christ. This latter group returned to Independence, Missouri, in the "appointed year" of 1867, and began purchasing "temple lots."

These temple lots (the subject of controversy and court action between the Church of Christ and the Reorganized Church of Christ, finally resolved in favor of the Church of Christ) consist of land dedicated in 1831 by Joseph Smith and other Mormon leaders for the building of the Lord's temple. The belief is that the Lord himself will designate the time of building, and that while the men of the church cannot do this until the appointed time, they nevertheless believe that they have a sacred obligation to hold and keep this land free, "that when the time of building does come, it can be accomplished as the Lord sees fit."

Generally, the Church of Christ puts its faith in the pattern and thought of the church "as it existed in the time of Christ and His apostles." Hence the highest office in the church is that of apostle, and there are 12 apostles. They are charged with the missionary work and general supervision of the church. Temporal affairs are directly administered by the General Bishopric, under the direction of the General Conference and the Council of Apostles; local churches administer their own affairs, but must keep their teachings and practice in harmony with those of the denomination. Most of the membership is described as "Gentile," with several members among the Maya Indians of Yucatan, Mexico.

Church of Jesus Christ

The founders of this church were at one time members of a Mormon body led by Sidney Rigdon, in Pennsylvania. Rigdon and his followers refused to join the western march under Brigham Young, denouncing Young's teaching of polygamy, the plurality of gods, and baptism for the dead; in 1846 they purchased a farm (later lost at sheriff's sale) near Greencastle, Pennsylvania. A small group did not go to Greencastle; they remained at West Elizabeth, and under William Bickerton, who had been one of Rigdon's elders, were formally organized as The Church of Jesus Christ at Green Oak in 1862. The name "Bickertonites" is employed to distinguish them from other Mormon groups; they prefer to be known as "the Bickerton Organization." Current president is Gorie Ciaravino, elected in 1965.

Foot washing is practiced, and they salute one another with the holy kiss. Monogamy is required, "except in case of death," and obedience of all state and civil laws. They have their own edition of the *Book of Mormon* (in English and Italian), publish a monthly periodical, *The Gospel News*, and other denominational material at headquarters in Monongahela, Pennsylvania, where a general conference meets annually. Missionary work is conducted in Italy, Nigeria, Mexico, and among the Indians of the United States and Canada. There are 2,439 members in the United States and Canada, in 50 churches.

Church of Jesus Christ of Latter-Day Saints (Strangites)

The group claims that is is "the one and original Church of Jesus Christ of Latter-Day Saints" and that its founder, James J. Strang, is the only legal successor to church leadership with written credentials from Joseph Smith. Strang translated portions of the Plates of Laban; they, together with certain other revelations, are found in "The Book of the Law of the Lord." Strang also translated what is called "The Voree Record"—a record found under an oak tree near Voree, Wisconsin, dealing in hieroglyphic-like characters with "an ancient people . . . who no longer exist." He was crowned "king" of this church in 1850 and was murdered in 1856 during a wave of anti-Mormonism in the Great Lakes region.

Organized at Burlington, Wisconsin, in 1844, the church denies the virgin birth theory, holds that Adam fell by a law of natural consequences rather than in the breaking of a divine law and that the corruption thus caused could be removed only by the resurrection of Christ. They deny the Trinity and the plurality of gods, celebrate Saturday as the Sabbath day, and believe that baptism is essential for salvation. Due to "lack of prophetic leadership at the present time" they do not practice baptism for the dead.

Chief officer of the church is a high priest in the Melchizedek priesthood, chosen by the General Church Conference. Membership is given at about 300 in 6 churches or branches.

CHURCH OF OUR LORD JESUS CHRIST OF THE APOSTOLIC FAITH, INC.

Confident that it is "a continuation of the great revival begun at Jerusalem on the day of Pentecost in A.D. 33," this church was organized at Columbus, Ohio, in 1919 by R. C. Lawson. Doctrine is stated to be that of the apostles and prophets with Christ as the cornerstone. Perhaps the basic emphases are those laid upon Christ's resurrection and premillennial second coming, the resurrection and translation of the saints, the priesthood of all belivers, and the final judgment of mankind. Baptism is by immersion, and the baptism of the Holy Spirit is necessary to the second birth. Feet washing is practiced, but not as an ordinance.

Found in 32 states, the British West Indies, Africa, the Philippines, Haiti, the Dominican Republic, and London, England, the church reports a membership of 150,000 in 250 churches. Twenty-two elementary schools, one Bible College, 18 extension schools, one clinic, and one orphanage are maintained. A national convocation meets every other year at the headquarters church, Refuge Temple in New York City. Officers of the denomination include 5 Apostles, 32 Bishops, 27 District Elders, 3 secretaries, 1 Treasurer, and 1 Public Information officer.

CHURCH OF THE NAZARENE

The theological and doctrinal foundations of the Church of the Nazarene lie in the preaching of the doctrines of holiness and sanctification as taught by John Wesley in the eighteenth-century revival in England. Its physical structure is the result not so much of schism as of the merging of 3 independent holiness groups already in existence in the United States. An eastern holiness body, located principally in New York and New England and known as the Association of Pentecostal Churches in America, joined at Chicago in 1907 with a western (California) body called the Church of the Nazarene; the 2 merging churches agreed on the name "Pentecostal Church of the Nazarene." The southern group, known as the Holiness Church of Christ, united with this Pentecostal Church of the Nazarene at Pilot Point, Texas, in 1908. In 1919 the word Pentecostal was dropped from the name, leaving it as we know it today, the Church of the Nazarene. This was primarily a move to disassociate in the public mind any connection with other Pentecostal groups which taught or practiced speaking in tongues, a teaching and practice not endorsed by the Church of the Nazarene.

The background of the Nazarenes is definitely Methodist; they adhere closely to the original Wesleyan ideology. Most of the early holiness groups in this country came out of the Methodist Episcopal Church; 2 of the original 7 general superintendents of the Church of the Nazarene were ex-Methodist ministers, and the Nazarene *Manual* has been called a "rewritten and modified Methodist *Discipline*."

The doctrine of the church is built around santification as a second definite work of grace subsequent to regeneration; all ministers and local church officials must have undergone this experience. Other doctrines include belief in the plenary inspiration of the Scriptures as containing all truth necessary to Christian faith and living; in the atonement of Christ for the whole human race; in the justification, regeneration, and adoption of all penitent believers in Christ; in the second coming of Christ, the resurrection of the dead, and the final judgment. Members of this church believe in divine healing but never to the exclusion of medical agencies. The use of tobacco and alcoholic beverages is denounced. Two ordinances—baptism by sprinkling, pouring, or most often immersion and the Lord's Supper—are accepted as "instituted by Christ." Members are admitted on confession of faith and on agreement "to observe the rules and regulations . . . of the Church." It is a middle-of-the-road church, neither extremely ritualistic on the one hand nor extremely informal on the other; one church historian calls it the "right wing of the holiness movement."

There are 4988 local congregations grouped into 80 districts. Local pastors are elected by local churches; each district is supervised by a district superintendent who may be elected for a 4-year term by the members of the district assembly.

The general assembly also elects a general board, consisting of an equal number of lay and ministerial members, which is in turn divided into 8 administrative departments: world missions, home missions, evangelism, publication, pensions and benevolence, education and the ministry, church schools, and youth. Foreign missionary work is conducted in 45 world areas with 537 missionaries and 2,729 national workers. Home missions are carried on in all 80 districts and in 12 areas outside the continental United States; a strong emphasis is laid upon evangelism. Eight liberal colleges are maintained, 2 of which were started in 1968. A theological seminary in Kansas City and Bible colleges in the U.S., Canada, and the British Isles are supported by the church.

The books and periodicals of the church are produced at the Nazarene Publishing House in Kansas City; 54 periodicals are published, and the annual volume of business exceeds $7,000,000.

Membership in the United States is reported at 404,732, in Canada and the British Isles at 11,809, in overseas home missions areas at 1,570, with an additional 99,163 abroad, for a total membership of 517,274. There are 7,713 churches and stations at home and overseas.

CHURCHES OF CHRIST

Twelve thousand independent congregations with a total membership of about 2,000,000 constitute the Churches of Christ. They are located in 50 states with greatest concentrations in the South and West, have congregations in 65 foreign countries, and in the past 20 years have emerged as one of the top 10 non-Catholic bodies in North America.

There is a distinctive plea for unity at the heart of the Churches of Christ—a unity that is Bible based. It is believed here that the Bible is "the beginning place" in and through which God-fearing people can achieve spiritual oneness; it is an appeal to "speak where the Bible speaks and to be silent where the Bible is silent" in all matters pertaining to faith and morals; consequently, members recognize no other written creed or confession of faith than the Scriptures. In all religious matters, there must be a "thus saith the Lord."

In modern times the churches are related to the restoration movement—in the work and thinking of James O'Kelly in Virginia, Abner Jones, and Elias Smith in New England, Barton Stone in Kentucky, and Thomas and Alexander Campbell in West Virginia. (For a detailed discussion, see Christian Church and Disciples of Christ.) These four movements, all contending that "nothing should be bound upon Christians as a matter of doctrine which is not as old as the New Testament," and all completely independent at the start, eventually became one strong religious stream because of their common purpose and plea.

The leaders among the Churches of Christ in the nineteenth century were more conservative religiously than their counterparts among the Disciples of Christ. They contended for a strict adherence to the New Testament pattern of both worship and church organization. Congregations refused to join any intercongregational organization, such as a missionary society. Their worship was simple, and they opposed the addition of instrumental music on the grounds that the New Testament did not authorize it and that the early church did not use it. Around the turn of the twentieth century a recognition of differences between the conservative and more liberal wings of the restoration movements became evident, and in the 1906 Census of Religious Bodies, the Churches of Christ were listed separately for the first time. They disclaim being a denomination, but claim to be nondenominational with no headquarters, no governing bodies, and no clergy. They cooperate voluntarily in international radio programs sponsored by one congregation.

Today one of the outstanding features of the Churches of Christ lies in their acceptance of the Bible as a true and completely adequate revelation. This basic concept has resulted in such characteristic practices as weekly observance of the Lord's Supper, baptism by immersion, *a cappella* singing, a vigorous prayer life, support of church needs through voluntary giving, and a program of preaching and teaching the Bible. This concept also explains the autonomy of local churches, governed by elders and deacons appointed under New Testament qualifications, dignified worship services, enthusiastic mission campaigns, and far-flung benevolent programs all financed by the local churches.

The great scriptural doctrines usually classified as "conservative" are received in the Churches of Christ, including the concept of the Father, the Son, and the Holy Ghost as members of one Godhead; the incarnation, virgin birth, and bodily resurrection of Christ; the universality of sin after the age of accountability and its only remedy in the vicarious atonement of the Lord Jesus Christ. Strong emphasis is also laid on the church as the body and bride of Christ. A figurative rather than a literal view is prevalent with reference to the book of Revelation. Membership is contingent upon the faith of the individual in Jesus Christ as the only begotten Son of God, repentance, confession of faith, and baptism by immersion into Christ for the remission of sins. Church attendance is stressed.

While professing identity with the original church established by Christ and the apostles at Pentecost, the Churches of Christ maintain that the final judgment of all religious groups is reserved unto the Lord himself. Members believe they are "Christians only, but not the only Christians." This view, however, still allows for a vigorous evangelism which finds unacceptable the doctrines, practices, names, titles, and creeds which have been grafted into the original Christianity in the long post-apostolic period.

Ministers are ordained rather than licensed, and they hold tenure in their pulpits under mutual agreement with the elders of churches in which they preach. Their authority is moral rather than arbitrary, the actual government of the church being vested in its eldership.

A vigorous missionary program is carried on in 65 nations outside the United States, and in recent years a strong movement to extend the influence of the group in the northeastern United States has developed. Counting native workers in the foreign field and mission activities within the United States, there are over 1,000 missionaries, or evangelists, supported by others than the group to whom they preach. A quota of chaplains is maintained in the Air Force and the Army.

Properties owned by the group probably exceed $2,500,000,000 in value. There are 21 colleges, including one in Japan; 70 secondary and elementary schools; 40 homes for orphans or the aged; and 65 periodicals, newspapers, and magazines published throughout the country. Since all official status in these institutions is lacking, none of them being authorized to speak for the entire church, their conformity in ideas and teachings is all the more remarkable.

Another medium of evangelism has been put to use in the publication of articles in a number of big national magazines. This is the work of the Gospel Press of Dallas, Texas, and is supported entirely by voluntary contributions from individual members throughout the country. Many churches offer correspondence courses in connection with this advertising. A "Herald of Truth" radio and television program has nationwide coverage; it is sponsored by the Highland Church of Christ in Abilene, Texas, and support is found in hundreds of other churches and individuals throughout the country.

CHURCHES OF CHRIST IN CHRISTIAN UNION

This church originated in a defection from the Christian Union churches (see p. 84), at the 1909 meeting of the Council of Christian Union churches at Marshall, Ohio. It was organized "to allow a complete freedom in the preaching of full salvation as stated doctrinally by John Wesley"—a teaching and a freedom which the dissenters felt was being neglected in the parent body. Their first annual council was held at Jeffersonville, Ohio, in that year, and annual councils have been held since that date. In 1945 legislation was enacted to provide for the organization of additional councils in other states; it now reaches into 17 states and several countries abroad.

The Churches of Christ in Christian Union are generally evangelistic and revivalistic in faith and work; camp meetings, revival and soul-winning campaigns are held regularly throughout the denomination. Worship follows simple forms, with little that is ritualistic or traditional. It is characteristic that they place their emphasis "on the blessing of God rather than on the ingenuity of man." A general council meets every two years at Circleville, Ohio, and district councils meet annually. A publishing house is maintained at Circleville, issuing two official publications, *Advocate* and *Missionary Tidings*, and Sunday school materials. There is one college, Circleville Bible College, established to train ministers and lay workers. Headquarters are also located at Circleville.

The Reformed Methodist Church merged with this body in September of 1952, and is now known as the North Eastern District of the Churches of Christ in Christian Union. There is a total of 252 churches, with 8,687 members.

CHURCHES OF GOD, HOLINESS

The Churches of God, Holiness, began in 1914 with a group of 8 people in Atlanta, Georgia, under the preaching of K. H. Burruss. Large churches were founded in Atlanta and in Norfolk, Virginia, in 1916; and by 1922 there were 22 churches in 11 states, Cuba, the Canal Zone, and the British West Indies. In 1922 these churches were incorporated into what is currently known as the National Convention of the Churches of God, Holiness.

All doctrine within this group is tested strictly by New Testament standards; the Scriptures are accepted as inspired, and the New Testament "gives safe and clearly applied instructions on all methods of labor, sacred and secular," and on the conduct of the whole of life. The churches believe in the Trinity, in justification, entire sanctification and regeneration, and hold that the gift of the Holy Spirit is an act subsequent to conversion. Perfection is both *present* and *ultimate*. One must believe in divine healing to be acceptable as a member, but medicines and doctors are approved for those who desire them, not being expressly denounced by Scripture. Two ordinances, baptism and the Lord's Supper, are observed. The washing of feet is approved but not regularly practiced.

Pastors of all churches are assigned by the one bishop of the denomination; they are assisted in the local congregation by deacons. In direct supervision over the pastors in the state overseer, also appointed by the bishop. State conventions are held annually. The highest administrative body is the national convention, a delegate body that elects the national president, or bishop. The church reports 25,600 members and 32 churches.

CHURCHES OF GOD IN NORTH AMERICA (GENERAL ELDERSHIP)

John Winebrenner (1797-1860), a member of the Reformed Church in Maryland, was active in the religious revival which swept this country in the early years of the nineteenth century; his ardent evangelism proved unpopular in the Reformed Church, and he severed relations with it in 1826, forming an independent "church of God" in Harrisburg, Pennsylvania. In 1830 Winebrenner and 6 companion preachers organized the first eldership. The terms "eldership" and "conference" are used interchangeably today in this church. A General Eldership was organized in 1845, distinguishing the national body from other local or area elderships organized since 1830. The words "In North America" were added in 1845, and "Church" became "Churches" in 1903.

Arminian in theology, these churches consider the Bible to be the sole rule of faith and practice. They believe in justification by faith, repentance and regeneration, the Triune God, the office and work of the Holy Spirit, practical piety, observance of the Lord's Day, and the resurrection of the just and the unjust at the final judgment.

The churches were to be, according to Winebrenner, "spiritual, free, and independent churches consisting of believers only, without any human name or creed or ordinance or law." Each local church today is a Church of God. Sectarianism is held to be anti-scriptural. Two ordinances are "perpetually obligatory"—baptism by immersion (the church does, however, accept on transfer the baptismal forms of members from other churches) and the Lord's Supper. The ordinance of foot washing is not obligatory. The Lord's Supper is called Communion in many of the churches, and may be observed at any time, "as the time of observance is not of major importance nor is the posture of the communicant."

Organization consists of 15 elderships or conferences which meet annually in their respective states; there is also an India-Pakistan Eldership, and there is missionary work in Haiti. The General Eldership is composed of ministerial and lay delegates in equal numbers, with a proportionate number of youth from the annual elderships; it meets triennially and plans work in evangelism, education, and the other interests of the church. Local churches are presbyterian in government, but ministerial appointments follow a semi-itinerant system. There is a coeducational college (Findlay) and Winebrenner Theological Seminary at Findlay, Ohio, and a publishing house operates in Harrisburg, Pennsylvania, where headquarters are located. There are 364 churches and 35,833 members.

CHURCHES OF THE LIVING GOD

Two churches of common origin, similar in type but differing in details, bear the title Church of the Living God. Both came out of an organization formed at Wrightsville, Arkansas, in 1889 by William Christian, who "by virtue of a divine call, created the office of chief." Christian held that "Freemason religion" is the true expression of religion and insisted that his "organism" be known as "operative Masonry and [that] its first three corporal degrees shall be baptism, Holy Supper, and foot washing." Both groups are organized along fraternal lines; members tithe their incomes in support of the church and call their churches temples.

The first body, the larger, is known as the Church of the Living God (Motto: Christian Workers for Fellowship). It claims 43,572 members in 272 churches, stresses believer's baptism by immersion, foot washing, and the use of water and unleavened bread in the celebration of the Lord's Supper. A chief bishop is the presiding officer; there is an annual assembly, and a general assembly meets every 4 years to elect other officers and determine the laws for the church. Membership is biracial.

The second body, called the House of God, Which is the Church of the Living God, the Pillar and Ground of the Truth, Inc., is also episcopal in polity and generally follows the form and thought of the Workers for Fellowship group. They have 2,350 members in 107 churches.

111

CHURCHES OF THE NEW JERUSALEM

Commonly called Swedenborgian, the Churches of the New Jerusalem are based upon the teachings of Emmanuel Swedenborg and exist in three main bodies: the General Convention of the New Jerusalem in the U.S.A. (the older United States body); the General Church of the New Jerusalem, which broke from the older group in 1890; and the General Conference in England.

Swedenborg, who was born in Stockholm in 1688 and died in London in 1772, was a Swedish scientist distinguished in the fields of mathematics, geology, cosmology, and anatomy before he turned seriously to theology. Items in his theology dealing with the nature of the one God, heaven and hell, human freedom, the Bible, marriage, etc., are held to have been revealed of God to man's rational mind through things heard and seen by Swedenborg in the spiritual world; he was "uniquely permitted to have communication with the other world." His writings disclaim spiritism, but claim almost daily vision of heaven and hell, which he describes in full detail. He wrote also of frequent conversations with spirits, through whom he learned that a new Christian church was to be born and that his written works would be the basis of its teachings. He died and was buried a Lutheran, but his teachings were definitely different.

Certain that he was divinely commissioned to teach the doctrines of this "New Church," Swedenborg taught that God is man, meaning that the origin of all that is truly human is in one God. The Divine Humanity is, however, Christ's glorified and risen Humanity, in which man is manifested and which is God. These doctrines are accepted and preached by his followers, who consider him to be a divinely illuminated seer and revelator. Against the background of his concept of "correspondence" of the natural world with the spirit world, he expounded an additional sense of the Scriptures considered to be consistent with science and reason. Swedenborg himself never preached, or founded a church, but his followers felt that the need for a separate denomination was implicit in the New Revelation.

The New Church as an organization started in London in 1783 when Robert Hindmarsh, a printer, gathered a few friends together to discuss the writings of Swedenborg; they formed a general conference of their societies in 1815. The first Swedenborgian Society in America was organized at Baltimore in 1792; in 1817 the General Convention of the New Jerusalem in the U.S.A. was established.

The doctrines of the General Convention as set forth in the liturgy are as follows:

1. That there is one God, in whom there is a Divine Trinity; and that He is the Lord Jesus Christ.
2. That saving faith is to believe in Him.
3. That evils are to be shunned, because they are of the devil and from the devil.

4. That good actions are to be done, because they are of God and from God.

5. That these are to be done by a man as from himself; but that it ought to be believed that they are done from the Lord with him and by him.

The societies are grouped into a general convention meeting annually; there are also state regulations. Each society is self-regulating. They have ministers and general pastors (in charge of state associations). Services are liturgical but with a wide latitude, based upon the Book of Worship issued by the General Convention. The convention now has 5,096 members active in 62 societies; a theological school is located at Newton, Massachusetts; the Swedenborg Foundation in New York City distributes the writings of Swedenborg.

The General Church of the New Jerusalem accepts the full divine authority of the "Writings," acknowledging them as being not really *his*, but rather "from the Lord alone." There is no fixed constitution in this church; polity is based upon "essential unanimity" in free council and assembly. There are ministers, pastors, and bishops, the latter being chosen by a general assembly meeting every 3 or 4 years; 3,297 members are reported in 21 organized circles and 15 organized groups. Eight of these societies have parochial elementary schools with an enrollment of 627; there is a theological school, a college, and a secondary school. Headquarters are at Bryn Athyn, Pennsylvania, where a cathedral church has been built.

CONGREGATIONAL CHRISTIAN CHURCHES (NATIONAL ASSOCIATION)

This Association was organized in 1955 by a group of churches desiring to "preserve historic Congregational forms of freedom and fellowship (the Congregational Way)." With 340 churches and an estimated 90,000 members, it is the largest of several Congregational bodies which did not participate in the merger of the General Council of Congregational Churches and the Evangelical and Reformed Church in the United Church of Christ in 1957.

The National Association brings local churches together for counsel, inspiration, and fellowship, but still preserves the independence and autonomy of the local churches. Member churches are either established Congregational Christian churches or affiliated associations of local churches in sympathy with the purposes of the Association. A moderator presides over an annual meeting of all the churches; an Executive Committee of 12, elected for 4 years, acts for the Association between meetings. Eight commissions (Christian education, congregational fellowship, the ministry, publications, women's work, youth, world Christian relations, and spiritual resources) work under the direction of the Executive Committee. Three divisions of the Corporation of the National Association provide a Missionary Society, a Building and Loan Fund, a Foundation for Theological Studies. A unique feature of the organization is found in its Referendum Council, which on call of 10 percent of the churches and by a two-thirds vote may modify any action or proposal of any of the national bodies or officers of the Association.

There is no binding ecclesiastical authority and no required subscription to any creed or program. ("We are bound together not by uniformity of belief but by the acceptance of a covenant purpose to be 'the people of God.'") The Association tends to avoid involvement in controversial social and political questions and action. It does a widespread missionary work at home and overseas in the Philippines, Hawaii, Alaska, Mexico, Hong Kong, Formosa, Greece, Italy, Germany, Brazil, and South India. *The Congregationalist*, a denominational periodical founded in 1849, was revived in 1958 as the monthly journal of the Association. National offices are maintained in Oak Creek, Wisconsin.

CONGREGATIONAL HOLINESS CHURCH

Founded in 1921 by a group of ministers withdrawing from the Pentecostal Holiness Church in an effort to retain holiness doctrines and to establish a more democratic church polity, this church is Trinitarian, emphasizing the inspiration of the Scriptures, justification, sanctification, divine healing (without objection to medicine), the second coming of Christ, eternal punishment and rewards, the merits of the atonement, and the salvation of the entire church.

The Bible is held as the sole rule of conduct; slang, tobacco, membership in oath-bound secret societies, and other forms of worldliness are condemned. Ordinances include baptism, foot washing, and the Lord's Supper. The crowning blessing of religious experience is held to be the baptism of the Holy Ghost and speaking with other tongues "as the Spirit [gives] utterance."

Church government is, as the name suggests, congregational. Local churches are grouped in annual associations from which delegates are elected to a general association. Local church officers, elected annually, consist of deacons, trustees, a secretary, and a treasurer. Pastors are called by a majority vote of the congregation; women are licensed to preach but are not ordained. There are 147 churches and 4,859 members in the United States; newer churches and conferences have been established in Mexico, Honduras, Costa Rica, Brazil, and Cuba.

CONSERVATIVE CONGREGATIONAL
CHRISTIAN CONFERENCE

The origins of the "CCCC" go back to 1935 and the labors of H. B. Sandine, a pastor in Hancock, Minnesota, who was convinced that the denominational establishment of the Congregational Christian Churches had departed from the beliefs, polity, and practices of historic Congregationalism. He carried on a mimeographed educational effort until 1939, when his efforts were consummated in a monthly publication, *The Congregational Beacon* (now *The Congregational Christian*). A Conservative Congregational Christian Fellowship was organized at Chicago in 1945. The prospect of still another merger (involving Congregational Christian and Evangelical and Reformed churches) precipitated reorganization into the Conservative Congregational Christian Conference in 1948.

Today there are 123 member churches in the conference, with a total of 21,200 members. There are also 20 "regional" fellowships and associations with some 250 churches, made up of Congregational Christian churches which are in sympathy with the Statement of Faith and general polity of the conference but not directly involved in its official work and actions.

The Statement of Faith is conservatively evangelical; it includes items of belief in the infallibility and authority of the Scriptures; the Trinity; the deity, virgin birth, sinlessness, atoning death, resurrection, ascension, and promised return of Christ; regeneration by the Holy Spirit; the resurrection of both saved and lost; and the spiritual unity of all believers in Christ.

Local churches are completely autonomous; national officers include a president, 2 vice-presidents, a recording and an executive secretary (missionary-at-large), a treasurer, an editor, and a historian, all elected for 3 years. A Board of Directors manages the property and directs the general business of the conference, through an Executive Committee composed of the officers, with the president as chairman. Under the Executive Committee there are 13 subordinate committees guiding the various efforts of the conference. Work is largely in the areas of missions, youth, and Christian education, carried on through recognized evangelical home and foreign mission agencies, Bible institutions, colleges, seminaries, and Sunday school publishing houses. An annual meeting is held, usually in August. The CCCC is especially active in the fields of church extension, pastoral placement, and regional activities.

The conference is a member denomination of the National Association of Evangelicals, and has recently entered into an international alliance with the Union of Evangelical Congregational Churches of Brazil; the new alliance is known as the International Evangelical Congregational Union, and similarly minded Congregational groups are at work in Brazil, England, and Australia. Headquarters are in Hinsdale, Illinois.

DIVINE SCIENCE

Three sisters—Alethea Brooks Small, Fannie Brooks James, and Nona Lovell Brooks—of Denver, Colorado, and Mrs. Malinda E. Cramer of San Francisco in the late years of the last century worked out independently of one another the principles and practice of Divine Science. They met and joined forces in 1898, incorporating the Divine Science College; their first church—the First Divine Science Church of Denver—was organized in Denver.

The core of its teaching is the principles of the all-inclusive God-mind:

God [is] the Omnipresence, the Universal Presence, Life, Love, Intelligence and Substance; man, a child of God, is of God, is like God; knowledge of this truth frees man into a larger concept of God and the understanding of man's higher nature; the practice of the Presence of God in daily life results in man's right attitude towards negative thinking; evolution is God's method of accomplishing, and love, conscious unity, is the fulfilling of the law.

The founders had all had the experience of divine healing, and the emphasis upon healing naturally persists. Healing comes through an understanding of the nature of God and the Universal Law and is "the cleansing of the inner man from all that is unlike God." Divine Science does not deny the existence of visible matter but interprets both form and substance as manifestations of God.

Divine Science further stands for: (1) the Fatherhood of God as Omnipresent Life, Love, Intelligence and Wisdom; (2) the brotherhood of man; (3) the unity of all life; (4) the higher thought in science, philosophy and religion; (5) the awareness of man's relation to God released into expression in each individual life man's divine inheritance—health, abundance, peace, and power; (6) the transcendance and immanence of God manifested in all created things.

For many years local churches and colleges of Divine Science were independent of one another. In 1957, some of the ministers and key workers of existing Divine Science churches and colleges met and organized the Divine Science Federation International. This new movement serves as a meeting ground and clearing house for determining standards of teaching and conduct for the workers and churches of the movement. Churches, centers and study groups are found in major cities of the United States and abroad; headquarters are located in Denver, where all publications are printed and a monthly periodical, *Aspire*, is issued.

EASTERN CHURCHES

When in A.D. 330 Constantine moved his capital from Rome to Byzantium and began to rule his vast empire from the new Constantinople, the most important split in the history of Christianity was under way. Up to this time the church in the West, in Rome, and the church in the East, formed one body. In the East there were four patriarchs, each traditionally equal with the fifth—the patriarch or pope of Rome; all five patriarchs accepted the Nicene Creed; all were sacramental and apostolic. There were, however, certain basic differences which made for confusion; racially, socially, linguistically, mentally, morally, and philosophically there were deep gulfs between the two. The East was Greek in blood and speech; the West was Latin. The transference of the capital from West to East meant a shifting of the center of political, social, and intellectual influence. When the Goths swept down upon Rome, that city turned for help— not to Constantinople, but to the Franks; in gratitude for his aid the pope crowned Charles the Great as emperor on Christmas Day in 800, and the Roman Church became coterminous with the Holy Roman Empire.

Conflict deepened between the pope at Rome and the patriarch at Constantinople. In 857 Ignatius in Constantinople refused to administer the sacrament to Caesar Bardas on the ground that he was immoral. Tried and imprisoned by the Eastern emperor, Ignatius was succeeded by Photius, an intellectual giant for whom the weaker pope was no match. Their increasing friction broke into flame at the Council of St. Sophia, where Photius bitterly condemned the Latin Church for adding the word 'filioque" to the Nicene Creed. The Eastern Church held that the Holy Spirit proceeded directly from the Father; the Western Church had adopted the view that the Spirit proceeded from the Father *and* the Son—filioque. Political and ecclesiastical jealousies fanned the flame until, in 1054, the pope excommunicated the patriarch and the patriarch excommunicated the pope, the result being that there were finally two churches, Eastern and Western, instead of one. The pope remained head of the Western Church; at the moment, in the East, there were 4 patriarchs, or heads, guiding the destinies of Eastern Orthodoxy. This is important to an understanding of the Eastern Orthodox Church. It is not a monarchy with one all-powerful ruler at the top: it is "an oligarchy of patriarchs," based on the body of bishops and responsible to local or general (ecumenical) church councils. No one patriarch is responsible to any other patriarch, yet all are within the jurisdiction of an ecumenical council of all the churches in communion with the patriarch of Constantinople, who holds the title of Ecumenical Patriarch.

Today Christendom remains divided into 3 principal sections: Roman Catholic, Eastern Orthodox (frequently referred to as the Greek Church), and Protestant. The Eastern Orthodox Church con-

117

sists of those churches which accept the decisions and decrees of the first 7 general church councils—2 at Nicea, 3 at Constantinople, 1 at Ephesus, and 1 at Chalcedon—and of such other churches as have originated in the missionary activities of these parent churches and have grown to self-government but still maintain communion with them. Certain Eastern Church bodies refused to accept the Christological definition of the Council of Chalcedon (451) and are generally referred to as the Ancient Eastern Churches, viz., Syrian-Antiochian, Malabar Syrians, the Armenians, the Copts of Egypt, and the Ethiopians.

Claiming to be "the direct heir and true conservator" of the original primitive church, Eastern Orthodoxy has tended historically to divide into independent national and social groups—Syrian, Russian, Serbian, Bulgarian, Romanian, Albanian, Greek, Georgian. These groups have had a bitter struggle for existence, caught as they have been between Arab, Tatar, Turkish, and Western armies in endless wars. Generally it may be said that Greek Christianity became the faith of the people of the Middle East and the Slavs in Europe, while Latin Christianity became the religion of Western Europe and the New World.

There are at present the 4 ancient Eastern Orthodox patriarchates (Constantinople, Alexandria, Antioch, and Jerusalem), with the modern patriarchates of the Russians, the Serbs, the Romanians, the Bulgarians, and the Georgians. In 1970, the former Russian Orthodox Greek Catholic Church in North America was granted autocephaly with the new name, Orthodox Church in America. Mount Sinai, Cyprus, the National Orthodox churches of Greece, Albania, Finland, Poland, Japan, and Czechoslovakia have autonomous national status.

The Turkish conquest of Constantinople greatly depleted the power of the patriarchate in that city, although it has retained its primacy among the Orthodox—while the First World War and the Russian Revolution of 1917, with the attendant disruption of the Russian Empire, led the Eastern Orthodox churches in Poland, Finland, Estonia, and Latvia to assert their independence. (Lithuania continued loyal to Moscow.) After World War II, Estonia and Latvia were reintegrated into the Russian Orthodox Church. Widely separated, they are all still in essential agreement in doctrine and worship, and together they make up what we know as the Holy Eastern Orthodox Church. Nearly all of the European and Asiatic bodies of the Eastern Orthodox Church have established dioceses in America, some of which are governed by one or another of the 5 major patriarchates, while others have declared themselves to be independent and self-governing.

In the United States today Albanian, Bulgarian, Greek, Romanian, Russian, Serbian, Ukrainia, Carpatho-Russian, and Syrian churches are under the supervision of bishops of their respective nationalities, mostly related to their respective mother churches in tradition and spirit, if not in administration. A Patriarch of Moscow and Alexandria each has jurisdiction over a few parishes in the United States.

Doctrine in Eastern Orthodoxy is based on the Bible, on the holy tradition, and on the decrees of the 7 ecumenical councils. The Nicene Creed is recited in all liturgies and at vespers and matins—the Eastern churches holding that a "creed is an adoring confession of the church engaged in worship"; its faith is expressed more fully in its liturgy than in doctrinal statements. Actually the basis lies in the decisions and statements of the 7 councils which defined the ecumenical faith of the early undivided church against the heresies of the period, and in the later statements defining the position of the Orthodox Church of the East with regard to the doctrine and practices of the Roman Catholic and Protestant churches. The Nicene Creed is held in its original form without the "filioque" clause. The dogma of the pope as the sole "vicar of Christ on earth" is rejected, together with the dogma of papal infallibility. Members of Orthodox churches honor the Virgin Mary as *theotokos*, but do not dogmatize on the immaculate conception. They also honor the saints and 9 orders of angels. They reject the teaching of the surplus merits of the saints and the doctrine of indulgences but reverence the saints, ikons (consecrated pictures) of revered persons or events, and the cross. The use of carved images is forbidden. Bas-relief is permitted in some Orthodox groups.

They have 7 sacraments: baptism, anointing (confirmation or chrismation), Communion, penance, holy orders, marriage, and holy unction. Both infants and adults are baptized by threefold immersion. The sacrament of anointing with chrism or holy oil (confirmation) is administered immediately after baptism. Holy unction is administered to the sick but not always as a last rite. The Holy Eucharist is the chief service on all Sundays and holy days, and all Orthodox churches believe and teach that the consecrated bread and wine are the body and blood of Christ. Purgatory is denied, but the dead are prayed for; and it is believed that the dead pray for those on earth. For justification, both faith and works are considered necessary.

Government is episcopal. There is usually a council of bishops, clergy, and laymen and a synod of bishops over which an elected Archbishop, metropolitan, or patriarch presides. In the United States each Orthodox jurisdiction is incorporated, with a church assembly of bishops, clergy, and laity. There are 3 orders in the ministry: deacons (who assist in parish work and administering the sacraments), priests, and bishops. Deacons and priests may be either secular or monastic; candidates for the deaconate and the priesthood may marry before ordination, but they are forbidden to marry thereafter. Bishops are chosen from members of the monastic communities; all belong to the same monastic rule, that of St. Basil the Great, and are under life-long vows of poverty, chastity, and obedience.

Church services are elaborately ritualistic; the liturgy of Holy Communion is a reenactment of the Gospel story. Of their worship Frank Gavin has said:

In the details of Eastern worship is a rough epitome of the history of Eastern Christendom: the *ikons*, about which a bitter controversy once raged; the service in the vernacular as against Latin; the existence of both a married and a celibate priesthood; the strong and passionate loyalty to the national allegiance evidenced by the provision of special prayers for the rulers by name—all these mark the characteristics, peculiarities, and contrasts with the customs of the West.

In the United States they pray for the President, Congress, the armed forces, and for all in places of lawful civil authority.

Membership statistics are confusing and often unreliable, inasmuch as membership is based on baptismal record rather than communicant status. Infants are confirmed (chrismation) immediately after baptism and are given their first Communion; after the age of 7 they must go to confession before taking Communion. Parish membership, however, is more frequently determined by the number of males over 21 than by communicants (the male head of each family is the voting member in the parish organization). There are probably well over 3,000,000 Orthodox church members in the United States.

It must be kept clear, however, that there are other so-called Orthodox churches in the United States which are not recognized as canonically "Orthodox." These are members and churches which never had or have lost canonical and historical connection with valid, recognized, ancient Orthodoxy. Orthodox churches must be in canonical relationship with the Patriarch of Constantinople and with each other. These irregular Eastern churches might be called autogenic, or self-starting, but they cannot properly be called "Orthodox."

Albanian Orthodox Archdiocese in America

The Albanian Orthodox Church in America is the spiritual descendant of the ancient ecclesiastical Western Illyricum (the Holy Illyria) of early Christianity and the early church, and it has suffered a bewildering series of persecutions and changes in the religio-political struggles of the Balkan area. Under the Peace of Constantine, at the time of the division of the Roman Empire, it was placed under the jurisdiction of the Western Church; under the Byzantine (Greek) emperors it was assigned to that of the Patriarch of Constantinople. Christianized by both Latin and Greek missionaries, Albania, as part of Illyricum, had both Latin and Greek Rite Christians. There were close ties with both Rome and Constantinople until the Moslem Turks became the masters of Albania in 1478-79, when half its people became Moslems and a small minority remained divided between Latin Rite Christians in the North and Greek Rite Christians, subordinated to Constantinople, in the South. Four centuries of oppression ended in the political and religious revolts in the nineteenth and twentieth centuries, when Albania became independent and its people demanded a church independent of Constantinople.

Meanwhile thousands of Albanians had emigrated to America. The Turkish rulers had long refused to allow the maintenance of Albanian language churches by the church authorities in Constantinople, and accordingly the Russian Greek Orthodox Catholic Church in America set up Albanian dioceses here under an Albanian archimandrite-administrator, the Right Rev. Theophan S. Noli, with a liturgy translated into Albanian in 1908. With the outbreak of the Russian Revolution these ties with the Russian Church were severed, and Theophan Noli became the first bishop of a completely independent Albanian Rite Church—a "mother church" which, strangely enough, spread its influence back into the motherland of Albania. Noli was consecrated in the Korche Cathedral in Albania as the Archbishop and Metropolitan of Durazzo, and Albanian candidates for the priesthood in America were ordained in Albania. He returned to America to establish a metropolitan throne, with its see in Boston. All Albanian Orthodox in the New World are under this see; it includes 13 organized territorial parishes and some thousands of unorganized, scattered communicants visited by priests on mission circuits. There are 67,100 members in 2 Albanian church groups.

They have made outstanding contributions in liturgy, the most notable of which is the production of a liturgical literature in a language which has developed as a composite of ancient Pelasgo-Illyrian dialects, Latin, Greek, and Turkish. Their "Albanian Rite" liturgy actually preceded the liturgy of the Albanian Rite Church in Albania. Uniquely, this church has never depended upon the church of its native land. Thanks to communism and the dropping of the Iron Curtain, communication between the two churches is no longer possible, but the strong influence of the American church remains.

American Carpatho-Russian Orthodox Greek Catholic Church

The Carpatho-Russians are Carpatho in that their homeland is in the Carpathian Mountain regions of eastern Czechoslovakia; they are Russian because historically they and their homeland have been a part of the Russian nation, and their religious allegiances have been bound to the Russian and Orthodox churches. Their mother church endured for long years a strife between Eastern Orthodoxy and Roman Catholicism; under political pressure in the seventeenth century it became a Uniat church, with Eastern rites and customs but under the Uniat or "Union" plan, recognizing the supremacy of the Roman pope. The desperate struggle to separate from Rome and to become completely Eastern was transferred to the United States with the immigration of large numbers of their people, especially to our coal-mining and industrial areas. In 1891 the Rev. Dr. Alexis Toth, a Carpatho-Russian Uniat priest, led his church in Minneapolis back to the Orthodox Church, and with several other pastors and parishes was absorbed in the Russian Orthodox Church in America. In 1938 the New Carpatho-

Russian Orthodox Greek Catholic Diocese was formed, and the Rev. Orestes P. Chornock was elected bishop. (He was elevated to metropolitan in 1965.) The diocese was canonized by his Holiness Patriarch Benjamin I in Constantinople.

They now have 68 churches and an inclusive membership of 108,400. Headquarters, a seminary, and a new cathedral have been established at Johnstown, Pennsylvania.

American Holy Orthodox Catholic Apostolic Eastern Church
(Affiliated with the Orthodox Catholic Patriarchate of America)

Instituted in 1932 and incorporated in 1933, this church is self-governing, "maintaining the Eastern Orthodox faith and rite for all men indiscriminately." Spiritually it "owns no head but the head of the Christian faith, Jesus Christ our Lord," but considers itself "inseparably joined in faith with the great church of Constantinople and with every other orthodox eastern church of the same profession." The Greek Rite is used in all worship services, but it receives into Communion and affiliates with other churches of Eastern Orthodox persuasion and belief which desire to retain their national and individual characteristics.

Government is autocephalous; the archbishop does not acknowledge the authority or jurisdiction of any other church or bishop. He is responsible to the National Council, the supreme legislative, administrative, and judicial authority, which is made up of bishops, clergy, and laity. It meets every third year. Two lower ecclesiastical bodies, the Holy Synod and the Supreme Ecclesiastical Council, manage the affairs of the church between councils.

The work of the church is not only religious but social and educational. It represents an effort, fairly successful, to draw together those of Eastern Orthodox faith into one group regardless of race, nationality, or language. A provisional synod was set up in 1935 to encourage coordination between the national groups in the various Eastern Orthodox churches, and the Patriarchal Holy Synod was fully established in March, 1951, in the state of New York. The church and patriarchate has 10 bishops, 25 clergy, 30 churches, and an inclusive membership of approximately 9,000 members.

Antiochian Orthodox Churches

Of Syrian background, these churches are found in two groups in the United States—the Antiochian Orthodox Archdiocese of Toledo, Ohio, and Dependencies in North America, and the Antiochian Christian Archdiocese of New York and All North America. Both are constituents of the Eastern Orthodox Church and were chartered in Ohio under a Praxis issued by the Patriarch of Antioch and are still both under his jurisdiction. Faith and structure are the same in both bodies and both belong to the same Holy Synod.

The Toledo body was established in Ohio in 1935 and is composed of 20 churches and 5 missions. It is in "spiritual communion" with the Greek Orthodox Patriarchate of Antioch, with headquarters in Damascus, Syria. Membership is reported at 30,000.

Formerly known as the Syrian Antiochian Archdiocese of New York and North America but now as the Antiochian Orthodox Christian Archdiocese of New York and all North America, this Church is made up of former residents of Syria, Lebanon, Palestine, Egypt, and Iraq now living in the United States. At first they were under the supervision of a Syrian archbishop appointed by the Russian archbishop in America. In September of 1934 the Patriarch of Antioch appointed the Very Reverend Archimandrite Antony Bashir as patriarchal vicar for all Syrian Orthodox people in North America, with authority to unite all parishes into one organization to be known as the Syrian Antiochian Orthodox Archdiocese of New York and All North America. There are currently 100,000 members in 92 churches. Doctrine and polity are typically Eastern Orthodox.

In 1961 the American Orthodox Church, formed originally in 1940, merged with the Syrian Antiochian Church as the Western Rite Vicariate of that body.

Bulgarian Eastern Orthodox Church

Before the outbreak of the Macedonian revolution in 1903 there was very little Bulgarian immigration to the United States; in 1940 there were only 9,000 Bulgarians resident here. Coming out of the Bulgarian Orthodox Church, which is the state church of the country, they brought with them memories of the long struggle for independence of that church from the domination of Constantinople. It was in 1872 that the Bulgarian Church won its freedom and self-government.

The church started in this country as the Bulgarian Orthodox Mission in 1909 and established a bishopric in 1938. It is attached directly to the Holy Synod of Bulgaria, with a membership made up of immigrants from Bulgaria, Macedonia, Thrace, Dobruja, and other parts of the Balkan peninsula. Services are in the Bulgarian and English languages, and doctrine is in accord with that of other Eastern Orthodox churches.

Membership is reported at 86,000 members in 13 churches, under the leadership of the Metropolitan Archbishop of North and South America and Australia.

Eastern Orthodox Catholic Church in America

American in background, the Eastern Orthodox Catholic Church began its work in America under the leadership of Bishop Raphael Hawaweeny, who was consecrated by permission of the Holy Synod of Russia. Raphael was succeeded in 1917 by Bishop Aftimos, and in turn by Bishop Sophronios and Bishop Morendi, who established (in 1951) what is now known as the Eastern Orthodox Catholic Church in America.

With 265 members in 2 churches, it maintains a mission program, a study center for prospective clergymen, and publishes a monthly periodical, *The American Review of Eastern Orthodoxy.*

The church is governed by what is called the Governing Synod. It is the only orthodox jurisdiction in the United States that uses English exclusively in its worship.

Greek Archdiocese of North and South America

Greeks arrived in the United States in increasing numbers between 1890 and 1914, coming from the Greek mainland, the Greek islands of the Aegean Sea, Dodecanese, Cyprus, Constantinople, Smyrna, and other sections of Asia Minor. They asked for and secured the services of Orthodox priests sent to them by the Holy Synod of Greece or the Ecumenical Patriarchate of Constantinople. Each priest maintained his relation with the synod or patriarchate from which he came; there was at first no central organization to unite them.

Following a period of confusion (1908-1922), during which jurisdiction of the American churches was shifted from the Ecumenical Patriarchate of Constantinople to the Holy Synod of Greece and then back again, an act known as the Founding Tome of 1922 established the Greek (Orthodox) Archdiocese of North and South America, consisting of 4 bishoprics under the supervision of the Archbishop Alexander and the Patriarchate of Constantinople. Alexander's successor, Archbishop Athenagoras, was elected Patriarch of Constantinople in 1948, and was succeeded in turn by Archbishop Michael and Archbishop Iakovos, the present incumbent.

Doctrine, polity, and worship are of the usual Orthodox patterns. There are 1,950,000 members in 502 churches and 11 Archdiocesan districts, 18 parochial schools, 9 summer camps, 1 teachers college, 3 homes for teenage boys, and 1 home for the aged.

Holy Apostolic and Catholic Church of the East (Assyrians)

This is the ancient Church of Persia. Its patriarch originally resided in Chaldea, near the Persian Gulf. It is said that at its peak, throughout most of Asia, it had better than 80,000,000 members, but with the exception of the church which still exists in India, it was almost completely annihilated in the wars of Ghengis Khan and Tamerlane, and later by the Portuguese and Turks in 1915; they scattered through Iraq, Syria, Persia, and Lebanon.

The church claims as founders Thomas, Thaddeus, Peter, and Batholomew of the apostles, and Mari and Addai of the seventy. Its theology stresses the 2 natures of Christ, holding that he was "man and God, 2 natures and 2 substances united in 1 person and 1 will," and insists that Mary should not be granted the status or name of "Mother of God." ("Mary did not give birth to the divinity, but to the humanity, the temple of divinity.") Accordingly, she is not the mother of God, but the mother of Christ. They believe that it was the man in Christ that died, not the God in Christ.

The American branch of this church began during the wave of immigration in 1911, and nearly all of its adherents have come here during the last half-century. In 1940 the head of the church, then in exile in England, came to the United States; he is Mar Eshai Shimun XXIII, Catholicos Patriarch of the East and Supreme Head of the Assyrian people in the Republic of Iraq. Some 250,000 members are still active in the Middle East, Russia, and India; in the United States there are 5,000 members in 10 churches.

Holy Orthodox Church in America (Eastern Catholic and Apostolic)

An interchurch movement rather than a denomination, this body was instituted in 1927-28 to present the Eastern liturgies in the English language, to offset the disadvantages of the use of foreign languages in America, and to establish an autocephalous Orthodox church in America for English-speaking people with American customs and traditions.

The movement stems from the authorization of the late Patriarch Tikhon of the Russian Orthodox Church and the acts of his successors to propagate Orthodoxy among English-speaking people around the world. For its first 15 years in this country it was a program of translating, lectures, classes, and writings.

Services are based on the original liturgy composed by James, first bishop of Jerusalem, as abbreviated and arranged in the fourth century by John Chrysostom into the local usage it has today in all Orthodox bodies, varying only in local custom and language. This liturgy is used throughout the year with the exception of the weekdays of the Great Feast (Lent). The liturgy of Basil the Great is used 10 days of the year.

The faith and order of the Holy Orthodox Church in America rest on the Holy Scripture, holy tradition, the canons of the 7 councils, and the teachings of the anti-Nicene Fathers. Concessions have been made to Western custom in the installation of seats in its churches, in the use of organs and mixed choirs, and in conformity to the Western calendar. It wishes to be known as an independent unit of the Holy Eastern Orthodox Greek Catholic Church, following strictly, however, the ancient traditional doctrines and dogmas of that church. There are 260 members in 4 churches.

Romanian Orthodox Episcopate of America

The Romanian Orthodox Episcopate of America was organized at a Church Congress convened in Detroit, on April 25, 1929, by clergy and laity voting as representatives of Romanian Orthodox parishes in the United States and Canada. It was at first under the canonical jurisdiction of the Romanian Orthodox Patriarchate in Bucharest, until political conditions (the advent of communism) forced its separation from that body, and it is now under the jurisdiction of the autocephalous Orthodox church in America. The Romanian Orthodox bishop is a member of the Holy Synod of the Orthodox Church in America, and the Romanian diocese is recognized as an administratively self-governing body.

The episcopate is headed by a bishop elected for life by a special Electoral Congress made up of clerical and lay delegates from the parishes of the episcopate. With the aid of an Episcopate Council composed of 10 laymen and 5 clergymen (elected for 3 years by the Church Congress), he supervises all matters of administration. The bishop presides at all council meetings, which are held as need arises. The Church Congress is the chief legislative body; it is composed of 1 clerical and 1 or 2 lay representatives from each parish and meets annually in July.

There are 5 "deaneries" or districts in the U.S.; some Romanian Orthodox parishes in South America, Western Europe, and Australia are under the jurisdiction of the episcopate. There are 45 churches and 50,000 members in the United States.

Russian Orthodox Church

Eastern Orthodoxy came to Russia with the baptism of Vladimir in A.D. 988. Government of the church at first was ruled by metropolitans appointed or approved by the Patriarch of Constantinople. About 500 years ago Job became the First Patriarch of All Russia. The office of patriarch was suppressed, and a Holy Synod was substituted during the reign of Peter the Great; the other Orthodox churches recognized this synod as being patriarchal in effect. From 1721 to 1917 the Holy Synod was made up of 3 metropolitans and other bishops from various parts of Russia, who sat in rotation at its sessions. A civil officer of the tsar, known as the Chief Procurator of the Holy Synod, attended its sessions as the tsar's representative, sitting at a small side desk. This pre-1917 church, like every public organization in Russia, was administratively dominated by the tsarist regime.

In 1917 dramatic changes were instituted by the Great Sobor, or church assembly. Administration was changed, the office of chief procurator was abolished, and plans were made to return to the old patriarchal form of government. These reforms were put into effect. As the Great Sobor held its sessions, however, the gunfire of the revolution was heard in the streets, and once the followers of Lenin had taken over the state, they immediately applied their Marxist-Leninist principles: separation of church from state, of school from church, and restriction of church activity in large measure to worship. The patriarch and the synod resisted, but the government found some priests and a few bishops who were ready to support the new regime.

These held a rigged assembly which deposed the patriarch, endorsed communism, and declared itself the governing body of the Russian church. Calling themselves the Renovated or Living Church, they changed the ancient disciplinary rules of the church and instituted liturgical reforms. With the support of the Soviet authorities who hoped thus to divide and weaken the church, they held control for several years. Although they misled some of the Russian people, they were never recognized by the great body of clergy or people. The government considered opposition to the Living Church a civil offense, and on this basis banished thousands of bishops, clergy, and laymen to hard labor camps. In 1927 the Soviet government again recognized the central administration of the Russian Orthodox Church, but not until 1943 did it permit the holding of a church assembly to elect a patriarch.

When the Germans invaded Russia, it was the aged metropolitan, later Patriarch Sergius, who called on his people to support the Soviet government in the defense of their country. This marked a turning point in the Soviet government's policy toward the church; the Living Church was discarded and the patriarch's authority was recognized by the state. Many surviving clergy and bishops who had been banished to Siberia were permitted to return, and gradually the patriarchal administration became again the sole authority in the Orthodox Church of Russia.

The main missionary efforts of Russian Orthodoxy were historically directed toward the Moslem, Buddhist, animistic populations of Central Asia and Siberia. In the late nineteenth century an Orthodox mission was begun in Japan. Eight Russian Orthodox monks entered Alaska in 1792; they established headquarters at Kodiak and built there the first Eastern Orthodox church in America. "K" is known today as the Orthodox church in America; it claims a membership of 1,000,000.) Twelve thousand natives were baptized within two years' time. Orthodox monks and bishops created an alphabet and printed a grammar in the Aleutian language, translated portions of the Bible, and built a cathedral at Sitka.

A chapel was built in the early years of the century at a Russian trading post near present-day San Francisco, in California. An episcopal see was established in San Francisco in 1872 and moved in 1905 to New York City, as Russian immigration brought thousands of Orthodox to the eastern states. Immigrants from other countries with Orthodox churches—Serbia, Syria, Greece—were for many years cared for by the Russian hierarchy in America. Many Orthodox from the old Austro-Hungarian empire, traditionally having been in a Uniat church which had grown to impressive numbers, came to this country and found themselves in an embarrassing situation, being placed under the direction of Irish and German Roman Catholic bishops. Torn between conflicting demands and loyalties, many of these Uniat parishes returned to the jurisdiction of the Russian Orthodox Church.

Hard days were ahead, however. The Russian revolution of 1917 cut off the financial support that had come from the mother church, which was now fighting for its life. The Living Church faction in Russia, supported by the Communist government, sent an emissary to secure control of the church property in the United States, and he succeeded by action in the civil courts in securing possession of the Russian cathedral in New York City. Further seizures were prevented by the declaration of the Russian Orthodox in America at a Sobor (church assembly) at Detroit in 1924, recognizing its spiritual heritage but asserting its administrative, legislative, and judicial independence of Moscow. This church thus became an autonomous Orthodox church and has made great progress in the support and loyalty of its people. It now has 13 archbishops and bishops, and reports 755,000 members in 352 churches. Its official title was the Russian Orthodox Greek Catholic Church of America but is now the Orthodox Church in America.

In addition to this Russian Orthodox jurisdiction (or administrative unit), with its continuous history in this country since 1792, there are now 2 other Orthodox jurisdictions that have come to America within recent years. No doctrinal differences separate these 3 groups; their disagreement is exclusively on the question of recognizing the authority of the Patriarch of Moscow. A second body, the Russian Orthodox Church Outside Russia, holds that the Moscow patriarchate has forfeited its right to be considered a true Orthodox Church because its accepts the authority of the atheist Soviet government. The metropolitan and synod of this body administers all like-minded Russian Orthodox all over the world.

The second body is made up largely of Russian exiles of the revolution and displaced persons of World War II. When armed resistance to the Soviet revolution was finally put down, many sought refuge abroad. A number of bishops and clergy gathered at Constantinople and later transferred to Sremski Karlovici in Yugoslavia, and there they set up a synod to give spiritual leadership to these refugees. After World War II, the establishment of a Communist regime in Yugoslavia and the increase in the number of Russian refugees (including some of the bishops of this synod) gathered in displaced-persons camps led the synod to move its headquarters to Munich. Relief programs of the churches brought great numbers of the "displaced persons" to America, and the headquarters of the synod (now called the Russian Orthodox Church Outside Russia) were moved to New York City in 1952. Its complete rejection of the Moscow patriarchate conformed to the attitude of many of these new arrivals and kept them from uniting with the Russian church already established in North America, which claimed in 1951 some 55,000 members and 81 churches. In addition, it maintains bishops and clergy wherever Russian refugees are resettled—in Canada, South America, Australia, Africa, and Europe.

The third body is called the Patriarchal Parishes of the Russian Orthodox Church in the U.S.A. It accepts the full authority of the

Moscow patriarchate and is its representative in America. De facto occupancy of the old Russian cathedral in New York City was established when the former emissary of the Living Church faction made his submission to the patriarch's representative. It is governed by four bishops appointed by the patriarch, and an assembly elected by the parishes.

Serbian Orthodox Church in the U.S.A. and Canada

The church in Serbia from the seventh century to the thirteenth was under the jurisdiction of the Greek Patriarchate of Constantinople and became the independent National Serbian Church in 1219. It made notable contributions to art and architecture and played an important part in the Serbian struggle for independence all through the long period of Turkish invasion and domination (1389-1876), during which it suffered an unbelievable persecution.

Serbian immigrants to the United States, coming here more for political than economic reasons, began to arrive in large numbers about 1890. They worshiped at first in Russian churches, accepting the ministrations of Russian priests and the supervision of Russian bishops. The Serbian Patriarchate of Yukoslavia approved the organization of the Diocese of the United States and Canada in 1921, and sent its first bishop in 1926. Headquarters are located in Chicago. There are today 52 parishes and 65,000 members. Doctrine and polity are in harmony with other branches of the Orthodox Church.

Ukrainian Orthodox Churches

Eastern Orthodoxy was established as the state religion in the Ukraine by a unique procedure. In the tenth century Vladimir the Great, ruler of Kiev, sent investigators abroad to study the doctrines and rituals of Islam and Judaism as well as those of Christianity. They came back to report that the Eastern Orthodox faith seemed best suited to the needs of their people. Vladimir was immediately baptized in that faith, and by 988 the entire Ukraine population had become Orthodox Christian.

For more than 600 years the Ukrainian Church was under the jurisdiction of the Ecumenical Patriarchate of Constantinople. In 1686 it was placed under the supervision of the Russian Patriarch of Moscow. Rejecting the authority of Moscow after the 1917 revolution, Ukrainians in the United States are still engaged in a bitter dispute among themselves; attempts at union have been made, but to date have been unsuccessful. Three groups are in competition. The first, known as the Ukrainian Orthodox Church of the U.S.A., was formally organized in this country in 1919; Archbishop John Theodorovich arrived from the Ukraine in 1924. This group has 107 churches and 87,745 members. The secondy body is known as the Ukrainian Orthodox Church of America (Ecumenical Patriarchate), was organized in 1928, has 23 churches and 30,000 members. The third body is known as the Holy

Ukrainian Autocephalic Orthodox Church in Exile. It broke from the Ukrainian Church in the U.S.A. in 1951 in a dispute over administrative matters and is made up largely of Ukrainian laymen and clergy who came to America after World War II. There are 4,800 members in 15 churches.

EPISCOPAL CHURCH

It is stated in the preface of the *Book of Common Prayer* of the Protestant Episcopal Church (now known generally as the Episcopal Church) that "this Church is far from intending to depart from the Church of England in any essential point of doctrine, discipline, or worship." Therein lies the hint of its origin: the Protestant Episcopal Church constitutes the "self-governing American branch of the Anglican Communion." For a century and a half in this country it bore the name of the Church of England.

Its history runs back to the first missionaries who went to the British Isles from Gaul prior to the Council of Arles in A.D. 314. It is traced down through the days when Henry VIII threw off the supremacy of the pope (Henry, according to Anglican scholars, did not found the Church of England; it was a church that had always been more British than Roman); through the reign of Edward VI, when the *Book of Common Prayer* and 42 Articles of Religion were written; through the period of Catholic restoration under Bloody Mary and through her successor Elizabeth, who put the united church and state under the Protestant banner and sent Sir Francis Drake sailing to build an empire.

Drake came ashore in what is now California in 1578. His Church of England chaplain, Francis Fletcher, planted a cross and read a prayer while Drake claimed the new land for the Virgin Queen. Martin Frobisher had reached Laborador in 1576, also with a chaplain. After them came colonists to Virginia under Sir Humphrey Gilbert and Sir Walter Raleigh; Raleigh's chaplain baptized an Indian named Manteo and a white baby named Virginia Dare before the settlement vanished. With Captain John Smith came Chaplain Robert Hunt, who stretched a sail between 2 trees for a shelter and read the service from the *Book of Common Prayer.*

In the South the transplanted Church of England quickly became the established church. It was at heart a tolerant and catholic church, but the control of the crown brought an almost ruthless authority which made the church suspect in the eyes of those colonists who had come here seeking freedom from all such authority. The Virginia House of Burgesses set the salary of the Virginia clergyman at "1,500 pounds of tobacco and 16 barrels of corn." It was a British clergy supported by public tax and assessment and by contributions from the church in England through the Society for the Propagation of the Gospel. And it was technically under the jurisdiction of the Bishop of London. In that fact lay one of its almost fatal weaknesses; colonial ministers had to journey to England for ordination, and few could afford it. This, coupled with the rising tide of the American Revolution, placed the colonial Church of England in an unenviable position.

Yet the church did well. Membership grew rapidly. William and Mary College was established in 1693, and the Church of England became the predominant church in the South. King's Chapel in Boston, the first Episcopal church in New England, was opened in 1689; in 1698 a church was established at Newport, Rhode Island, and another, called Trinity Church, in New York City. In 1702 a delegation from the Society for the Propagation of the Gospel came from England to survey the colonial church and found about 50 clergymen at work from the Carolinas to Maine. The visitors sensed the need for American bishops to ordain American clergymen; they also sensed the increasing opposition of the American patriot to a British-governed church.

The Revolution almost destroyed the colonial Church of England. Under special oath of allegiance to the king the clergy either fled to England or Canada or remained as Loyalists in the colonies in the face of overwhelming persecution. That many of them were loyal to the American cause meant little; the Rev. William White was chaplain of the Continental Congress, the Rev. Charles Thurston was a Continental colonel, and in the pews of the Episcopal Church sat Washington, Jefferson, Patrick Henry, John Jay, Robert Morris, John Marshall, Charles and "Light-Horse Harry" Lee, and John Randolph. But their presence could not stem the tide. The Anglican house was divided, and it fell. At the war's end there was no episcopacy, no association of the churches, not even the semblance of an establishment. Few thought of any future for this church, which suffered between Lexington and Yorktown more than any other in the colonies.

There was, however, a future—and a great one. In 1782 there appeared a pamphlet entitled *The Case of the Episcopal Churches in the United States Considered*, written by William White. It was a plea for unity and reorganization, and it proposed that the ministry be continued temporarily without the episcopal succession since the latter "cannot at present be obtained." In 1783 a conference of the Episcopal churches met at Annapolis, Maryland, and formally adopted the name Protestant Episcopal Church—"Protestant" to distinguish it from the Roman Catholic Church, "Episcopal" to distinguish it from the Presbyterians and the Congregationalists. In 1967 the general convention adopted the Episcopal Church as an alternate name for the Protestant Episcopal Church in the U.S.A.

Also in 1783 the clergy in Connecticut elected Samuel Seabury as their prospective bishop; he went to England and waited a year for consecration at the hands of English bishops. This was denied, and he then went to Scotland to be consecrated bishop in 1784. Ultimately Parliament and the Church of England cleared the way, and two other bishops-elect from New York and Pennsylvania were consecrated by the Archbishop of Canterbury in 1787. In 1789 the constitution of the Protestant Episcopal Church was adopted in Philadelphia, the *Book of Common Prayer* was revised for American use, and the Protestant Episcopal Church became an independent, self-governing body.

There were complete harmony and expansion for the next half century. There were established new churches and church institutions: Sunday schools, Bible, prayer book, and tract societies, theological seminaries, colleges, boarding schools, guilds for men and women, and a domestic and foreign missionary society. Diocesan organizations replaced state organizations; new bishops moved into the new West. Bishop J. H. Hobart in New York, A. V. Griswold in New England, Richard Channing Moore in Virginia, and Philander Chase in Ohio worked miracles in overcoming the revolutionary prejudices against the church. W. A. Muhlenberg, one of the great Episcopalian builders,

organized the first free church of any importance in New York, introduced the male choir, sisterhoods, and the fresh air movement, while his church infirmary suggested to his mind the organization of St. Luke's Hospital [in New York], the first church hospital of any Christian communion in the country.

Muhlenberg was a man of wide vision; he inspired a "memorial" calling for a wider catholicity in the Protestant Episcopal Church, which resulted in the famous Lambeth Quadrilateral on Church Unity in 1888 and the movement which produced the further revision of the American *Book of Common Prayer* in 1892.

With the outbreak of the Civil War disruption again threatened the Protestant Episcopal Church, but it did not come. Among the major Protestant churches this one alone suffered no division. New England churchmen may have been abolitionists, and a Louisiana bishop, Leonidas Polk, may have been a general under Lee, but Polk prayed for Bishop Charles Pettit McIlvaine of Ohio in public, and the Ohioan prayed for Polk, and they were still in 1 church. A temporary Protestant Episcopal Church in the Confederate States was organized to carry on the work in the South, but the names of the southern bishops were called in the general convention in New York in 1862; and once the war was over, the Episcopal house was in 1865 quickly reunited.

The years following Appomattox were years of new growth. A dispute over churchmanship, rising out of the Oxford Movement in England, resulted in the separation of a group into the Reformed Episcopal Church in 1873, but otherwise Episcopal unity held fast. New theological seminaries were established and old ones were reorganized and strengthened. This period saw the organization of a church congress, the Brotherhood of St. Andrew, and numerous other church agencies. The expansion continued into the next century; two world wars failed to halt it. In 1830 the Protestant Episcopal Church had 12 bishops, 20 dioceses, 600 clergymen, and 30,000 communicants;

in 1930 it had 152 bishops, 105 dioceses, 6,000 clergymen, and 1,250,000 communicants.

The Episcopal form of government closely parallels that of the federal government. It is a federal union, now consisting of 112 dioceses (originally coterminous with the states of the Union), each of which is autonomous in its own sphere, associated originally for the maintenance of a common doctrine, discipline, and worship, to which objectives have been added the unification, development, and prosecution of missionary, educational, and social programs on a national scale.

Of the 112 dioceses, 20 are overseas missionary dioceses. Most of the overseas jurisdictions will become either independent Anglican churches or parts of existing Anglican churches in their areas.

Each diocese functions through a bishop (elected locally, with the approval of the whole episcopate and of representatives of the clergy and laity of the whole church), who is the spiritual and administrative head. There is a diocesan legislative body (convention, council, or synod) made up of the clergy of the diocese and representatives of the local congregations, meeting annually; a standing committee of clergymen and laymen who are advisers and assessors to the bishop; and, usually, a program board.

The normal pattern for the local congregation is the parish, which elects its own minister (called a rector) who is vested with pastoral oversight of the congregation and who, with the warden and vestrymen (comprising the vestry) administers also the temporal affairs and the property of the parish.

Each parish and parochial district (mission or chapel) is represented in the annual diocesan convention by its clergy and by elected lay delegates of the congregations (usually in proportion to their constituency); each diocese and missionary diocese is represented in the triennial general convention of the church by its bishop or bishops and clerical and lay deputies elected in equal numbers (at present 4 of each). The general convention is a bicameral legislature, and the 2 houses of the convention, bishops and deputies, meet and deliberate separately. Either house may initiate, but the concurrence of both is required to enact legislation.

Between sessions of the general convention, the work of the church is carried on by the presiding bishop (elected for a 12-year term by the House of Bishops with the concurrence of the House of Deputies) and an elective executive council of 41 members—30 elected by the general convention, 9 elected by the provinces (regional groups of dioceses and missionary districts), and 2 ex officio (the presiding bishop and the president of the House of Deputies).

Established in 1919 to unify the work of 3 previously independent boards, the council in 1968 took the further step of abolishing a more-or-less rigid departmental structure in favor of a functional operation guided by a management team: Executive Vice President, the Administrative Officer, the Overseas Relations Officer, the Deputy for Jurisdictions, the Empowerment Officer, the Program Officer and the Vice President for Development.

The Episcopalian accepts 2 creeds—the Apostles' and the Nicene. The articles of the Church of England, with the exception of the twenty-first and with modification of the eighth, thirty-fifth, and thirty-sixth, are accepted as a general statement of doctrine, but adherence to them as a creed is not required. The clergy make the following declaration:

I do believe the Holy Scriptures of the Old and New Testaments to be the Word of God, and to contain all things necessary to salvation, and I do solemnly engage to conform to the doctrine, discipline, and worship of the Protestant Episcopal Church in the United States of America.

The church expects of all its members "loyalty to the doctrine, discipline and worship of the one holy Catholic Apostolic Church, in all the essentials, but allows great liberty in nonessentials." It allows for variation, individuality, independent thinking, and religious liberty. Liberals and conservatives, modernists and fundamentalists, find cordial and common ground for worship in the prayer book, which next to the Bible has probably influenced more people than any other book in the English language.

There are 2 sacraments, baptism and the Lord's Supper, recognized as "certain sure witnesses and effectual agencies of God's love and grace." Baptism by pouring or immersion is necessary for either children or adults; baptism by any church in the name of the Trinity is recognized as valid baptism; baptized children are confirmed as members of the church by the bishop, and those not baptized in infancy or childhood must accept the rite before confirmation. Without stating or defining the holy mystery, the Episcopal Church believes in the real presence of Christ in the elements of the Supper. The church also recognizes the sacramental character of confirmation, penance, orders, matrimony, and unction.

Some Episcopalians are high churchmen with elaborate ritual and ceremony; others are described as low churchmen with a ritual less involved and with more of an evangelistic emphasis. All, however, high or low, have a loyalty to their church which is deep and lasting. In more than 300 years this church has known only 1 minor division; today it stands sixth among all denominations: it has 3,062,734 members in 6,891 churches in the United States.

Stanley I. Stuber has called this the "church of beauty," and it is an apt description. Its prayer book is matchless in the literature of religious worship, containing the heart of the New Testament and Old Testament devotions. Members have built stately cathedrals in this country, among them the Cathedral of St. John the Divine in New York City, which is the third largest cathedral in the world, and the National Cathedral at Washington, sometimes called the American Westminster Abbey. Stained-glass windows, gleaming altars, vested choirs, and a glorious ritual give the worshiper not only beauty but a deep sense of the continuity of the Christian spirit and tradition. Next to their stress on episcopacy their liturgical worship is a distinguishing feature; varying in degree according to high or low church inclinations, it has its roots in the liturgy of the Church of England and includes the reading, recitation, or intonation by priest, people, and choir of the historic general confession, general thanksgiving, collects, Psalter, and prayers, all of which are written in a beauty and cadence second only to that of the King James Version of the Bible.

Home missions, supported or aided by national missionary funds, are found in 32 dioceses and missionary districts in the United States. Special emphasis is placed upon work in town and country areas, in college communities, and in Negro, Indian, and Spanish-speaking fields. Overseas missions are located in all American territories—the Panama Canal Zone, Guam, the Virgin Islands, and Puerto Rico—and in the Dominican Republic, Haiti, India, Japan, the Near East, Liberia, Mexico, Okinawa, Taiwan, Central America, and the Philippines. The church sponsors or maintains 17 theological seminaries, 8 colleges, 1 university, 1 training school for deaconesses, 130 secondary schools for boys and girls, 105 homes for the aged, 79 institutions and agencies for child and youth care, 69 hospitals, homes and convalescent clinics, and work for seamen in 5 dioceses in American. This church is unique in Protestantism for its orders of monks and nuns; there are 11 orders for men and 14 for women, employed in schools, hospitals, and various forms of missionary work.

The Episcopal Church has an undeserved reputation for exclusiveness and noncooperation with other Protestant bodies; actually it has been most cooperative. The Lambeth Quadrilateral, already mentioned, was adopted by the house of bishops at the general convention of 1886 and accepted with modifications 2 years later. It had 4 points for world unity of the churches: the Scriptures as the Word of God, the Apostles' and the Nicene creeds as the rule of faith, the 2 sacraments of baptism and the Lord's Supper, and the episcopate as the central principle of church government. In 1910 the general convention appointed a commission to arrange for a World Conference on Faith and Order; the first conference was held at Geneva in 1920, the second in 1927 at Lausanne, the third at Edinburgh in 1937. The church is active in the National Council of the Churches of Christ in the U.S.A. and in the World Council of Churches. An unusually effective intercommunion has been established among the Anglican, Old Catholic, Polish National Catholic, and Philippine Independent churches, which may be the first step toward a merger of these bodies.

Reformed Episcopal Church

The Reformed Episcopal Church was organized in New York City in 1873 by 8 clergymen and 20 laymen who formerly had been priests and members of the Protestant Episcopal Church. A long debate over the ritualism and ecclesiasticism of the Protestant Episcopal Church lay behind the separation; the immediate cause of the division lay in the participation of Bishop George David Cummins of Kentucky in a Communion service held in the Fifth Avenue Presbyterian Church in New York City. In the face of criticism and in the conviction that the catholic nature and mission of the Protestant Episcopal Church were being lost, Bishop Cummins withdrew to found the new denomination.

Doctrine and organization are similar to that of the parent church with several important exceptions. The Reformed Episcopal Church rejects the doctrine that the Lord's table is an altar on which the body and blood of Christ are offered anew to the Father, that the presence of Christ in the Supper is a presence in the elements of bread and wine, and that regeneration is inseparably connected with baptism. It also denies that Christian ministers are priests in any other sense than that in which all other believers are a "royal priesthood." Clergymen ordained in other churches are not reordained on entering the ministry of the Reformed Episcopal Church, and members are admitted on letters of dismissal from other Protestant denominations.

Worship is liturgical; at the morning services on Sunday the use of the prayer book, revised to remove certain objectionable sacerdotal elements, is required. At other services its use is optional, while at any service extempore prayer may be used by the minister.

Parish and synodical units prevail in the administration of the church; the triennial general council of the Reformed Episcopal Church is not like the general convention of the Protestant Episcopal Church, however, as its bishops do not constitute a separate house.

Foreign missions are maintained in India, Congo, Uganda, northern Rhodesia, and Germany. In India and Africa there are 20 primary schools, 2 hospitals, and 1 orphanage. There is 1 seminary in the United States located at Philadelphia. There are 6,890 members in 65 local churches.

EVANGELICAL CHURCH OF NORTH AMERICA

When the Methodist Church and the Evangelical United Brethren churches merged into the United Methodist Church in Dallas, Texas, in 1968, a number of churches in the Brethren body, dissatisfied with the merger, withdrew to form a denomination of their own—the Evangelical Church of North America. In June of 1968 the new Church was incorporated at Portland, Oregon, and eventually came to include congregations across the country, including those of the former Holiness Methodist Church.

The doctrinal position is of the Wesleyan-Arminian persuasion; in organization, there are Conference Superintendents over each district and Annual Conferences; the general administration of each conference is carried on by the Annual Conference sessions, the Conference Council of Administration and program agencies such as Evangelism, Missions, Christian Education, and Stewardship. There is an inclusive membership of 9,451 in 115 churches.

EVANGELICAL CONGREGATIONAL CHURCH

Objecting to the "usurpation of powers in violation of the discipline" by bishops, 7 annual conferences and from 60,000 to 70,000 members of the Evangelical Association—later known as the Evangelical Church —withdrew from that body in 1894 to organize the United Evangelical Church. The two churches were reunited in 1922, but again a minority objected and remained aloof from the merger. The East Pennsylvania Conference, together with several churches in the Central, Pittsburgh, Ohio, Illinois, and West Virginia Conferences, continued their separate existence under the old name. This was later changed to the Evangelical Congregational Church.

Today the boundaries of the Eastern Conference are larger than at the time of the merger; the midwest churches are joined in a Western Conference. They are, like their parent Evangelical Church, "Methodists in polity, Arminian in doctrine." There is emphasis upon the inspiration and integrity of the Bible and the "fellowship of all followers of Christ." There are annual and general conferences with equal lay and clerical representation, bishops and district superintendents, and an itinerant ministry. Pastors are appointed yearly by the annual conferences. Local congregations, as the name implies, have more freedom—especially in temporal matters—than congregations in either Evangelical or Methodist churches. The Board of Missions with 2 women's auxiliaries and 2 conference missionary societies supervises the home and foreign missionary programs. There are 40 missionaries abroad and 36 at home, and 154 nationals at work in various lands.

Large summer assemblies are held in 6 camp sites strategically located in the conferences. Church headquarters, the publishing house, the infirmary, the home for the aging, and the school of theology are located at Myerstown, Pennsylvania. There are nearly 30,000 members and approximately 160 churches.

EVANGELICAL COVENANT CHURCH OF AMERICA

This church traces its roots to the Protestant Reformation, to the biblical instruction of the Lutheran State Church of Sweden, and to the great spiritual awakenings of the nineteenth century. These 3 in-

influences have in large measure shaped its development and are to be borne in mind in seeking to understand its distinctive spirit.

The Covenant Church adheres to the affirmations of the Protestant Reformation regarding the Holy Scriptures as the Word of God and the only perfect rule for faith, doctrine, and conduct. It has traditionally valued the historic confessions of the Christian church, particularly the Apostles' Creed, while at the same time it has emphasized the sovereignty of the Word over all creedal interpretations. It has especially cherished the pietistic restatement of the doctrine of justification by faith as basic to its dual task of evangelism and Christian nurture, the New Testament emphasis upon personal faith in Jesus Christ as Saviour and Lord, the reality of a fellowship of believers which recognizes but transcends theological differences, and the belief in baptism and the Lord's Supper as divinely ordained sacraments of the church. While the denomination has traditionally practiced the baptism of infants, in conformity with its principle of freedom it has given room to divergent views. The principle of personal freedom, so highly esteemed by the Covenant Church, is to be distinguished from the individualism that disregards the centrality of the Word of God and the mutual responsibilities and disciples of the spiritual community.

The local church is administered by a board elected by the membership; it calls its ministers (ordained by the denomination) generally with the aid and guidance of the denominational pastoral relations commission and the conference superintendent. There are 11 geographical districts known as regional conferences, each of which elects its own superintendent. The highest constituted authority is vested in an annual meeting composed of ministers and laymen elected as delegates by the constituent churches. An executive board, elected by the annual meeting, implements its decisions.

Mission fields are in Africa (Republic of Congo, Kinshasa), Alaska, China (Taiwan), Ecuador, Colombia, Indonesia, Japan, and Hong Kong. There is a Bible Institute in Canada, Minnehaha Academy in Minneapolis, and at Chicago the church supports the Swedish Covenant Hospital School of Nursing and North Park College and Theological Seminary. There are 2 homes for orphaned children, 1 sailors' home, 2 hospitals, and 13 homes for aged. There are 68,428 adult members in 526 churches.

EVANGELICAL FREE CHURCH OF AMERICA

The church began with a group of independent congregations and several churches of the old Swedish Ansgarii Synod and Mission Synod, which met together at Boone, Iowa, in 1884 to form a fellowship of "free" congregations, to be known as the Swedish Evangelical

Free Mission (later changed to Swedish Evangelical Free Church, and still later to Evangelical Free Church of America). In 1950 the Swedish Evangelical Free Church and the Evangelical Free Church Association (formerly the Norwegian and Danish Evangelical Free Church Association) were merged into the present body.

By agreement, in the organization of the fellowship in 1884, this was to be a body of self-governing congregations, each left free to establish its own doctrine; the several churches elected delegates to an annual conference which was purely advisory in character. A society of ministers and missionaries was organized in 1894 to guide the denomination in doctrine and practice. This is still the guiding principle of the church; the only qualification for membership lies in evidence of conversion and the living of a Christian life. Polity is congregational. A 12-point doctrinal statement, in 1950, is incorporated into the bylaws of most local congregations.

There are 83,337 members and 600 churches, 13 district organizations (11 in the United States, 2 in Canada), mission stations in Japan, the Philippines, Hong Kong, Republic of Congo (Leopoldville), Singapore, Germany, and Venezuela. Three schools of higher education—Trinity College in Chicago, Trinity Evangelical Divinity School in Bannockburn, Illinois, and Trinity Junior College in Langley, British Columbia—are maintained, and the church is a member of the International Federation of Free Evangelical Churches and the National Association of Evangelicals.

FEDERATED CHURCHES

Federated churches in the United States are largely a rural or village phenomenon, strongest in New England and the West. They are churches, 2 or more in number and representing different denominations, which unite for mutual conduct of their work while continuing their connections with the denominations involved. The first federated church of which we have any record was formed in Massachusetts in 1887; another was founded in Vermont in 1899. By 1936 there were 508 federated churches in 42 states, with 88,411 members. There may be double that number now; further statistics are unavailable because of the lack of any national organization or office. Dr. Ralph Williamson, conducting a survey for Cornell University, listed over 800 federated churches in 1952.

Economic pressure, conviction that the community is overchurched, flow of population, the inspiring example of the consolidated school, and the increased cost of church maintenance have been influential in forcing such federations. Ralph A. Felton in *Local Church Cooperation in Rural Communities* (Home Missions Council, 1944) describes the usual circumstances under which the average federated church is created:

Two churches in the same locality begin to have financial difficulties. Their memberships are too small to carry on thriving individual churches. They feel that if they could unite into one local congregation they could provide a more efficient religious program. Neither church wants to give up its affiliation with its denomination. For years they have been saying, "We should unite, but who's going to give up?" Finally they unite locally, hire one minister instead of two, but continue their separate "overhead" or denominational affiliations. The two or more separate churches thus become a federated church.

Usually there are joint religious services and a common Sunday school, and policy is determined by a joint official board. In some cases one minister is chosen to serve continuously; in others the minister is chosen alternately from the denominations represented. In approximately half of the federated churches in this country all the Protestant churches in the community have entered the federation. Presbyterians seem to have the highest percentage of cooperation, with Congregationalists and Christians, Methodists, and Baptists following in that order. There is still a real conflict of loyalties in the federated churches; its conclusion depends upon a slow educational process. There is a noticeable trend toward eventual denominationalization. Majority groups have a way of absorbing minorities; and usually when denominationalization comes, people go to the denomination that continues to provide a minister. It is also clear that if a federated church lasts 5 years, it is seldom abandoned.

Doctrine, polity, and membership requirements correspond in some cases to the standards of the denominations included; in other instances they are completely independent. No blanket statement is possible in these matters.

FIRE BAPTIZED HOLINESS CHURCH

A Negro Pentecostal sect, this church was for the first 10 years of its existence a part of the white Fire Baptized Holiness Association of America; the Negro membership separated in 1908. In 1922 it became the Fire Baptized Holiness Church.

This church teaches the standard Pentecostal and holiness doctrines of repentance, regeneration, justification, sanctification, Pentecostal baptism, speaking with other tongues, divine healing, and the premillennial Second Coming. It stands opposed to the "so-called Christian Scientists, Spiritualists, Unitarians, Universalists and Mormons." Adventism, immorality, antinomianism, the annihilation of the wicked, the glorification of the body, and "many other modern teachings of the day" are denounced as false, wicked, and unscriptual. Government is by a bishop, 2 overseers, a general secretary, treasurer, and a board of trustees. Ruling elders, ordained ministers, and pastors are in charge of local churches; and a general convention is held yearly. In

1958, 988 members were reported in 53 churches. Headquarters are in Atlanta, Georgia.

FIRE BAPTIZED HOLINESS CHURCH (WESELYAN)

Preaching on the doctrine of holiness inspired the organization of this church about 1890; its first members were dissenters within the Methodist churches of southeastern Kansas. They called themselves at first the Southeast Kansas Fire Baptized Holiness Association; the present name was adopted in 1945.

Doctrine is primitive Wesleyan, emphasizing sanctification and complete holiness. The church government and organization follow the Methodist episcopal pattern, and there is strong emphasis upon evangelism. There are 988 members in 53 churches.

FREE CHRISTIAN ZION CHURCH OF CHRIST

Led by E. D. Brown, a local Methodist missionary, a small group of Methodist and Baptist Negro ministers formed this church in 1905 at Redemption, Arkansas. They objected to the taxing of any church membership to provide support for any ecclesiastical organization, feeling that the care and relief of the needy and the poor were the first responsibility of the church. Such relief activities characterize their local churches today.

Doctrine is completely Methodist and so is government except for minor titles and details. Chiefs or superintendents perform the functions of bishops; a chief pastor is chosen as top administrative officer, making all assignments to pastorates and appointing all church officers. Pastors and deacons head local churches and are responsible for the aid of the poor in their congregations. Laymen share in the conduct of the churches and in the annual General Assembly. The latest membership report (1956), listed 22,260 members in 742 churches.

FRIENDS

With a membership in the United States and Canada of only 123,000 and with 200,000 around the world, the Religious Society of Friends, better known as Quakers, has had a deep and lasting influence upon Western society. Contributions in both religious and humanitarian spheres have won the Quakers universal respect and admiration, and their amazing history and loyalty to their quiet faith offer a challenge and inspiration to all the churches.

Their vicissitudes and victories began with George Fox (1624-91), a British "seeker" after spiritual truth and peace. Failing to find such in the churches of his time, Fox found them in a new, intimate, personal relationship with Christ. He said: "When all my hopes in [churches and churchmen] were gone . . . then I heard a voice which said, 'There is one, even Christ Jesus, that can speak to thy condition.'" This is the Inner Voice or Inner Light of Quakerism, based upon the description of John 1:9—"the true Light, which lighteth every man that cometh into the world"—a voice available to all men, having nothing to do with outward forms or ceremonies, rituals or creeds. Every man to the Quaker is a walking church; every heart is God's altar and shrine.

Quakerism was revolutionary, and it was treated as revolution by the state Church of England. To tell this united state and church that they were both wrong, that their theology and dogma meant nothing, that men need not attend the "steeple houses" to find God, and that it was equally wrong to pay taxes in support of state church clergymen—this was rebellion.

Fox and his early followers went even further. They not only refused to go to church but insisted upon freedom of speech, assembly, and worship; they would not take oaths in court; they refused to go to war; they doffed their hats to no man, king or commoner; they made no distinction among people in sexes or social classes; they condemned slavery and England's treatment of the prisoner and the insane. The very names they took—Children of Truth, Children of Light, Friends of Truth, and finally the Religious Society of Friends—roused ridicule and fierce opposition. Fox, hauled into court, advised one judge to "tremble at the Word of the Lord," and heard the judge call him "Quaker." It was derision, but it was not enough to stop them. Persecution unsheathed its sword.

The Quakers were whipped, jailed, tortured, mutilated, murdered. Fox spent 6 years in jail; others spent decades, dying there. From 1650 to 1689 more than 3,000 suffered for conscience' sake, and 300 to 400 died in prison. Thanks to that persecution they prospered, founding the society in 1652. When Fox died, there were 50,000 Quakers.

Some were already in America. Ann Austin and Mary Fisher arrived in Massachusetts from Barbados in 1656, were promptly accused of being witches and deported. Two days later 8 more came from England. Laws were passed hastily to keep them out; the whipping post worked overtime and failed. Four were hanged in Boston. Quakers kept coming into New England, New York, New Jersey, Maryland, Virginia, and Pennsylvania. Rhode Island and Pennsylvania welcomed them from the start. The long horror in the communities that did not welcome them ended with the passage of the Toleration Act of 1689.

With the Act and Fox's death a new phase began. Persecution waned and died and so did a great deal of Quaker revolutionary zeal. They settled down as business men and farmers known for their pacifism and honesty and became quite prosperous.

Yet there were lights in this period of quiet. The meeting organization and community life became well organized. Closely knit family life was emphasized. It was a time of creativeness and mystical inwardness. The period of withdrawal was one in which Quaker philanthropy became widely respected and even admired; their ideas on prison reform began to take effect. Quaker schools increased; as early as 1691 there were 15 Quaker boarding schools in England.

In 1682 William Penn came to Philadelphia. He sat under an elm at Shackamaxon and made a treaty with the Indians—the "only treaty never sworn to and never broken." Treated like human beings, the Indians reacted in kind. If all our cities had been Philadelphias and all our states Pennsylvanias, our national history would have been vastly different.

But even here the holy experiment had to end. Quakers controlled the Pennsylvania legislature until 1756, when they refused to vote a tax to pay for a war against the Shawnees and the Delawares and consequently stepped down and out of power.

They looked within rather than without, and began enforcing discipline on their membership so strictly that they became in fact a "peculiar people." Members were disowned or dismissed for even minor infractions of the discipline; thousands were cut off for "marrying out of Meeting." Pleasure, music, and art were taboo; sobriety, punctuality, and honesty were demanded in all directions; dress was painfully plain, and speech was biblical. They were different and dour; they gained few new converts and lost many old members.

Some few "fighting Quakers" went to battle in the American Revolution, but they were few; most of them remained pacifists. They worked quietly for peace, popular education, temperance, democracy, and against slavery. In 1688 the Friends of Germantown, Pennsylvania, said that Negro slavery violated the Golden Rule and encouraged adultery; they protested against the "traffic in the bodies of men" and called it unlawful. Their first attitude of toleration changed slowly to one of outright opposition; it took nearly a century for the Quakers to rid their society of slavery, but they did it years in advance of any other religious body in America. Sellers or purchasers of slaves were forbidden membership in the society by the close of the eighteenth century. Persistently all across the years the Quakers dropped their seeds of antislavery agitation into the body politic. First John Woolman and then the poet Whittier wielded tremendous influence in the fight; and once the Civil War was over, they threw their strength into such organizations as the Freedman's Aid Society. Ever since, they have been active in education and legislative protection for the free Negro.

Divisions arose within their ranks during these years: the Hicksites separated in 1827, the Wilburites in 1845; and the Primitives (a small group now extinct) in 1861. Of these separations, the one led by Elias Hicks was of primary concern. Hicks was a rural Long Island

Quaker whose liberal and rational theological views brought him into conflict with those of more orthodox and evangelical persuasion. The division came in 1827; basically, while it had personal and sociological emphases, the split was due to the widespread nineteenth-century conflict between liberalism and rationalism on the one hand and an orthodoxy based on Methodist ideas of evangelism and salvation on the other. Two thirds of the Philadelphia Yearly Meeting withdrew with the Hicksites (a nickname never officially adopted by any Quaker group) and similar divisions followed in New York, Ohio, Indiana, and Baltimore yearly meetings. A second series of separations resulted from the Wesleyan Methodist influence, led by Joseph John Gurney and John Wilbur (see Religious Society of Friends [Conservative], below).

The twentieth century thus far has been a century of Quaker unity and outreach. A Five Years Meeting (now the Friend's United Meeting) was organized in 1902, merging a large portion of the pastoral yearly meetings. The 2 Philadelphia meetings, separated since 1827, were united in 1955. In the same year the 2 New York Yearly Meetings were merged, and the 3 Canada Yearly Meetings came together to form 1 body. In 1968 two Baltimore Yearly Meetings reunited. Southeastern Meeting, newly founded, affiliated with both Friends United Meeting and Friends General Conference in 1972.

In 1917, before the guns of World War I had stopped firing, Friends from all branches of the society were at work in the American Friends Service Committee in relief and reconstruction efforts abroad. The A.F.S.C. remains today one of the most effective of such agencies in the world. Its volunteers erected demountable houses, staffed hospitals, plowed fields, reared domestic animals, and drove ambulances. Famine relief and child-feeding programs were instituted in Serbia, Poland, Austria, Russia, and Germany; at one time the Friends were feeding more than 1,000,000 German children every day; Greek refugees, earthquake victims in Japan, needy miners' families in Pennsylvania, West Virginia, and Kentucky were helped. Thousands would have perished but for the A.F.S.C.

Quakers drove ambulances and served in the medical corps of both world wars, and some were in combat; probably more young Quakers volunteered or accepted military service in these conflicts than resisted on grounds of religious principle. They also worked to relieve our displaced Japanese-Americans, and they cooperated with the Brethren and Mennonites in locating our conscientious objectors in work of real importance on farms, in reformatories, hospitals, and insane asylums. They were in Spain soon after the outbreak of the Spanish Civil War and later fed the child victims in Spain, southern France, Italy, Austria, Holland, North Africa, and Finland. In one year, 1945, they sent 282 tons of clothes, shoes, bedding, and soap to Europe and still more to China and India. Counting gifts, both of cash and materials, the income of the A.F.S.C. is apt to exceed $7,500,000 annually. At home and abroad summer camps of young volunteers have inspired an incalculable good will among nations and minority groups within nations.

Nor have they been satisfied with work merely in relief. Peace conferences have been a prominent part of their work, conferences ranging from local to international and covering all age groups. Lake Mohonk in New York was founded by a Friend. Scores of youth conferences and camps at home and in foreign fields testify to their devotion to the way of Christ; it is little wonder that they are known as a "peace church."

Worship and business in the society are conducted in monthly, quarterly, and yearly meetings. The monthly meeting is the basic unit, made up of one or more meetings in a neighborhood. It convenes each week for worship and once a month for business. It keeps records of membership, births, deaths, and marriages; appoints committees; considers queries on spiritual welfare; and transacts all business of the group. Monthly meetings in a district join 4 times a year in the quarterly meeting to stimulate spiritual life and to pass on whatever business they feel should be brought to the attention of the yearly meeting. The yearly meeting corresponds to a diocese in an episcopal system; there are 27 of them in the United States and Canada. They are in touch with Friends all over the world and have standing committees on such subjects as publications, education, the social order, missions, peace, charities, and national legislation; they allocate trust-fund incomes and generally supervise the work of the society.

Group decisions await the "sense of the meeting." Lacking any unity of opinion, the meeting may have a "quiet time" for a few minutes until unity is found, or it may postpone consideration of the matter or refer to a committee for study. Minorities are not outvoted but convinced. Every man, woman, and child is free to speak in any meeting; delegates are appointed at quarterly and yearly meetings to ensure adequate representation, but they enjoy no unusual position or prerogatives. Women have as much power as men and hold a position of absolute equality in Quaker polity.

There are, contrary to popular misunderstanding, church officers—elders and ministers—among the Quakers; they are chosen for recognized ability in spiritual leadership, and they, too, stand on equal footing with the rest of the membership. All members are ministers to the Quaker. A few full-time workers are paid a modest salary, and "recorded" ministers serving as pastors in those meetings having programed worship also receive salaries (about 1,000 meetings have no paid pastors).

Quaker worship is of 2 kinds: programed and unprogramed. The two, however, are not always distinct. The former more nearly resembles a simple Protestant service, but there are no rites or outward sacraments. While believing in spiritual communion, partaking of the elements is thought unnecessary. In the unprogramed meetings there is no choir, collection, singing, or pulpit; the service is devoted to quiet meditation, prayer, and communion. Any vocal contributions are spontaneous. There is no uniform practice; some of the so-called "churches" greatly prefer to be called "meetings."

In business meetings there is often frank inquiry into the conduct of business, treatment of others, use of narcotics or intoxicants, reading habits, and recreation. No true Quaker gambles, plays the stock market, bets, owns race horses, or engages in raffles, lotteries, or the liquor business. Some follow conservative religious or theological patterns and others are liberal; all are guided by the Inner Light.

The Inner Light is highly important in Quaker belief. Grace, power from God to help man resist evil, is to Quakers universal among all men. They seek not holiness but perfection—a higher, more spiritual standard of life for both society and the individual—and they believe that the truth is unfolding and continuing. They place high evaluation on the Bible but try to rely on individual fresh guidance from the Spirit of God which produced the Bible, rather than to follow only what has been revealed to others. Some modern groups accept the Bible as the final authority in all religious matters.

Rufus Jones says:

They believe supremely in the nearness of God to the human soul, in direct intercourse and immediate communion, in mystical experience in a firsthand discovery of God. . . . It means and involves a sensitiveness to the wider spiritual Life above us, around us, and within us, a dedication to duty, a passion for truth, and an appreciation of goodness, an eagerness to let love and the grace of God come freely through one's own life, a reverence for the will of God wherever it is revealed in past or present, and a high faith that Christ is a living presence and a life-giving energy always within reach of the receptive soul.

No Quaker body has ever departed from the Declaration to Charles II in 1661: "We utterly deny all outward wars and strife and fighting with outward weapons, for any end or under any pretense whatever. . . . The spirit of Christ, which leads us into all Truth, will never move us to fight and war against any man with outward weapons, neither for the Kingdom of Christ, not for the kingdoms of this world." However, there is great tolerance toward individual variations in this position. In World War II formal Quaker positions favored applying for conscientious objector status, either as noncombatants within the military or in alternate service; during the Vietnam War corporate positions shifted toward encouraging men to practice draft refusal and go to jail if necessary. In both cases a wide variety of positions were seen as acceptable; the emphasis was on following individual conscience. Quakers who enter military service are no longer disowned from membership but many leave the Society and join a Church that does not profess pacifism. Conversely, pacifists brought up in other traditions tend to join the Society of Friends in young adulthood.

Marriage is not necessarily a ceremony to be performed by a minister; in cases where the traditional Quaker marriage is observed the bride and groom simply stand before a meeting and make mutual vows of love and faithfulness and are thereby married. In certain sections of the country the pastor of the meeting officiates.

The Friends have never been great proselytizers; they depend almost entirely upon birthright membership and membership by "convincement." In many of their bodies, though not in all of them, every child born of Quaker parents is declared a member of the society. This has resulted in a large number of nominal or paper members who contribute little; efforts are being made to correct this custom by establishing a junior or associate membership for children. This reliance upon birthright membership, has seriously depleted their numbers. There are 30 yearly meetings in America, including one in Canada, one in Cuba, one in Jamaica, and a small group in Mexico. There are also 20 yearly meetings overseas.

If the Friends were ever "exclusive" they are not now; a world outreach has been evident and growing in recent years. The Friend's United Meeting and the Friends' General Conference are members of the World Council of Churches; with the Philadelphia Yearly Meeting it also belongs to the National Council of Churches. A Friends World Committee for Consultation, organized at Swarthmore, Pennsylvania, following the Second World Conference of Friends in 1937, functions as an agent or clearinghouse for the interchange of Quaker aspirations and experiences by way of regional, national, and international intervisitation, person-to-person consultations, conferences, correspondence, and a variety of publications. The committee has headquarters in Birmingham, England, and offices in Philadelphia, Pennsylvania; Plainfield, Indiana; and Edinburgh, Scotland. The American section has helped some 50 small Friends groups in the United States to monthly meeting status. The F.W.C.C. is a nongovernmental organization related to the Economic and Social Council of the United Nations through cooperation with the A.F.S.C.; it helps operate a program at the U. N. headquarters to forward world peace and human brotherhood. Something of a world brotherhood, or "Franciscan Third Order," has been set up in the organization of the Wider Quaker Fellowship, in which non-Quakers in sympathy with the Quaker spirit and program may participate in the work of the Friends without coming into full Quaker membership. This is not so much an organization as it is "a fellowship of kindred minds— a way of life, a contagion of spirit"; it has 4,200 members, 360 of whom live abroad.

An Evangelical Friends Alliance was formed in 1965 in the interests of evangelical emphasis and denominational unity; it seeks to bring together those interested in an evangelical renewal within Christianity and a renewal of interest in the evangelical emphases of seventeenth century Quakerism, and includes the Association of Evangelical Friends. Theology here is conservative; local pastors are elected. There are 254 churches and 23,683 members.

A further movement toward unity is found in the Religious Society of Friends (Unaffiliated Meetings), which also stresses elements and teachings of early Friends movements. This group is unique in its wide variety and experimentation in worship and polity; it is not associated with the larger bodies in the Society. There are 72 churches with 2,896 members.

Friends General Conference

This is a national organization of yearly meetings (Baltimore, Lake Erie, South Central, Canada, New England, Illinois, Indiana, South Eastern, New York, and Philadelphia). It was established in 1868 as a Sunday school conference and matured in 1900 as a general conference for fellowship across yearly meeting boundaries as an instrument for deepening the spiritual and social testimonies of the Society. One of its main features is an annual conference; in 1972 it had 1,500 members, about one third of whom were children and young people. There are 33,200 members and 335 churches in the General Conference, a fraction of who also belong to the Friends United Meeting (described below); this is explained by the dual membership in Canada, New York, and New England in the General Conference and the Friends United Meeting.

Friends United Meeting (Five Years Meeting)

With 67,086 members and 492 churches in 1972, this is the largest single Quaker body in the United States. (The largest yearly meetings in the world are the East Africa with 32,000 members and London with 20,625.) Organized in 1900, it brought together in one cooperative relationship 12 yearly meetings and 3 yearly meetings abroad—East Africa, Cuba, and Jamaica—with a somewhat different status. They work together in many departments—such as missionary service and the production of Sunday school materials—and while each yearly meeting in the body is autonomous, they come together for spiritual stimulation, business, and conference every 3 years.

The ministries of the "FUM" are carried forward in the interim between Triennial Sessions by 3 planning commissions and the General Board, which convene semiannually. Affirming the importance of personal religious experience which goes beyond theory or speculation, it embodies a creative balance of central Quaker accents, evangelism and social concern, mission and service, worship and ministry. Friends of various persuasions work together within the FUM spectrum.

Religious Society of Friends (Conservative)

Known also as Wilburites, this group resulted from a second division. Joseph John Gurney, a British evangelical Quaker, came to America in the mid-1800's and began preaching and teaching the final authority of the Bible, and acceptance of the doctrines of the atonement, justification, and sanctification. John Wilbur, a Rhode Island conservative Friend, while not denouncing the authority of the Bible and its teachings, felt that Gurney's preaching substituted a creed for the immediate revelation of the Divine Spirit available to man. Both men had large followings; the outcome was separation in Kansas, Iowa, Indiana, Ohio, New England, North Carolina, and Canada, between 1845 and 1904.

The conservative pattern, generally, was one "set forth by the Society in the beginning," calling for a silent waiting before God in Quaker meetings, in expectation that his spirit would instruct and move them to speak or pray without program or ritual. In New England in 1945, and in Canada in 1955, differences were resolved between these conservatives, and they were reunited. There are still conservative yearly meetings in Iowa, Ohio, and North Carolina; they cooperate with other Friends groups in various areas of service and in intervisitation. There are 26 Monthly Meetings and 1,806 members.

HOUSE OF DAVID

Benjamin Purnell, who founded the House of David at Benton Harbor, Michigan, in 1903, claimed to be the seventh messenger prophesied by the book of Revelation; the other six, of whom Johanna Southcott (1792) was the first, had all been British. Purnell set up his Benton Harbor colony as a "commonwealth, according to apostolic plan" and was accepted there as the supreme ruler over all the community's spiritual and temporal matters. All who joined the colony put their earthly funds and possessions into the commonwealth treasury and contributed their work and services thenceforth to the cause. They lived in anticipation of the ultimate establishing of the kingdom of God on this earth; Purnell therefore called them "Israelites" and his movement an ingathering, because they were the direct lineal descendants of the 12 lost tribes of Israel, to be restored at the last days to their rightful places as judges and rulers in the kingdom of God.

Charges of dishonesty and immorality were brought against "King Benjamin" Purnell, and he died at the height of the scandal just before the supreme court of Michigan brought in a verdict in his favor; the movement, however, survived and continues on the original location. There are about 150 members at the Benton Harbor headquarters, and other members in Australia, New Zealand, England, Ireland, Scotland, and in every state in this country. Members are required to contribute all their earthly possessions and labor to the House of David. A common treasury provides for the needs of all "as they severally have need." The colony is financed by the sale of produce from the farms, dairies, vineyards, greenhouses, cold storage and fruit-preserving plants, and other shops and industries maintained by the members. They are strict vegetarians (a practice based on Gen. 1:29). They never shave their heads or faces (a practice based upon "what Jesus did," and on the Nazarene injunction that man is the head of the woman and the heads of women must never be "uncovered").

In belief, they shun all use of the word "religion," because "there has been so much cruelty and bloodshed and all kinds of bitter strife under the name of religion. We would rather say that we believe and teach the same doctrine as Jesus Christ . . . and which Gospel was the redemption of the body." They hold Sunday to be "a type of the coming Millennial Sabbath Day"; that "a perfect creation of men and women are going to inhabit the earth during the Millennium and bring forth a perfect creation, in the image of God"; that there is a great ultimate salvation of spirit, body, and soul. "We believe in God and Jesus Christ; and that Benjamin is the Seventh Messenger or Seventh Angel spoken of in Revelation 10:1." In this salvation "thousands of people now on earth will never die." The immortality of the natural body, together with the conviction that we are living in the last 6,000 years of God's time, "in the great and dreadful day when the Lord will overthrow the wicked kingdoms of the earth," is strongly emphasized. They believe that automobiles, telephones, radios, and motion pictures are prophesied in the Bible as signs of the end of the evil powers and of Satan's kingdom, but at Colony Park, east of Benton Harbor, they maintain a picnic ground and entertainment area with rodeos, dancing, billiards, and midget auto rides for the amusement of visitors.

The House of David is controlled by a board of directors who conduct all spiritual and temporal affairs of the association.

INDEPENDENT ASSEMBLIES OF GOD INTERNATIONAL

A holiness and Pentecostal group, this is more an unorganized association or fellowship of Pentecostal ministers than a denomination. Sometimes called "Philadelphia" churches, they have a Swedish background and work closely with the Swedish Pentecostal Movement, with which they conduct an extensive missionary program. It is claimed that their missionary church in Brazil is the largest Protestant movement in that country, having "close to half a million followers (and) really converted people."

Doctrine is, of course, Pentecostalist, and government follows the loosely local autonomy of other Pentecostal churches and assemblies. They have 200 churches, 12 Bible schools, and 200 missionaries in the Philippines.

INDEPENDENT CHURCHES

It is difficult, if not impossible, to classify properly all those churches in the United States calling themselves independent. Generally they may be identified as churches not controlled by any denominational or ecclesiastical organization, but even this does not hold in all cases. The following groupings are possible:

1. Churches called union, community, nondenominational, undenominational, or interdenominational. Community and nondenominational churches together constitute nearly one half the number of so-called independent churches.

2. Churches using a denominational name but working without denominational supervision.

3. Churches organized by individuals: holiness, evangelistic churches or movements, gospel churches or halls, "storefront" churches, and so forth.

4. United churches of all types.

5. Federated churches (already discussed; see p. 139).

Many of these churches shift from one classification to another; one listed as United one year may be listed as Community (Methodist) the next. Free as they are of denominational control, they are as widely different in doctrine and polity as the preferences of the individuals and groups involved are different.

The most effective community church organization in this country is found in the Council of Community Churches, founded in 1946. This is a fellowship of participating churches, rather than a denominational or ecclesiastical body—a "clearinghouse" or forum for the cooperative activities of the churches. Membership is on an annual basis. Upon invitation the council helps overchurched communities to federate or unite in one community-centered church; it encourages denominations to set up procedures to alleviate overchurched situations, helps to find community-minded ministers, and distributes relevant literature. Many of their churches have a denominational relationship, and some of them have multiple denominational relationships, as in federated churches. There are 203 member churches in the council; services are rendered to about 450-500 other churches.

Policies are established by registered delegates of the churches in the council and/or by a board of trustees elected for one year at their annual conference. An executive director is active in field work, correspondence, and as general supervisor or director of various appointed committees. He is liaison officer between the Community Council and the National Council of Churches and the World Council of Churches, in both of which the Community Council is represented as a consultative member.

INDEPENDENT FUNDAMENTAL CHURCHES OF AMERICA

Organized in 1930 at Cicero, Illinois, by representatives of various independent churches anxious to safeguard fundamentalist doctrine, this body has 2 types of membership—1 for organizations, the other for ministers, missionaries, and evangelists. The organization membership accounts for 600 churches directly affiliated with 296 other independent churches whose pastors are affiliated. There are 4 Bible camps, 3 Bible institutes, 1 Christian school and children's home, 11 church extension missions, 10 home and 3 foreign missionary projects. More than 1,200 ministers, missionaries, and evangelists are members; total membership is 77,794.

The president of the body presides over an annual conference in which the members have voting power. An executive committee of 12 serves for 3 years; the constituent churches are completely independent, but are required to subscribe to the statement of faith of the organization.

INTERNATIONAL CHURCH OF THE FOURSQUARE GOSPEL

Rising out of the evangelistic work of Aimee Semple McPherson, this church is a tribute to the organizing genius and striking methods of its founder. Born in Ontario in 1890, Mrs. McPherson was converted under the preaching of her first husband, Robert Semple, an evangelist. He died in China, and she returned to the United States in 1911 to tour the country in a series of gospel meetings which were spectacular even in war years. She settled in Los Angeles in 1918, building the famous Angelus Temple which was opened January 1, 1923, and founding the Echo Park Evangelistic Association, the L.I.F.E. Bible College, and International Church of the Foursquare Gospel religious corporations. The headquarters are still located at Angelus Temple in Los Angeles.

With her great speaking ability and her faith in praying for the healing of the sick, Mrs. McPherson attracted thousands to her meetings. Her more irreverent critics felt that her meetings were too spectacular, but others appreciated her type of presentation. There was great interest in the sick and the poor; "more than a million and a half" are said to have been fed by the Los Angeles organization.

The teaching of the church is set forth in a 21-paragraph Declaration of Faith written by Mrs. McPherson. Strongly fundamentalistic, it is premillennalist, holiness, and Trinitarian, advocating that the Bible is as "true, immutable, steadfast, unchangeable, as its author, the Lord Jehovah." The Holy Spirit baptism with the initial evidence of speaking in other tongues is subsequent to conversion, and there is the power to heal in answer to believing prayer. There are the usual doctrines on the atonement, the second coming of Christ "in clouds of glory," reward for the righteous at the judgment, and eternal punishment for the wicked. Baptism and the Lord's Supper are observed.

Mrs. McPherson was president of the church during her lifetime and was, with a board of directors, its ruling power and voice; her son, Rolf K. McPherson, became president at the time of her death. Today the official business of the church is conducted by a board of directors, the missionary cabinet, and an executive council. The highest seat of authority is the Convention Body, which alone has the power to make or amend the bylaws of the church. District supervisors are appointed for 10 districts, and are ratified by the pastors of the respective districts every 4 years. Each church is governed by a church council and contributes monthly to home and foreign missionary work. There are 230,134 members, 2,637 churches and meeting places in 29 different countries, 3,003 missionaries and national pastors, 30 day schools, 41 Bible schools, 4 orphanages on the foreign field, and a net property valuation of $55,478,854. All members are required to subscribe to the Declaration of Faith. The young people are organized into bands of Foursquare Crusaders. A church flag—red, gold, blue, and purple with a red cross on a Bible background bearing a superimposed "4"—is prominently displayed in the churches and at rallies and assemblies; their radio station, KFSG, broadcasts from Los Angeles.

JEHOVAH'S WITNESSES

The people called Jehovah's Witnesses believe that they have in their movement the true realization of the "one faith" mentioned by the apostle Paul in Eph. 4:5. Their certainty of this and their zeal in proclaiming it have made them at least in point of public interest an outstanding religious phenomenon in modern America.

They were not known as Jehovah's Witnesses until 1931. Up to this time they had been called Millennial Dawnists, International Bible Students, and earlier Russellites, after the man who brought about their first incorporation in 1884. Pastor Charles Taze Russell, their first president, is acknowledged not as founder (there is no "human" founder) but as general organizer; Judge Rutherford, Russell's successor, claimed that the Witnesses had been on earth as an organization for more than 5,000 years and cited Isa. 43:10-12; Heb. 11; and John 18:37 to prove it.

Russell was deeply influenced by belief in Christ's second coming; he studied the Bible avidly and attracted huge crowds to hear him expound it. The first formal organization of his followers came in Pittsburgh in 1872; his books, of which 13,000,000 are said to have been circulated, laid the foundations of the movement. Russell was president; to assist him, a board of directors was elected by vote of all members subscribing $10 or more to the support of the work (a practice discontinued in 1944).

Under Russell's direction headquarters were moved to Brooklyn, New York, in 1909 and another corporation formed under the laws of the state of New York. In 1956 the name was changed to the Watchtower Bible and Tract Society of New York, Inc. When Pastor Russell died in 1916, Joseph F. Rutherford was made president. Known widely as Judge Rutherford, he had been a Missouri lawyer who occasionally sat as a circuit court judge. He wrote tirelessly; his books, pamphlets, and tracts supplanted those of Russell; and his neglect of some aspects of the teaching of Russell brought dissension.

Government of the group became more theocratic in the days of Rutherford's presidency; the governing body of the Witnesses today is in the hands of older and more "spiritually qualified" men who base their judgments upon the authority of the Scriptures. This is considered not a governing hierarchy by the Witnesses but a true imitation of early apostolic Christian organization. Under this governmental system, 3 corporations eventually came to serve the society: the Watchtower Bible and Tract Society of New York, Inc., the Watchtower Bible and Tract Society of Pennsylvania; and the International Bible Students Association of England. Judge Rutherford as president was a moving power in all of them.

Under the direction of these leaders at headquarters local congregations of Witnesses (they are always called congregations and never churches) are arranged into circuits with a traveling minister visiting the congregations, spending a week with each. Approximately 22 congregations are included in each circuit. Circuits are grouped into districts, of which there are 23 in the United States. District and circuit organizations are now found in 208 countries and islands across the world.

Meeting in kingdom halls and not in churches, they witness and "publish" their faith not only in testimony in their halls, but in a remarkably comprehensive missionary effort. All of them are ministers; they do not believe in any separation into clergy or laity for the simple reason that "Christ Jesus did not make such a separation." They never use titles such as "Reverend" or "Rabbi" or "Father"; this, they feel, is not in accordance with the words of Jesus in Matt. 23:6-10. Every member is a minister, and all of them give generously of their time in proclaiming their faith and teaching in private homes. Called "Publishers of the Kingdom," most of them devote an average of 15 hours a month in kingdom preaching work, preaching only from the Bible. Pioneers are required to give at least 100 hours per month; special pioneers and missionaries devote a minimum of 150 hours per month and are sent out to isolated areas and foreign lands where new congregations can be formed. All pioneers provide for their own support, but the society gives a small allowance to the special pioneers in view of their special needs. The headquarters staff, including the president of the society, are housed at the Bethel Home in Brooklyn, engage primarily in editorial and printing work, and receive an allowance of $14 a month in addition to room and board. The literature they write, print, and distribute is of almost astronomical proportions. The official journal, *The Watchtower*, has a circulation of 7,850,000; more than 1,000,000,000 Bibles, books, and booklets have been distributed since 1920; Bibles, books, booklets, and leaflets are available in more than 176 languages. More than 1,658,990 Witnesses are active in this work throughout the world.

In this literature (all of which is circulated without an author's by-line or signature) is contained the teaching of the society. It all rests firmly upon the idea of the theocracy, or rule of God. The world in the beginning, according to the Witnesses, was under the theocratic rule of the Almighty; all then was "happiness, peace, and blessedness." But Satan rebelled and became the ruler of the world, and from that moment on mankind has followed his evil leading. Then came Jesus, "the beginning of the creation by God," as the prophets had predicted, to end Satan's rule; Jesus' rule began in 1914. In 1918 Christ "came to the temple of Jehovah"; and in 1919 when Rutherford reorganized the movement shattered by the war, Jesus, enthroned in the temple, began illuminating the prophecies and sending out his followers to preach.

God, in Witness thinking, will take vengeance upon wicked man in our times; at the same time he is now showing his great love by "gathering out" multitudes of people of good will whom he will give life in his new world which is to come after the imminent battle of Armageddon is fought. This is to be a universal battle; Christ will lead the army of the righteous, composed of the "host of heaven, the holy angels," and will completely annihilate the army of Satan. The righteous of the earth will watch this battle but will not participate. After the battle a great crowd of people will remain on the earth; these will be believers in God and will be his servants. Those who have proved their integrity under test in this old world will multiply and populate the new earth with righteous people. A resurrection will also take place and will be an additional means of filling the cleansed earth with better inhabitants. After the holocaust, "righteous princes" are to rule the earth under Christ as "King of the Great Theocracy." The willfully wicked, being incorrigible, shall not be resurrected at all; once dead, they never awake. One special group—the 144,000 Christians mentioned in Rev. 7 and 14—will become the "bride of Christ" and rule with him in heaven.

Judge Rutherford said often that "millions now living will never die"—which meant that Armageddon was close and that the Kingdom was at hand. He died in 1942, leaving guidance of the movement in the hands of the present president, Nathan H. Knorr; and Armageddon had not yet been fought. But the certainty of its imminence persists.

All this is based upon the Bible; Witnesses quote elaborately from the Scriptures, using the proof-text method in verifying their beliefs. All other teachings and interpretations are to them suspect and unreliable. They oppose and attack the teachings of the various churches as false and unscriptural, insisting as they do so that they are attacking or denouncing not churches or church members as such, but only doctrines and interpretations of scripture which they consider false. They have been especially active in opposing what they consider to be 3 allies of Satan: the false teachings of the churches, the tyranny of human governments, and the oppressions of business. This "triple alliance" of ecclesiastical, political, and commercial powers has misled and all but destroyed humanity, the Witnesses claim, and must be destroyed at Armageddon before the new world can be born. They refuse, for instance, to salute the flag or to bear arms in war or to participate in the affairs of government not because of any pacifist convictions but because they consider these to be expressions of Satan's power over men. This attitude has brought them into conflict with law-enforcing agencies; and they have endured jailings, whippings, assault by mobs, even stonings and tar-and-featherings and the burning of their homes. This they have accepted in a very submissive spirit; their position is that they will obey the laws of men when those laws are not in conflict with the laws of God; their guide is Acts 5:29.

The ranks of active "publishers" across the world has grown to 1,658,990, of which approximately 431,179 are in the United States. There are 5,794 congregations in the United States and 28,407 throughout the world. Branch offices are maintained in 95 countries, and work is reported in 208 lands. There are 276 established missions and 2,516 Watchtower trained foreign missionaries. The Bible School of Gilead was established at South Lansing, New York, in 1943 to train their missionaries, and since 1961 has operated at international headquarters at 124 Columbia Heights, in Brooklyn, New York. Since 1959 the society has operated in all the major countries of the world a Kingdom Ministry School, designed to provide a 2-week training course for all congregation overseers; in the United States this school is now located at international headquarters.

JEWISH CONGREGATIONS

Jews arrived early in the American colonies; some were here before 1650. A small group of Portuguese Jews found safety if not complete understanding in Peter Stuyvesant's New Amsterdam, where they established the first official congregation in North America, Shearith Israel (Remnant of Israel) in 1654. Three years later there was a small group of Jews at Newport, Rhode Island. Jews came to Georgia with Oglethorpe and in 1733 organized a synagogue at Savannah. By 1850 there were 77 Jewish congregations in 21 states, and at the end of the century more than 600 congregations of over 1,000,000 Jews. Today 5.5 million American Jews have a widely varying synagogue membership estimated at anywhere from a minimum of 2,000,000 upward in 3,990 congregations.

The historic sense of unity among the Jewish people soon demonstrated itself here as it had abroad. That unity had defied centuries of dispersion and persecution, and it now welded the followers of Judaism into one of the best-organized religious groups in America. In *The Truth About the Pharisees* it has been described by R. T. Herford as a "detailed system of ethical practices by which its adherents consecrated their daily lives to the service of God. The cornerstone of Judaism was the deed, not the dogma."

There are, however, 2 pillars upon which Judaism rests. One is the teaching of the Old Testament, particularly of the Pentateuch, the 5 books of Moses. This is known in Judaism as the Torah. It is the revelation of God, divine in origin and containing the earliest written laws and traditions of the Jewish people. The other is the Talmud, which is a rabbinical commentary and enlargement of the Torah, an elaborate, discursive compendium containing the written and the oral law of the faith.

In Torah and Talmud are the Judaistic foundation principles of justice, purity, hope, thanksgiving, righteousness, love, freedom of the will, divine providence and human responsibility, repentance, prayer, and the resurrection of the dead. At the heart of it all lies the Hebrew concept of the oneness of God. Every day of his life the good Jew repeats the ancient biblical verse, "Hear, O Israel, the Lord our God is one Lord." All other gods are to be shunned; there is but one Creator of man and the world, holding the destiny of both in his almighty hands.

Man, created by this one God, is inherently good. There is no original sin, no instinctive evil or fundamental impurity in him; he is made in God's image and endowed with an intelligence which enables him to choose for himself between good and evil. He has and needs no mediator such as the Christians have in Christ; he approaches God directly. Men—Jews and Gentiles alike—attain immortality as the reward for righteous living.

Judaism looks forward to the perfection of man and to the establishment of a perfect divine kingdom of truth and righteousness upon this earth, the messianic era, in which all will be peace and bliss. To work toward this kingdom, the Jews have been established of God as a deathless, unique people, a "kingdom of priests and a holy nation," and as the "servant of the Lord."

Some of their laws provide for the great festivals of the Jewish year: Pesach, or Passover, in late March or early April, a memorial of the Jewish liberation from Egypt; Shabuoth, the Feast of Weeks, or Pentecost, in late May or early June, commemorating the giving of the Ten Commandments to Moses; Sukkoth, or the Feast of Tabernacles, or Booths, in October, marking the years of Jewish wandering in the wilderness; the Feast of Lights, or Hanukkah, in late November or December, celebrating the purification of the temple by the Maccabees after its defilement by Antiochus Epiphanes; the Feast of Lots, or Purim, in February or March, honoring the heroine Esther. Three principal minor fasts are observed: the Fast of Tebeth in January, commemorating the siege of Jerusalem; the Fast of Tammuz in July, observing the breach of Jerusalem's walls; and the Fast of Ab also in July, memorializing the fall of the city and the destruction of the temple. The most important days in the Jewish religious calendar are the great fasts of Rosh Hashanah, or New Year's Day, and Yom Kippur, the Day of Atonement, in September or early October, closing the Ten Days of Penitence which begin with Rosh Hashanah.

Other laws are kept as reminders of God's covenant with Israel; these include the laws of circumcision and Sabbath observance. Still others are held as marks of divine distinction and are kept to preserve the ideal of Israel as a chosen, separate people.

Within the local congregation there is full independence. There are no synods, assemblies, or hierarchies of leaders to control anything whatsoever in the synagogue. The Jews are loosely bound by the "rope of sand" of Jewish unity, with wide variation in custom and procedure. They have been influenced deeply by the many peoples and cultures with which they have come in contact and have made adjustments accordingly. Because of differences in historical background over the centuries some congregations use a German-Polish version Hebrew prayer book; others use a Spanish version. Some use English at various points in their services, such as the sermon; but all use Hebrew in their prayers. Sermons may be heard in English or Yiddish, a Jewish language derived from Middle High German with Hebrew-Aramaic and Slavic components. Traditional Orthodox synagogues have no instrumental music in their services; the congregation worships with covered head; and the men and women sit separately. In Reform temples these traditions are not observed.

At the head of the congregation stands the rabbi, trained in college and seminary and fully ordained. He is preacher and pastor. He officiates at marriages and grants divorce decrees in accordance with Jewish law after civil divorce has been granted by the state. He conducts funerals and generally supervises the burial of Jews as Jewish law requires. Congregations usually own their own cemeteries or organize cemetery societies; there are also many private cemetery or burial associations owned and controlled by Jewish benevolent groups. Orthodox rabbis are also charged with the supervision of slaughtering animals for food and with the distribution of kosher meat products in accordance with the Levitical dietary laws. Many congregations engage readers or cantors, but it is the rabbi who is the leader and authority on Jewish law and ritual.

There is no examination for synagogue membership, all Jews being readily accepted as congregants. However, married women and unmarried children are not usually recognized as voting members. Men are almost always the corporate members. There are sometimes also pewholders, who contribute to and engage in the work of the synagogue, but without the authority of corporate members. A third class of synagogue membership consists of those who merely pay for the use of a synagogue seat during the high holidays. Corporate members are supposed to control all synagogue property and to guide congregational policy and activity, but the other members often participate on almost equal footing.

There are 3 divisions in American Judaism: (1) Orthodox Judaism, represented nationally by the Union of Orthodox Jewish Congregations of America, the Rabbinical Council of America, and the Union of Orthodox Rabbis of the United States and Canada. (2) Reform Judaism, with the Central Conference of American Rabbis and the Union of American Hebrew Congregations—the first national organization of synagogues in America, established in 1873—as spokesmen. (3) Conservative Judaism, organized in the United Synagogue of America and the Rabbinical Assembly of America. These national Jewish organizations are constituent members of the Synagogue Council of America.

Synagogue membership is difficult to determine; no comprehensive comparison seems available or possible. It is probable that each of the 3 branches of Judaism—Orthodox, Conservative, and Reformed—has about a million members. In addition to this, many Orthodox congregations are not affiliated with any national organization, and some estimates of their number run as high as 2,000. Percentages of increase are unusually high; congregations are being formed faster than the various seminaries can ordain rabbis to fill their pulpits.

The multiplicity of Jewish national organizations is bewildering. The American Jewish Year Book lists them in the following categories:

community relations and political, 19; overseas aid, 13; religious and educational, 61; social and mutual benefit, 19; cultural, 27; social welfare, 25; Zionist and pro-Israel, 47. American Jews live in more than 700 communities. In over 225 of the larger cities and towns the Jewish population maintains at least 1 central local organization: a federation, welfare fund, or community council. There are more than 200 Jewish periodicals and newspapers in 43 states and the District of Columbia, and 2 Jewish news syndicates. *American Judaism* is the quarterly Reform organ, the bimonthly *Jewish Life* speaks for the Orthodox Branch, and *Conservative Judaism* is a quarterly for the Conservatives. Of general interest are *Commentary, Midstream, The Reconstructionist Judaism, Jewish Frontier, Jewish Spectator,* and *National Jewish Post and Opinion*.

Education on all levels is a major Jewish concern. Children are enrolled in Sunday schools, weekday schools, all-day schools, Yiddish schools, and released-time schools. In 1966 there was a total of 554,468 children in all weekday and Sunday schools, but it was still estimated that not more than 53 percent of available Jewish children were enrolled in Jewish schools.

Institutions of higher learning are largely limited to schools for the training of rabbis. The most important of these schools are the Rabbi Isaac Elchanan Theological Seminary of Yeshiva University in New York City (Orthodox); the Hebrew Union College in Cincinnati and the Jewish Institute of Religion in New York City (Reformed institutions that were merged in 1948 into what is now called H.U.C.-J.I.R.); and the Jewish Theological Seminary in New York City (Conservative). The Jewish Theological Seminary has a branch in Los Angeles called the University of Judaism; Dropsie College ("a postgraduate, nonsectarian institution of Semitic learning") in Philadelphia and the Yivo Institute for Jewish Research in New York City are the only 2 institutions of higher learning working independently of Jewish seminaries; Yeshiva University in New York City and Brandeis University in Waltham, Massachusetts, are the only Jewish colleges awarding a B.A. degree.

Jewish charity is amazingly efficient. Jewish federations and welfare boards maintain programs costing over $500,000,000 per year; this money is divided among local agencies (health, welfare, education, and recreation), national agencies (civic defense, cultural, religious, and service), and overseas (mainly to help settle refugees in Israel and other countries).

The American Jewish Committee is organized to protect the civil and religious rights of all Jews around the world. It seeks equality for Jews in economic, social, and educational opportunities and gives aid and counsel in cases where intolerance or persecution are evident.

Among the Zionist groups, the Zionist Organization of America still remains the largest single body numerically, except for Hadassah, the women's Zionist group, which is the largest and most active among

Zionists in philanthropic and educational programs. In the last decade the most influential spokesman on behalf of aid to Israel has been the Conference of Presidents of major American Jewish organizations, a coordinating body and forum of 22 major American Jewish organizations, on all questions affecting American-Israeli affairs.

Three trends are noticeable: There is a trend toward a relaxation of strict or letter observance of the time-honored Jewish law; one practical expression of this is found in the Reconstructionist movement, a religious-philosophical development of some influence in both Conservative and Reform Judaism. There is also a trend toward "emphasis upon youth," in which young Orthodox Jews are organized as Young Israel in the interests of future leadership in the synagogue. Third, there is a tendency among all 3 groups to consider the inner spiritual strength of Judaism as its only hope for the future; under this drive, American Jews are moving toward fewer divisions and more cooperation and unity.

Orthodox Judaism

Orthodox Judaism has been called "Torah-True" Judaism; it is the branch which preserves the theology and traditions of Old World Jewry in the New World. It assigns equal authority to the written and oral law and to the ancient Jewish codes embodied in the Torah and the Talmud and their commentaries. The Torah is all-important and basic to all the rest: the Torah is of God, given to Moses, and there is no way to God except through obedience to the laws of the Torah; Torah is a revelation of the Fatherhood of God and the brotherhood of man, and it explains the place of the Jews as the chosen people of God. Everything a Jew needs to know is in the Torah; it governs every moment of his life. Moses is believed to have transmitted it down to the time when it was first committed to writing. There are, however, 2 slightly variant emphases in Orthodoxy; the East European, Hasidic Orthodoxy stemming from Hungary opposes resolutely *all* change or innovation in speech, dress, and education; that coming from Germany and western Europe is a bit less severe, attempting to preserve the more important elements of traditional Jewish life, but accepting modern changes and ideas in these 3 areas.

Orthodox Jews believe in the political rebirth of their nation, in the return of the Jew to Palestine to rebuild his temple on Mount Zion and to reestablish his ancient sacrificial ritual. They look forward to the coming of the Messiah, who is to be a descendant of David. The biblical dietary laws are strictly observed, and the traditional holy days and festivals are faithfully kept. The Hebrew language is used in their synagogue prayers; English, in their sermons. They are the fundamentalists of Judaism.

Reform Judaism

Reform Judaism is liberal Judaism. It began in Germany just after the Napoleonic emancipation, when "reformers" within Judaism shortened the synagogue services, made use of the vernacular and of organs in those services, and established group in place of individual confirmation. Some reformers at that time advocated a complete break with Judaistic traditional forms, but that did not come.

Isaac Mayer Wise, one of their outstanding leaders in the United States, founded here the Union of American Congregations (1873), the Hebrew Union College (1875), and the Central Conference of American Rabbis (1889); these important groups sum up the aim of Reform Judaism in their conviction that Judaism should "alter its externals to strengthen its eternals."

Reform holds that there is divine authority only in the written law of the Old Testament; this is its main distinction from Orthodox Judaism. But revelation in Reform is not confined to the Old Testament; it is progressive. The Reform Jew limits himself to the practice of the ceremonial laws of the Pentaeuch, with the exception of those laws which, like the law of sacrifice, he regards as having no application or purpose in the present day. The sacrifices of the Mosaic era, he insists, were merely concessions to the customs of the times. Claiming that the mission of Judaism is the spiritualization of mankind, he sees such practices as covering the head at worship, dietary laws, the wearing of phylacteries as anachronisms which isolate the Jew from the rest of mankind and make such spiritualizing impossible, and hence should be abolished. In other words, the Orthodox Jew accepts the entire body of oral and written law as sanctified by tradition; the Reform Jew has simplified the ritual and adapted it to modern needs.

Unlike his Orthodox brothers, he does not believe in the Messianic restoration of the Jewish state and return to Jerusalem; he is abandoning belief in a personal Messiah, but he still holds to his faith in the coming of a Messianic age. He does, however, support the return to Israel under the Zionist movement, not so much on spiritual or Talmudic grounds as on the ground that Israel offers a place of refuge for persecuted Jews of the world. He advocates the preservation in the new state of Israel of such Jewish values, customs, and traditions as have inspirational value.

Conservative Judaism

Conservative Judaism holds middle ground between Orthodox and Reform, and seeks preservation of the values and ideals of both. From Orthodoxy is takes its belief in the Torah, observance of dietary laws, and use of the Hebrew language; from Reform comes its tendency to reconcile the old beliefs and practices with the cultures in which it finds itself at work. To the Conservative, Judaism is not static but the deepening, growing, widening faith of a people who take into their culture many different influences from other cultures, and yet retain their own racial and religious aspects. Extreme changes in Jewish traditions are opposed, but some notable innovations are evident: the English language is often used in synagogue prayers, men and women sit together in family pews, and modern methods of education are applied in their development schools for children and youth. Adult education is a primary interest here; there has been a marked increase in adult schools and studies across the last 2 decades.

Black Jews

There are a number of small black "Jewish" sects in Harlem and across the country which claim "official" recognition as bona fide sects, but only one is so recognized by white Jews. There is an organization called Hazaad Harishon, at 515 Park Avenue, New York City, which offers help to Negro Jews; its activities include welfare, religious, and educational programs, and the Black Jews associated with this group have been accepted "halakically"—that is, according to the traditional Jewish law—by the Orthodox rabbinate. Hazaad Harishon actively engages the white Jewish community in efforts on behalf of these Black Jews; Black Jewish children participate with white Jewish children in citywide Jewish educational activities. There are other programs involving college-age youth.

KODESH CHURCH OF IMMANUEL

Formed in 1929 and incorporated in April, 1930, by the Rev. Frank Russell Killingsworth and 120 laymen, some of whom were former members of the African Methodist Episcopal Zion Church, this is an interracial body of approximately 3,000 members, most of whom are Negroes. The 9 churches of the denomination are located in Pennsylvania, Virginia, and the District of Columbia; a missionary station has recently been established in Liberia, West Africa. Teachings are Wesleyan and Arminian, stressing entire sanctification, or the baptism of the Holy Spirit, and premillennialism. Divine healing is practiced, but not to the exclusion of medicine.

As the church was founded for the purpose of "conserving and propagating Bible holiness," the use of alcoholic liquors and tobacco is forbidden; pride in dress and behavior, Sabbath desecration, secret societies, dissolute dancing, and attendance at inferior and obscene theaters are denounced. Divorce is recognized only on the biblical ground of adultery. Water baptism is by the optional modes of sprinkling, pouring, or immersion.

The churches are under the charge of ministers and oversight of supervising elders. Ministers are elected and ordained by annual assemblies, to which they report. Supervising elders are elected and consecrated by general assemblies, which meet quadrennially to enact all the laws of the church. The work of the entire church, including the support of foreign missionaries, is maintained by freewill offerings and tithes.

LIBERAL CATHOLIC CHURCH

Tracing its beginnings to the Old Catholic Church movement in Great Britain, which began in Holland, and its orders to an apostolic succession running back to the Roman Catholic Church under the reign of Pope Urban VIII, and even to the 12 apostles, the Liberal Catholic Church aims at a combination of traditional Catholic forms of worship with the utmost freedom of individual conscience and thought. It claims to be neither Roman Catholic nor Protestant, but still "catholic" in the broadest sense of the word. It was established during the reorganization of the British Old Catholic Movement in 1915-16, and its founders were allied with the Theosophist movement of Helena Blavatsky and Mrs. Annie Besant. The first bishops sent out to Australia and the United States were co-workers with Mrs. Besant.

In the United States, in 1947, a division occurred which separated them into 2 groups, 1 holding firm to the original Theosophical emphases (with headquarters in Minneapolis), and the other standing for a more Christian outlook and philosophy (with headquarters in Miranda, California). There are about 1,200 of them in 5 churches, the majority in the larger Miranda group. Another liberal Catholic group with headquarters in London lists 1,500 members in 18 churches. The Nicene Creed is used in their services, generally, but there is no requirement of submission to any creed, scripture, or tradition; they seek not a common profession of belief but a corporate worship in a common ritual. The Theosophical emphases tend to be played down today; they stress a central inspiration from faith in the living Christ, based on the promises of Matt. 18:20 and 28:20. These promises are regarded as "validating all Christian worship," but special channels of Christ's power are found in the sacraments of the church, of which there are 7: baptism, confirmation, the Holy Eucharist, absolution, holy unction, holy matrimony, and holy orders.

The liturgy for the Eucharist is a free translation of the Latin rite of the Roman Catholic Church, with modifications drawn from other liturgies; other services have been similarly translated and modified. No images of the dead Christ are permitted in Liberal Catholic churches. Priests and bishops may or may not marry, as they choose, and they exact no fee for the administration of the sacraments; many of them are employed in lay occupations. Divine healing is practiced through "the revifying power of the Holy Spirit, the grace of absolution, the sacred oil for the sick, and the sacrament of holy unction," but not to the exclusion of physicians and medicines.

Bishops are in charge of regional areas; they are elected by the General Episcopal Synod, which is the chief administrative and legislative body.

LIGHT OF THE WAY OPEN DOOR CHURCH FELLOWSHIP, INTERNATIONAL

As the name suggests, this is more of a fellowship than a denomination. Founded in May, 1969, they are described as "a last day revival church made up largely of Baptist and Pentecostal (and some Methodist and Presbyterian) ministers who were tired of denominational bondage . . . a group of independent churches and ministers worldwide to spread the gospel of our Lord Jesus Christ." A born-again experience is required of all applicants for membership, to whom, on admission, baptism by immersion and Holy Ghost baptism, the Lord's Supper and foot-washing are "open."

They are conservative in theology, stressing Baptist and Pentecostal beliefs. No report on membership is available, but they do report 2,500 churches in the United States, 2,000 ordained ministers, 4 Bible colleges and recently established Fellowships in 15 other countries. The Fellowship works in cooperation with the International Council of Christian Churches and publishes two magazines, *Miracle Light* and *Open Door Pentecostal World*, from their headquarters in Columbus, Ohio.

LUTHERANS

"Lutheran" was a nickname fastened upon the followers of Martin Luther by their enemies in the days of the Protestant Reformation; today it stands for something far more comprehensive. "It is clear," said Abdel R. Wentz, "that 'Lutheran' is a very inadequate name to give to a movement that is not limited to a person or an era but is as ecumenical and abiding as Christianity itself." Luther's teachings of justification by faith and of the universal priesthood of believers might be called the cornerstone of Protestantism.

The story of Luther's rebellion against the Roman Catholic Church is well-known history. His position was, briefly, that the Roman Catholic Church and papacy had no divine right in things spiritual; that the Scriptures, and not the Roman Catholic priest or church, had final authority over conscience. "Whatever is not against Scripture is for Scripture," said Luther, "and Scripture is for it." Men were forgiven and absolved of their sins, he believed, not by good works or by imposition of church rite—and especially not through the purchase of indulgences offered for sale by the Roman Catholic Church—but by man's Holy-Spirit-empowered action in turning from sin directly to God. Justification came through faith and not through ceremony, and faith was not subscription to the dictates of the church but "by the heart's utter trust in Christ." "The just shall live by faith" was the beginning and the end of his thought. He held the individual conscience to be responsible to God alone; he also held that the Bible was the clear, perfect, inspired, and authoritative word of God and guide of man. God, conscience, and the Book—on these was Lutheranism founded.

In 1529 Luther wrote his Longer and Shorter Catechisms. A year later a statement of faith known as the Augsburg Confession was authored by his scholarly associate Philip Melanchthon; 1537 brought the Smalcald Articles of Faith written by Luther, Melanchthon, and other German reformers. In 1577 the Formula of Concord was drawn up. These documents in explanation of Luther's ideology and theology form the doctrinal basis of Lutheranism.

The Reformation resulted, not in a united Protestantism, but in a Protestantism with two branches: Evangelical Lutheranism with Luther and Melanchthon as leaders; and the Reformed Church, or branch, led by John Calvin, Ulrich Zwingli, and John Knox. Evangelical Lutheranism spread from its birthplace in Germany to Poland, Russia, Lithuania, Czechoslovakia, Austria, Hungary, Yugoslavia, France, and Holland; it became in time the state church of Denmark, Norway, Sweden, Finland, Iceland, Estonia, and Latvia. It was mainly from Germany and Scandinavia that Lutheranism came to the United States.

A Lutheran Christmas service was held at Hudson's Bay in 1619; the first European Lutherans to come here and stay permanently arrived on Manhattan Island from Holland in 1623. They had a congregation worshiping in New Amsterdam in 1649, but they did not enjoy full freedom in their worship until the English took over control of "New York" in 1664. The first independent colony of Lutherans was established by Swedes along the Delaware at Fort Christiana in the colony of New Sweden in 1638.

The New York Lutherans were largely Germans. German exiles from Salzburg also settled in Georgia, where in 1736 they built the first orphanage in America. Lutherans from Württemberg settled in South Carolina. The great influx, however, came to Pennsylvania, where by the middle of the eighteenth century there were 30,000 Lutherans, four fifths of them being German and one fifth Swedes. From Philadelphia they swept over into New Jersey, Maryland, Virginia, and North Carolina.

Their first churches were small, often without pastors; and because only a minority of the immigrants joined the church, they were poor churches. The situation was relieved with the coming of Henry Melchoir Muhlenberg from the University of Halle to effect the first real organization of American Lutherans; in 1748 he organized pastors and congregations in Pennsylvania, New Jersey, New York, and Maryland into what came to be called the Ministerium of Pennsylvania; it was the first of many Lutheran synods in America. Other synods followed slowly: New York in 1786; North Carolina in 1803; Maryland in 1820;

and Ohio in 1836. Each synod adjusted itself to its peculiar conditions of language, national background, previous ecclesiastical relationship with Lutheran authorities abroad, and geographical location. The need for even further organization, aggravated by the ever-increasing immigration of Lutherans from Europe, resulted in the formation of the General Synod in 1820; with that the last real bonds with European Lutheranism began to break, and American Lutheranism was increasingly on its own.

The General Synod was obliged to extend its efforts farther and farther west as German, Swedish, Norwegian, Danish, Icelandic, and Finnish Lutherans came pouring into the new country. The Missouri Synod was formed in 1847. From 1850 to 1860, 1,000,000 Germans arrived, and the majority of them were Lutherans; the German Iowa Synod was organized in 1854, and in the same year the Norwegian Lutheran Church was established. The Augustana Synod was created in 1860 to care for the Swedes in the new West. By 1870 the Lutherans had the fourth largest Protestant group in the country, with approximately 400,000 members.

The Civil War brought the first serious break in the Lutheran ranks with the organization of the United Synod of the South in 1863; 3 years later a number of other synods led by the Ministerium of Pennsylvania withdrew from the General Synod to form the General Council. To increase the complexity, Lutheran immigrants arrived in larger and larger numbers; from 1870 to 1910 approximately 1,750,000 came from Sweden, Norway, and Denmark; and in those years the Lutheran church membership leaped from less than 500,000 to nearly 2,250,000. New Lutheran churches, colleges, seminaries, and publications were established from coast to coast.

Since 1910 there has been an almost constant effort toward the unification of Lutheran churches and agencies. Three of the large Norwegian bodies united in 1917 in the Norwegian Lutheran Church of America; some of the Midwest German synods merged in the Joint Synod of Wisconsin in 1918; the synods of Iowa, Ohio, and Buffalo merged in the American Lutheran Church in 1930. The General Synod, the General Council, and the United Synod of the South merged into the United Lutheran Church in 1918, and no less than 8 Lutheran churches were included in mergers in 1960-62. In addition to these, the Lutheran Council in the U.S.A. (consisting of the American Lutheran Church, the Lutheran Church in America, the Lutheran Church—Missouri Synod, and the Synod of Evangelical Lutheran Churches) operates through 5 divisions (Educational Services, Mission and Welfare Services, Public Relations, Service to Military Personnel, and Theological Studies). Perhaps the most cooperative effort in the history of American Lutheranism is found in Lutheran World Action, through which over $300,000,000 in goods and cash (inclusive of U.S. government-donated commodities) have been distributed across the world.

In spite of their organization division there is real unity among American Lutherans; it is a unity based more upon faith than upon organization. All Lutheran churches represent a single type of Protestant Christianity. Their faith is built upon Luther's principle of justification by faith alone in Jesus Christ; it centers in the gospel for fallen men. The Bible is the inspired Word of God and the infallible rule and standard of faith and practice. Lutherans confess their faith through the 3 general creeds of Christendom, the Apostles', the Nicene, and the Athanasian, which they believe to be in accordance with the Scriptures. They also believe that the Unaltered Augsburg Confession is a correct exposition of the faith and doctrine of Evangelical Lutheranism. The Apology of the Augsburg Confession, the 2 catechisms of Luther, the Smalcald Articles, and the Formula of Concord are held to be faithful interpretations of Evangelical Lutheranism and of the Bible.

The 2 sacraments, baptism and the Lord's Supper, are not merely signs or memorials to the Lutheran, but channels through which God bestows his forgiving and empowering grace upon men. The body and blood of Christ are believed to be present "in, with, and under" the bread and wine of the Lord's Supper, and are received sacramentally and supernaturally. Consubstantiation, transubstantiation and impanation are rejected. Infants are baptized, and baptized persons are believed to receive the gift of regeneration from the Holy Ghost.

The congregation is usually administered between its annual meetings by a church council consisting of the pastor and a number of elected lay officers, some of whom are called elders, some deacons, and some trustees. There is a growing tendency to call all lay officials deacons. Pastors are elected and called by the voting members of the congregation, but a congregation itself may never depose a pastor from the ministry. As a rule, ministers are ordained at the annual meetings of the synods; they are practically all trained in college and seminary.

Congregations are united in synods; these are composed of the pastors and lay representatives elected by the congregations and have only such authority as is granted by the synod constitution. In some other instances there are territorial districts or conferences instead of a synod, operating in the same manner and under the same restrictions; some of these may legislate, while others are for advisory or consultative purposes only.

Synods (conferences or districts) are united in a general body which may be national or even international, and which is called variously "church," "synod," or "conference." Some of these general bodies are legislative in nature, some consultative; they supervise the work in worship, education, publications, charity, and missions. Congregations have business meetings at least annually; synods, districts, and conferences hold yearly conventions; the general bodies meet annually or biennially.

168

Worship is liturgical, centering on the altar. "No sect in Western Christendom outside the Church of Rome," said the late Lutheran Archbishop Nathan Söderblom of Sweden, "has accentuated in its doctrine the Real Presence and the mysterious communion of the sacrament as has our Evangelic Lutheran sect, although our faith repudiates any quasi-rational magical explanation of the virtue of the sacrament."

Non-Lutherans are often critical of the divisions among American Lutherans, but actually they are not as divided as they seem. At one time there were 150 Lutheran bodies in this country; consolidation, unification, and federation have now reduced the number to 12. Six of the bodies in the United States account for about 95 percent of all Lutherans of North America. With the old barriers of speech and nationality disappearing, the tendency toward union becomes constantly stronger. Even on the international front united efforts are noticeable; groups of lay and ministerial delegates from major Lutheran churches in 22 countries formed a Lutheran World Federation in 1947, for the purposes of relief and rehabilitation among Lutherans on a global scale.

Historically the Lutherans have shown a tendency to remain apart from the rest of Protestantism. In the United States they are identified with churches founded by immigrant groups deeply conscious of their national and linguistic origins, conservative, confessional, nonrevivalistic, and suspicious of anything that might tend to modify their Old World faith and traditions. These traits seem to be vanishing, however, as the older membership passes and an English-speaking generation takes over. The mother tongues of Lutheranism are still used occasionally, but English is predominant. The large Lutheran Church in America is a constituent member of the National Council of the Churches of Christ in the U.S.A. Four bodies—the United Lutheran Church, the American Lutheran Church, the Augustana Evangelical Lutheran Church, and the American Evangelical Lutheran Church—participated in the organization of the World Council of Churches. A fifth body, the Evangelical Lutheran Church, affiliated with the World Council in 1957. Lutheran groups participating in interdenominational organizations have always insisted upon the operation of 2 principles within those organizations: the evangelical principle that the churches in the association should be those confessing the deity and saviorhood of Jesus Christ, and the representative principle that the governing and operating units of the organizations should be made up of officially chosen representatives of the churches.

American Lutheran Church

At a constituting convention held July 22-24, 1960, in Minneapolis, 3 major Lutheran churches were formally merged into the body now known as the American Lutheran Church. They were the American

Lutheran Church, which had a German background and which began with the formation of the Ohio Synod in 1818; the Evangelical Lutheran Church, of Norwegian heritage, which at the time of the merger was the third largest Lutheran church in America; and the United Evangelical Lutheran Church, founded in 1896 by Danish immigrants. A fourth body, the Lutheran Free Church of Norwegian background, joined these 3 on February 1, 1963, giving the new American Lutheran Church an inclusive membership of 2,521,930 in 4,823 churches. Headquarters have been established at Minneapolis.

This was a merger across ethnic lines, and the problems involved were complex in areas of both polity and doctrine, but they were successfully resolved. In government, the highest constitutional authority is vested in a general convention which meets every 2 years and has approximately 1,000 delegates (500 lay, 500 clergy) elected from the 18 districts into which the Church is geographically divided. There are 3 national officers—a general president, vice-president and general secretary. A Church Council composed of the general officers and a lay and clergy representative from each district together with the district presidents, 2 representatives from the Board of Trustees and 2 from the Luther League serving in advisory capacity, meets as the interim body between general conventions and makes recommendations to the general convention on all matters directed to it by the districts and the boards and standing committees of the Church. Five divisions are maintained as churchwide agencies responsible for mission in behalf or directly in service to member congregations. The Division of Life and Mission in the Congregation is to develop resources for and provide services to the congregations. The Division of Service and Mission in America is to implement the mission of the Church within the United States. The Division for World Mission and Inter-Church Cooperation is responsible for the missions of the Church abroad. These 3 divisions are the responsibility of 21-person boards with 18 elected by the districts and 3 members elected by the Church Council. The other 2 divisions are the Division for Theological Education and Ministry and the Division for College and University Services, each directed by a board of 9 members elected by the general convention.

There are 3 service boards established to provide specific services. The Board of Trustees has responsibility for the general management of business affairs, financial controls, and property transactions. The Board of Pensions provides for retirement income for the clergy and eligible clergy. The Board of Publications is a nonbudgetary production and distribution unit. Each of its service Boards is composed of 9 members elected by the general comvention.

There are 3 administrative offices maintained as agencies responsible to the general president. The Office of Communications and Mission Support is to interpret the mission of the Church and to provide support for that mission. The Office of Research and Analysis is organized to keep the Church informed regarding the effects of changes in society and to coordinate research efforts. The Office of Support to Ministry is to provide support to the various ministries of the Church and to provide staff services to the Council of Presidents. The offices have standing committees to which they relate.

District and national committees on Appeals and Adjudication exercise judicial authority for the Church.

The Confession of Faith of this Church accepts the Bible as divinely inspired, revealed, and inerrant; the 3 ancient ecumenical creeds (Apostles', Nicene, and Athanasian); the Unaltered Augsburg Confession; Luther's Larger and Shorter Catechisms; the Book of Concord of 1580; the Apology; the Smalcald Articles, and the Formula of Concord.

In the field of education there are 3 theological seminaries, 11 senior colleges, 1 junior college, and 1 academy. In the area of social services there are 18 group care homes for the emotionally disturbed, 7 homes for the mentally and physically handicapped, 126 homes for the aged, 2 alcohol treatment centers, 3 homes for unwed mothers, 13 hospitals, 34 multi-service agencies (case work, etc.), 14 other group services. Foreign missionaries are supported in 15 countries overseas and home missionaries work in 47 states.

Lutheran Church in America

With well over 3,000,000 members, this is the largest Lutheran church in the United States; it represents a consolidation of 4 Lutheran bodies (the United Lutheran Church in America, the Augustana Evangelical Lutheran Church, the American Evangelical Lutheran Church, and the Finnish Evangelical Lutheran Church) which came about on June 28, 1962.

The United Lutheran Church was the youngest of the 4 uniting bodies, having been formed in 1918 in the uniting of 45 synods previously found in the General Synod, the General Council, and the United Synod of the South. Some 13 of these synods later withdrew or formed along new lines in the following 44 years, but the United Church brought a total of almost 2,500,000 members in 4,600 congregations into the 1962 merger.

The Augustana Evangelical Lutheran Church began in the work of scattered Swedish families and congregations in Iowa and Illinois in the mid-1800's; their Augustana Synod was formed in 1860, with 5,000 communicants and 49 congregations, of which 36 were Swedish and 13 Norwegian. The name "Augustana" affirmed the group's loyalty to the doctrine of the Augsburg Confession (*Augustana*, in the Latin). Ten years later the Norwegians withdrew to form a church of their own; at the time of the 1962 merger the Augustana body had better than half a million communicants in 1,200 congregations.

The Finnish Evangelical Lutheran Church (better known as the Suomi Synod), was organized at Calumet, Michigan, in 1890; it was strictly a confessional church, using the 3 ecumenical creeds and the unaltered Augsburg Confession. Until quite recently the Finnish language was employed in the services of this church, which had 36,000 members and 153 congregations in 1962.

The American Evangelical Lutheran Church was the smallest of the uniting bodies numerically, with 25,000 members in 79 congregations. It was of Danish origin, founded under the direction of ministers sent from Denmark in 1872 and under the name *Kirkelig Missionsforening*. It was a church deeply concerned with the place and meaning of the Bible in Lutheran theology, yet it had a strong tradition of ecumenical interest, and was represented in the National Lutheran Council, the National Council of Churches, and the World Council of Churches.

To bring these 4 churches into 1 body seemed at first impossible, but it was accomplished. A new confession was worked out which preserved the historic creeds and confessions of Lutheranism, and yet established a new, broad base of emphasis upon full acceptance of Christ and the Scriptures. This statement of faith is found in Article Two of the Constitution of the Lutheran Church in America; it reads, in part:

This church holds that the Gospel is the revelation of God's sovereign will and saving grace in Jesus Christ, . . . acknowledges the Holy Scriptures as the norm for the faith and life of the church, . . . accepts the Apostles', the Nicene, and the Athanasian creeds as true declarations of the faith of the church, . . . accepts the Unaltered Augsburg Confession and Luther's Small Catechism as true witnesses to the Gospel, and acknowledges as one with it in faith and doctrine all churches that likewise accept the teachings of these symbols. . . . [It] accepts the other symbolical books of the evangelical Lutheran church, the Apology of the Augsburg Confession, the Smalcald Articles, Luther's Larger Catechism, and the Formula of Concord as further valid interpretations of the confession of the church. . . . [It] affirms that the Gospel transmitted by the Holy Scriptures . . . is the true treasure of the church, the substance of its proclamation, and the basis of its unity and continuity.

In administration, the chief officer is a president elected for 4 years by a biennial convention; he presides over the convention and over an executive council of 33 members (3 officers, 15 ministers, and 15 laymen) which supervises the work of the synods, and the following churchwide agencies: Division for Mission in North America, Division for Parish services, Division for Professional Leadership, Division for World Mission and Ecumenism, Office for Administration and Finance, Office for Communication, and Office for Research and planning.

A full-time president serves each of the 33 synods which coordinate and direct the work of local congregations; these synods hold annual meetings of which each minister, whether active or retired is a member and in which each congregation is represented by 1 or more lay delegates; each synod is subdivided into regional districts, under the direction of a pastor-dean.

The LCA is active in missions in 24 foreign countries, Nearly 200 social institutions (hospitals, homes for the aged and children, nurseries, etc.) are supported by the Church; there are 28 colleges and seminaries.

Church of the Lutheran Brethren of America

This is an independent church body, with churches located in Minnesota, Wisconsin, North and South Dakota, Iowa, Illinois, and on both East and West coasts. Organized in Milwaukee in 1900, it differs from other Lutheran churches in accepting as members only those who profess a personal experience of salvation and in stressing nonliturgical worship and lay participation. They have 2 years of confirmation instruction, but no vow is used at the confirmation service; they instruct children and wait until there is an individual experience and conversion before receiving them as communicant members. Communion is received in the pew; there are no altars in church buildings. Free prayer and personal testimony are stressed.

The church as a body is the supreme administrative unit, with a president, 2 vice-presidents, secretary, and treasurer. Foreign missions are supervised by a board of 9 members, and home missions by a board of 9. With a total membership of some 9,010 in 97 congregations, the church conducts foreign missionary work in Africa, Japan, and Formosa. There are 58 adult missionaries abroad. On an annual budget of $475,250 (high among Lutherans in proportion to the membership), the church supports a 3-year high school, a 2-year Bible course, a 3-year seminary course—all operated by the Synod at Fergus Falls, Minnesota. Sarepta Home for the Aged and the Broen Memorial Home are also controlled by the church. Synodical headquarters are located at Fergus Falls.

Evangelical Lutheran Synod (Formerly the Norwegian Synod)

The synod was formed in 1918 by a minority group which declined to join the union of other Norwegian groups into the Norwegian Lutheran Church (the former Evangelical Lutheran Church) in 1917. The name was changed as above in 1958.

The jurisdiction of the synod is entirely advisory; all synod resolutions are accepted or rejected by the local congregations. The officers and boards of the synod, however, direct the work of common interest insofar as they do not interfere with congregational rights or prerogatives.

For some years the synod used the facilities of the colleges and seminaries of the Missouri and Wisconsin synods, within the framework of the Synodical Conference; in 1963 the Evangelical Lutheran Synod withdrew from the Synodical Conference because of doctrinal differences with the Missouri Synod and now maintains its own junior college and seminary at Mankato, Minnesota, and works in fellowship with the Wisconsin and some smaller synods overseas. It has 12 home mission stations in the United States and 2 foreign missions in South America and Nicaragua, 1 preparatory school, and 17,426 members in 89 churches.

Apostolic Lutheran Church of America

Sometimes called the "Church of Laestadius," after Lars Levi Laestadius, a minister of the state church of Sweden, this church originated with Finnish immigrants in and around Calumet, Michigan, in the middle years of the nineteenth century. They worshiped at first in the Lutheran Church of Calumet under a Norwegian minister; however, differences between the 2 national groups led to the forming, in 1872, of a separate Finnish congregation led by Solomon Korteniemi and called the Solomon Korteniemi Lutheran Society. The first incorporated church in Michigan was incorporated in 1879 under the name of the Finnish Apostolic Lutheran Church of Calumet. The national church was formed and incorporated in 1929, under the name of the Finnish Apostolic Lutheran Church of America; this body was actually a merger of independent Apostolic Lutheran congregations into the one national body. Spreading over Michigan, Minnesota, the Dakotas, Massachusetts, Oregon, Washington, and California, the new church was divided into 2 districts—Eastern and Western. Foreign missions work in Nigeria, Liberia, and Guatamala.

A scriptural Christian experience is required as a condition for voting membership in spiritual matters; supporting members may vote on temporal matters only. The church accepts the 3 ecumenical creeds and puts strong emphasis upon the confession of sins, absolution, and regeneration. Confession may be made to a Christian brother, but if someone has fallen into sins unknown to other people, private confession is not sufficient, and "he should confess them publicly before the congregation and receive absolution."

The 64 local congregations of this church are quite free to govern themselves; at the annual church convention where every congregation has 1 vote, 3 members are elected to a 9-member executive board for 3-year terms; the board elects a president, vice-president, secretary, and treasurer. Three members are also elected to the Eastern and Western mission boards and to the Elder's Home Board. As of 1961, there were 6,994 members.

The Lutheran Church—Missouri Synod

With 2.8 million members and 5,774 churches, this is the second largest Lutheran church in the United States. The "Missouri" in the name comes from the founding of the denomination in that state by Saxon immigrants; these were later joined by Hanoverians in Indiana and Franconians in Michigan. From the start all 3 of these groups were devoted to the maintance of orthodox Lutheranism. They were Germans who had fought the trend toward rationalism in the old country and who came here for the sake of religious freedom and to establish a synod in which the sovereignty of the local congregation would be recognized.

This synod was organized in 1847 with 12 congregations and 22 ministers under the name German Evangelical Lutheran Synod of Missouri, Ohio, and Other States. Under the constitution adopted at the time, all symbolical books of the Lutheran Church were considered to be the "pure and uncorrupted explanation of the Divine Word," and doctrinal agreement was required for exchange of pulpits and altars with other churches.

The doctrinal standard of the Missouri Synod is strictly observed and enforced. That standard is found in the Bible "as it was interpreted by the Book of Concord," plus the 3 ecumenical creeds—the Apostles', Nicene, and Athanasian—and the 6 Lutheran confessions: the Augsburg Confession, the apology of the Augsburg Confession, the Smalcald Articles, the Formula of Concord, and the 2 catechisms of Martin Luther. All across the years the synod has been unswerving in its allegiance to this conservative Lutheranism.

There are the usual Lutheran districts and district conventions, and the general convention meet biennally.

A startling work is done in education; the Missouri Synod has 1,177 parochial schools, 27 high schools, and 5,889 day schools. The Synod's world mission work is done in cooperation with sister churches in India, Ceylon, New Guinea, the Philippines, Taiwan, Korea, Ghana, Nigeria, and Hong Kong. The Middle East Lutheran Ministry, with headquarters in Lebanon, concerns itself chiefly with radio work. The Synod serves colleges and universities in North America through its Department of Campus Ministry with 100 full-time pastors and 70 others on a part-time basis. It has 30 hospitals, 11 homes for the aged and 13 homes for children, 3 convalescent homes, 10 junior colleges, 3 teachers' colleges, and 1 senior college. Concordia Seminary in St. Louis and Concordia Seminary in Springfield, Illinois, and Valpariso University at Valparaiso, Indiana, the largest Lutheran college in this country.

Affiliated with the Missouri Synod are the Walther League (a youth organization), the Lutheran Missionary League, and the Lutheran Laymen's League. This Synod carries on the most extensive work among the deaf in American Protestantism, with 44 full-time pastors serving 55 congregations.

The Synod has been disturbed in recent years over questions of orthodoxy. One group, known as The Lutheran Churches of the Reformation, split off from the Synod in the early 1960's because of what the group felt to be a trend toward liberalism; it has an estimated 20 congregations and 3,000 members, stresses the principle of congregational autonomy, and refuses fellowship with other conservative Lutheran bodies on this account. The LCR operates several day schools and a seminary in Shepherd, Michigan. A more recent deviation from the Synod is that of the Federation for Authentic Lutheranism (FAL), formed following the 1971 convention of the Missouri Synod in protest against "heretical practices" including altar and pulpit fellowship with the American Lutheran Church and woman sufferage. It has 7 congregations, and an estimated membership of 8,000.

Protestant Conference (Lutheran)

A protest against alleged "high-handed" tactics of church officialdom and against the inroads of leaglism in the life of the Wisconsin Evangelical Lutheran Synod led to the suspension of 47 pastors in 1927 and to the formation of the Protestant Conference (Lutheran). Their aim was to

break down within our Lutheran Church, and wherever else it may flourish, the spirit of self-righteousness and self-sufficiency through a re-emphasis upon the Gospel of forgiveness of sins . . . coupled with the warning of the hardening of hearts and of judgment upon those who reject this message and its implications.

A baptized membership of 2600 was reported in 1972 in 7 churches. A general conference meets 3 times a year, and 1 publication, *Faith-Life*, is issued from Mosinee, Wisconsin.

Wisconsin Evangelical Lutheran Synod

Organized in 1850 under the name First German Lutheran Synod of Wisconsin, 3 synods—Wisconsin, Minnesota, and Michigan—merged in an organic union in 1918 as the Evangelical Lutheran Joint Synod of Wisconsin and Other States. This name was changed in 1959 to the Wisconsin Evangelical Lutheran Synod. Very close to the theological pattern of the Missouri Synod, they stand for an orthodox, confessional Lutheranism and are opposed to tendencies toward union without doctrinal unity among Lutheran groups.

The Synod is divided into 9 districts in Arizona, California, the Dakotas, Montana, Michigan, Minnesota, Nebraska, and Wisconsin. The districts meet in convention every even year, in joint synodical conference in odd years, with pastors, teachers, and laymen as delegates. With an inclusive membership of 383,263 in 987 churches, it has 207 home mission stations. Its world missions are conducted among the Apache Indians in Arizona and in Germany, Japan, Zambi,

Malawi, Mexico, Canada, Puerto Rico, Hong Kong, Taiwan, Indonesia, and India.

There are 2 senior colleges, 4 junior colleges and academies, 1 theological seminary, 1 teacher's seminary, 9 area Lutheran high schools with an enrollment of 3,198, approximately 26,458 children in 256 parochial schools, 6 homes for the aged, and 1 child and family agency.

A splinter group, the Church of the Lutheran Confession, separated from the Wisconsin Synod in the early 1960's, following a dispute over relationships with the Missouri Synod; it now has about 9,000 members.

MENNONITES

The first Mennonite congregation of historical record was organized at Zurich, Switzerland, in 1525; it consisted of Swiss Brethren, or *Täufer*, who disagreed with Ulrich Zwingli in his readiness to consent to a union of church and state. They also denied the scriptural validity of infant baptism and hence were labeled Anabaptists, or Re-Baptizers. Anabaptists congregations were organized in Holland by Obbe Philips as early as 1534; Philips baptized Menno Simons (*ca.* 1496-1561) in 1536.

Menno was a converted Roman Catholic priest; he organized more Anabaptist congregations in Holland, and his contemporaries gave his name to the movement. Many of his Flemish adherents crossed the channel on the invitation of Henry VIII. In England as well as in Germany, Holland, and Switzerland they met opposition largely because of their determined distrust of any union of church and state. An impressive martyr roll was created; it might have been much larger had it not been for the sudden haven offered in the American colony of William Penn. Thirteen families settled in Germantown, near Philadelphia, in 1683. Eventually they established a Mennonite congregation there, although many of them had left the Mennonite fold and united with the Quakers before they left Crefeld, Germany. Mennonite immigrants from Germany and Switzerland spread over Pennsylvania, Ohio, Virginia, Indiana, Illinois, farther west, and into Canada; these were later joined by others coming from Russia, Prussia, and Poland. Thanks to their historic insistence upon nonresistance their colonial settlements were comparatively peaceful and prosperous.

The faith of these Mennonites was based upon a confession of faith signed at Dortrecht, Holland, in 1632. In 18 articles the following doctrines were laid down: faith in God as creator; man's fall and restoration at the coming of Christ; Christ as the Son of God, redeeming men on the cross; obedience to Christ's law in the gospel; the necessity of repentance and conversion for salvation; baptism as a public testimony of faith; the Lord's Supper as an expression of common union and fellowship; matrimony as permissible only among those "spiritually kindred"; obedience to and respect for civil government except in the use of armed force; exclusion from the church of those who sin willfully and their social ostracism for the protection of the faith of others in the church; and future rewards and punishments for the faithful and the wicked.

The Lord's Supper is served twice a year in almost all Mennonite congregations, and in most of them baptism is by pouring. Most of them observe the foot washing ordinance in connection with the Supper, after which they salute each other with the "kiss of peace." The sexes are separated in the last 2 ceremonies. All Mennonites baptize only on confession of faith, refuse to take oaths before magistrates, oppose secret societies, and follow strictly the teachings of the New Testament. They have a strong intrachurch program of mutual aid and a worldwide relief and elemosynary service through an all-Mennonite relief organization called the Mennonite Central Committee.

The local congregation is more or less autonomous and authoritative, although in some instances appeals are taken to district or state conferences. The officers of the church are bishops (often called elders), ministers, and deacons (almoners). Many ministers are self-supporting, working in secular employments when not occupied with the work of the church. There are other appointed officers for Sunday school, young people's work, and so forth.

The Amish movement within the ranks of the Mennonites takes its name from Jacob Amman, a Swiss (Bernese) Mennonite bishop of the late seventeenth century who insisted upon strict conformation to the confession of faith, especially in the matter of the ban, or expulsion of members. This literalism brought about a separation in Switzerland in 1693; about 200 years later the divided bodies, with the exception of 3 Amish groups, were reunited.

Amish immigrants to the United States concentrated early in Pennsylvania and moved from there into Ohio, Indiana, Illinois, Nebraska, and other western states; some went into Canada. They have today a common literature. Many of the Amish, distinguished by their severely plain clothing, are found in the Conservative Amish Mennonite Church and the larger Old Order Amish Mennonite Church. They are still the "literalists" of the movement, clinging tenaciously to the "Pennsylvania Dutch" language and to the seventeenth-century culture of their Swiss-German forbears. They oppose automobiles, telephones, and higher education, but are recognized as very efficient farmers.

Beachy Amish Mennonite Churches

These churches are made up of Amish Mennonites who separated from the more conservative Old Order Amish over a period of years, beginning in Somerset County, Pennsylvania, in 1927. They were led by Bishop Moses M. Beachy, who died in 1946. There are today 60 congregations and 4,069 members.

They resemble to some degree the Old Order Amish in garb and general attitudes, but their discipline is more mild and relaxed. They worship in church buildings, have Sunday schools, and are active in supporting missionary work.

Church of God in Christ (Mennonite)

This church grew out of the preaching and labors of John Holdeman, a member of the Mennonite Church in Ohio, who became convinced that his church was apostate and in error in many of its teachings and practices. He preached ardently on the necessity of the new birth, Holy Ghost Baptism, more adequate training of children in the fundamentals, the discipline of unfaithful members, avoidance of apostates, and the condemnation of worldly minded churches. He separated himself, finally, from the Mennonite Church, and in 1859 began holding meetings with a small group of followers who were formally organized into the Church of God in Christ, Mennonite.

The church believes that the same confession of faith must be believed and practiced by all churches, "from the time of the apostles to the end of the world," and that the Bible as the inspired, infallible Word of God must govern all doctrine and teaching. It accepts the Eighteen Articles of Faith drawn up at Dortrecht, Holland, in 1632. It practices the mode form of baptism, and teaches nonresistance and nonconformity to the world in dress, bodily adornment, worldly sports, and amusements. Missions are operated in the United States, Canada, Mexico, Haiti, India, and Nigeria; there are 6,204 members in 38 congregations spread from the United States to Africa.

Conservative Mennonite Conference

Known as the Conservative Amish Mennonite Church until 1954, when the present name was adopted, this conference subscribes to the Dortrecht Confession of Faith and the 1963 Mennonite Confession of Faith. Its first general conference was held at Pigeon, Michigan, in 1910. It separated gradually from the Old Order Amish, installing such innovations as meetinghouses, Sunday schools, evening and "continued" meetings, and the use of English rather than German in worship. Holding strictly to the Mennonite principles of nonresistance and nonconformity, it promotes missions and various types of social work in the United States, Central America, and Europe. There are 6,900 members in 103 mission stations and congregations.

Evangelical Mennonite Brethren

Formerly called the Conference of Defenseless Mennonites of North America, this group now has 3,784 members in 33 churches. It was established by Russian Mennonite immigrants in 1873-74 and concentrates on a strong missionary program under which some 110 missionaries are at work overseas.

Evangelical Mennonite Church

Formerly the Defenseless Mennonite Church, this body was founded about 1865 under the leadership of Henry Egly, to emphasize teachings on regeneration, separation, nonconformity to the world, and nonresistance. Their program today is largely one of missions and evangelism. There is a children's home in Flanagan, Illinois; 3,200 members are in 20 churches.

General Conference Mennonite Church

A group of local Mennonite congregations in Iowa, anxious to improve upon and enlarge foreign missionary efforts, offer better training for prospective leaders, and to establish a church periodical, organized at Wayland, Iowa, in 1860 to form the General Conference Mennonite Church. The desire to unite all Mennonite churches and conferences was strong among them, and still is. They accept established Mennonite doctrine but place strong emphasis upon the autonomy of the local congregation, and in their insistence upon freedom from the traditional Mennonite regulations on dress and attire for both men and women they are marked as "liberal in conduct."

Six district conferences meet annually, and a general conference meets triennially for fellowship and the transaction of official business. Elected commissions—overseas mission, home ministries, education, communication, and administration—direct the work of the general conference. The conference maintains 2 liberal arts colleges, 1 Bible college, 1 junior college, 1 theological seminary, several homes for children and the aged, hospitals, and nurses' training schools. There are 36,314 members in 187 churches in the United States, 20,553 members in 103 churches in Canada, and additional churches in Latin America. Mission work is carried on in ten overseas countries, where the membership totals about 40,000.

Hutterian Brethren

These are disciples of Jacob Hutter, a sixteenth-century Tyrolean Anabaptist who advocated communal ownership of property. He was burned as a heretic in Austria in 1536. Many of the Hutterites came from Russia to Canada and the United States about 1874; they have moved back and forth across the border ever since. Most of them today are of German ancestry and use the German tongue in their homes and churches. Aside from the common-property idea, they are quite similar to the Old Order Amish: they have a Bible-centered faith which they seek to express in brotherly love; they aim at the recovery of the New Testament spirit and fellowship; they feel that this requires nonconformity to the world, and accordingly they practice nonresistance; refuse to participate in local politics, dress differently, make no contributions to community projects, and have their own schools, in which the Bible is paramount. Their exclusiveness has made them unwelcome in certain sections of the country, and their status is uncertain at the moment. There are 20,000 of them in 200 colonies in South Dakota, Minnesota, Montana, Washington, and Canada.

Mennonite Brethren Church of North America

Russian in background, this church was organized in 1860 on withdrawal from the Mennonite Church in the Ukraine of a small group seeking a rigid enforcement of the ban and closer attention to prayer and Bible study. Pietistic in orientation, the group adopted a Baptistic policy. Small bodies of these German-speaking Russians reached Kansas in 1876, and spread to the Pacific coast and into Canada.

A general conference meets triennially as the chief administrative body, gathering delegates from 2 areas (Canada and the United States). Each area has a number of districts. The area conferences supervise work in home missions, education, and publications. Foreign missions (a department of the general conference) are found in Africa, Asia, Europe, South America, and Mexico.

The Krimmer Mennonite Brethren merged with this church in 1960, bringing the total membership to 30,000 in 160 churches.

Mennonite Church

This is the largest single group of Mennonites in the United States, with about 90,000 members in 1,041 churches; it is the church founded by German immigrants in Germantown, Pennsylvania, in 1683. The Dortrecht Confession was adopted at a conference of the Pennsylvania Mennonite ministers in 1725, and this remained the official statement of faith until a 1921 Mennonite general conference adopted a restatement on the Fundamentals of the Christian Faith consisting of 18 articles. In 1963 the general conference of the Mennonite Church adopted a new, revised confession of faith which seeks, without attempting to make Mennonites into a creedal church, to set forth the major doctrines of Scripture as understood in the Anabaptist-Mennonite tradition. The attempt was made to write with simplicity and clarity, to be more biblical than philosophical or even theological. This 1963 Confession of Faith stresses faith in Christ, the saved status of children (without any ceremony), the importance of proclaiming God's Word and "making disciples," the baptism of believers, the ethic of absolute love and nonresistance to injustice and maltreatment, the church as a nonhierarchical brotherhood, and the practice of church discipline.

The General Assembly meets every 2 years; deacons and ministers who are not elected delegates from the district or state conference may debate but not vote; the bishops and other delegates from the district conferences render decisions by a majority vote. The district conferences set the disciplinary standards for their respective congregations. Bishops, ministers, and deacons serve as delegates; some districts also have lay delegates. Three conferences of the former Amish Mennonite Church have been merged with district state conferences of this church.

A number of churchwide boards and committees are in charge of missionary, educational, publishing, and philanthropic work; they are now under the direction of a general church board. Home missions stress evangelism; foreign missions are found in India, Japan, Africa, and South America. There are 2 colleges, 2 seminaries, several academies, 1 hospital, 2 nurses' training schools, 3 orphans' homes, and 4 homes for the aged.

Old Order Amish Mennonite Church

Continuous with the Amish immigrants of 1720-40, the church adheres to the older forms of worship and attire, using hooks and eyes instead of buttons, worshiping in private homes, and having no conferences. Members do not believe in conferences, missions, or benevolent institutions, and oppose centralized schools; some of them, however, do contribute to the missions and charities of the Mennonite Church. There are 29,750 members in 398 churches.

Old Order (Wisler) Mennonite Church

This church was named for the first Mennonite bishop in Indiana, Jacob Wisler, who led a separation from the Mennonite Church in 1872. Those who separated did so in protest against the use of English in the services and the introduction of Sunday schools. Joined in 1886, 1893, and 1901 by groups with similar ideas from Canada, Pennsylvania, and Virginia, they still maintain their church on the basis of these protests. Each section of the church has its own district conference; there are no benevolent or missionary enterprises, but some contribute to the work of the Mennonite Church in those fields. There are 8,000 members in the U.S. and Canada.

Reformed Mennonite Church

Organized under the leadership of John Herr in Lancaster County, Pennsylvania, in 1812, Reformed Mennonites hold closely to New Testament teachings and believe that there can be but one true church for all believers. They have 4 ordinances: baptism, the Lord's Supper, foot washing, and the kiss of peace; these are "for edification and not as a means of salvation." Baptism, by pouring or sprinkling, is considered an outward testimony of the baptism of the Holy Spirit within the heart, which must precede the reception of water baptism. The Communion service signifies unity with God and with one another and is observed only by members of the church. They practice foot washing as taught in John 13, carry out strictly the instructions in Matthew 18 regarding laboring in love with an erring brother, greet each other regularly with the kiss of peace, insist upon modest and plain uniform clothing, and require their women to wear head coverings.

They are nonresistant, pacificistic, do not vote or hold any governmental office, and refuse to worship with those with whom they are not united in faith and practice. They have 14 churches and a membership of about 500. Their bishops, ministers, and deacons are chosen from the local congregations and are not paid. They have no Sunday schools, believing it obligatory upon the parents to teach their own children.

Unaffiliated Mennonites

A number of small Mennonite groups hold an unaffiliated status with all other Mennonite bodies. These unaffiliated Amish Mennonite and Mennonite churches claim 4,425 members enrolled in 87 churches. There is such a wide variety of emphasis on doctrines and practice that no general statement can be made in respect to their faith and polity.

METHODISTS

England's famed old Oxford University has been called the "cradle of lost causes," but at least one cause was born there which was not lost. This was Methodism. Known and ridiculed at Oxford in 1729, it claims today some 14,000,000 adherents in North America and more than 18,000,000 around the world.

The Oxford Methodists (also dubbed "Bible Bigots," "Bible Moths," and the "Holy Club") were a tiny group of students who gave stated time to prayer and Bible reading; prominent among them were John and Charles Wesley and George Whitefield. They were methodically religious, talking of the necessity of being justified before they could be sanctified and of the need of holiness in human living, reading and discussing William Law's *A Serious Call to a Devout and Holy Life* and *A Treatise on Christian Perfection*. The 2 Wesleys were sons of a clergyman of the Church of England; with the other members of the Holy Club they stood their ground against jeering students and went out to preach and pray with the poor and desperate commoners of England—prisoners in jail, paupers in hovels, bitter and nearly hopeless "underdogs of a British society that was perilously close to moral and spiritual collapse." Methodism started on a campus and reached for the masses.

The Wesleys came to Georgia in 1736. Charles came as secretary to General Oglethorpe, and John was sent by the Society for the Propagation of the Gospel as a missionary to the Indians. It was an unsuccessful and unhappy 2 years for John Wesley with but one bright spot; on shipboard en route to the colonies he met a group of Moravians and became deeply impressed by their piety and humble Christian living. Later when he returned to London, he went one night to meet with a religious society in Aldersgate Street, heard the preacher read Luther's preface to the Epistle to the Romans and felt his heart "strangely warmed" as the meaning of the reformer's doctrine of "justification by faith" sank into his soul. It was the evangelistic spark that energized his life and started the flame of the Wesleyan revival in England. From the pious Moravians via Wesley came the warmhearted emphases upon conversion and holiness which are still the central themes of Methodism.

Whitefield and the Wesleys were too much afire to remain within the staid Church of England. When its doors were closed to them, they took to the open air, John preaching and Charles writing the hymns of the revival in streets, barns, and private homes and in the mining pits of Cornwall, preaching repentance, regeneration, turning from sin and the wrath to come, justification, holiness, and sanctification. The upper classes laughed, and the lower classes listened to the first words of hope they had heard in many a year. Converts came thick and fast; it became necessary to organize them into societies. The first Methodist society was attached to a Moravian congregation in Fetter Lane, London, in 1739, and later moved to its own quarters in an old, abandoned government building known as the Foundry, where the first self-sustaining Methodist society in London was organized in 1740.

Between 1739 and 1744 the organizational elements of Methodism were instituted; we read of a "circuit system" and of an "itinerant ministry," of class meetings and class leaders, of lay preachers and annual conferences. There was a phenomenal growth in membership; more than 26,000 Methodists were worshiping in England, Ireland, Scotland, and Wales in 1767. Their impact upon British society was startling; the crudities and barbarisms of the times were alleviated and a "French revolution" averted. It was primarily a lay movement.

Wesley did his best to keep the movement within the Church of England; an evangelical party grew within the church, but the greater numbers recruited from among the unchurched made a separate organization imperative. In 1739 Wesley drew up a set of general rules which are still held by modern Methodists and an ideal delineation of Bible rules and conduct. A Deed of Declaration in 1784 gave legal status to the yearly Methodist conference. But John Wesley was dead in 1791 before Methodism in England had the name of a recognized church, the Wesleyan Methodist Connection.

Meanwhile the movement had invaded the American colonies. Wesley had begun to send out leaders; the first of them were Joseph Pilmoor and Richard Boardman. Philip Embury, an Irish lay leader, encouraged by his cousin Barbara Heck, preached in New York and inspired the organization of the first Methodist society overseas about 1766. By 1769 the New York Methodists had built Wesley Chapel, now known as John Street Methodist Church. To the south Captain Thomas Webb, a veteran of Braddock's ill-fated army, established societies in Philadelphia, and Robert Strawbridge started a revival in Maryland and built a log-cabin church at Sam's Creek. Devereux Jarratt, a transplanted evangelical Anglican minister, led a revival in Virginia which won thousands. The true center of Methodism in those days did indeed lie in the South; out of 3,148 Methodists in the colonies in 1775 about 2,000 lived south of Mason and Dixon's Line. Wesley, aware of the rapid spread of the movement in America, sent emissaries to take charge, among them Francis Asbury and Thomas Rankin, the latter as the first full-fledged "superintendent of the entire work of Methodism in America." Rankin presided over the first conference in America, called at Philadelphia in 1773 and attended by 10 ministers.

There were about 1,160 Methodists represented in the conference of 1773; when the Liberty Bell rang in 1776, there were less than 7,000 in all the colonies, and they seemed doomed to disappear as quickly as they had been gathered. The majority of their preachers had come from England and were incurably British; they were so roughly handled by the patriots that by 1779 nearly every one of them had fled either to Canada or home to England. Wesley's pro-British attitude also roused resentment, and Francis Asbury working almost singlehanded had a difficult time keeping some of the churches alive. But a miracle happened; of all the religious groups in the colonies the Methodists alone actually seemed to prosper during the Revolution. When the surrender came at Yorktown, their membership had grown to 14,000 and there were nearly 80 preachers. They were, after Yorktown, an American church, free of both England and the Church of England. Wesley accepted the inevitable; he ordained ministers for the colonies and appointed Asbury and Thomas Coke as superintendents.

Coke brought with him from England certain instructions from Wesley, a service book and hymnal, and authority to proceed with the organization. A Christmas Conference held at Baltimore in December of 1784 organized the Methodist Episcopal Church, elected Coke and Asbury as superintendents (later called bishops), and adopted the Sunday Service (an abridgment of the Book of Common Prayer) and Articles of Religion as written by John Wesley, adding another article that as good patriots Methodists should vow allegiance to the United

States government. The first general conference of the new church was held in 1792, made up solely of ministers. It was not until 1872 that laymen were admitted to what had become by that time a quadrennial general conference. Membership soared: from 37 circuits and 14,000 members at the close of the Revolution there came a membership of 1,324,000 by the middle of the following century.

Methodism not only swept through the cities; it developed an amazing strength in small towns and rural areas. Everywhere there were circuit riders—ministers on horseback riding the expanding frontier and preaching in mountain cabins, prairie churches, schoolhouses, and camp meetings of free grace and individual responsibility and the need of conversion and regeneration. Their itinerant ministry was perfectly adapted to the democratic society of the frontier. The Methodist Book Concern was established in 1789, putting into the saddlebags of the circuit riders a religious literature which followed the march of American empire south and west. The camp meeting, born among the Presbyterians though not always carried on by them, was adopted by the Methodists and exploited to the limit. Its revivalistic flavor and method were made to order for the followers of Wesley and Whitefield. There are still camp meetings in Methodism.

All was not peaceful, however, among all the Methodists; divisions came. Objecting, like good democrats, to what they considered abuses of the episcopal system, several bodies broke away: the Republican Methodists, later the Christian Church, withdrew in Virginia; Methodist Protestants seceded in 1830. Between 1813 and 1817 large Negro groups formed independent churches: the African Methodist Episcopal Church; the Union Church of Africans, now the Union American Methodist Episcopal Church; and the African Methodist Episcopal Zion Church. In 1844 came the most devastating split of all, the bisecting of the Methodist Episcopal Church into 2 churches, the Methodist Episcopal Church, the northern body; and the Methodist Episcopal Church, South.

The cause of this major split was, of course, slavery. Bishop Andrew, a Georgian, owned slaves through inheritance; and his wife was also a slaveholder. It was not possible for him or his wife to free their slaves under the laws of Georgia. The general conference of 1844, held in New York City, requested him to desist from the exercise of his office so long as he remained a slaveholder. Incensed, the southern delegates rebelled, a provisional plan of separation was formulated, and the Southerners went home to organize their own church in 1845. Basic to the separation was the constitutional question of the power of the general conference, which, the Southerners maintained, assumed supreme power in virtually deposing a bishop against whom no charges had been brought, who had violated no law of the church, and who had been given no trial. It was a split that concerned neither doctrine nor polity; it was purely political and social, and it was a wound that waited until 1939 for healing. In that year the Methodist Episcopal Church, the Methodist Episcopal Church, South, and the Methodist Protestant Church were reunited at Kansas City, Missouri.

The uniting conference of 1939 adopted a new constitution in 3 sections: the Articles of Religion, drawn up by John Wesley and based on the 39 Articles of Religion of the Church of England; the General Rules, covering the conduct of church members and the duties of church officials; and the Articles of Organization and Government, outlining the organization and conduct of conferences and local churches. This constitution cannot be changed by any general conference unless and until every annual conference has acted on the changes proposed.

In matters of faith there has been very little occasion for confusion or difference among Methodists; heresy trials and doctrinal quarrels have been noticeably absent. Historically they have never built theological fences or walls to keep anyone out; they have stressed the great foundation beliefs of Protestantism and offered common theological ground. Some of the churches repeat the Apostles' Creed in their worship, but not all of them, though the discipline of the church provides for its use in formal worship. Their theology is Arminian, as interpreted by Wesley in his sermons, his notes on the New Testament, and his Articles of Religion.

They preach and teach doctrines of the Trinity, the natural sinfulness of mankind, man's fall and need of conversion and repentance, freedom of the will, justification by faith, sanctification and holiness, future rewards and punishments, the sufficiency of the Scriptures for salvation, perfection and the enabling grace of God. Two sacraments, baptism and the Lord's Supper, are observed; baptism is administered to both infants and adults, usually by sprinkling. Membership—full, preparatory, or "affiliate" (the latter arranged for people away from their home church who wish to affiliate where they live)—is based upon confession of faith or by letter of transfer from other evangelical churches; admission of children to membership is usually limited to those 13 years of age or over, though in the South the age may be 2 or 3 years younger. There is wide freedom in the interpretation and practice of all doctrine; liberals and conservatives work in close harmony.

The local churches of Methodism are called charges; their ministers are appointed by the bishop at the annual conference, and each church elects its own Administrative Board, which initiates planning and sets goals and policies on the local level. It is composed of staff people, chairmen of various committees, persons representing various program interests, and members at large. Charge, annual, and general conferences prevail in most Methodist bodies; while Methodist government is popularly called episcopal, it is largely governmental by this series of conferences. The charge conference meets in the local charge or on the circuit with the district superintendent presiding. It fixes the salary of the pastor, elects the church officers, and sends delegates to the annual conference. The charge conference may delegate to the administrative board of the local church responsibility for many of these duties. Some areas have district conferences between the charge and the annual conference, but it is not a universal arrangement in the church. Annual conferences cover defined geographical areas, ordain and admit ministers to the ministry, vote on constitutional questions, supervise pensions and relief, through act of the bishop exchange pastors with other annual conferences, and every fourth year elect lay and ministerial delegates to the general conference. The general conference is the lawmaking body of the church, meeting quadrennially; the bishops preside, and the work of the conference is done largely in committees, whose reports when adopted by the general conference become Methodist law.

Worship and liturgy are based upon the English prayer book with widespread modifications. The language of the prayer book is much in evidence in the sacraments of the Methodist churches. In many forms of worship, however, each congregation is free to use or change the accepted pattern as it sees fit.

There are 23 separate Methodist bodies in the United States of which The United Methodist Church is numerically the strongest.

The United Methodist Church

Two mergers of major importance produced The United Methodist Church (the largest Methodist Church in this country, with 10,334,521 members in 39,395 local churches). The first was actually a rejoining of three existing Methodist groups; at a uniting conference in Kansas City in 1939, the Methodist Episcopal Church, the Methodist Episcopal Church, South, and the Methodist Protestant Church were reunited under a new name, The Methodist Church. In 1968 The Methodist Church merged with the Evangelical United Brethren Church to form The United Methodist Church.

The histories of the Methodist Episcopal Church and the Methodist Episcopal Church, South, have already been outlined above. The Methodist Episcopal Church, South, was organized at Louisville, Kentucky, in 1845 and held its first general conference a year later in Petersburg, Virginia, under the presidency of Bishops James Andrew and Joshua Soule; it brought a membership of 3,000,000 to the reunited church. The Methodist Protestant Church was organized at a conference in Baltimore in 1830, in protest against the almost total rule of the clergy in the Methodist Episcopal Church and the exclusion of laymen from its councils. It had about 200,000 members in 1939.

The Evangelical United Brethren Church came out of a series of mergers in 2 groups: the United Brethren in Christ and the Evangelical Church. The Evangelical Church began with the labors of Jacob

Albright (1759-1808) among the German people of Pennsylvania, in what at first was called the Evangelical Association; preaching first as a Lutheran and then as a Methodist exhorter, Albright was made a bishop at the first annual conference of the Association in 1807. He used the Methodist *Discipline* until 1809, preached Methodist doctrine, and was so effective that for some time his followers were known as "the Albrights." A split in the membership in 1891 resulted in a separate denomination known as the United Evangelical Church; the two groups were reunited in 1922 under the name of the Evangelical Church.

Another group, known as the Church of the United Brethren in Christ, had a parallel development which began with the preaching of William Otterbein and Martin Boehm among the Germans in Pennsylvania, Maryland, and Virginia; they were elected bishops at a conference in September, 1800, which created the Church of the United Brethren in Christ, and which was also strongly Methodistic in polity, doctrine, and practice. Both groups had a *Discipline* modeled on the Methodist *Discipline*, and had too much in common to remain separated. These two bodies—the Church of the United Brethren in Christ and the Evangelical Church—were merged into the Evangelical United Brethren Church at Johnstown, Pennsylvania, in 1946.

Both Methodist and "E.U.B." churches, across the years, had been deeply conscious of their common historical and spiritual heritage. Their doctrines were similar; both were episcopal in government; both traced their origins back to John Wesley; both had nearly the same book of *Discipline*. Their preachers exchanged pulpits and congregations, often worked together and shared the same buildings. The only major difference between them was that of language—German among the Brethren, English among the Methodists. As new, native-born generations appeared, this barrier meant less and less. Conversations concerning the merging of the two churches began as early as 1803, and were consummated when the two came together as The United Methodist Church at Dallas Texas, on April 23, 1968.

There was some dissent at Dallas; 51 congregations and 79 ministers of the Evangelical United Brethren withdraw from the Pacific Northwest Conference to establish the Evangelical Church of North America; 18 of 23 E.U.B. congregations in Montana left to establish the Evangelical Church of North America in Montana, and 13 other congregations in the Erie and Ohio Southeast Conferences petitioned to leave; these petitions were denied. The split occurred mainly over theological issues and the question of church ownership. But there were still roughly 750,000 Brethren who accepted the merger; their strength gave the new United Methodist Church a membership of nearly 11 million.

In this union no significant changes were made in either doctrine or polity. The Confession of Faith of the Evangelical United Brethren Church, adopted in 1962, was placed beside the Methodist Articles of Religion; Wesleyan standards dominate both statements, and both are used as the congregations of the church elect to use them. The Methodist system of bishops and conferences, already in use in both denominations, is maintained. There are now 73 annual conferences in the United States with a total of 39,395 organized churches and 34,885 ministers. Above the annual conferences are 5 jurisdictional conferences, established for geographical convenience in administrative matters, meeting quadrennially at times determined by the Council of Bishops, to elect new bishops and to name the members of the larger boards and commissions. In lands outside the continental United States, there are central conferences which correspond to the jurisdictional conferences; they meet quadrennially, and when authorized to do so, may elect their own bishops. All bishops are elected for life (except in autonomous overseas conferences where the term is 4 years) with retirement set at 72; there are 45 of them in the United States and abroad in charge of the areas of the church, such as the New York Area, the Denver Area, etc. Together they constitute the Council of Bishops, which meets at least once a year and usually twice a year "for the general oversight and promotion of the temporal and spiritual affairs of the entire church."

The general conference consists of over 800 delegates, half laymen and half ministers, elected on a proportional basis by the annual conferences. A judicial council has been created to determine the constitutionality of any act of the general conference which may be appealed, and to hear and determine any appeal from a bishop's decision on a question of law in any district, annual, central, or jurisdictional conference. It is made up of 5 ministerial and 4 lay members, and has become so important that it is often called "the Supreme Court" of the church.

The General Conference of 1972 "restructured" the administrative bodies of the Church. The Council of Bishops and a Council on Finance and Administration were made responsible to the General Conference, and a new Council on Ministries was set up as a coordinating body between the Conference and various other Commissions, support services and program boards. The Commissions now include those on Archives and History, Religion and Race, Status and Role of Women; the Support Services include a Joint Committee on Communications, a Board of Publication, and a Board of Pensions. The program Boards were rearranged to include Boards on Church and Society, Discipleship, Higher Education and Ministry, and Global Ministries. In this restructuring, the church's 21 major boards and agencies were reduced to 6.

This General Conference also broadened the basis of doctrine in the Church, in the first restatement on doctrine since the 18th century. The classic statements of the merging Methodist and Evangelical United Brethren churches were maintained, but the doctrinal door was left open to theological change and revision. Typical of the openness that has always characterized Methodism is the statement in the new *Discipline* that the four main sources and guidelines for Christian theology are Scripture, tradition, experience and reason: "These four are interdependent; none can be defined unambiguously. They allow for, indeed they positively encourage, variety in United Methodist theologizing."

This Church has property valued at $6,576,006,234, not including educational plants, hospitals, or homes for the aged. There are 13 schools of theology, 1 school of medicine, 1 school of business and electronics, 1 conservatory of music, 7 universities, 81 colleges, 20 junior colleges, and 17 secondary schools. There are 190 homes for the aged, 65 homes for children and youth, 78 hospitals. It is at work in 48 countries; 15 bishops administer the work overseas, where there is a total of 814 missionaries.

The United Methodist Publishing House is the oldest and largest religous publishing concern in the world. *United Methodists Today* is the denomination's most widely circulated magazine, and there are 41 other periodicals sponsored, exclusive of Sunday school materials.

The World Methodist Council, organized in 1881 and designed to draw the whole Wesleyan movement close together in fellowship and devotion to their mutual heritage, has become increasingly active in recent years. Nine Ecumenical Conferences have been held by this Council since 1881. Headquarters have been established at Lake Junaluska, North Carolina.

African Methodist Episcopal Church

With 1,166,301 members and 5,878 churches (as of 1951) this is the second largest Methodist group in the United States. Its genesis lies in the withdrawal in 1787 of a group of Negro Methodists from the Methodist Episcopal Church in Philadelphia; their objection was directed largely against practices of discrimination. They built a chapel and ordained a Negro preacher through the assistance of Bishop William White of the Protestant Episcopal Church. In 1793 Bishop Francis Asbury dedicated Bethel Church in Philadelphia, a church whose members prohibited any white brother from "electing or being elected into any office among [them], save that of a preacher or public speaker." In 1799 Bishop Asbury also ordained Richard Allen to preach. Other similar Methodist Negro bodies were formed; the African Methodist Episcopal Church was formally organized in 1816. In the same year Richard Allen was consecrated as its first bishop, again by Bishop Asbury. It was a church confined in the years preceding the Civil War to the northern states; following the war its membership increased rapidly in the South, and today it is represented in nearly every state in the union.

Both doctrine and polity follow that of other Methodist bodies. General boards are constituted by nomination of the bishops, of which there are 13 appointed at the general conference. The general conference also examines all judicial power and prerogatives. Each department of church work is supervised by the board of 45 members, from each episcopal district. The church has a widespread home missionary program, foreign missionary work in Africa and the West Indies, 17 educational institutions, and 4 periodicals.

African Methodist Episcopal Zion Church

This church dates from 1796, when its first organization was instituted by a group of Negro members protesting discrimination in the John Street Church in New York City. Their first church, built in 1800, was called Zion; the word was later made part of the denominational name. The first annual conference of the body was held in this church in 1821 with 6 Negro Methodist churches in New Haven, Philadelphia, and Newark, New Jersey, represented by 19 preachers and presided over by the Rev. William Phoebus of the white Methodist Episcopal Church. James Varick, who led the John Street dissension, was elected for their first bishop at this conference. The name African Methodist Episcopal Zion Church was aproved in 1848.

This church spread quickly over the northern states; by the time of the general conference of 1880 there were 15 annual conferences in the South. Livingstone College at Salisbury, North Carolina, the largest educational institution of the church, was established by that conference. Departments of missions, education, and publications were established in 1892; later came administrative boards to direct work in church extension, evangelism, finance, ministerial relief, and so on. Home missions are supported in Louisiana, Mississippi, and in several states beyond the Mississippi, principally in Oklahoma. Foreign missionaries are found in Liberia, Ghana, Nigeria, South America, and the West Indies. There are 5 secondary schools, 2 colleges (Livingstone, in Salisbury, North Carolina, and Crinton, in Rock Hill South Carolina), several foreign mission stations, and there are 1,342,427 members in 5,000 churches.

African Union First Colored Methodist Protestant Church, Inc.

A Negro body organized in 1866, this is a union of 2 former churches known as the African Union Church and the First Colored Methodist Protestant Church. Doctrine is in accord with most of Methodism, but there are differences in polity; there are no bishops, and ministers and laymen have equal power in annual and general conferences. There is no foreign missionary program; home missions are maintained by a group of women known as the Grand Body. A general board, with a president, secretary, and treasurer, directs the denominational effort; the board meets annually and the general conference quadrennially. There are 8,000 members and 41 churches.

Christian Methodist Episcopal Church

Known until 1954 as the Colored Methodist Episcopal Church, this church was established in 1870 in the South in an amicable agreement between white and Negro members of the Methodist Episcopal Church, South. There were at the time at least 225,000 Negro slave members in the Methodist Episcopal Church, South, but with the Emancipation Proclamation all but 80,000 of these joined the 2 independent Negro bodies. When the general conference of the Methodist Episcopal Church, South, met at New Orleans in 1866, a commission from the Negro membership asked for a separation into a church of their own. The request was granted, and in 1870 the organization of the Colored Methodist Episcopal Church was realized. They held this name until the meeting of their general conference at Memphis in May of 1954, when it was decided to change it to the Christian Methodist Episcopal Church.

Their doctrine is the doctrine of the parent church; this denomination adds a local church conference to the quarterly, district, annual, and general conferences usual in Methodism. Seven boards supervise the national work, each presided over by a bishop assigned as chairman by the College of Bishops. The general secretaries of the various departments are elected every 4 years by the general conference. There were 466,718 members and 2,598 churches in 1965.

There are 2 periodicals, and 5 colleges are maintained.

Congregational Methodist Church

This church was constituted in Georgia in 1852 by a group withdrawing from the Methodist Episcopal Church, South, in objection to certain features of the episcopacy and the itineracy. Two thirds of its membership in turn withdrew to join the Congregational Church in 1887-88.

Local pastors are called by the local churches; district conferences grant licenses, ordain ministers, and review local reports. District, annual, and general conferences are all recognized as church courts, ruling on violations of church law, citing offending laymen or ministers, and holding the power of expulsion over unworthy members. There is a restricted home and foreign missionary program. A senior college and denominational headquarters and a publishing-house are located at Florence, Mississippi. There are 16,00 members in 250 churches.

First Congregational Methodist Church of the U.S.A.

Organized at Forsythe, Georgia, in 1852, this group claims to be the parent body from which the Congregational Methodist Church dissented to form its own organization. Originally under the jurisdiction of the Methodist Episcopal Church, South, they withdrew from that church in disagreement over the episcopal and itinerant systems, claiming that the system lacked biblical authority and democratic principles, to set up a church that would be congregational in government. There are local, district, state, and general conferences, and about 7,500 members in 100 churches, in Alabama, Mississippi, Georgia, Tennessee, Texas, Missouri, Arkansas, and Oklahoma.

Cumberland Methodist Church

This is a small Methodist body, listing currently 4 churches and an inclusive membership of 65. Its leaders withdrew from the Congregational Methodist Church in protest against certain elements of polity and doctrine. It was organized at Laager, Grundy County, Tennessee, on May 5, 1950. A general board is the chief administrative body, and a president is elected instead of the usual bishop. The membership is limited to the state of Tennessee.

Evangelical Methodist Church

Organized at Memphis, Tennessee, in 1946, this church is "fundamental in doctrine, evangelistic in program, and congregational in government." It represents a double protest against what were considered autocratic and undemocratic government on the one hand and a tendency toward modernism on the other in The Methodist Church, from which the body withdrew. There is great emphasis placed upon the protest against modernism.

The church is Arminian in theology and Wesleyan in doctrine. Members seek a return to the original revivalistic thought and program of Wesleyanism; extremely fundamentalist, they oppose the "substituting of social, educational, or other varieties of cultural salvation."

Local churches own and control their own property and select their own pastors. There are 6 districts and 6 district superintendents in the Western Conference, 6 districts with 6 district superintendents in the Eastern conference; a general superintendent presides over both conferences. Mexico constitutes a mission conference. The general conference meets quadrennially. International headquarters are in Wichita, Kansas. There are 148 churches, with a membership of over 10,000.

Free Methodist Church of North America

This is one of the more conservative among the larger bodies of American Methodism, both in doctrine and in standards of Christian practices. Its founder was the Rev. B. T. Roberts, who with his associates objected to what was called "new school" Methodism, which they considered destructive to the Wesleyan standards of the church. They were "read out" of their churches and organized the Free Methodist Church in Pekin, New York, in 1860. The Genesee Conference, of which Roberts had been a member, restored his credentials to his son in 1910, but no reunion of the group with The United Methodist Church has yet been effected. A merger with the Holiness Movement Church in Canada was approved in 1960.

Doctrinally, the Free Methodists call for a return to primitive Wesleyan teaching; they stress the virgin birth and deity of Jesus and his vicarious atonement and resurrection. No one may be received into membership without an experience of confession and forgiveness of sin, and the experience of entire sanctification is sought in all members. Strict adherence to the general rules of Methodism is demanded, and membership in secret societies is forbidden.

The Free Methodist Church has become a world fellowship consisting of three general conferences—Egypt, Japan, and North America—with a common constitution formally ratified by each general conference in 1964. All legislative actions are reviewed by a Constitutional Council with members elected from each general conference. There are 70,755 members in the United States and Canada in 1,147 churches, and a world membership of 123,606. Foreign missions are maintained in Africa, India, Japan, the Dominican Republic, Formosa, Hong Kong, the Philippines, Egypt, Brazil, Paraguay, Mexico, and Haiti. There are 4 senior colleges, 1 junior college, a cooperative program with other denominations in another senior college, and a seminary foundation maintained in cooperation with Asbury Theological Seminary.

Fundamental Methodist Church, Inc.

Known until August, 1956, as the Independent Fundamental Methodist Church, this church was instituted on August 27, 1942, at Ash Grove, Missouri, organized under its original title in 1944, and chartered under its present title in 1948. Its origin is traced back to the Methodist Protestant Church, of which it was a part until the merging of the 3 major Methodist churches in 1939. Dissatisfaction with the merger and the conviction that the primitive Wesleyan principles and theology would suffer thereby led to the withdrawal and the establishment of the new church. As the name suggests, there is an insistence here upon fundamental teaching.

There are no bishops in this church; it has only a district superintendent and a secretary. Government is more representative than in most Methodist groups, with an annual conference made up of ministers and laymen, voting equally. Conferences are divided into districts, with an annual conference for each district. There are 15 churches, 725 members.

Independent African Methodist Episcopal Church

This group was formed in 1907 at Jacksonville, Florida, by 12 ministers who left the African Methodist Episcopal Church following disputes with the district superintendents of that church. A new book of discipline, doctrines, and laws was written; the *Book of Discipline* is revised from time to time by the quadrennial general conference, but the 25 articles of religion it contains remain unchanged.

There are quarterly, annual, and general conferences. The annual conference ordains ministers as deacons, and the general conference ordains elders and bishops. In 1940 there were 1,000 members and 12 churches.

New Congregational Methodist Church

This church originated in an administrative quarrel in the Georgia conference of the Methodist Episcopal Church, South, over the consolidation of certain rural properties in the southern section of the state. Protesting, the New Congregational Methodist Church was organized in 1881 on the general plan of the Congregational Methodist Church. (There has in recent years been a division of this church, with a number of congregations uniting with the Congregational Methodist Church.) There are at present 773 members in 15 churches —7 of which are in north Florida and 8 in south Georgia. There are 2 smaller groups in central Georgia and Indiana.

Government is a combination of Methodist and Congregational systems; the episcopacy is rejected, and congregations call and elect their own pastors; there are the usual (Methodist) local, district, and general conferences. An unusual feature of this church lies in their practice of foot washing.

People's Methodist Church

Conservative and "holiness," the founders of this church left The Methodist Church in North Carolina at the time of the merger of the 3 major Methodist churches. There are approximately 25 congregations and 1,000 members, and a Bible school in Greensboro, North Carolina. No information on doctrine or polity is available.

Primitive Methodist Church, U.S.A.

This church had its initial organization in England, under the influence of Lorenzo Dow, an American camp-meeting revivalist, who went to England early in the nineteenth century to hold a series of meetings which resulted in the formation of a number of societies among his converts. The leaders of these societies were dropped from the Wesleyan Connection and formed the Primitive Methodist Church in 1810. Four missionaries came to America in 1829, settling in New York City and Philadelphia.

Today there are annual conferences (administrative in nature) and a general conference (legislative). There is only one salaried officer— an executive secretary. Ministers, who have no time limit set upon their pastorates, are invited by the local churches, who designate their first, second, and third choices and extend their invitations in that order. All invited pastors are assigned to charges by the annual conference, and no ministerial candidates are received unless there are churches open to them. Doctrinally, modified Wesleyan Articles of Religion are accepted.

Work in education and missions is directed by the general conference; foreign missionaries are stationed in Guatemala. There are about 12,805 members in 90 churches. An official organ, *The Primitive Methodist Journal*, is published monthly.

Reformed Methodist Union Episcopal Church

This church was started in 1885 at Charleston, South Carolina, in a withdrawal from the African Methodist Episcopal Church, the immediate cause of the division being a dispute over the election of ministerial delegates to the general conference. Intended at first as a nonepiscopal church, the body adopted the complete polity of the Methodist Episcopal Church in general conferences of 1896 and 1916. Its first bishop was consecrated in 1899 by a bishop of the Reformed Episcopal Church. Class meetings and love feasts are featured in the local congregation; there are 5,000 members and 20 churches.

Reformed Zion Union Apostolic Church

This church was organized at Boydton, Virginia, in 1869 by Elder James R. Howell, a minister of the African Methodist Episcopal Zion Church in New York, in a protest against white discrimination and against the ecclesiasticism of other Negro Methodist churches. This was originally known as the Zion Union Apostolic Church; internal friction completely disrupted the body by 1874, and in 1881-82 it was reorganized under the present name. There are no basic departures from standard Methodist doctrine or polity except that only 1 ordination, that of elder, is required of its ministers. There are 16,000 members, 50 churches.

Southern Methodist Church

Doctrinally, the Southern Methodist Church remains the same as the body from which it came—The Methodist Episcopal Church, South. They opposed the merger of that Church with the northern Methodist Episcopal Church, in 1939, on grounds of "alarming infidelity and apostacy found therein." They regard their Southern Methodist Church not as a separatist body but as a Church "brought into existence to perpetuate the faith of John Wesley."

There are no bishops here, but there are the usual Methodist annual (4) and general conferences; a president, usually a clergyman, is elected every four years. Laymen and clergy have equal voice and voting privileges in these conferences. Unique among Methodist bodies is their position on the question of racial segregation: "The Southern Methodist Church is a segregated church. We do not believe that integration . . . is the answer to current social problems. . . . It is our opinion that integration would produce more problems that it would solve."

Local churches own and control their own property and buildings and call their own ministers. There are 10,000 members in 163 churches from Virginia to Texas. There is one college, Southern Methodist College, and a publishing house (Foundry Press) located at Orangeburg, South Carolina.

Union American Methodist Episcopal Church

This was one of the first Negro bodies to establish an independent Methodist church. A group of members left the Asbury Methodist Church in Wilmington, Delaware, in 1805; they worshiped out of doors and in private homes until 1813, when they built their first church and incorporated as the Union Church of Africans. Defections from the membership in this church were responsible for the formation of another body known as the African Union Church, which forced the change to the present name—the Union American Methodist Episcopal Church.

General, annual, district, and quarterly conferences are held; general conferences are called only to consider proposed changes in name, law, or polity. There are 2 educational institutions, and the church claims 27,560 members in 256 churches.

METROPOLITAN CHURCH ASSOCIATION

Springing from a revival in the Metropolitan Methodist Church of Chicago in 1894, this association was originated primarily to carry on a local evangelistic work in the poorer and more densely populated sections of the city. It has since grown into a widespread work in this country and abroad.

Foreign missionaries are now stationed in the United Provinces of India, South India (under the ministry of native pastors, serving 7,000 members), the Union of South Africa, and Switzerland. Home missionaries are at work in Mexico.

The founders of the association sought a return to the teaching of primitive Wesleyan holiness, and that emphasis is still strong. There is no creed "except such as may be found in the Scriptures themselves." Inasmuch as this is an off-shoot of Methodism, its government closely resembles the Methodist pattern. The association was chartered under the laws of Wisconsin in 1918. There are 443 members in 15 churches.

MISSIONARY CHURCH

The Missionary Church is made up of two groups merged in March, 1969: the Missionary Church Association and the United Missionary Church. The new denomination claims 360 congregations, 23,500 members, and 50,000 Sunday school pupils. It has missionaries in 15 countries, and total assets of about $35,000,000.

Up to 1947 the United Missionary Church was "the Mennonite Brethren in Christ Church," but in that year it dropped all its Mennonite connections in a new organization. They stressed the Wesleyan-Arminian message of holiness, and were, generally, fundamentalist in theology. The Missionary Church Association was founded at Berne, Indiana, in 1889, and was quite similar to the United Missionary Church in theology and practice.

Local churches in the new Missionary Church will be independent in managing their own affairs, but they will recognize the authority of a general conference made up of ministers, missionaries, and laymen, and held biennially. Working under the general conference is a general board, made up of the officers of the administrative boards of the church: Christian Education, Evangelism and Church Extension, Higher Education, Overseas Missions, Publications and Social Concerns. A president, vice-president, secretary, and treasurer are elected for a term of four years.

Missions are highly evangelistic; missionaries are serving in Africa, India, South America, Egypt, Japan, Mexico, Haiti, Hawaii, Jamaica, and Sierra Leone. More than $1,150,000 was given by the membership last year to the missionary program; the average member contributed more than $347 to the total work and program of the church.

The church operates two educational institutions in the United States—Bethel College in Mishawaka, Indiana, and Fort Wayne Bible College in Fort Wayne, Indiana, with a combined enrollment of 1,100 students. There are also two Bible colleges in Canada.

MORAVIANS

In a sense the Moravian Church had its first apostles in Cyril and Methodius, who were missionaries among the Slavs in the ninth century. As early as this Moravians and Bohemians in old Czechoslovakia were struggling for political and religious freedom. Later they followed John Huss, martyred in 1415, and Jerome of Prague, martyred in 1416. Their first association was formed in Bohemia in 1457. At the beginning of the Reformation there were more than 400 Brethren, or Moravian, churches with about 175,000 members.

As a church they opposed the corruption of the Roman Catholic Church and stressed purity of morals, apostolic discipline, and true scriptural teaching. For a time they inclined toward a very literal interpretation of the Sermon on the Mount and denounced war, the taking of oaths, and all unions of church and state. They called themselves *Jednota Bratrska*, the Church (or Communion) of Brethren; this is the correct translation of their later term *Unitas Fratrum*. They accepted the Apostles' Creed, rejected the purgatory and worship of the saints of the Roman Catholic Church as well as its authority, practiced infant baptism and confirmation, and put conduct above doctrine.

The Thirty Years' War all but annihilated their first societies, persecution drove them into Hungary, Holland, Poland, and Saxony. A small band found refuge on the estate of Nicholas Louis, Count of Zinzendorf, in Saxony, where they built the town of Herrnhut (1722-27). Zinzendorf was a Lutheran who had close contact with the Pietist movement, and he became so influential among the Moravians that they used for a time the Augsburg Confession of Faith of Lutheran Saxony. They adopted the name *Unitas Fratrum* from their ancient church and in 1735 again established the episcopacy which had been preserved through John Amos Comenius and his son-in-law Jablonsky. The *Unitas Fratrum* came to be popularly known as the Moravian Church because the leaders of the renewal had come from Moravia.

Moravian Church (Unitas Fratrum)

The Moravian Church arrived in America in 1734, when a group of the Brethren from Germany came to Georgia to carry on missionary work among the Indians. John Wesley was a passenger on the same ship with them, and this was the beginning of his important relations with the Moravians. Political disturbances in Georgia soon disrupted their colony; and a group accompanied George Whitefield to Pennsylvania, where they settled in 1740. Three uniquely and exclusively Moravian towns grew swiftly in Pennsylvania at Bethlehem, Nazareth, and Lititz, based on the communities in Germany, Holland, and England. They remained basically Moravian until the middle years of the nineteenth century.

Zinzendorf came to America in 1741, attempted to merge all the colonial Germans into 1 body, and failed. He stayed on for a year to help with the establishment of Bethlehem and Nazareth and to lay the foundations of the Moravian missionary work among the Indians. By 1775 there were 2,500 Moravians in Pennsylvania alone.

The Moravians have no doctrine peculiar to them; they are broadly evangelical, insisting upon a principle of "in essentials unity, in nonessentials liberty, and in all things charity." Their scriptural interpretations agree substantially with the Apostles' Creed, the Westminster and Augsburg confessions, and the Articles of Religion of the Church of England. They hold the Scriptures to be the inspired Word of God and an adequate rule of faith and practice; and they have doctrines dealing with the total depravity of man, the real Godhead and the real humanity of Christ, justification and redemption through the sacrifice of Christ, the work of the Holy Spirit, good works as the fruits of the Spirit, the fellowship of all believers, the second coming of Christ, and the resurrection of the dead to life and judgment. Their main doctrinal emphasis may be said to be upon the love of God manifested in the redemptive life and death of Jesus, the inner testimony of the Spirit, and Christian conduct in everyday affairs.

The sacrament of infant baptism by sprinkling is practiced, through which children become noncommunicant members until confirmation. There are 60,574 members in 161 churches. Members are admitted by vote of the congregational board of elders. The Lord's Supper is celebrated at least 6 times a year, and the old custom of the love feast is preserved. A variety of liturgies is used in worship: the church is notable for 1 especially beautiful outdoor service held at Easter.

The Moravian Church is divided in the United States into 2 provinces, northern and southern. Congregations are grouped into provincial and district synods; internationally they are joined in a "unity" with a unity synod meeting as a world body every 10 years. The highest administrative body in each American province is the provincial synod. Composed of ministers and laymen and meeting every 5 years, it directs missionary, educational, and publishing work, and elects a provincial elders' conference, or excutive board, which functions between synod meetings. Bishops are elected by provincial and general synods. They are spiritual, but not administrative, leaders in the church.

Missionary work has always been a first concern of the Moravians; with a comparatively small membership they conducted the most efficient missionary work among the Indians of any of the early colonial churches. The worldwide Moravian Church now supports work in 13 foreign missionary fields, including North, Central, and South America, Africa, Tibet, and Israel. A home missions work among the Eskimos of Alaska has been carried on since 1885. The church maintains 2 colleges, a theological seminary, and a coed Moravian academy. The latter trace their origins back to the prerevolutionary period.

Unity of the Brethren

Known until 1962 as the Evangelical Unity of the Czech-Moravian Brethren in North America, this body originated among Czech and Moravian immigrants arriving in Texas in the late nineteenth century. The present name (*Unitas Fratrum*, or *Jednota Bratrska*) is the original name used in 1457.

There are few departures from the doctrine and polity of the Moravian Church in America (*Unitas Fratrum*), except that their synod meets every 2 years. The church has no colleges or seminaries. In 1964 there were 6,142 members in 32 churches.

MUSLIMS

It is estimated that there are from 10,000 to 20,000 Muslims worshiping in 15 or 20 local centers in the United States; officially, there are 1,166,000 Muslims in North and South America and Australia and over 704,000,000 around the world. There is no national organization (there is, indeed, no titular head nor priesthood in all of Islam), but there are Islamic Centers in Washington, Toledo, Detroit, New York, etc. The Center in Washington includes a beautiful mosque, library, classrooms for study, and administrative offices; it is open for daily prayer and offers lectures and publications on the literature, philosophy, religion, and art of Islam.

The word "Islam" means "purity, peace, submission to God's will and obedience to his laws." It does not claim to be a new religion formulated by the prophet Mohammed, but rather to be "the continuation of all former religious principles decreed by God through his revelations to all prophets," and the prophets include Jesus Christ (they accept him as prophet, but not as divine) and many of the Jewish prophets and leaders of the Old Testament, from Noah to Zephaniah.

They revere and honor Mohammed, but they do not worship him; their creed is that "there is no deity worthy of worship except God (Allah), and Mohammed is God's Messenger." This is "the religion of the Book," and the Book is the Koran ("Quran," to the Mohammedans), said to have been dictated to Mohammed (born A.D. 571) by the angel Gabriel. The Koran contains the faith of Islam, and describes the manner in which God is to be worshiped; it also outlines legislation concerning civil and criminal laws, laws of war, peace treaties between nations, and laws ruling in such matters as marriage, divorce, inheritance, and wills. The Ten Commandments are embodied in the Koran, and it contains "the Six Articles of Belief" and "the Five Pillars of Faith" which are the heart of Islam. The Five Pillars are: (1) the recital of the creed; (2) recital of prayer 5 times daily, facing Mecca (the Cebba at Mecca is held to be the first house built by Abraham for his son Ishmael, for the worship of God); (3) the giving of tithes for the support of the poor and the expansion of the faith; (4) the observation of Ramadan, the ninth month of the Moslem calendar, fasting during daylight in commemoration of the first revelation of the Koran; (5) a pilgrimage to Mecca, when financially able. The Six Articles of Belief are: (1) God is One, and this is Allah; (2) the Koran is God's truly inspired book; (3) God's angels are heavenly beings created to serve God, and they are opposed to evil spirits; (4) God sent his prophets to earth at stated times for stated purposes; the last of these was Mohammed, and God makes no distinctions between his messengers; (5) the Day of Judgment will find good and evil weighed in the balance; (6) the lives and acts of men are foreordained (predestined) by an all-knowing God. Islam, however, still leaves man as "the architect of his own destiny, free to make or mar his own future through a life of honest endeavor."

Mohammed accomplished his mission, which was primarily to proclaim the unity of God; when he died at 62, the precepts of the Koran became the great unifying force around which, eventually, 500,000,000 people were to become the followers of Islam (Moslems, or Muslims), with Mecca as their holy city and ardent in their faith in the Islamic trinity of the Koran, Moslem tradition, and the Prophet Mohammed. Some divisions and sects have appeared (Shiites, Sunnites, Sufis) with variations in interpretation and practice, but by and large there is and has been a firm allegiance to the Koran and to traditional Moslem practices.

The true Moslem prays 5 times daily, has a service of congregational prayer preceded by a sermon on Friday at noon, eats no pork, drinks no intoxicating liquors, shuns gambling, adultery, and the breaking of one's word. In some countries he practices polygamy and (with less and less insistence) the custom which demands the veiling of Moslem women. He removes his shoes upon entering the mosque and is meticulous in washing feet, hands, head, and arms before prayer. In his mosque there are no icons, statues, symbols, pews, chairs, or musical instruments; there is only a constant repetition and echo of the fundamental Koran approach to prayer: "In the name of God, the Beneficent, the Merciful, praise be to God, Lord of the worlds."

Outside the mosque he is a student. There is a saying that God created the pen as his first creation, and that the first word God revealed to Mohammed was the word "read." To read and to study and to seek knowledge are obligatory in Islam; the ink of the scholar is more valuable to them than the blood of a martyr.

NATIONAL DAVID SPIRITUAL TEMPLE OF CHRIST CHURCH UNION (INC.), U.S.A. (The Universal Christian Spiritual Faith and Churches for All Nations)

This is a body founded in 1932 by Dr. David William Short, a former minister of the Missionary Baptist Church. Dr. Short wished to "proclaim the Orthodox Christian spiritual faith"; he was convinced that no man had the right or spiritual power "to make laws, rules, or doctrines for the real church founded by Jesus Christ," and that the denominational churches had been founded in error and in disregard of the apostolic example. He held wisdom, knowledge, faith, healing, miracles, prophecy, discerning of spirits, and diverse kinds of tongues to be spiritual gifts of the Holy Ghost and parts of the church of

Christ. He believed that all races should and must be accepted in the true church.

The members of this church consider themselves to be the true and universal church of Christ and not just another denomination. They rely entirely upon the Holy Ghost for inspiration and direction; their church constitution they claim to be found in I Cor. 12:1-31 and Eph. 4:11. Their organization is made up of pastors, prophets, prophetesses, bishops, archbishops, elders, overseers, divine healers, deacons, and missionaries. Archbishop Short is the chief governing officer; there is a national executive board, which holds a national annual assembly.

A restricted home missionary work is conducted in hospitals, and a nursing home is maintained. A monthly newspaper, *The Christian Spiritual Voice,* is published at Kansas City, Missouri. Archbishop Short is also founder, president, and mentor of the St. David Orthodox Christian Spiritual Seminary, which was dedicated in 1949 at Des Moines, Iowa; in 1952 he was elected archbishop and chief apostle of a new Universal Orthodox Christian Spiritual Faith and Church of All Nations, representing a merger of the National David Spiritual Temple, the St. Paul's Spiritual Church Convocation and King David's Spiritual Temple of Truth Association. The original National David Spiritual Temple has a membership of 40,816 in 66 churches, prayer bands, and missions.

NEW APOSTOLIC CHURCH OF NORTH AMERICA

The New Apostolic Church of North America is a variant or schism of the Catholic Apostolic Church movement in England. It claims common origin with the Catholic Apostolic Church in the appointment of an apostle in the parent body in 1832. Debate arose in 1860 over the appointment of new apostles to fill vacancies left by death. Insisting on 12 apostles at the head of the true church, Bishop Schwarz of Hamburg was excommunicated from the Catholic Apostolic Church in 1862 for proposing the election of new apostles. A priest named Preuss was elected to the office of apostle "through the spirit of prophecy" to lead the dissenting body; Bishop Schwarz served under him until his own elevation to the apostolic office.

Under Preuss and Schwarz the New Apostolic Church spread from Europe to America, where today it is organized into apostles' districts, bishops' districts, and elders' districts. Each church has a rector and one or more assistants (priests, deacons, and so forth), who serve usually without remuneration. All ministers and other "office-bearers" are selected by the apostleship. The American church is a constituent part of the international organization supervised by Chief Apostle Walter Schmidt in Dortmund, Germany.

Just as the true church must be governed on the scriptural pattern by 12 apostles, members of this church believe that only the apostles have received from Christ the commission and power to forgive sin. The New Apostolic Church of North America accepts the Apostles' Creed and stresses the authority and inspiration of the Bible, the apostolic ordinances of the laying on of hands, the necessity of gifts of the Holy Spirit (which include prophecy, visions, dreams, diverse tongues, songs of praise, wisdom, discrimination of spirits, the power of healing and performing wonders), tithing, and the speedy, personal, pre-millennial return of Christ. Three "means of grace" are found in 3 sacraments: baptism (including children), Holy Communion, and Holy Sealing (the dispensing and reception of the Holy Spirit). Work "along broader interior and missionary lines" is conducted in the United States, Canada, Mexico, and Puerto Rico. The United States has 21,000 members in 205 churches and 65 missions; the international organization about 1,000,000 in 6,000 branches in 46 countries.

OLD CATHOLIC CHURCHES

Old Catholic churches in the United States are outgrowths but unconnected branches of the Old Catholic movement and churches of Europe. The European bodies originated in a protest against the doctrine of papal infallibility adopted by the Roman Catholic Vatican Council of 1870; Roman priests in Germany who refused to accept the doctrine were excommunicated and organized the Old Catholic Church under the leadership of Dr. Ignatz von Döllinger in 1871. A similar break occurred in Holland and Switzerland, where other Old Catholic churches were established.

This revolt did not break completely with Roman Catholicism. It rejected papal infallibility, the doctrine of the immaculate conception, compulsory celibacy of the priesthood, and in some instances the filioque clause of the Nicene Creed, but kept much of the other doctrine, creeds, customs, and liturgy of the Roman Catholic Church. It was also most anxious to preserve the orders and the apostolic succession of its priests and bishops inasmuch as they considered apostolic succession as vital in a valid Christian ministry. Much confusion has resulted in conflicting claims of succession and validity of orders, especially in American Old Catholic churches. All Old Catholic bodies in this country were at one time or another connected with European bodies, but that is not true today; most American groups have severed their connections with churches abroad. Someone has said that most of the Old Catholics in America are either dissatisfied Anglicans or former Roman Catholics; and there is some truth in that, if not all the truth. Several attempts have been made, however, to merge Old Catholic churches with those of the Church of England or the Greek Church, and gestures have been made toward membership in the World Council of Churches.

Old Catholic missionaries were in America soon after 1871, establishing scattered congregations. Father Joseph René Vilatte, a French priest ordained by the Old Catholics in Switzerland, attempted to organize these congregations and at once became the storm center of the rising confusion. Vilatte himself vacillated between rival bodies; he studied at a Presbyterian college in Montreal and twice returned to submit to the Roman Catholic Church, dying at last in a French monastery. Vigorously opposed within his own church and by American Protestant Episcopalians, whose ranks he refused to join, he went to Switzerland in 1885 for ordination as an Old Catholic bishop and was finally consecrated as an archbishop by Archbishop Alvarez of Ceylon, who claimed orders through the Syro-Jacobite Church of Malabar. He returned to America to found the American Catholic Church.

Separated and competing as they are, the Old Catholics in the United States have a firm common doctrinal basis. The doctrine is similar to that held by the Greek and Latin churches before those 2 bodies separated; among the Old Catholics it is now more Eastern Catholic than Western. They accept the 7 ecumenical councils of the church held before the division into Eastern and Western bodies. Bible reading is encouraged, and national tongues rather than Latin are used in all worship. There is a strange blend here of orthodoxy and rationalism both in doctrine and in ritual.

There are 4 main divisions of Old Catholic churches in the United States, with an approximate total of 97,000 members in 100 churches—the American Catholic Church (Archdiocese of New York), the North American Old Roman Catholic Church, Christ Catholic Church of America and Europe (no information available aside from membership, which is 7,100 in 24 churches), and the American Catholic Church (Syro-Antiochian). The African Orthodox Church, a Negro group, is listed often as an Old Catholic body, but is actually Protestant Episcopalian in origin and connection. The Polish National Catholic Church may be said to have certain Old Catholic origins and doctrines, but it has been listed separately in this book in consideration of their distinctively nationalistic character. The Liberal Catholic Church is also related to the Old Catholic movement.

American Catholic Church, Archdiocese of New York

This church was organized by its present archbishop, the Most Rev. James Francis Augustine Lashley, in 1927 and incorporated in 1932. Its orders are derived from the Syrian Church of Antioch through Father Vilatte, and it has a membership of 200 in 14 churches, 10 in Manhattan and Brooklyn, 4 in Trinidad, W.I. Roman Catholic forms of ordination and consecration are followed in the investing of holy orders.

American Catholic Church (Syro-Antiochian)

Deriving its orders from the Syrian Patriarch of Antioch, this church is better known as the Jacobite Apostolic Church. It was organized in the United States in 1915 and is a Monophysitic body. Armenian Coptic and Jacobite Syrian churches are all Monophysitic. The word "Jacobite" was borrowed from the name of Jacobus Baradeus (died in 578), the Syrian monk who founded the movement. Historically, a bitter quarrel has raged between the Jacobites and the Orthodox Christians.

Syrian Jacobites are found in Mesopotamia, Iran, Syria, India, and Kurdistan, where they claim something over 80,000 members. It is from this section of the Middle East that they have migrated to America, where today they are found in 1 of 2 churches—the Assyrian Jacobite Apostolic Church with about 1,400 members and 4 churches, and the American Catholic Church (Syro-Antiochian), with 450 members in 5 churches. They use Western rites.

North American Old Roman Catholic Church

Two Old Catholic groups bear this name, typical of the confusion and debate among Old Catholics. One body, identical in faith, thought, and worship with the Roman Catholic Church but differing in discipline, was "received into union" with the Eastern Orthodox Church by the Archbishop of Beirut in 1911, and again by the Orthodox Patriarch of Alexandria in 1912.

The second Church, still in existence as an Old Catholic Church, claims proven succession of Catholic orders; the Knott Missal is used for all masses, but the Pontificale is used for all Order Rights. It is not under Papal control or jurisdiction. Some 60,000 members are reported, in 121 churches.

Old Roman Catholic Church in Europe and America (English Rite)

Archbishop Arnold Harris Mathew, who had been consecrated to the Episcopacy by Archbishop Gerard Gul of the Old Catholic Church of Utrect, Holland, in 1911, consecrated Prince de Landes Berghes de la Rache, a Hungarian, in 1912, and sent him to America to consolidate the small, scattered Old Catholic churches in this country. De Landes settled in Waukegan, Illinois, and on October 3, 1916, consecrated William Henry Francis Brothers as an Old Catholic Bishop, and on the following day he also consecrated Carmel Henry Carfora as Bishop. Less than a month later, at the suggestion of Mgr. Mathew, and in a dispute over the question of Minor Orders, de Landes excommunicated Brothers. Carfora then organized and incorporated the North American Old Roman Catholic Church, which remained the official name of the Church until 1963, when it was changed to The Old Roman Catholic Church (English Rite), following the death of Carfora.

Many Poles and Lithuanians in the country were brought into the membership of this Church; in 1972 it had a membership of 65,128 in 186 churches. It is similar to the Roman Catholic Church in worship and discipline (but denies papal infallibility) and differs slightly in doctrine. They celebrate the Mass, have 7 sacraments, teach transubstantiation, "the Veneration and Invocation of the Glorious and Immaculate Mother of God, of the Angels and of the saints." They offer prayers for the dead, advocate celibacy for their priests, but permit them to marry. Worship services are in the English language.

In 1963, the present Archbishop Metropolitan for North America, Robert Alfred Burns, led the Church into union with the Old Roman Catholic Church (English Rite) in Great Britain.

OPEN BIBLE STANDARD CHURCHES, INC.

Open Bible Standard Churches, Inc. was originally composed of 2 revival movements: namely, Bible Standard, Inc., founded in Eugene, Oregon, in 1919; and Open Bible Evangelistic Association, founded in Des Moines, Iowa, in 1932. Similar in doctrine and government, the 2 groups amalgamated on July 26, 1935, taking the combined name, "Open Bible Standard Churches, Inc.," with headquarters in Des Moines.

The Pacific coast group, with activities centered in Oregon, spread through Washington, California, and into the Rocky Mountain areas of the West; the Iowa group expanded into Illinois, Missouri, Ohio, Florida, and Pennsylvania. There are now churches in 24 states, with the main concentration in the central and far-western states.

The teachings are "fundamental in doctrine, evangelical in spirit, missionary in vision, and pentecostal in testimony"; they include emphasis on the blood atonement of Christ, divine healing, baptism of the Holy Spirit, personal holiness, the premillennial return of the Lord, and baptism by immersion.

Churches are grouped into 5 geographical divisions, subdivided into 24 districts. Twenty-four district superintendents guide the work under the supervision of divisional superintendents. Individual churches are congregationally governed, locally owned, and are affiliated by a charter with the national organization. The 10 departments function under the leadership of departmental heads with the advice of a committee and are represented on the general board of directors. The highest governing body is the general conference, which meets annually and is composed of all licensed and ordained ministers and 1 lay delegate from each church.

There are 50 missionaries at work in 8 foreign countries, and 4 Bible training colleges for the training of national workers. In the United States there are 3 Bible institutes and Bible colleges, with a total enrollment of about 300 students, located at Des Moines, Iowa; Eugene, Oregon; and Dayton, Ohio.

A board of publications is responsible for the preparation of conference publications; a nationally owned book store and press, known as "Inspiration Press and Book Store," is located in Des Moines and circulates a monthly periodical, *The Message of the Open Bible*, and lesson materials for their Sunday schools.

The denomination is a constituent member of the Pentecostal Fellowship of North America and of the National Association of Evangelicals. As of 1972, there were approximately 25,600 constituents in 275 churches.

PENTECOSTAL BODIES

Pentecostalism is a most inclusive term applied to a large number of revivalistic American sects, assemblies, and churches. Many of them have come out of either Methodist or Baptist backgrounds, and they are primarily concerned with perfection, holiness, and the Pentecostal experience.

They offer statements of faith which are often long and involved and highly repetitious, but through which may be traced certain common strains and elements. Most of them believe in the Trinity, original sin, man's salvation through the atoning blood of Christ, the virgin birth and deity of Jesus, the divine inspiration and literal infallibility of the Scriptures, manifestations and "blessings" of the working of the Holy Spirit—the fiery Pentecostal baptism of the Spirit, premillennialism, and future rewards and punishments. Two sacraments are found in most of their sects—baptism, usually by immersion, and the Lord's Supper. Foot washing is frequently observed in connection with the Supper. Many practice divine healing, and speaking in tongues is widespread.

Ultrafundamentalistic, varying in size from small group meetings to huge mass meetings, Pentecostalists are found in every state in the Union with their greatest strength in the South, West, and Middle West. They use a great variety of names, and do not always include the word "Pentecostal" in their names—for instance, the largest single group of all, the Assemblies of God, with over half a million members, and the Church of God groups. No accurate count of their total membership is possible, as many of them never issue statistical reports of any kind.

Calvary Pentecostal Church, Inc.

This church was founded at Olympia, Washington, in 1931 by a group of ministers who sought a ministerial fellowship rather than a separate denomination and freedom from the sectarian spirit. The body was incorporated in 1932, and a home and foreign missionary society was incorporated in the same year. Home missions work today consists mainly of evangelistic work, relief to weak churches, and the establishment of new churches. A general superintendent and executive presbytery board administer the work of the church; the general body meets in convention annually or semiannually. Seminary, college, or even Bible school education is considered beneficial but no requisite for ministers of this church, who may be either men or women; those who give evidence of having heard the call of God to preach are qualified by ordination. There are 22 churches and 8,000 members.

Elim Fellowship

Established in 1947, this body is an outgrowth of the missionary-oriented Elim Ministerial Fellowship, formed in 1932, and of the work of graduates of the Elim Bible Institute in Lima, New York (founded in 1924). The organizational pattern is Congregational, and doctrine is basically premillenial, holding the usual tenets of belief in an inspired and infallible Bible, the Trinity, sanctification, the baptism of the Holy Spirit, divine healing, and the resurrection of both saved and unsaved for eternal reward or punishment. Some 5,000 members are found in 70 churches, and 100 missionaries are at work in 18 countries of Africa, Asia, Europe, and South America. Headquarters are located at the institute, on the former campus of Genesee Wesleyan Seminary, purchased in 1951. The assemblies hold membership in the Pentecostal Fellowship of North America and the National Association of Evangelicals.

Emmanuel Holiness Church

The founders of this church had come to a general conference of the Pentecostal Fire-Baptized Holiness Church in 1953, but withdrew from that church in protest against certain positions taken by the conference of doctrine and polity. They now have 1,200 members in 56 churches and tabernacles located in Alabama, Florida, Georgia, North and South Carolina, Indiana, and Michigan; there is missionary activity in Mexico. Their chief administrative body is a general assembly and their ruling church officer is a general overseer. A periodical, *Emmanuel Messenger*, is published at Anderson, South Carolina.

International Pentecostal Assemblies

This body is the successor to the Association of Pentecostal Assemblies (founded in 1921) and the National and International Pentecostal Union (founded in 1919). Doctrine follows the usual Pentecostal standards; the sick are anointed with oil, and prayer is offered for their healing; foot washing is optional; and this group is not opposed to participation in government or in defensive war. There are ap-

210

proximately 10,000 members in 55 churches, under the general supervision of a 9-member general board and several district superintendents who direct the work in 24 states and 13 foreign countries. The entire work is supported by membership tithes and offerings. A Bible College is maintained at Atlanta, Georgia.

Pentecostal Assemblies of the World, Inc.

This was an interracial body at the time of its organization in 1914; some of the white members withdrew in 1924 to form the Pentecostal Church, Inc., which became a constituent body of the United Pentecostal Church, Inc. in 1945. Origin is traced "directly back to Pentecost, A.D. 33." Doctrine reveals no important departure from that of Pentecostalism in general. Secret societies are opposed. Divorce is perimtted, but only on the grounds of fornication when both man and wife have had the "baptism of the Holy Ghost"; but when the unbeliever in a marriage contract procures a divorce, the believer may remarry.

Organization is similar to that of the Methodists: a general assembly meets annually under a presiding bishop; there is a secretary for foreign missions, a committee of 3 on evangelism, and 78 district elders. An executive board is composed of bishops (of whom there are 20), directors, the general secretary, and general treasurer. An election of officers is held every 3 years by the ministerial members of the national assembly. Local assemblies are under the direction of district elders. There are 45,000 members in 550 churches.

Pentecostal Church of Christ

Founded by John Stroup at Flatwoods, Kentucky, in 1917, and incorporated at Portsmouth, Ohio, in 1927, this church subscribes to the usual Pentecostal doctrines of the Trinity, regeneration, sanctification, baptism of the Spirit, and puts strong emphasis upon divine healing. They have 1,365 members in 45 churches, missionary work in Brazil, and churches in the United States located in Ohio, Kentucky, West Virginia, Virginia, and Maryland. American headquarters are in London, Ohio.

Pentecostal Church of God of America, Inc.

This church was organized at Chicago in 1919, incorporated in Missouri in 1936, and held its first national convention in 1938. The words "of America" were added to its name to distinguish it from a Colorado Springs body bearing a similar name. It is typically Pentecostalist in faith, with baptism by immersion, Holy Spirit baptism, physical evidence of speaking in tongues, divine healing, and the second coming of Christ.

Officers include a general superintendent, secretary-treasurer, director of world missions, director of Christian education, district superintendents, and district presbyters. A general convention meets biennially; the 34 districts have annual meetings.

With 250,000 communicants, 2,160 churches are maintained in 21 countries; there are 3 Bible colleges, and 12 Bible colleges located abroad; children's homes are located in Pettit, Texas, and Mexico. A large publishing-house is located at Joplin, Mo.

Pentecostal Fire-Baptized Holiness Church

This church was organized in 1911 by a small group who declined to continue in the union of the Fire-Baptized Holiness Church and the Pentecostal Holiness Church; their objection had to do mainly with matters of discipline in the wearing of ornaments and elaborate dress. They withdrew from the union in 1918.

Members of this church are forbidden to buy or sell, or to engage in any labor or business for which they may receive "pecuniary remuneration." They are also forbidden "filthiness of speech, foolish talking or jesting, slang, attendance at fairs, swimming pools, or shows of any kind, the use of jewelry, gold, feathers, flowers, costly apparel, neckties."

The sect is strongly premillennialist and perfectionist; "joyous demonstrations" are prominent, finding expression in hand clapping, crying, and shouting. State conventions support convention evangelists, and there is a general convention which elects a 7-member board of missions. Foreign missions are supported in Mexico. There are 545 members and 41 churches.

Pentecostal Free-Will Baptist Church, Inc.

As the name suggests, this is a Pentecostalist group with a Free-Will Baptist background; it came into existence through the merging of 3 Free-Will Baptist conferences in North Carolina in 1959. Doctrine is, naturally, a mixture of Baptist and Pentecostalist beliefs; they include regeneration through faith in the shed blood of Christ, sanctification as a second definite work of grace (subsequent to regeneration), Pentecostal baptism of the Holy Ghost, divine healing, and the Premillennial second coming of Christ.

Officials include a general superintendent, general secretary, and general treasurer. A general meetings is held annually, on the last Wednesday of August, composed of both lay and ministerial representatives.

There are 13,500 members and 150 churches.

Pentecostal Holiness Church

This church was organized in 1898 at Anderson, South Carolina, by a number of Pentecostal associations which at the time used the name Fire-Baptized Holiness Church. A year later another group organized as the Pentecostal Holiness Church; the 2 bodies united in 1911 at Falcon, North Carolina, under the latter name. A third body, the Tabernacle Pentecostal Church, joined them in 1915. There are 74,108 members in the United States, in 1,340 churches, and 27,383 in 481 churches in foreign mission fields.

The theological standards of Methodism prevail here, with certain modifications. It accepts the premillennial teaching of the Second Coming and believes that provision was made in the atonement for the healing of the body. Divine healing is practiced, but not to the exclusion of medicine. Three distinctive experiences are taught: 2 works of grace—justification by faith and sanctification, as a second work of grace—and the Spirit baptism, attested by speaking in other tongues. Services are often characterized by "joyous demonstrations."

Polity also is Methodistic; there are annual conferences and a quadrennial general conference which elects 1 general superintendent (bishop) to hold office for 4 years only. The general conference also elects 4 assistant general superintendents, a general secretary, and a general treasurer of the church, these constituting the general executive board. There is a general board of administration composed of the executive board and the superintendents of all annual conferences in the United States and Canada. There are 32 annual conferences in the United States, 3 in Canada, 1 in England, and 7 in South Africa. Foreign missions are found in Hong Kong, India, South Africa, Central Africa, West Africa, South America, Central America, Mexico, and Cuba. There is a junior college (Emmanuel College) at Franklin Springs, Georgia; a junior college (Southwestern College) at Oklahoma City, Oklahoma; a theological seminary (Holmes Theological Seminary) at Greenville, South Carolina; a children's home (Falcon Children's Home) at Falcon, North Carolina; homes for the aged at Carmen, Oklahoma, and Falcon, North Carolina.

There is a publishing house which also houses general offices for the church (Advocate Press) at Franklin Springs, Georgia, the international headquarters of the denomination.

United Pentecostal Church International

The product of a union of 2 Pentecostal organizations (the Pentecostal Assemblies of Jesus Christ and the Pentecostal Church, Inc.) at St. Louis, Missouri, in 1945, this church stresses the necessity of repentance, water baptism in the name of Christ, and the receiving of the baptism of the Holy Ghost with the initial sign of speaking in tongues. It has 300,000 members in 2,550 churches; the superintendents of geographical districts make up their general board, which is the international administrative body. One hundred fifty thousand missionaries are supported in a foreign missions program which has 2,450 ministers and 2,670 congregations in 64 countries; 37 summer campgrounds are maintained in the United States and Canada. Headquarters and a publishing house which issues the official *Pentecostal Herald* are located in St. Louis.

The Church also sponsors an international radio broadcast on 275 stations, maintains a Youth Redemption Training Center for drug addicts in Lincoln, Nebraska, has 8 affiliated Bible Colleges, and a children's home in Tupelo, Mississippi.

PILLAR OF FIRE

The Pillar of Fire originated from the evangelistic efforts of its founder, Mrs. Alma White. The wife of a Methodist minister in Colorado, Mrs. White often preached from her husband's pulpit. Her fervent exhortations on regeneration and holiness—and especially her habit of organizing missions and camp meetings on her own authority —brought her into sharp conflict with the bishops and other leaders of Methodism, and she withdrew to become an evangelistic free lance. She established the Pentecostal Union in 1901 and changed the name to Pillar of Fire in 1917.

Mrs. White's first headquarters were located at Denver; they were later moved to Zarephath, near Bound Brook, New Jersey. In both Denver and Zarephath the body has a college, preparatory school, Bible seminary, radio station, and publishing house. Other schools are located in Cincinnati, Los Angeles, Jacksonville, Pacifica, San Francisco, Seattle, Philadelphia, Liberia (Africa), and London.

Modernism in theology is condemned by Pillar of Fire; its teaching is based upon primitive Wesleyanism, with doctrines on the inspiration and inerrancy of the Scriptures, repentance, justification, second blessing holiness, premillennialism, and future judgment. Sacraments include baptism and the Lord's Supper; marriage is a "divine institution."

Mrs. White was the first bishop of Pillar of Fire; on her death authority passed to her 2 sons. The membership is divided into 4 classes: probationary, associate, regular, and full, with only regular and full members being allowed to vote on administrative matters. There are deacons and deaconesses, and both men and women are ordained as ministers; there are also consecrated deaconesses, licensed preachers, and missionaries, and as in Methodism, presiding elders (district superintendents), and bishops. Considerable literature is printed and distributed in the United States, and there are regular broadcasts from WAWZ, Zarephath, KPOF, Denver, and WAKW, Cincinnati, Ohio. There were approximately 5,000 members and 61 branches as of 1949.

POLISH NATIONAL CATHOLIC CHURCH
OF AMERICA

A strictly American church born on American soil, the Polish National Catholic Church of America was formally organized at Scranton, Pennsylvania, on March 14, 1897; behind this formality lay a long period of conflict between the Roman Catholic Church and many of the Poles who had immigrated to the United States around the turn of the century. Roman Catholic in homeland background, they objected that in the United States they had no bishops and few priests who were Polish, that they could not teach in Polish in their parish schools, and that under the ruling of the Roman Catholic Council of Baltimore in 1884 they had not right to establish parishes of their own. All this, they felt, gave the Roman hierarchy and priesthood an unwarranted religious, political, financial, and social power over their parishioners, and permitted "an unlawful encroachment upon the ownership of church property and [paved] the way for the political exploitation of the Polish people." (Some scholars feel that the cause of dissension has roots further back, in the demand in Poland in the Reformation era for a Polish National church.) Resentment smoldered gradually into open revolt in Chicago, Detroit, Cleveland, Buffalo, and Scranton and gradually resulted in the founding at Scranton of an independent Polish body with approximately 20,000 members mainly in the eastern states. This is the only break of any considerable size from the Roman Catholic Church in the United States; but there are other groups among Slovaks, Lithuanians, Ruthenians, and Hungarians which have also broken away. Several of the Slovak and Lithuanian parishes have merged with the Polish National Catholic Church.

A constitution for the new church was adopted by the Scranton parish in 1897, claiming the right for the Polish people to control all churches built and maintained by them, to administer such church property through a committee chosen by the parish, and to choose their own pastors. The first synod was held at Scranton in 1904, with 147 clerical and lay delegates representing parishes in Pennsylvania, Maryland, Massachusetts, Connecticut, and New Jersey. The Rev. Francis Hodur, the organizer and dominant figure in the group, was chosen bishop-elect; he was consecrated bishop in 1907 at Utrecht, Holland, by 3 bishops of the Old Catholic Church. This synod also ordered all Latin service books translated into Polish and established a seminary at Scranton.

The doctrine of this church is founded on "the Scriptures, the holy traditions and the 4 ecumenical synods of the undivided church . . . but not rejecting the next 3." The Apostles' and Nicene Creeds are accepted. Doctrine is expanded in a Confession of Faith which includes statements of belief in the Trinity; the Holy Spirit as the ruler of the world and the source of grace, power, and peace; the necessity of

215

spiritual unity of all Christians in one body of Christ's church, apostolic and universal; the church as teacher, steward of grace, and a light unto salvation; the equal right of all men to life, happiness, and growth in perfection and equal responsibility toward God, all people, and nations; immortality and the future justice and judgment of God. The doctrine of eternal damnation and punishment is supplanted by an expressed hope and surety of universal salvation as taught in the church by Origen, Jerome, and Gregory of Nazianzus.

"Even sinful man, after undergoing an intrinsic regeneration through contrition, penance and noble deeds, may have a chance to regain the grace of God. . . . Man, by following the Supreme Being, is in this life capable of attaining a certain degree of the happiness and perfection which is possessed of God in an infinite degree."

Faith is absolutely necessary to salvation, but it must be manifest in good works. Sin is

a lack of perfection, a consequence resulting from a lack of spiritual, godly life within the being in whom predominates a mean, animal life, and as mankind progresses in this knowledge of the causes of life and the nature of God, and comes nearer and nearer to him, sin will gradually grow less and less until it vanishes entirely. Then man will become the true image and child of God, and the kingdom of God will prevail upon earth.

Seven sacraments are observed, with baptism and confirmation as one sacrament (confirmation is regarded as a completion of baptism). The seventh sacrament here is the hearing of the Word of God proclaimed by the church from the Scriptures. Two forms of confession are in general use—a private confession for children and youth and a general confession for adults only.

A general synod is the highest authority in the government of the church. It meets every 4 years, except for such special sessions as may be considered necessary, and is composed of bishops (of whom there are now 7), clergy, and lay delegates from every parish. Administrative power rests with the Prime Bishop. A church council meets annually, or on call, and is composed of all the bishops, 4 clerical, and 4 lay delegates elected by the general synod. In like manner the authority of the diocese is vested in a diocesan synod which meets every 4 years. Each parish is governed by an elected board of trustees. There are 282,411 members in 162 churches in the United States. The Polish language is used in the worship and in the educational program in parish schools, taught largely by pastors; but English may be used if necessary for the Mass, sacraments, sermons, gospel, and other church rites, with permission of the bishop. The clergy may marry, but only with the knowledge and permission of the bishops.

The Polish National Union, a fraternal and insurance organization, was established by the church at Scranton in 1908, set up on parish lines and as an adjunct to parish life. It consists of 12 districts divided into 257 branches and has 35,000 members, all of whom are not required to be members of the church.

A missionary work was begun in Poland in 1919, and by 1951 had 119 parishes and a theological seminary in Krakow. Missionary Bishop Padewski was arrested by the Communists and died in prison during the same year; since that tme, the church in Poland has severed all physical ties with the American body, but the 2 remain in complete harmony in theology and ideology. At home, there is a theological seminary in Scranton and a home for the aged and disabled at Spojnia Farm, Waymart, Pennsylvania. In 1964 the Lithuanian National Church merged with the Polish National Catholic Church. An unusually effective intercommunion has been established between this church and the Protestant Episcopal, Anglican, and Old Catholic churches.

PRESBYTERIANS

Presbyterianism has 2 firm and deep roots: one goes back to the Greek word *presbuteros* (elder) and has to do with the system of church government of ancient and apostolic times; the other goes back to John Calvin and the Protestant Reformation and has to do with the form of government used by all people calling themselves Presbyterian and holding the faith of the Reformed churches.

Calvin (1509-64) was a Frenchman trained for the law. Turning to theology, his keen, legalistic mind and his lust for freedom from the rigid, confining forms of Roman Catholicism drove him as a fugitive from Roman reprisal to the city of Geneva, where he quickly grasped the reins of leadership in the Reformed sector of the Reformation. Resolute and often harsh with those who opposed him, he established himself and his theological systems at the heart of a "city of God" in the Swiss capital, making it, according to Macaulay, the "cleanest and most wholesome city in Europe."

Calvin's whole thought revolved about the concept of sovereignty:

the sovereignty of God in his universe, the sovereignty of Christ in salvation, the sovereignty of the Scriptures in faith and conduct, the sovereignty of the individual conscience in the interpretation of the Will and Word of God.

His system has been summarized in 5 main points: human impotence, unconditional predestination, limited atonement, irresistible grace, and final perseverance. God, according to Calvinism, is sovereign and eternal ruler of the world; man is completely dominated by and dependent upon him.

217

The doctrine of God's eternal decree is held in harmony with the doctrine of his love to all mankind, his gift of his Son to be the propitiation for the sins of the whole world, and his readiness to bestow his saving grace on all who seek it; that concerning those who perish, the doctrine of God's eternal decree is held in harmony with the doctrine that God desires not the death of any sinner, but has provided in Christ a salvation sufficient for all, adapted to all, and freely offered in the gospel to all; that men are fully responsible for their treatment of God's gracious offer; that his decree hinders no man from accepting that offer; and that no man is condemned except on the ground of his sin. All dying in infancy are excluded in the election of grace, and are regenerated and saved by Christ through the Spirit, who works when and where and how he pleases. (Quoted from the declaratory statement in the Constitution of the United Presbyterian Church.)

Out of this Calvinism came miracles of reform. Few reformers have made as many contributions as John Calvin in so many fields at once—in education, in the building of an intelligent ministry, in the liberation of the oppressed and persecuted, and in the establishment of democratic forms of government in both church and state. In his thought lay the germ which in time destroyed the divine right of kings. He gave a new dignity to man, and representative government to man's parliaments and church councils. He struck the final blow at feudalism and offered a spiritual and moral tone for drawing capitalism.

Strictly speaking, John Calvin did not found Presbyterianism; he laid the foundations upon which it was reconstructed in Switzerland, Holland, France, England, Scotland, and Ireland. He inspired fellow Frenchmen out of whose ranks came the Huguenots; by 1560 there were 2,000 churches of Presbyterian complexion in France. He influenced the Dutchmen who established the Dutch Reformed Church in Holland. He gave courage to British Presbyterians in their bitter struggle against Catholic Bloody Mary. To him came Scots who became Covenanters; to him came John Knox, who went home to cry "Great God, give me Scotland, or I die." Knox and the Covenanters set Scotland afire and made it Protestant and Presbyterian.

A delegation of Scots sat in the Westminster Assembly of Divines along with 121 English ministers, 10 peers, and 20 members of the House of Commons, resolved to have "no bishop, and no king." This Westminster Assembly is a milestone in Presbyterian history. Meeting at the call of Parliament to resolve the struggle over the compulsory use of the Anglican *Book of Common Prayer*, it sat for nearly 5 years (1643-48) in 1,163 sessions, produced a Larger and a Shorter catechism, a directory for the public worship of God, a form of government, and the Westminster Confession of Faith, which, built upon the Old and New Testaments, became the doctrinal standard of Scottish, British, and American Presbyterianism.

Dominant in the Wesminster Assembly, the Presbyterians soon

dominated the British government. Cromwell completed the ousting of a monarch and established a commonwealth; the commonwealth crashed, the monarchy rturned, and the fires of persecution flamed again. British Presbyterians fled to America with the Puritans; an attempt to establish episcopacy in Scotland after 1662 sent many Presbyterians out of Scotland into Ireland, where economic difficulties and religious inequalities drove them on to America. The Presbyterian British, and even more the Presbyterian Scotch-Irish, became the founders of Presbyterianism in America. Beginning in 1710 and running into mid-century, from 3,000 to 6,000 Scotch-Irish came annually into the American colonies, settling at first in New England and the middle colonies, then spreading out more widely than any other racial group ever to reach our shores.

There were Presbyterian congregations in the colonies long before the Scotch-Irish migration of 1710-50. One was worshiping in Virginia in 1611; others were worshiping in Massachusetts and Connecticut in 1630. Long Island and New York had congregations by 1640 and 1643. Francis Makemie ranged the coast from Boston to the Carolinas, planting churches and giving them unity with one another; 6 groups were united into the first presbytery in Philadelphia in 1706; in 1716 this first presbytery had become a synod made up of 4 presbyteries and held its first meeting in 1717.

United Presbyterian Church in the U.S.A.

Overwhelmingly the largest single body of Presbyterians in America, this church is the result of a merger (1958) of 2 groups in the United States: the Presbyterian Church in the U.S.A., and the United Presbyterian Church of North America. We shall consider them first separately, under their original names, and then as a united church.

The Presbyterian Church in the U.S.A. dates back to the organizing of the general presbytery in 1706. The first general synod of its spiritual forefathers, meeting in 1729, adopted the Westminster Confession of Faith with the Larger and Shorter catchisms "as being, in all essential and necessary articles, good forms of sound words, and systems of Christian doctrine." The same synod denied to the civil magistrates any power whatever over the church or any right to persecute anyone for his religious faith.

Free in the new land with their Scotch-Irish fire and Covenanter background, the Presbyterians quickly set about procuring trained ministers; creeds and colleges have been their stock in trade from the earliest days. William Tennent, Sr., organized a "log college" in a cabin at Neshaminy, Pennsylvania. He started with 3 of his 4 sons as his first pupils, and this family school grew into the most important Presbyterian institution of higher learning in America. Out of it came the College of New Jersey (now Princeton University) and a stream of revivalistic Presbyterian preachers who played leading roles in the

Great Awakening of the early eighteenth century. Prominent among them were William Tennent, Jr., and his brother Gilbert, who met and liked the British revivalist George Whitefield and followed him in preaching an emotional "new birth" revivalism which came into conflict with the old creedal Calvinism. The camp-meeting revival grew out of the Great Awakening enthusiasm; it was born as a Presbyterian institution and was continued by the Methodists when the Presbyterians dropped it.

Presbyterian objection to emotional revivalism went deep; it split their church. Preachers took sides; those of the "old side" opposed revivalism, while those of the "new side" endorsed it, claiming that less attention should be paid to college training for the ministry and more to the recruiting of regenerated common men into the pulpit. The 2 sides quarreled until 1757, when they reunited; in 1758, the first year of the united synod, there were 98 ministers in the Presbyterian Church in the colonies, 200 congregations, and 10,000 members. One of the ablest of the new-side preachers was John Witherspoon, president of Princeton (founded in 1746), member of the Continental Congress, and the only ministerial signer of the Declaration of Independence.

Witherspoon may have been instrumental in the call of the general synod upon the Presbyterian churches to "uphold and promote" the resolutions of the Continental Congress. The Scotch-Irish accepted the revolution with relish; the persecution they had experienced in England and Ulster left them as natural dissenters and solidly anti-British. Their old cry, "No bishop and no king," was heard as far off as England; Horace Walpole supposedly remarked that "Cousin America" had run off with a Presbyterian parson.

The Presbyterians moved swiftly to strengthen their church after Yorktown, meeting as a synod at Philadelphia in 1788 at the same time that the national constitutional convention was in session in the same city. The national administrative bodies of American Presbyterianism were known as The Presbytery from 1706-16; as The Synod from 1717-88, and as The General Assembly from 1789 to the present time.

From 1790 to 1837 membership in the Presbyterian Church in the U.S.A. increased from 18,000 to 220,557. This growth was due to the revival which swept the country during those years and to the plan of union with the Congregationalists. Under this plan Presbyterian and Congregational preachers and laymen moving into the new western territory worked and built together; preachers of the 2 denominations preached in each other's pulpits, and members held the right of representation in both Congregational association and Presbyterian presbytery. The plan worked well on the whole, absorbing the fruits of the national revivals and giving real impetus to missionary work both at home and abroad. Then came disagreements between Old School and New School factions within the church over matters of discipline and the expenditure of missionary money. The General Assembly of 1837 expelled 4 New School presbyteries, which promptly met in their own convention at Auburn, New York. The Presbyterian Church in the U.S.A. was split in two between New School men who wanted to keep the plan of union and old-school men who were suspicious of the "novelties of New England [Congregational] theology."

These years promised to be an era of expansion for the Presbyterians. Marcus Whitman drove the first team and wagon over the south pass of the Rockies into the great Northwest. After him came hosts of Presbyterian preachers and laymen building churches, schools, colleges, and seminaries. From 1812 to 1836 the Presbyterians in the United States built their first great theological seminaries: Princeton, Allegheny, Auburn, Columbia, Lane, McCormick, Union in Virginia, and Union in New York City. They also set up their own missionary and educational societies. But the era of unity suddenly became an era of schism. Even earlier than the old-school–new school division the Cumberland presbytery had broken away in 1810, following a dispute over the educational qualifications of the ministry, to form the Cumberland Presbyterian Church. Antislavery sentiment was increasing. A strong protest was made in 1818, but it was later modified. In 1846 the Old School assembly regarded slavery in the southern state as no bar to Christian communion; but the New School assembly took action in the same year, condemning it without reservation. By 1857 several New School southern synods had withdrawn to organize the United Synod of the Presbyterian Church, and the greater and final break came in 1861 when 47 Old School southern presbyteries formed their General Assembly of the Presbyterian Church in the Confederate States of America. In 1865 the United Synod and the Confederate churches merged into what is now known as the Presbyterian Church in the United States. The Synod of Kentucky united with it in 1869 and the Synod of Missouri in 1874.

The Old School and New School bodies, holding separate assemblies since 1837, were united in 1870 on the basis of the Westminster Confession; they were joined in 1906 by a large majority of the Cumberland churches and in 1920 by the Welsh Calvinistic Methodists.

From the 1920s through the 1950s, 2 strong emphases were noticeable in this church: one was the emphasis upon theology, seen in the struggle between liberals and conservatives; and the other was the emphasis upon Presbyterian unity. The latter was evident in the proposed merger with the Protestant Episcopal Church, which was not realized, and in the 1958 merger of the Presbyterian Church in the U.S.A. with the United Presbyterian Church of North America.

The United Presbyterian Church of North America was formed by the merging of the Associate Presbyterian Church and the Associate Reformed Presbyterian Church at Pittsburgh in 1858. The doctrines, traditions, and institutions of the 2 combining bodies were preserved; government in the united church followed the Presbyterian form with session, presbytery, synod, and a general assembly which met annually.

In matters of faith this church rested upon the broad foundation of the Westminster Confession with certain modifications, one of which amended the chapter in the confession on the power of civil magistrates. A confessional statement of 44 articles was drawn up by the United Presbyterian Church in 1925; it contained the substance of the Westminster standards and symbols but restricted divorce cases to marital unfaithfulness, denied infant damnation, extended sacramental privileges to all who professed faith in Christ and led Christian lives, withdrew the protest against secret or oath-bound societies, abandoned the exclusive use of the Psalms, maintained insistence upon the verbal inspiration of the Scriptures, affirmed the sufficiency and fullness of the provisions of God for the needs of Christ, emphasized the renewing and sanctifying power of the Holy Spirit, and held salvation to be free to all sinners.

There were no insurmountable doctrinal differences when the United Presbyterian Church of North America and the Presbyterian Church in the U.S.A. merged in 1958; there were the usual disagreements between theological conservatives and liberals, but on the whole they found agreement and unity in the doctrine of the Westminster Confession, which had been the accepted doctrinal statement of Presbyterianism in the United States since its adoption here in 1729. But as time passed, the conviction grew in the united church that a new statement or confession, written not against the background of seventeenth century language, thought, and culture but in the language of the twentieth century, was needed and necessary to proclaim the gospel. The Westminster document was 300 years old; many felt that it was too much "bound by time." Accordingly, a special committee was appointed to prepare and present a new statement. Climaxing nearly 8 years of study and discussion, the 179th General Assembly of the church, meeting at Portland, Oregon, approved the Committee's new "Confession of 1967" as a contemporary statement of faith. It was the first major change in three centuries.

Presbyterians now have a *Book of Confessions* containing not 1 creed or confession but 9: The Nicene Creed of 325, the second-century Apostles' Creed, the Scots Confession of 1560, the Heidelberg Catechism of 1563, the Second Helvetic Confession of 1566, the Westminster Confession of 1647, the Shorter Catechism of 1647, the Theological Declaration of Barmen (1934), and the Confession of 1967. The purpose of this arrangement of creeds and confessions was to trace the development of the great affirmations of the Christian faith, particularly through the Reformed tradition, to make clear the great common confessional belief of the majority of Christians in the world and to offer common ground for unity among those churches holding the Reformed position.

The Confession of 1967 is brief (4,200 words), avoids the confusing terminology of the Westminster Confession, and stresses the concepts of love, sin, eternal life, and (especially) the work of reconciliation in God, Christ, and the church. It is Christ-centered, emphasizing faith in Christ as Messiah and Lord and, generally, repeats in modern speech the standards of the Westminster Confession. While there is still some opposition (on the ground that it waters down some of the traditional statements of the Westminster Confession), an overwhelming majority in the church has accepted it, convinced that it not only reflects the mind and faith of true Presbyterianism but offers as well a wide theological base upon which all Presbyterians can stand together.

Under the Presbyterian system of government, each congregation has its local session, which acts in receiving and disciplining members and in the general welfare of the church. Congregations in limited districts are grouped in presbyteries which examine, ordain, and install all ministers; review reports from the sessions and hear cases of complaint brought before them. The synod supervises the presbyteries of a larger district, reviews the records of its contituent presbyteries, organizes new presbyteries, and functions in an administrative capacity in all denominational matters lying within its jurisdiction. The highest judiciary is the annual general assembly, made up of clerical and lay delegates elected by the presbyteries on a proportional plan. The general assembly settles all matters of discipline and doctrine referred to it by the lower bodies, establishes new synods, appoints agencies and commissions, and reviews all appeals. Its decisions are final except that it cannot of itself amend the constitution of the Church. The officers of the general assembly are the stated clerk (the chief executive officer), elected for five years with the privilege of reelection, and the moderator, chosen each year to preside over the sessions of the general assembly.

On the national level, a program of restructure concentrated direction of the work of the denomination in three new agencies—the Program Agency, the Vocation Agency, the Support Agency—and the General Assembly Mission Council. The General Assembly Mission Council recommends goals, objectives, policies, and the best possible use of all resources to the general assembly; overseas the implementation of decisions made by the general assembly; appropriates funds to agencies and synods; assesses the effectiveness of mission undertakings; coordinates policies, procedures, and practices established by the assembly. The Program Agency trains and deploys people in mission on all six continents—missionaries, fraternal workers, volunteers, church leaders, service people in human ministries; provides money and consultation that enable other units of the church at home and abroad to conduct programs in church development, evangelism, church education, and issue-responsive ministries; serves people with particular needs—refugees, disaster victims anywhere in the world, and people with needs related to military service; maintains relationships with Presbyterian education and health care institutions around the world, with world and national ecumenical groups, and relates to other UPC councils and agencies at the national level. The Vocation Agency works in developing new ministries, providing dossier services, training ministerial relations committees, providing placement counseling, training judicatory staff, setting guidelines for enlistment, career counseling, remuneration, and retirement (pensions). The Support Agency works in the general areas of communications and finance; it provides news and information through the channels of press, radio, and television; publishes *A.D.*, a magazine serving both the United Presbyterian Church in the U.S.A. and the United Church of Christ; provides accounting counsel and functions and budget operations, oversees treasury functions including payments made to and by all agencies, foreign accounting, banking, and insurance management; supervises and informs on property management, the sale, rental, lease, and assigned use of property; records management, central purchasing, marketing and distribution, office services, travel, and overseas shipping; renders legal services such as property transfers, mortgages, church loans, and legal opinions.

Historically, it is interesting to note the Presbyterian concern with Christian higher education. From the start, in this country, this Church has insisted upon high standards of academic training for its ministers, and has developed an admirable educational program for both clergy and laity. Today there are 52 United Presbyterian-related colleges and universities, 7 theological seminaries in the U.S. and 21 abroad; a total of 1,131 ministers and chaplains are serving on 700 college campuses.

The membership of the United Presbyterian Church stands at 2,908,958 in 8,732 churches (as of 1972). There are 10 different Presbyterian denominations in the United States, with a total membership of over 4 million. Of these, no less than well over 3 million are found in the United Presbyterian Church and the Presbyterian Church in the U. S. (Southern). (This figure already needs revision, due to the recent defection of about 273 churches with 70,000 members from the southern group, who call their new denomination the Presbyterian Church in America.) Of the 10 groups, 5 are working together in the North American area of the Alliance of Reformed Churches Throughout the World Holding the Presbyterian Order, organized in 1875.

Presbyterian Church in the United States

The establishment and historical background of this church have already been described (see p. 219). Popularly known today as "Southern Presbyterians," they are still separated from the "Northern Presbyterians" in the United Presbyterian Church in the U.S.A., in differences which are theological, ecclesiastical, administrative, and social in nature, but there are still evidences of cooperation in missionary planning, in 2 colleges and 1 theological seminary. Probably more than either of the other 2 churches in "the big 3," Presbyterians, Methodists and Baptists), the Presbyterian Church in the U.S. has led the effort to integrate Negro churches into the denomination, and to open the doors of their conferences, colleges, and seminaries to those of both races.

Through all its history, the Presbyterian Church in the United States has been characterized by a continuing demand for freedom and intelligence in both politics and religion—a fundamental concept and drive brought here by the Scotch-Irish Presbyterian dissenters who migrated from the north of Ireland to settle in the American South. Their influence in the establishment of the American commonwealth has run wide and deep. Virginia and North Carolina presbyteries were calling for American independence long before the Boston riots and the Liberty Bell; the Mecklenberg (North Carolina) presbytery was the first ecclesiastical body in the colonies to approve the Declaration of Independence. Presbyterian civic leaders brought law and order to many areas of the South before colonial officials could be appointed or elected; with their distinguishing passion for education, Presbyterian ministers taught school before there was any organized system of public education in the region. In parallel patriotic passion they were prominent in both French and Indian and Revolutionary Wars and in the long struggle for religious liberty and the rights of religious dissenters. With the Baptists, they laid in church and school the spiritual, political, moral, and intellectual foundations of the famous Jeffersonian "Act for Establishing Religious Freedom" in Virginia, which preceded similar statements concerning the same rights and freedoms in the Constitution of the United States. Their missionary zeal was evident in their presence in the first wagons and wagon trains that moved out through the Mississippi Valley to the West.

Doctrinally they are of course Calvinistic. As in most Reformed churches, ministers, elders, and deacons are required to give adherence to a confessional statement. Women are now admitted to the ministry and eldership and are encouraged to enlist in other government fields of Christian work. Polity government and doctrine follow the Presbyterian pattern.

There are 7 synods, 4,214 churches, and 946,526 members in 18 states. The church supports 4 theological seminaries—Austin, Columbia, Loisville, and Union (Richmond)—15 colleges and 1 other affiliated college, 5 junior colleges, 4 secondary schools, 2 missions schools, and 1 school of religious education, 18 children's homes, and 20 homes for the aged. Home missionary work is conducted among the Indians and Latin-Americans in Texas and Oklahoma, in the Ozarks and Appalachians; the work is marked not only by financial support, but by concern for comity in churching the several areas, in urban problems, etc. Abroad, a missionary force of 519 is at work in Mexico, Ecuador, Brazil, Taiwan, Korea, Japan, Portugal, Iraq, Vietnam, and the Congo; they serve not only Presbyterian churches and missions, but many indigenous projects as well. There are 29 periodicals published by the Board of Education, which also operates the John Knox Press.

Associate Presbyterian Church of North America

This church maintains the traditions of the secession movement of 1733 in the Church of Scotland. Missionaries from Scotland organized the Associate Presbytery in America in 1754. This presbytery merged with the Reformed Presbytery in 1782; 2 ministers and 3 ruling elders refused to accept the union and continued the organization of the Associate Presbytery of Pennsylvania. Other presbyteries joined the Pennsylvania group, which in 1801 was named the Associate Synod of North America. In 1858 this associate synod and the Associate Reformed Presbyterian Church of North America consummated a union under the name United Presbyterian Church of North America. Eleven ministers refusing to enter this union continued the Associate Presbyterian Church.

This church believes in restricted Communion, expels members who join secret orders, and uses the Psalms exclusively in worship services. It follows the Westminster Confession and has an associate testimony of its own explaining its doctrinal position. Polity differs in no essential elements from that of other Presbyterian churches. Home missions are conducted by itinerant pastors, and foreign missionary work is supported in India. There are no colleges or other schools; there are 650 members and 4 churches.

Associate Reformed Presbyterian Church

This is a synod of the former Associate Reformed Presbyterian Church; it is a body of Covenanter origins and traditions. ("Covenant" here refers to the Reformed branch of the church. The Associate Presbyterian Church of North America, in distinction, is of Seceder origin; the Associate Reformed Church is a result of the union of the Associate and Reformed groups.) Feeling that the distances which separated them from their fellow members in the North were too great, the synod of the Carolinas withdrew in 1822 from the Associate Reformed Church to form the Associate Reformed Synod of the South. Following the creation of the United Presbyterian Church in 1858 (which this group never joined), they dropped the phrase "of the South," thereby becoming the Associate Reformed Presbyterian Church. They became a general synod in 1935.

The standards of the Westminster Confession are followed. For some years the only music in this church was the singing of the Psalms; this was modified in 1946 to permit the use of selected hymns. Foreign mission stations are located in Pakistan and Mexico. *The Associate Reformed Presbyterian* is published weekly at Due West, South Carolina; Erskine College and Erskine Theological Seminary are also maintained there. The William Dunlap Orphanage is located at Brighton, Tennessee. There is a summer assembly ground, "Bonlarken," at Flat Rock, North Carolina. Total membership is placed at 28,427 in 144 churches.

Bible Presbyterian Church

In 1936, during the fundamentalist-modernist controversy in the Presbyterian churches, a group of about 100 ministers, led by Dr. J. Gresham Machen of Princeton Theological Seminary, withdrew from the Presbyterian Church in the U.S.A. to establish the Presbyterian Church in America, later renamed the Orthodox Presbyterian Church. Two years later, with the controversy still raging and complicated by the formation of an American Council of Christian Churches and an International Council of Christian Churches, a group led by Dr. Carl McIntire withdrew from this Orthodox Presbyterian Church to organize the Bible Presbyterian Church; the group also withdrew from both councils in 1955. A majority of the local churches, however, continued in the councils through the Bible Presbyterian Church Association. The General Synod of the next year, 1956, divided into two synods—the Bible Presbyterian Church (Columbus Synod) and the Bible Presbyterian Church (Collingswood Synod). So from 1956 to July, 1961, there were two separate Bible Presbyterian churches representing the two different Synods. In 1961 the Bible Presbyterian Church (Columbus Synod) changed its name to the Evangelical Presbyterian Church, which later (1965) united with the Reformed Presbyterian Church in North America to become the Reformed Presbyterian Church, Evangelical Synod. In the same year the Collingswood body dropped that name and continued as the Bible Presbyrian Church.

The word "Bible" is included in the name of this church to emphasize its conservative, Bible-based position. It is thoroughly fundamentalist, subscribing to the Westminster Confession of Faith (including the Larger and Shorter Catechisms); it opposes all "social gospel" teaching and refuses to have fellowship with "that which compromises and which represents unbelief" in such doctrines as those of the verbal and infallible inspiration of the Bible, the virgin birth, the blood atonement, and the bodily resurrection of Christ. Through the American Council of Christian Churches it carries on a continuing debate with the National Council of the Churches of Christ in the U.S.A., which it considers apostate, and through the International Council of Christian Churches it stands opposed to the ecumenical policies and liberal doctrine of the World Council of Churches.

There are distinct breaks here with the usual Presbyterian polity. The property of the local church is guaranteed to the church itself. Local congregations may call their pastors "without interference" (by presbyteries, synods, etc.). Any church may withdraw at any time "for reasons sufficient to themselves." The work of the church is carried on through independent agencies, such as the Independent Board for Foreign Missions and Faith Theological Seminary, "leaving the presbyteries and synods as places for fellowship." There are about 8,000 members.

Cumberland Presbyterian Church

An outgrowth of the great revival of 1800, the Cumberland Presbytery was organized on February 4, 1810, in Dickson County, Tennessee, by 3 Presbyterian ministers, the Revs. Finis Ewing, Samuel King, and Samuel McAdow. Contributing factors to the organization were a rejection by the founders of the doctrine of fatality of the Westminster Confession of Faith and an insistence that the rigid standards of the Presbyterian Church for the education of the clergy be relaxed in the light of extraordinary circumstances existing on the American frontier. A union with the Presbyterian Church, U.S.A., in 1906 was only partially successful. A considerable segment, to whom the terms of union were unsatisfactory, perpetuated the Cumberland Presbyterian Church as a separate denomination.

This church reports 88,738 members in 877 congregations located for the most part in 11 southern states, with some congregations in the state of Indiana, Illinois, Ohio, Michigan, Iowa, Kansas, New Mexico, and California.

The church sponsors missionaries in Colombia, Japan, and the Hong Kong area. The Cumberland Presbyterian Theological Seminary is located at Memphis, Tennessee. Bethel College is located at McKenzie, Tennessee. There is a Cumberland Presbyterian children's home at Denton, Texas; publishing house and headquarters are at Memphis.

Second Cumberland Presbyterian Church in the United States (Formerly Colored Cumberland Presbyterian Church)

This church was built on the 20,000 Negro membership of the pre-Civil War Cumberland Presbyterian Church with the full approval of the general assembly of that church held in 1869. The first 3 presbyteries were organized in Tennessee, where the first synod, the Tennessee Synod, was organized in 1871. In doctrine this church follows the Westminster Confession with 4 reservations: (1) there are no eternal reprobates; (2) Christ died for all mankind, not for the elect alone; (3) there is no infant damnation; and (4) the Spirit of God operates in the world coextensively with Christ's atonement in such manner "as to leave all men inexcusable." There were 19 presbyteries, 4 synods—Alabama, Tennessee, Kentucky, and Texas—121 churches, and 30,000 members found in all sections of the country in 1949. In May of 1940 the general assembly accepted an overture from a presbytery of 17 churches and 1 school in Liberia, Africa, and voted to make it a part of the Second Cumberland Presbyterian Church.

Orthodox Presbyterian Church

This church was organized June 11, 1936, in protest against what were believed to be modernistic tendencies in the Presbyterian Church in the U.S.A. (now the United Presbyterian Church in the U.S.A.).

Led by Dr. J. Gresham Machen, the dissenters had formed a foreign missionary society which they were ordered to disband; refusing, they were tried, convicted, and suspended from the Presbyterian Church in the U.S.A. They organized the Presbyterian Church of America; an injunction brought against the use of that name by the parent body resulted in the change in 1938 to the name Orthodox Presbyterian Church.

The Westminster Confession and the Westminster Larger and Shorter Catechism are accepted as subordinate doctrinal standards or creedal statements. Strong emphasis is laid upon the infallibility and inerrancy of the Bible (the books of the Bible were written by men "so guided by Him that their original manuscripts were without error in fact or doctrine"); original sin; the virgin birth, deity, and substitutionary atonement of Christ; his resurrection and ascension; his role as judge at the end of the world and the consummation of the Kingdom; the sovereignty of God; and salvation through the sacrifice and power of Christ for those "whom the Father purposes to save." Salvation is "not because of good works, [but] it is in order to do good works."

The Presbyterian system of government is followed; a general assembly meets annually. The church constitution contains the creedal statement of the group, a form of government, book of discipline, and directory for the worship of God. The church has published the *Trinity Hymnal*, which is probably the only hymnal designed as a worship supplement to the Westminster Confession of Faith. Committees appointed by the general assembly conduct work in home missions, Christian education and general benevolence. With 14,871 members in 123 churches and 24 chapels, the church is a constituent member of the Reformed Ecumenical Synod, an international association of churches holding the Reformed faith.

Reformed Presbyterian Church, Evangelical Synod

Merged in April of 1965 at Lookout Mountain, Tennessee, this church is the result of a merger in 1965 of the Reformed Presbyterian Church in North America (General Synod) and the Evangelical Presbyterian Church. The Reformed Church was founded in 1774, when its first presbytery was constituted in Dolphin County, Pennsylvania. More than a century later (1965), this Reformed Church merged with the Evangelical Presbyterian Church, which had split from the Orthodox Presbyterian Church in 1937.

This church is active in protest against apostasy and worldliness and has no affiliation with any church councils or associations. It operates Covenant Theological Seminary in St. Louis and Covenant College in Lookout Mountain, Georgia. Their National Presbyterian Missions Board assists in establishing new local churches in the U. S. and Canada, and World Presbyterian Missions works in 11 nations with 85 missionaries. They have 10 chaplains on active duty with the armed forces; they report a total membership of 15,262 communicant members in 138 churches located in the United States, Canada, and India. The Church is now considering reuniting with the Orthodox Presbyterian Church.

Reformed Presbyterian Church of North America

A body of direct Covenanter lineage, its first minister came to this country from the Reformed Presbytery of Scotland in 1752. Most of the early membership joined the union with the Associate Presbytery in 1782, but a small group remained outside the union and reorganized at Philadelphia under the name Reformed Presbytery in 1798. A synod was constituted at Philadelphia in 1809, only to split in 1833 into Old Light and New Light groups in a dispute over citizenship and the right of its members to vote or participate generally in public affairs; the general synod of the Reformed Presbyterian Church (New Light) imposed no such restriction. This restriction was finally removed in 1964; members are free to participate in civil government and to vote on issues and for candidates who are committed to Christian principles of civil government.

The government of this Church is thoroughly Presbyterian except that there is no general assembly. The Westminster Confession is the doctrinal standard. Members observe closed communion, use only the Psalms and permit no instrumental music in their services. Members cannot join any secret society.

Home missionaries are currently opening new work in seven states under a Board of Home Missions and Church Extension; foreign missionaries are at work in Cyprus, Japan, and Taiwan. There is a college at Beaver Falls, Pennsylvania (Geneva College), a theological seminary at Pittsburgh, and 1 home for the aged. There are 5,621 members in 70 churches.

REFORMED BODIES

When the Belgic Confession was written in 1561 as the creedal cornerstone of the Reformed churches in Belgium and Holland, the "Churches in the Netherlands which sit under the Cross" gave thanks to their God in the preface of that document, where they said, "The blood of our brethren . . . crieth out." There was real cause for crying out, but the Reformation was spreading into the Netherlands from Switzerland in the midst of the long Dutch struggle against Catholic Spain. The Dutch Reformed Church was cradled in cruelty.

Those Reformation-founded churches called Reformed, as distinguished from those called Lutheran, originated in Switzerland under Zwingli, Calvin, and Melanchthon; they were Reformed in Switzerland, Holland, and Germany; they were Presbyterian in England and Scotland and Huguenot in France; still others in Bohemia and Hungary used national names. As they moved overseas to the American colonies, they formed into 4 groups of churches; 2 from Holland became the Reformed Church in America and the Christian Reformed Church; 1 from the German Palatinate became the Reformed Church in the United States, later known as the Evangelical and Reformed Church and now merged with the Congregational Christian churches in the United Church of Christ; the fourth, coming from Hungary, became the Free Magyar Reformed Church in America. All of them were and still are Calvinistic and conservative, basing their doctrine generally upon the Heidelberg Catechism, the Belgic Confession, and the Canons of the Synod of Dortrecht, and using a modified Presbyterian form of government.

Reformed Church in America

This church had an unorganized membership along the upper reaches of the Hudson River in the neighborhood of Fort Orange (Albany), New York, in 1614. Members had no regularly established congregations or churches; but they were numerous enough to require the services of Reformed ministers, 2 of whom came from Holland in 1623 as "comforters of the sick." By 1628 the Dutch in New Amsterdam had a pastor of their own in Dominie Jonas Michaelius and an organized Collegiate Church, which was to become the oldest church in the middle colonies and the oldest church in America with an uninterrupted ministry.

When the English took New Amsterdam in 1664, Dutch churches were thriving in Albany, Kingston, Brooklyn, Manhattan, and at Bergen in New Jersey. As the immigration from Holland ceased, there were perhaps 8,000 Dutch churchmen and churchwomen in the country, holding their services in Dutch and served by either native clergymen or pastors sent from Holland. It was difficult and expensive to send native-born ministerial candidates to Holland for education and ordination; the question rent the Reformed Church and was finally resolved in the building of a college and seminary at New Brunswick (Queen's College, later Rutgers). It was the first theological seminary to be built in this country, and it was fathered by the famous Dominie Theodore Frelinghuysen, who also took a leading part in the revival called the Great Awakening.

A sharp controversy disputing the authority of the classis of Amsterdam resulted in the complete independence of the Dutch churches in America; a general body and 5 particular bodies were created, a constitution was drawn up in 1792, and the general synod was organized in 1794. The names Dutch Reformed Church in North America and Reformed Dutch Church in the United States of America were both in use in 1792; in 1819 the church was incorporated as the Reformed

Protestant Dutch Church, and in 1867 it became the Reformed Church in America.

The American Revolution had little effect upon the Reformed Church in America except to offer the Dutchmen a chance to even matters with the English. Once the war was over, Scottish, English, and Germans began joining the church, creating a problem in the use of the Dutch tongue which took years to resolve. A second Dutch immigration from the Netherlands started in the middle of the nineteenth century, bringing whole Dutch congregations with their pastors. One group, led by Dominie Albertus van Raalte, settled in western Michigan and established the community called Holland, known today for Hope College, Western Theological Seminary, and an annual tulip festival. Van Raalte and his group became part of the Reformed Church in America in 1850. Another colony, led by Dominie Scholte, settled in Pella, Iowa, in 1947-48 and in 1856 merged with the Reformed Church in America except for a small dissenting group.

Domestic missions began in 1786; actually, missionary work among the Indians had begun much earlier. Needy and destitute churches in New York, Pennsylvania, and Kentucky were assisted by the domestic missionaries of the classis of Albany for many years, and in 1806 the general synod took over administration of all missionary agencies. This church cooperated with the American Board of Commissioners for Foreign Missions. In 1832 the Board of Foreign Missions was created but continued to work through the American Board until 1857, from which time it has operated independently. Insisting from the start upon 7 years of college and seminary training for its ministers, the church established the Education Society of the Reformed Church in America in 1828 and changed it to the Board of Education of the General Synod in 1831.

The explicit statements and principles of the Belgic Confession, the Heidelberg Catchism, and the Synod of Dortrecht are still the doctrinal standard of the Reformed Church in America. The mild and gentle spirit of the confession with its emphasis upon salvation through Christ is a central theme; the primacy of God and his power in human life are at the heart of the preaching of the church as they are at the heart of the canons of Dortrecht; and the Heidelberg Catechism, based as it is on the Apostles' Creed, is employed in many catechetical classes. The divine authority of the Scriptures is important here; "the final authority in the Reformed faith is the Holy Scripture, the living Word of God, spoken to every man through the Holy Spirit of God."

Worship is semi-liturgical, but it is an optional liturgy; only the forms for baptism and the Lord's Supper, the 2 recognized sacraments of the church, are obligatory. It is a corporate or congregational way of worship, blending form and freedom and distinguishing this church from other Protestant communions. A new edition of the Liturgy and Psalter was published in 1968.

Government of the church stands midway between the Episcopal and Presbyterian forms; it might be called "modified Presbyterian." The governing body in the local church is the consistory, made up of elders, deacons, and the pastor, who is always president. Elders are charged with the guidance of the spiritual life of the church, and deacons are in charge of benevolences; but they generally meet and act as one body. A number of churches in a limited area are grouped into a classis, which has immediate supervision of the churches and the ministry, and is composed of all the ministers of the area and an elder from each consistory. Classes are grouped into particular synods, of which there are 6, meeting annually and made up of an equal number of ministers and elders from each classis, and supervising the planning and programing of the churches within the area. The higher court of the church is the general synod, representing the entire church, meeting once a year and composed of delegations of ministers and elders from each classis; the size of the delegation depends upon the size of the classis.

In 1968 this church underwent a process of "restructure" which drastically changed its form of government. Formerly there were 4 national boards (world missions, North American missions, education, and pensions) together with agencies working under these boards; the boards have now been unified in a general program council, which has taken over their responsibilities. There are fewer board members under this plan, but each of the 44 classes in the United States has a representative on the council. The program staff is assisted by 3 "service offices" (administration and finance, promotion and communications, and human resources). As of 1973, a further process of decentralization is taking place: new "Centers" will be organized on a regional basis, to expedite work peculiar to those regions.

Foreign missionaries are appointed to work in 11 areas abroad; home missionaries work among Dutch immigrants in Canada, and among Chinese, Japanese-Americans, Negroes, Indians, migrants, and sharecroppers. Scholarships and student aid are provided in 3 colleges and 2 theological seminaries. Membership in 1973 stood at 225,000 in 911 churches.

Christian Reformed Church

With a membership of 287,114 in 750 churches, this Reformed group began in Michigan in 1847 and was affiliated with the Reformed Church in America from 1850 to 1857, when they found themselves in disagreement with the parent church on matters of doctrine and discipline. A conference held at Holland, Michigan, in 1857, effected the separation of the True Holland Reformed Church from the Reformed Church in America. Through a series of changes in name, the True Holland Reformed Church became the present Christian Reformed Church. Immigration from Holland and anti-Masonic agitation in the Reformed Church in America brought several other groups into the new organization and rapidly increased its membership.

233

The Christian Reformed Church today is largely an English-speaking church, although Dutch, German, Navajo, and Spanish are used in some of their churches. Doctrine shows no important differences from accepted Reformed standards; the 3 historic creeds are accepted. Organization bears the usual Reformed markings, including 37 classes which meet every 4 months (in some cases every 6 months) but with no intermediate or particular synods between the classes and a general synod made up of 2 ministers and 2 elders from each classis meets annually.

One hundred and eighty-five home missionaries in Canada and the United States maintain ministries among the unchurched, Navajo and Zuni Indians, blacks, Chinese, Spanish-Americans, and on many university campuses. One hundred fifty-eight foreign missionaries are stationed in Japan, South America, Northern Nigeria, Cuba, Taiwan, Mexico, Guam, Korea, Puerto Rico, the Philippines, Australia, Honduras, and Liberia. The Christian Reformed World Relief Committee carries on a worldwide relief program.

The "Back to God Hour" radio broadcast from a chain of stations in the United States reaches Canada, Europe, and Arabia, and a Spanish broadcast covers all of South America. There are 3 colleges—Calvin College and Seminary in Grand Rapids, Dordt College in Sioux Center, Iowa, and Trinity College in Palos Heights, Illinois. A publishing house is located in Grand Rapids, providing literature for the church at large and for the unique Christian school societies made up of parents who work to support a national educational program.

Hungarian Reformed Church in America

The Hungarian Reformed Church in America is the successor to a work begun in the United States by the Reformed Church of Hungary in 1904. Work among Hungarian Reformed people had actually begun in 1891, under the auspices of other interested Calvinistic groups, but that sponsored by the parent body in Hungary soon became the most vital and popular, and by 1912 there were 2 classes affiliated with the church in Hungary. With the break-up of the Austro-Hungarian Empire and the impoverishment of Hungary, the Reformed Church in that country transferred jurisdiction of its churches in the United States to the Reformed Church in the United States, in an agreement reached at Tiffin, Ohio, in 1921. Three of the original congregations and 4 more recently organized refused to accept the agreement, and united to form the Free Magyar Reformed Church in America at Duquesne, Pennsylvania, in 1924. The present name was adopted in 1958.

The church's polity is a combination of Episcopal and Presbyterian elements developed in Hungary in the eighteenth century. It is made up of 3 classes—New York, Eastern, and Western—which form a diocese headed by an elected bishop and lay curator. Doctrinal standards are those of the Heidelberg Catchism and the Second Helvetic Confession. Diocesan meetings are held annually, and a "constitutional" meeting is held every 3 years. There are 27 congregations with 11,250 baptized members, in 10 states: Connecticut, New York, New Jersey, Pennsylvania, Ohio, Michigan, Florida, Kansas, Colorado, and California. There are also 2 congregations in Onterio, Canada. The church is a constituent member of the World Alliance of Reformed Churches, the National Council of Churches, and the World Council of Churches.

Netherlands Reformed Congregations

This is the smallest of all Reformed groups in the United States; it has 22 churches and 7,319 communicants and 4,195 baptized members. Its short history began with a secession from the state church in Holland; Dutch immigrants formed their first 2 churches in South Holland, Illinois (1865), and Grand Rapids, Michigan (1870), basing their belief on the Belgic Confession, the Heidelberg Catechism, and the Canons of Dortrecht. There are 9 additional churches in Canada, with a total of 8 Sunday schools and 7 clergymen; a synod meets every 2 years.

Protestant Reformed Churches of America

Three consistories of the Classis Grand Rapids East and Grand Rapids West of the Christian Reformed Church, with their pastors, were deposed from that church as the result of a disagreement over the doctrine of common grace (Arminianism). The debate began in 1923; the dissenters were formally organized as Protestant Reformed Churches of America in 1926. They stand for particular grace, for the elect alone, and hold to the 3 Reformed confessions—the Heidelberg Catechism, the Belgic or Netherlands Confession, and the Canons of Dortrecht—as the basis of their belief in the infallible Word of God. In government they are Presbyterian, subscribing to the 87 Articles of the Church Order of Dortrecht. Their general synod meets annually, in June.

A small theological seminary is maintained at Grand Rapids. An association of Protestant Reformed men in the same city publishes a bimonthly periodical known as *The Standard Bearer;* and another publication, a monthly called *Beacon Lights,* is issued by the denomination's young people's federation. There are 3,256 members in 19 churches located in Michigan, Illinois, Iowa, Wisconsin, Minnesota, Colorado, California, Washington, North and South Dakota.

Reformed Church in the United States

When the original Reformed Church in the United States (see p. 231) merged with the Evangelical and Reformed Church in 1934, one protesting body, the Eureka Classis in the Dakotas, decided to continue as the Reformed Church in the United States and exists today under that name. Their doctrines are those set forth in the Heidelberg Catechism; they have 22 churches and an inclusive membership of 4,008 baptized and communicant members, and 24 churches.

ROMAN CATHOLIC CHURCH

For the first 1,500 years of Christendom, up to the time of the Protestant Reformation, the Western world was almost solidly Roman Catholic. The eleventh-century separation left the faith divided between Roman Catholic and Eastern Orthodox sectors. The Reformation left continental Europe and the British Isles divided among Roman Catholic, Lutheran, Anglican, and Reformed Churches, with the prospect of still further division as denominationalism increased.

The Roman Catholic Church dates its beginning from the moment of Christ's selection of the apostle Peter as guardian of the keys of heaven and earth and as chief of the apostles, and it claims this fisherman as its first pope. It gained temporal authority and power when it arose as the only body strong enough to rule after the fall of the city of Rome in A.D. 410. A house of terror ravaged first by Goths, Vandals, and Franks, and then by Saxons, Danes, Alemanni, Lombards, and Burgundians, Europe found its only steadying hand in the church. Without the church, anarchy would have been king from Britain to the Bosphorus.

The first mention of the term Catholic (meaning universal) Church was made by Ignatius about A.D. 110-15, but the first real demonstrations of its Roman authority came as it won the barbarians to its banners while it kept the flame of faith burning in its churches and the candle of wisdom alive in its monastic schools. Augustine deeply influenced its theological and philosophical structure, and he gave papacy its finest justification and defense. He left it strong enough to give crowns or deny them to Europe's kings.

The church beat back the threats of its enemies at home and from afar; it converted the barbarian, won against the Saracen, and employed the Inquisition against the heretic boring from within. It brought the hopeful interval known as the Peace of God; it also supported chivalry and feudalism, fought the Crusades, built schools, created a noble art and literature. For long centuries the Benedictine monasteries guarded and preserved learning and culture in Europe; this order of monks was founded in 529 in Italy by St. Benedict; since its founding more than 4 million men have practiced the Benedictine rule of life. Centuries later (1209) St. Francis of Assisi established the Franciscan order, and at about the same time St. Dominic began his Order of Friars Preachers (Dominicans).

Inevitably there came the temptations of power and prosperity from without. Then came the Reformation. Roman Catholic scholars readily admit that there were corrupt individuals within the church and that reform was necessary. Indeed, reform was under way before the Reformation broke; Martin Luther himself was a Catholic reformer within the church before he became a Protestant. Erasmus and Savonarola wrote and preached against the corruption and worldliness of certain Roman Catholic leaders and laymen, but they stayed within the church. That all these reformers had a case against the members of the Roman Church is not denied by the Roman Catholics; they do, however, maintain that while priests and bishops and even popes may err, the one true church cannot err, and that Luther was wrong in rebelling against the church. But rebel he did, and the Roman church suffered its most fateful division.

There were, too, other reasons for the revolt. There was the growth of nationalism and secularism, the ambitions of political princes and rulers with great personal ambitions who wanted no interference from the church. And there was the Renaissance, with its revival of Greek and Roman pagan influences and emphases. All these forces worked together to produce the Reformation. The Counter Reformation was effective in halting the spread of the new Protestantism in Europe and won back some areas to the Roman Catholic Church and faith; one of its chief instruments was the Society of Jesus (Jesuits), an educational and missionary order founded by Ignatius of Loyola in 1534.

But long before Luther, Roman Catholics had reached America. The first Roman Catholic diocese on this side of the Atlantic was established in Greenland in 1125; there were bishops in residence there until 1377. Priests of Catholic Spain came with Columbus in 1492; missionaries came with Coronado and with the other early Spanish explorers. Most of them perished; one of them started the first permanent parish in America at St. Augustine, Florida, in 1565.

French explorers, *voyageurs*, and colonizers—Cartier, Joliet, Marquett, and others—were generally Roman Catholics accompanied by missionary groups. Among them were the Recollects, Jesuits, Sulpicians, Capuchins, and the secular clergy. New France became a vicariate apostolic in 1658 with Bishop Laval at its head. The See of Quebec (1674) had spiritual jurisdiction over all the vast province of France in North America, reaching down the valley of the Mississippi to Louisiana.

In 1634 the Roman Catholics founded Maryland; later they were restricted by law in Maryland and in most other colonies, and the restrictions were not removed until after the Revolution. In the face of these restrictions and in view of the fact that most of the colonial immigrants were Protestants, the Roman Catholic Church grew slowly. In 1696 there were only 7 Catholic families in New York, and 80 years later they were still traveling to Philadelphia to receive the sacraments. In 1763 there were less than 25,000 Catholics in all the colonies; they were under the jurisdiction of the vicar apostolic of London.

Among the signatures on the Articles of Confederation, the Declaration of Independence, and the Constitution are found those of Thomas Fitzsimmons, Daniel Carroll, and Charles Carroll of Carrollton, all of whom were Catholics. The Revolution brought them religious as well as political freedom; religious equality became the law with the adoption of the Constitution in 1787.

There was no immediate hierarchal superior in the United States when the war ended, and the vicar apostolic in London refused to exercise jurisdiction over the "rebels." After long investigation and delay and an appeal to Rome the Rev. John Carroll was named superior, or prefect apostolic, of the church in the 13 original states. At that time there were 15,800 Catholics in Maryland, 700 in Pennsylvania, 200 in Virginia, and 1,500 in New York, unorganized and with no priests. At the turn of the century there were 80 churches and about 150,000 Roman Catholics; by 1890 there were 6,231,417—a growth due primarily to the flood tide of immigration from the Catholic countries of Europe.

Baltimore became the first American diocese in 1789 and an archdiocese in 1808; other dioceses and archdioceses were formed as the church expanded. Three plenary or national councils were held at Baltimore in 1852, 1866, and 1884. Archbishop John McCloskey became the first American cardinal in 1875, and Archbishop Gibbons of Baltimore was elevated to the same rank in 1877.

The Civil War and two world wars failed to disturb the work of the church or to interrupt its growth; indeed World War I produced one of the ablest hierarchal Roman Catholic agencies in the country—the National War Council, now known as the United States Catholic Conference. There were 18,608,003 Catholics in the United States in 1926; by 1972 the Roman Catholic Church was the largest church in the United States, with 48,390,990 members in approximately 18,250 churches. About 23 percent of the American people identified themselves as Roman Catholics.

The faith and doctrine of Catholicism are founded upon "that deposit of faith given to it by Christ and through his apostles, sustained by the Bible and by tradition." Thus, they accept as official creeds the Apostles' Creed, the Nicene-Constantinople Creed, the Athanasian Creed, and the Creed of Pius IV, also called the Creedal Statement of the Council of Trent. In 1968, Pope Paul VI proclaimed a "Creed of the People of God," which was offered in explanation of the creedal position of the church, but in view of the amazing reforms and changes which have swept the Roman Catholic Church since Pope John XXIII, it has become almost impossible to emphasize any detail in doctrine; a new era of open discussion and broad interpretation is prevalent in the whole church, and changes come swiftly. Doctrine remains, however, deeply rooted in the rock of the 4 historic creeds.

Baptism, necessary for membership in the church, is administered to both infants and adults by pouring, and all baptized persons are considered to be members of the church. Confirmation by the laying on of hands by a bishop and anointing with the holy chrism in the for of a cross follows baptism. The laity usually receive the Eucharist (Lord's Supper) in the form of bread alone; the body and blood of Christ are considered as actually present in the eucharistic elements. The sacrament of penance is one through which postbaptismal sins are forgiven. The anointing of the sick is for those seriously ill or injured. The sacrament of holy orders is one of ordination for deacons, priests, and bishops. Marriage is a sacrament which "cannot be dissolved by any human power"; this rules out divorce with remarriage. Members are required to attend Mass on Sundays and obligatory holy days, to fast and abstain on certain appointed days, to confess at least once a year, to receive the Holy Eucharist during the Easter season, to contribute to the support of pastors, and to observe strictly the marriage regulations of the church.

The government of the Roman Catholic Church is hierarchal and authoritarian, but laymen are frequently consulted on certain phases of parish work. (The trend is toward more and more lay participation, since Pope John.) At the head of the structure stands the pope, who is also Bishop of Rome and "Vicar of Christ on earth and the Visible Head of the Church." His authority is supreme in all matters of faith and discipline. Next to him is the College of Cardinals. Although laymen were once chosen to be cardinals, the office has been limited to priests since 1918; the last lay cardinal died in 1876. Many of the cardinals live in Rome, acting as advisors to the pope and as heads or members of the various congregations or commissions supervising the administration of the church. When a pope dies, the cardinals elect his successor; they hold authority in the interim. The Roman Curia is the official body of papal administrative offices through which the pope governs the church; it is composed of congregations, tribunals, and curial offices.

In the United States there are 9 cardinals, 53 archbishops, 320 bishops, and nearly 57,500 priests. The archbishop is in charge of the archdiocese and has precedence in his province. There are 31 archdioceses and 131 dioceses. Bishops are the ruling authority in the dioceses, but appeals from their decisions may be taken to the apostolic delegate at Washington and even to Rome. The parish pastor is responsible to the bishop; he is appointed by the bishop or archbishop and holds authority to celebrate Mass and administer the sacraments with the help of such other priests as the parish may need. Bishops are appointed from Rome, usually upon suggestions from the hierarchy in the United States.

The clergy of the church includes deacons, priests, and bishops. Candidates for orders studying in divinity schools are called seminarians; there are 23,000 of them in 106 diocesan seminaries and 326 religious and scholasticate seminaries. The usual seminary course covers a period of 8 years of study after high school—4 years of philosophy and 4 years of theology. Those in religious orders also spend 1 or 2 years in a novitiate.

Since the restoration of the permanent deaconate in 1967, hundreds of men have completed the training course and been ordained deacons. Most of these men are married and over 35. They are empowerd to preach, baptize, distribute Holy Communion, and officiate at weddings. Most deacons support themselves in secular jobs and exercise their ministry on weekends and evenings. Another 600 men in the U.S. are preparing for ordination as deacons.

In 1972 there were 26,727 diocesan or secular priests in the United States and 20,694 priests who belonged to religious orders and congregations. Add to these the 9,740 lay brothers and the 146,914 sisters engaged in the work, and their importance in the overall task of the church becomes clear. The official *Catholic Directory* lists a total of 101 religious orders of priests and brothers, 24 religious orders for brothers only, and over 400 orders of women. They differ widely in their work. Some are "contemplative" orders, remaining in their monasteries or cloistered convents. Those in active or mixed religious orders engage in teaching, care of the sick, missionary work, writing, or social work. Some orders consist only of brothers who teach or nurse the sick, or otherwise assist the ordained leaders in the work of the order, or carry on their own labors in teaching or social work. Those in brotherhoods or sisterhoods are required to take vows of poverty, chastity and obedience, but are not ordained; they engage primarily in educational, philanthropic, and charitable work. (Technically, the only orders for ordained men are the Dominicans, Carmelites, Benedictines, Augustinians, and Jesuits, but ordinarily any religious community of men or women is called a religious order.)

Besides religious orders and congregations, Catholics may join secular institutions whose members also observe poverty, chastity, and obedience but do not wear any distinctive garb or live together in a community; before receiving approval as secular institutes engaged in apostolic work, these groups may operate as approved "pious unions." Worldwide membership in these institutes and unions exceeds 15,000. Some members are also ordained priests.

Three ecclesiastical councils form an important part of the Catholic system; they are known as general or ecumenical, plenary or national, and provincial councils. A general council is called by the pope or with his consent; it is composed of all Roman Catholic bishops of the world, and its actions on matters of doctrine and discipline must be approved by the pope. Plenary councils are made up of the bishops resident in a given country; their acts, too, must be submitted to the Holy See before promulgation. Below them are diocesan and provincial councils which make further promulgation and application of the decrees passed by the other councils and approved by the pope. Pope John XXIII summoned the bishop of the church to the twenty-first ecumenical council known as the Second Vatican Council. Following his death Pope Paul VI reconvened the council, which stimulated liturgical reform, Catholic participation in the ecumenical movement, updated many church practices, and inaugurated the idea of collegiality among the bishops. In 1968 Paul VI reaffirmed the official church position against any form of birth control except total or partial abstinence from sex relations in marriage; many theologians, priests, and laymen protested against this, voicing opposition to the encyclical *Humanae Vitae*, and the hierarchies of such countries as France, Canada, Belgium, Holland, Switzerland, Austria, and West Germany interpreted the papal position in the light of the freedom of the individual conscience.

The central act of worship is the Mass; its two principal parts are the Liturgy of the Word and the Eucharistic Liturgy. Some of the chief parts of the Liturgy of the Word are the readings from the Old and New Testaments, the homily or sermon, the Nicene Creed and the Prayer of the Faithful. The Eucharistic Liturgy includes the offering of the bread and wine, the consecration, the Lord's Prayer, and the communion. From the third century to 1963 the Western Church prescribed Latin as the liturgical language; now the entire Mass is recited in the vernacular by both priest and people. Besides the Mass, Catholics may participate in popular devotions such as the benedictions, rosary, stations of the cross, novenas, and Bible vigils.

With the most centralized government in Christendom, the Holy See at Rome has representatives in many countries of the world. Roman Catholic churches have been established in 217 countries with a total membership of over 633,000,000. The majority of Italians, Spanish, Irish, Austrians, Poles, Latin Americans, Belgians, Hungarians, Southern Germans, Portugese, French, and Filipinos are baptized Roman Catholics. The Society for the Propagation of the Faith is the overall representative missionary body. In 110 foreign countries there are 7,699 missionaries sent out from the United States.

Education has been a primary interest of Roman Catholics ever since the establishment of a classical school at St. Augustine, Florida, in 1606. As of 1972, there are 9,206 elementary parochial and private schools in this country with 3,105,470 students, 1,815 diocesan and parochial high schools with 961,996 students. More than 428,000 students attend the 273 Catholic colleges and universities, including Notre Dame, Fordham, Georgetown, Boston College, St. Louis, Marquette, Catholic Loyola, and Villanova. There are 188,527 full-time teachers in Catholic schools of whom 8,700 are priests, 4,302 are brothers, 70,664 are sisters, and 104,236 are lay teachers. An estimated total of 1,400,000 Catholics attend non-Catholic colleges and universities.

Almost every diocese publishes a weekly newspawer; there are 145 newspapers and 275 periodicals. The *National Catholic Reporter* is probably the most influential (and controversial) Catholic publication; others include *Commonweal, America, Catholic World, U.S. Catholic,* and *Sign.* Periodicals reflecting a more conservative position include *Triumph, Twin Circle,* and *National Catholic Register.*

Roman Catholic charity and welfare work is conducted by many different organizations, religious and otherwise. The National Conference on Catholic Charities acts more and more in coordinating work on state and national levels; work is also conducted by several religious orders of men and women devoting full-time to the relief of the poor in homes or in institutions; there are also bureaus of charities in many of the dioceses. The Society of St. Vincent de Paul is perhaps the largest and most effective charity organization; numerous others—the Little Sisters of the Poor, the Sisters of Charity, the Daughters of Charity of the Society of St. Vincent de Paul, the Sisters of Mercy, and the Third Order of Franciscans—are active among the poor in Catholic hospitals, orphanages, and homes for the aged. There are 930 general and special hospitals treating 19,543,727 patients annually; one out of every three beds in the nation's private hospitals has been provided by the Catholic hospital system. There are 432 homes for the aged and 206 orphanages.

The members of the hierarchy are also members of the United States Catholic Conference, which operates as a clearinghouse of information; this is not a council or a legislative body, so the resolutions of its meetings do not have the force of law. It faciliates discussion of all policies affecting the interests and activities of the church, and unifies, coordinates, and organizes work in social welfare education, and other activities. Every bishop in the United States and its territories and possessions has a voice in this conference.

A new phenomenon of the church will have important effect in the shaping of future structures: parish councils, created to aid the priests in the management of the parish and composed of laymen, have consultative powers; new diocesan senates, composed of priests, assist the bishop in the setting of policies in the diocese; and an entirely extracanonical institution is developing in the National Priests' Association, with chapters in each diocese, organized to aid the individual priest in his relation to his bishop and his ministry.

While most Roman Catholics belong to the Latin Rite, there are at least 20 groups of churches and an estimated 10 to 12 million other Catholics belonging to the Eastern Rites. These Catholics hold identical docrinal beliefs and recognize the authority of the pope, but they differ in language, liturgy, customs, church laws, and tradition. Generally they follow one of 5 historic rites: Byzantine, Alexandrian, Antiochian, Armenian, or Chaldean. Across the world the main Eastern Rite bodies are the Catholic Copts, Ethiopian Catholics, Syrians, Chaldeans, Catholic Armenians, Malabar Catholics, Byzantine Catholics, and Maronites.

Most of these Eastern Rite groups are represented in the United

States; there are about 735,000 of them here, all under the jurisdiction of one or another of the Eastern patriarchs. Largest of the Eastern Rites in the U.S. are the Ukranians with 285,000 members in 3 jurisdictions, the Ruthenians with 278,000, the Maronites with 152,406, and the Melkites with 55,000. Smaller rites serve Catholics of Romanian, Russian, or Armenian backgrounds.

Latin and Eastern Rite Catholics may attend Masses in either groups. Eastern Rite Catholics receive both bread and wine at Communion; they make the sign of the cross from the right to the left shoulder. Most of the Mass is said in the language of the congregation (Syrian, Armenian, etc).

SALVATION ARMY

William Booth, an ordained minister in the Methodist New Connexion body in England, regretfully left the pulpit of that church in 1861, to become a free-lance evangelistic preacher. This step led him, in 1865, to the slum areas in London's East End and to a dedication of his life to the poverty-stricken, unchurched masses in that area. His first plan was to make his work supplementary to that of the churches, but this proved impractical because many converts did not want to go where they were sent, often they were not accepted when they did go, and Booth soon found that he needed his converts to help handle the great crowds that came to his meetings. He began his work in Mile End Waste under the name of the Christian Mission; in 1878 the name was changed to the Salvation Army.

Being a Methodist, Booth first organized his movement along lines of Methodist polity, with annual conferences at which reports were made and programs planned. With the changing of the name to the Salvation Army, the whole organization became dominated by the new title. "Articles of War" (declaration of faith) were drawn up, and soon the mission stations became corps, members became soldiers, evangelists became officers, and converts were listed as seekers. Booth was designated as "general," and gradually he set up his organization on a military pattern which provided a direct line of authority and a practical system of training personnel for effective action. The leader reasoned that it was "just as valid to build an army of crusaders to save souls as it has been to send armies to recover a sepulchre."

The work spread quickly over England, Scotland, and Wales, and in 1880 it was officially established in the United States by a pioneer group under the direction of Commissioner George Scott Railton. Once committed to a policy of expansion, Booth lost no time in sending pioneering parties in different directions, reaching Australia and France in 1881; Switzerland, Sweden, India, and Canada in 1882; Iceland and South Africa in 1883; and Germany in 1886. Today the

Salvation Army is working in 79 countries and colonies with 24,969 officers, preaching the gospel in some 106 languages in 16,208 evangelical centers, and operating more than 3,003 social welfare institutions, hospitals, schools, and agencies. There is a general membership of about 360,000 in the Army.

Administratively the Army is under the command of "the General of the Salvation Army," with top leaders in charge of 50 territorial and departmental commands of which 23 encompass the work in "missionary" lands or subsidized areas. In this country the Army conducts its religious and social welfare program in all 50 states, implementing its purpose of preaching the gospel and effecting the spiritual, moral, and physical reclamation of persons coming under its influence through 9,320 centers of operation and including 6,983 service extension units. These are administered by more than 5,000 officers, assisted by about 16,000 employees.

The unit of the Army is the corps, of which there may be several in 1 city. Each corps is commanded by an officer—ranging in rank from lieutenant to major—who is responsible to a divisional headquarters. The 41 divisions in the United States each consist of a number of corps, and the work of each division is under the direct supervision of a divisional commander. The divisions are grouped into 4 territories—Eastern, Central, Southern, and Western—with headquarters in New York City, Chicago, Atlanta, and San Francisco. Territorial commanders are in charge of the work in each territory, and the 4 territorial headquarters are composed of departments to facilitate the supervision and direction of all phases of Army work. National headquarters is the coordinating office for the entire country, and the national commander is the chief administrative officer, official spokesman, and president of the Salvation Army Corporation established under the laws of New York and of local corporations in 15 other states. Property and revenues are in the custody of a board of trustees or directors, and citizens' advisory boards assist in interpreting the work of the Army to the general public.

Within the structure of the Army, converts who desire to become soldiers (members) are required to sign the Articles of War, after which, as members, they give volunteer service. The function of officers is similar to that of ministers of other churches, and officers are commissioned to full-time Salvation Army service.

Basic training for each officer, regardless of his field of service—evangelical or social—is a 2-year-in-residence course at one of the Army's 4 schools for officers' training located in New York, Chicago, Atlanta, and San Francisco. The chief source of officer candidates is the Salvation Army corps. After a soldier has served actively for at least 6 months, he may make application for officership and, if accepted, may enter the School for Officers' Training where his curriculum, in addition to formal study, includes practical field experience

in corps and social service institutions as well as orientation in all possible areas of Salvation Army service. He is graduated from the school
as a lieutenant and, following additional studies, is eligible thereafter
to attain the ranks of captain, major, lieutenant colonel, colonel, and
commissioner.

The motivating force of the Salvation Army in all of its work is
the religious faith of its officers and soldiers; and the fundamental
doctrines of the organization are stated in its Foundation Deed of
1878 in 11 cardinal affirmations. These statements document the
Army's recognition of the Bible as the only rule of Christian faith and
practice; of God who is the creator and Father of all mankind; the
Trinity of Father, Son, and Holy Ghost; Jesus Christ as Son of God
and Son of man; sin as the great destroyer of man's soul and society;
salvation as God's remedy for man's sins and man's ultimate and
eternal hope made available through Christ; sanctification as the
individual's present and maturing experience of a life set apart for
the holy purposes of the kingdom of God, and an eternal destiny
that may triumph over sin and death. While the Army has a dual
function of church and social agency, its first purpose is the salvation
of men "by the power of the Holy Spirit combined with the influence
of human ingenuity and love." To the Salvation Army, its social
services are merely a means of putting the socially disinherited—the
needy in both the physical and spiritual realm—into a condition to
be physically and spiritually uplifted. In meeting the needs of the
"whole man," the Army has established a widespread social welfare
program.

The work of the Army in the United States today includes: 121
treatment centers aiding 61,000 men annually. In 36 homes and
hospitals, 6,214 unwed mothers were cared for, in addition to
54,487 helped as outpatients. A total of 20,506 patients were admitted to the Army's 3 general hospitals and related institutions,
and 53,377 persons were given outpatient care; 55 camps, providing
camping facilities for 44,290 children, mothers, and senior citizens;
369 boys' and girls' clubs and community recreation centers, with
90,871 members; 19 Salvation Army-USO and Red Cross Shield
clubs for servicemen with a total attendance of 2,875,268; 399 can-
teens serving 687,770 persons in emergencies; Family Service Bureaus
serving 441,602 families; hotels and lodges for men and women, settlements, missing persons' bureaus and day care centers, care for the
alcoholics, correctional service bureaus working with prisoners and
their families, community centers for all ages, and other allied services.

These services were given without respect to race, color, creed, or
condition; the whole work is financed largely through voluntary sub-
scriptions, participation in federal funds, and annual maintenance
appeals from each service.

SCHWENKFELDER CHURCH

Kaspar Schwenkfeld von Ossig (1498-1561), a Silesian nobleman, was baptized and reared in the Roman Catholic Church and experienced a spiritual awakening in 1519. Disappointed in his hope to help reform the Roman Catholic Church from within, he played a leading role in the Reformation, advocating wider reading of the Bible by laymen, urging the need of the power, guidance, and leading of the Holy Spirit, and preaching that the sacramental eating in the Lord's Supper is a mystical partaking of Christ as food for the soul; the food is really bread. This interpretation of the Lord's Supper, together with his insistence upon complete separation of church and state, led him into disagreement with Luther and Lutheranism.

He founded a number of spiritual brotherhoods, whose members in time came to be known as Schwenkfelders.

The body has disappeared in Europe but persists in the United States in a church of 2,250 members in 5 local congregations. A large body of them arrived in this country in 1734; their first formal society of Schwenkfelders was organized in 1782. Their 5 churches today are all located within a radius of 50 miles of Philadelphia.

All theology, they hold, should be constructed from the Bible alone; but the Scriptures are considered as dead without the indwelling Word. Christ's divinity was progressive, his human nature becoming more and more divine without "losing its identity"; faith, regeneration, and subsequent spiritual growth work a change in human nature; but justification by faith is not to be permitted to obscure the positive regeneration imparted by Christ.

Their theology is thus Christocentric. In polity they are congregational, each church being incorporated, self-sustaining, and conducting its affairs through its district or local conference. A general conference composed of all the local churches meets twice a year to develop the larger program of education and missions. The general conference sponsored the founding of the Perkiomen School for boys at Pennsburg, Pennsylvania, in 1892; and a majority of the board of trustees of that school are still members of Schwenkfelder churches.

SOCIAL BRETHREN

This is a body organized in Illinois in 1867 by a small group of persons from various denominations, holding quite orthodox doctrines but disagreeing in certain matters of interpretation of Scripture, discipline, and decorum. In 1963 they reported 3 associations, each meeting annually, 1 general assembly meeting biennially, 31 churches located in Illinois, Michigan, and Indiana, and about 2,000 members.

Their confession of faith emphasizes the following points:

The infinite power, wisdom and goodness of God, in whom are united three persons of one substance, power and eternity, the Father, Son and Holy Ghost.

The authority and consistency of the Scriptures, comprising the Old and New Testaments, as containing all things necessary to salvation, "so that whatsoever is not read therein nor may be proved thereby is not required of any man that it should be believed as an article of faith or thought to be requisite or necessary to salvation."

Regeneration and sanctification through Christ.

Eternal salvation of the redeemed and eternal punishment for apostasy.

The ordinances of baptism and the Lord's Supper for true believers only. Baptism may be by sprinkling, pouring or immersion.

Lay members of the church should have the right of suffrage and free speech, but ministers are called to preach the Gospel and not for political speeches.

Polity is a fusion of Baptist and Methodist structures and customs; and the work of the Social Brethren, aside from efforts in mutual aid and assistance, is largely evangelistic.

SPIRITUALISTS

Spiritualism is as old as man's longing to communicate with his dead; as an organized religion it began at Hydesville, New York, in 1848 with the Fox sisters. The sisters heard repeated knockings or rappings in their cottage at Hydesville and later in Rochester, and believing them to be signals from the spirit world, worked out a code of communication. Their séances became famous, and interest in Spiritualism spread rapidly. However, in 1847 Andrew Jackson Davis had published a book entitled *Nature's Divine Revelations*, which stated the fundamentals and philosophy of Spiritualism; the séances of the Fox sisters only substantiated the writings of Davis.

The first Spiritualist organizations were small, scattered, and without legal sanction. Little groups gathered about the mediums, and in cities the congregations soon became large. The first attempt at national organization did not come until 1863 and lasted for only 9 years. In 1893 the National Spiritualist Association was organized in Chicago; it is today the outstanding Spiritualist body in the United States. Small, independent congregations are still scattered across the country, independent in polity and worship and unwilling to grant any real authority to a centralized government; but many state and sectional Spiritualist groups function under the general direction of the president and board of the N.S.A.

The movement is known popularly for its mediums, séances, clairvoyance, and so on. Ouija boards, table tipping, and spirit rappings and conversations have attracted thousands anxious to communicate with their departed ones. But Spiritualism has genuine religious bases and connotations as well as psychic experiments. The movement has become a church. The N.S.A. offers a Declaration of Principles, which reads as follows:

1. We believe in Infinite Intelligence.
2. We believe that the phenomena of Nature, both physical and spiritual, are the expression of Infinite Intelligence.
3. We affirm that a correct understanding of such expression and living in accordance therewith constitute true religion.
4. We affirm that the existence and personal identity of the individual continue after the change called death.
5. We affirm that communication with the so-called dead is a fact scientifically proven by the phenomena of Spiritualism.
6. We believe that the highest morality is contained in the Golden Rule. . . .
7. We affirm the moral responsibility of the individual, and that he makes his own happiness or unhappiness as he obeys or disobeys Nature's physical and spiritual laws.
8. We affirm that the doorway to reformation is never closed against any human soul, here or hereafter.
9. We affirm that the practice of Prophecy, as authorized by the Holy Bible, is a divine and God-given gift, reestablished and proven through mediumship by the phenomena of Spiritualism.

The teaching of God as love is central in Spiritualism; the Lord's Prayer is used in both public worship and private séance. Christ is recognized as a medium; the Annunciation was a message from the spirit world, the Transfiguration was an opportunity for the materialization of the spirits of Moses and Elias, and the Resurrection was evidence that all men live on in the spirit world. Man's soul is often called the "astral body"; at death the material body dissolves, and the soul as the body of the spirit progresses through a series of spheres to a higher and higher existence. There are 2 lower spheres in which those of lower character or sinful record are purified and made ready for the higher existences. Most of the departed are to be found in the third sphere, called the summer land; above this are the philosopher's sphere, the advanced contemplative and intellectual sphere, the love sphere, and the Christ sphere. All reach the higher spheres eventually; Spiritualists do not believe in heaven or hell, or that any are ever lost.

Services and séances are held in private homes, rented halls, or churches. Most Spiritualist churches have regular services with prayer, singing, music, selections read from the *Spiritualist Manual*, a sermon or lecture, and spirit messages from the departed. The churches and ministers are supported by freewill offerings; mediums and ministers also gain support from classes and séances in which fees are charged. The attendance at church services is invariably small; one authority estimates the average congregation at 20 to 25. But membership cannot be estimated on the basis of church attendance; for every enrolled member there are at least 15 who are not enrolled but are interested in the movement and in attending its services. Nearly 180,000 Spiritualists were reported as members of their churches in 1954, but this is not comprehensive or inclusive of all using the services of the church.

Administration and government differ slightly in the various groups, but most of them have district or state associations and an annual general convention. All have mediums, and most have ministers in charge of the congregations. Requirements for licensing and ordination also differ, but a determined effort is being made to raise the standards in education and character in the larger groups.

International General Assembly of Spiritualists

Organized at Buffalo, New York, in 1936, this is a cooperative body endeavoring to establish cohesion and unity in the Spiritualist movement. It had an inclusive membership of 164,072 and 209 churches in 1956 and was organized originally as an auxiliary of the General Assembly of Spiritualists in New York to care for churches outside that state. Its present purpose is to charter new Spiritualist churches; headquarters are located at Norfolk, Virginia.

National Spiritual Alliance of the U.S.A.

This body was founded in 1913 by the Rev. G. Tabor Thompson and has its headquarters at Lake Pleasant, Massachusetts, where it was incorporated. Holding general Spiritualist doctrines, the alliance stresses subnormal and impersonal manifestations and intercommunication with the spirit world. Salvation is held to be through the development of personal character; "one reaps as he sows, yet . . . all things are working together for good and evolution obtains perpetually in all persons."

The local churches of the alliance elect their own officers and choose their own ministers; a 3-day convention is held annually with delegates from all the churches electing their national officers—president, secretary, and treasurer. An official board of directors directs the missionary work of ministers and certified mediums; college training is not required of a minister, but he must have passed a course of study arranged by the alliance. Mediums may baptize, but only ministers may officiate at the ceremonies of ordination and marriage. The work of the alliance is mainly in benevolent, literary, educational, music, and scientific activities. There are 3,230 members and 34 churches.

National Spiritualist Association of Churches

With 5,811 members in 175 churches, this association is influential far beyond its immediate membership, furnishing literature for the whole movement and advocating higher qualifications in mediums and ministers. It has a seminary, the Morris Pratt Institute, for the training of its ministers; a great deal of the work of the seminary is by correspondence. A national director of education directs a training course for members, licentiates, lecturers, mediums, and ordained ministers. The N.S.A. holds an annual legislative convention which elects officers triennially. This is the orthodox body of American Spiritualism.

Progressive Spiritual Church

This church was founded in Chicago in 1907 by the Rev. G. Cordingley and has its own confession of faith. It was organized "to lift spiritualism above mere psychic research, to establish it upon a sound, religious basis, and to secure its recognition among other Christian denominations." The confession of faith states the members' belief in the communion of spirits, in man's restoration to everlasting life, in God as an absolute divine Spirit, and in angels who as departed spirits communicate with the living by means of mediums. Jesus Christ is recognized as a medium controlled by the spirit of Elias and the spirit of Moses and the spirit of John the Baptist. "The fingers of the hand of a medium under control can write and deliver divine messages and visions. . . . A divine understanding of dreams can be had. . . . The stars divine the pathway of life of every character." The Bible is acknowledged as the inspired word of God, a guide to the spirit life as well as to the phases and phenomena of Spiritualism—prophecies, spiritual palmistry, spiritual automatic writing, spiritual materialization, spiritual trumpet speaking, spiritual healing by magnetized articles, and so forth. Heaven and hell are believed to be conditions, not locations.

Four sacraments—baptism, marriage, spiritual communion, and funerals—are observed. Ministers, who may be of either sex, must pass a course of instruction in the church seminary. Church officers include a supreme pastor, secretary, treasurer, and board of trustees. Local churches elect their own officers but are subject to the constitution and bylaws of the mother church. The work of the church is largely benevolent, social, literary, scientific, and psychical. There are 11,347 members and 21 churches.

THEOSOPHY

Some call Theosophy a religion, and some call it a philosophy; it is both—a blending of Eastern and Western philosophical and religious teaching. Its founder was Madame Helena Petrovna Blavatsky, who was born in Russia in 1831 and who travelled over the world in search of "a knowledge of the laws which govern the universe." She arrived in the United States in 1872 and with Henry Steele Orcott and William Q. Judge founded the Theosophical Society of New York in 1875. Her purpose and aim in Theosophy was "to form a nucleus of the Universal Brotherhood of Humanity, without distinction of race, creed, sex, case or color; to encourage the study of comparative religion, philosophy and science; and to investigate the unexplained laws of Nature and the powers latent in man."

Mrs. Blavatsky made use of the teachings of the great thinkers of various religions, but her system depended mainly upon the precepts and teachings of Buddhism and Hinduism. Proceeding from the premise that God is "immanent" in the hidden forces of nature and that man can attain perfection through his own powers, she described God as impersonal. God is the Absolute Principle of pantheistic Hinduism, a creator (like Brahma), a preserver (like Vishnu), and a destroyer (like Shiva). He is also supreme over an earthly hierarchy which includes Jesus and other master-thinkers who have experienced a series of rebirths or reincarnations to ultimately attain divinity. Reincarnation is a great central theme in Theosophy; it is the experience through which men rid themselves of all impurities and reach the true heaven.

When Mrs. Blavatsky died in 1891, Mrs. Annie Besant took over leadership of the movement, with headquarters established in Adyar, India. Mrs. Besant went beyond her predecessor in claiming that Jesus was an incarnation of Buddha; later she identified a young Hindu, Jeddu Krishnamurti, as the reincarnated Jesus-and-Buddha. Conflicts developed during this period between Mrs. Besant as leader of the Adyar Society and the leaders of other Theosophical groups in Europe and the United States; in 1895 William Q. Judge, one of the 3 founders and president of the American Society, established the independent Theosophical Society in America; those loyal to Mrs. Besant worked in the Theosophical Society of New York. Other splits developed in the years following, and the fragmentation is still evident, but the basic teachings of Mrs. Blavatsky still hold in all the rival groups.

No accurate report of membership seems possible, among these groups, but it is estimated that there are upwards of 40,000 Theosophists worldwide, and perhaps 5,000 of them in the United States. Their influence, thanks to the current interest in Oriental philosophy and religion, is felt in may other occult groups unconnected with any Theosophical Society, here or abroad.

TRIUMPH THE CHURCH AND KINGDOM OF GOD IN CHRIST

Founded in Georgia in 1902 by Elder E. D. Smith, this church teaches the cleansing from sin in all "justified" believers through the shed blood of Christ; entire sanctification as an instantaneous, definite work of second grace obtained through the faith of the consecrated believer; the second coming of Christ; and baptism by fire as a scriptural experience also obtainable by faith. General overseers are the chief officers of the body; they meet quadrennially in what is called the International Religious Congress; otherwise the work of the church is carried on by state, county, and local officers. There are 54,307 members and 495 churches.

UNITARIAN UNIVERSALIST ASSOCIATION

In May, 1961, the Unitarian and Universalist churches in the United States and Canada were consolidated as the Unitarian Universalist Association. As one of the most influential liberal churches in this country they have separate and interesting origins and history.

It has always been claimed by the Unitarians that their thought reaches back into the early Christian centuries, before the concept of Trinitarianism was developed. Unitarianism as we know it today, however, began with the Protestant Reformation, among Arminians and Socinians. The movement spread from independent thinkers and Anabaptists in Switzerland, Hungary, Transylvania, Holland, Poland, and Italy to England, where it found champions in such leaders as Newton, Locke, and Milton. No attempt was made to organize the movement in England until late in the eighteenth century.

American Unitarianism, however, developed independently out of New England Congregationalism. Members of the liberal wing of the Congregational Church in eastern Massachusetts, asked only to join a covenant in that church and never to subscribe to a creed, were branded as Unitarian while still within the Congregational membership. The first organized church to turn to Unitarianism as a body, however, was not a Congregational church but the Episcopal King's Chapel in Boston in 1785.

In the second half of the eighteenth century many of the older and larger Congregational churches moving toward Unitarianism were known as Liberal Christian churches or groups; the name Unitarian was finally accepted in 1819.

The split within Congregationalism came into the open in 1805 with the appointment of Henry Ware as professor of theology at Harvard; it was made certain when William Ellery Channing of Boston preached his famous Baltimore sermon in 1819 and in it outlined the Unitarian view. In that sermon the liberals had their platform. A missionary and publication society known as the American Unitarian Association was formed in 1825, and with it began an activity looking forward to the formation of a separate denomination. A national conference was established in 1865.

Channing defined the true church in these words:

By his Church our Savior does not mean a party bearing the name of a human leader, distinguished by a form or an opinion, and on the ground of this distinction, denying the name and character of Christians to all but themselves. . . . These are the church—men made better, made holy, virtuous by his religion—men who, hoping in his promises, keep his commands.

The Unitarians proceeded from this to formulate their views. They have no creed; the constitution of the general conference stated that "these churches accept the religion of Jesus, holding in accordance with his teaching that practical religion is summed up in the love to God and love to man." Cardinal points in their doctrinal attitudes are those of the oneness of God (as opposed to Trinitarianism), the strict humanity of Jesus, the perfectibility of human character, the natural character of the Bible, and the ultimate salvation of all souls. They deny the doctrine of total depravity and believe in the divine nature of man; Trinitarianism is rejected as unscriptural, and they reject the deity of Christ but say that they believe in his divinity as all men are divine as the sons of God. Salvation is by character; character is not an end but a means, and salvation lies in being saved from sin here, not from punishment hereafter. Hell and eternal punishment are held to be inconsistent with the concept of a loving and all-powerful God; to admit that God would permit eternal punishment would be to admit that he was powerless to save. Heaven is a state, not a place. Unitarians do not accept the doctrine of the infallibility of the Bible; they believe that the Bible is not a book but a library of books, all of which cannot be accepted as of equal value and importance. These ideas have been prominent in Unitarianism, but within this ideological framework the widest possible freedom is encouraged in personal interpretation and belief; even students and teachers in Unitarian theological schools are not required to subscribe to any dogmatic teaching or doctrinal tests. Emphasis upon individual freedom of belief, democratic principles, hospitality to the methods of science in seeking truth, and less concern with traditional doctrinal matters characterize the Unitarian movement.

In accordance with its charter, the American Unitarian Association considered itself to be devoted to certain moral, religious, educational, and charitable purposes which to the non-Unitarian may be as enlightening as an analysis of their religious or doctrinal statements; under these purposes, the association felt obligated to:

(1) diffuse the knowledge and promote the interests of religion which Jesus taught as love to God and love to man;

(2) strengthen the churches and fellowships which unite in the association for more and better work for the kingdom of God;

(3) organize new churches and fellowships for the extension of Unitarianism in our own countries and in other lands; and

(4) encourage sympathy and cooperation among religious liberals at home and abroad.

Organization has always been liberally congregational; independent local churches were grouped in local, county, district, state, and regional conferences, and were united in an international association for purposes of fellowship, counsel, and promotion of mutual interests.

At the time of merger, there were 2 denominational seminaries and 2 preparatory schools, 386 churches, and approximately 115,000 members. Foreign work was conducted through the International Association for Liberal Christianity and Religious Freedom with headquarters at Utrecht, Holland; the International Association has correspondents in 22 countries.

The Universalists draw their inspiration and find evidence of their thinking and philosophy in many cultural streams; much that is basic with Universalism is discovered throughout the world's several religions. Universalism is not exclusively a Christian denomination, having roots in both pre-Christian and contemporary world faiths, yet within the Christian frame of reference Unversalists claim roots in the early Christian gnostics, Clement of Alexandria, Theodore of Mopsuestia, the Anabaptists of Reformation times, and the seventeenth- and eighteenth-century German mystical universalists. American Universalism has its direct origin in the work of Dr. George DeBenneville, one of the German mystics; in John Murray, the British anti-Calvinist, and in Hosea Ballou, an original universalist thinker.

DeBenneville, the English-educated son of French Huguenot *émigrés*, studied medicine in Germany, came under the influence of the early Brethren and Friends of God and the German pietists in Pennsylvania in 1741, and preached his gospel of universal salvation as he practiced medicine among the settlers and the Indians.

In 1759 James Relly of England wrote a book entitle *Union*, in which he opposed the Calvinistic doctrine of the election of the few. Relly's conviction of universal salvation deeply influenced John Murray, a Wesleyan evangelist who came to New Jersey in 1770; Murray found groups of universalist-minded people scattered along the Atlantic coast, and became minister to one such group in Gloucester, Massachusetts. The Independent Christian Church of Gloucester became the first organized Universalist church in America in 1779. One of its charter members was Gloucester Dalton, a Negro. Murray served briefly as a Revolutionary War chaplain in the armies of Washington and Greene.

The Universalists met at Philadelphia in 1790 to draft their first declaration of faith and plan of government. Government was established as strictly congregational; doctrinally, they proclaimed their belief in the Scriptures as containing a revelation of the perfections and the will of God and the rule of faith and practice, faith in God, faith in Christ as a mediator who had redeemed all men by his blood, in the Holy Ghost, and in the obligation of the moral law as the rule of life. War was condemned; statements approving the settlement of disputes out of the courts, the abolition of slavery and the education of the Negro, testimony by affirmation rather than by oath, and free public education were approved. This Philadelphia declaration was adopted by a group of New England Universalists in 1793; at about the same time Hosea Ballou, a schoolteacher and intinerant preacher in Vermont, was ordained to the Universalist ministry.

Ballou broke radically with Murray's thought; in 1805 he published a book, *Treatise on Atonement*, which gave Universalists their first consistent philosophy. Ballou rejected the theories of total depravity, endless punishment in hell, the Trinity, and the miracles. Man, said Ballou, was potentially good and capable of perfectibility; God, being a God of infinite love, recognized man's heavenly nature and extraction and loved him as his own offspring. The meaning of the atonement he found not in bloody sacrifice to appease divine wrath, but in the heroic sacrifice of Jesus, who was not God but a son of the eternal and universal God revealing the love of God and anxious to win all men to that love. It was an avowedly Unitarian-Universalist statement of theology which deeply influenced American Universalism. Ballou made another lasting contribution with his insistence that the base of Christian fellowship lay not in creeds but in mutual good faith and good will; from this principle came 2 consistent aspects of modern Universalism—a broad liberalism in theology and a universal concern for persons.

It must be kept clear that the Universalists have never had an *official* statement of faith or covenant. From time to time they have set down their basic principles, not as tests of membership nor to be used in any official way, but only to examine their emphases at a given moment in history. Accordingly, in 4 successive statements, they have grown progressively liberal and inclusive. The Philadelphia statement of 1790, for instance, had obvious trinitarian overtones and spoke in prevailing orthodox terms on the Scriptures, God, the Mediator, and the Holy Ghost; the Winchester Profession of 1803 humanized Jesus and thus directly opposed Trinitarianism and reemphasized salvation for the whole family of mankind; it also saw the Bible as one revelation of the character of God. A statement of 5 Universalist principles in Boston in 1899 liberalized their doctrine still further, and in 1935, in Washington, D. C., they adopted their latest statement, which reads as follows:

The bond of fellowship in this Convention shall be a common purpose to do the will of God as Jesus revealed it and to cooperate in establishing the kingdom for which He lived and died.

To that end we avow our faith in God as External and All-Conquering Love, in the spiritual leadership of Jesus, in the supreme worth of every human personality, in the authority of truth known or to be known, and in the power of men of good will and sacrificial spirit to overcome all evil and progressively establish the kingdom of God. Neither this nor any other statement shall be imposed as a creedal test, provided that the faith thus indicated be professed.

In 1942 the character of the Universalist Church of America was changed to read: "To promote harmony among adherents of all religious faiths, whether Christian or otherwise." This was the last of a long series of steps calculated to meet the challenges of intellectual and social developments, and to safeguard the Universalist conviction that no doctrinal statements should be employed as creedal tests. Consequently Universalism has become a harmonious body of theists, naturalists, humanists, mystics, Christians, and non-Christians, who find great significance and meaning in a universal approach to life.

A keen sense of ethical responsibility has accompanied this sense of the importance of freedom among Universalists. They were very early active in movements of reform for prisons and working women; they opposed slavery from their earliest days, stood for separation of church and state, maintained a continuing interest in the fields of science, labor management, civil rights, and human concern. They have placed medical workers in West Berlin and South German refugee centers in modern times; international student work camp teams are serving underprivileged children and refugee youth in Europe. American Universalists are feeding children in Japan; developing community centers in India; providing child care for Negro children in Virginia and a social center at an interracial public housing development in Chicago; and doing work in various state mental hospitals. They have founded several colleges or universities—Tufts, St. Lawrence, Lombard (now part of the University of Chicago), Goddard, California Institute of Technology, Akron, Dean Junior College, and Westbrook Junior College. Through membership in the International Association for Religious Freedom, they contributed to the support of liberal religious groups in 22 countries abroad, and they maintain a close affiliation with Universalist groups in Holland, Japan, Korea, and the Philippines. At the time of the formation of the Unitarian Universalist Association, they had 68,949 members in 334 churches.

Joined now in their new association, neither Unitarians nor Universalists seem to have lost anything of their original ideology, theology, or purpose. Except for matters of orgnization and government, the churches involved will continue as they have been across the years;

no minister, member, or congregation "shall be required to subscribe to any particular interpretation of religion, or to any particular religious belief or creed." The aims and purposes of the Association are set forth in a revised (1972) statement:

The Association, dedicated to the principles of a free faith, shall:

(a) Support the free and disciplined search for truth as the foundation of religious fellowship;

(b) Cherish and spread the universal truths taught by the great prophets and teachers of humanity in every age and tradition, immemorially summarized in the Judeo-Christian heritage as love to God and love to man.

(c) Affirm, defend and promote the supreme worth of every human personality, the dignity of man, and the use of the democratic method in human relationships.

(d) Implement the vision of one world by striving for a world community founded on ideals and brotherhood, justice and peace;

(e) Serve the needs of member societies;

(f) Organize new churches and fellowships and otherwise extend and strengthen liberal religion;

(g) Encourage cooperation among people of good will in every land.

Under the constitution a general assembly is the overall policy-making body for carrying out the purposes and objectives of the association. Both ministers and laymen are represented in this assembly. The general assembly meets annually, or in such special sessions as may be called by the board of trustees. The elected officers of the association (a moderator, president, 2 vice-presidents, secretary, and treasurer, all elected for 4-year terms), together with 20 other elected members, constitute the board of trustees, which appoints the executive and administrative officers of the association and generally carries out the policies and directives of the general assembly. Members of this board have the usual powers of corporate directors as provided by law. The trustees meet 4 times a year, between regular meetings of the general assembly. A series of committees is appointed to facilitate and coordinate the association's work. Under the general assembly there is a nominating committee, program and business committees, and a commission on appraisal; under the board of trustees, an executive committee, a ministerial fellowship committee, finance committee, and investment committee.

National headquarters are in Boston; 21 district offices have been established, on regional or geographical bases. There are 210,648 members in 1019 churches.

UNITED CHURCH OF CHRIST

Three churches of historic importance constitute the United Church of Christ: the Congregational Church, the Christian Church, and the Evangelical and Reformed Church. The first 2 were merged into the Congregational Christian Churches in 1931 and were joined by the Evangelical and Reformed Church in 1957. The union was completed in the adoption of a constitution at Philadelphia in July, 1961.

The backgrounds of these 3 churches are important enough to be studied separately.

Congregational Church

Congregationalism has been an issue in Christianity from the beginning; it began, as Gaius Glenn Atkins suggests, "without a name and with no sense of its destiny." Even before the Reformation broke over Europe, there were little dissenting groups of churchmen in England "seeking a better way" than that of the established church (Anglican Church or Church of England). As the Reformation developed in England, dissent took corporate form in the Puritan movement, of which Congregationalism was the most radical wing.

Until a few years ago it was generally believed that Congregationalism had its rise in separatism, a movement which began in the days of Queen Elizabeth and which held that the Church of England was unchristian; that to attempt to reform it from within was hopeless; and that the only course for a true Christian to take was to separate himself from it completely. Recent historians, however, have proved that though Robert Browne and other separatist leaders developed sundry ideas which were identical with those of early Congregationalism, the 2 groups were wholly distinct, the former being perfectionists who refused cooperation with other branches of the church, the latter being as cooperative as possible without giving up their principles.

John Robinson, one of their most influential early leaders, first enters church history as a separatist; in 1609 he fled persecution in England and settled at Leiden in the Netherlands with the exiled congregation from Scrooby in Nottinghamshire. There he met William Ames, Congregationalism's first great theologian, and Henry Jacob, its first great pamphleteer and organizer. These men were also fugitives from the ecclesiastical courts of Britain. By them Robinson was converted from rigid separatism to the position of Congregationalism.

For 12 years Robinson and his congregation enjoyed peace and freedom under the Dutch; but haunted by the conviction that their sons would not grow up as Englishmen, a large part of the company sailed for America in 1620 aboard the historic *Mayflower*. In a hostile new world, with the wilderness before them and the sea at their backs, they helped lay the foundations of the American common-wealth; the democratic ideals of their Plymouth colony, worked out slowly and painfully, were the cornerstone of the structure which gave us our free state, free schools, and free social and political life.

Other Congregational churches were established at Barnstable, Salem, and elsewhere along the Massachusetts coast. Between 1630 and 1640, 20,000 Puritans came to Massachusetts Bay. It was inevitable that the "Bay People" who came direct from England and the "Plymouth People" from the Netherlands should join forces, which they did, establishing thereby an all-powerful theocratic government over both settlements.

Church and commonwealth were this theocracy's 2 instruments. It was a stern—and at times an intolerant—regime. Suffrage was limited to church members; Anne Hutchinson and Roger Williams were banished; Baptists were haled into court; and 4 Quakers were hanged on Boston Common. It was a dark but a comparatively short period, ending with the Act of Toleration in 1689.

In 1636 Thomas Hooker led a company of 100 to what is now Hartford, Connecticut; the freeman's constitution drawn up by Hooker and his associates became the model of the American Con-stitution. Dissenting from the rigidity of current church worship, Congregationalists such as Jonathan Edwards of Northampton played leading roles in the Great Awakening which broke in 1734; that re-vival was marked not only by the eloquence of George Whitefield but by the vigorous writings and preaching of Edwards, whose books are now regarded as American classics.

Emerging stronger than ever from the Revolution, in the prepara-tion of which it played a great heroic part, Congregationalism was concerned for the next century with 5 significant developments: higher education, missions, the Unitarian separation, the formation of a national council, and the production of a uniform statement of be-lief. In the field of education this church had already made tremendous contributions: it had founded Harvard in 1636; Yale (1707) was a Congregational project for the education of its clergy; Dartmouth (1769) developed from Eleazer Wheelock's School for Indians. These, with Williams, Amherst, Bowdoin, and Middlebury, were among the first colleges in New England. By 1953 there were 48 colleges and 10 theological seminaries in the United States with Congregational Chris-tian origin or connection.

Interest in missions among American Congregationalists began the day the Pilgrims landed at Plymouth. The Mayhews, David Brainerd, and John Eliot were soon at work among the Indians. Eliot spent 7 years mastering the Indian tongue, put the Bible in their language, and published an Indian catechism in 1653, the first book to be printed in their language. By 1674 there were 4,000 "praying Indians" in New England, with 24 native preachers. When the wagon trains went West after the Revolution, the families of Congregational ministers and missionaries were prominent. Manasseh Cutler, a preacher from Hamilton, Massachusetts, was instrumental in framing the famous Northwest Territory Ordinance of 1787; and other ministers led in the founding of Marietta, Ohio, the first permanent settlement in the Northwest Territory.

The American Board of Commissioners for Foreign Missions was organized in 1810 and was concerned at first with both home and foreign missionary work. On it served not only Congregationalists but representatives of Presbyterian, Dutch Reformed, and Associate Reformed churches. This was the first foreign missionary society in the country, and it was interdenominational. The first 5 men ordained were the 5 young men who had participated in the famous "haystack" meeting at Williams College. After them came missionaries to more than 30 foreign countries and in American territories, not the least of which was Hawaii, where Congregational missionaries within 25 years taught a whole nation of people to read and write, laid the foundations of a constitutional democratic government, and made of their beautiful islands a sociological laboratory filled with many races. The Congregational achievement in Hawaii is one of the greatest in the whole history of Protestant missions.

The rise of denominationalism worked against the interdenominational complexion of the American Board, and by mid-century the non-Congregationalists had all withdrawn to go their separate ways. The American Board was no longer interdenominational.

Moving westward, Congregationalists from New England came into contact with Presbyterians moving out from the middle and southern states. To avoid competition and duplication of effort, a plan of union was worked out under which ministers and members from both churches were exchanged and accepted on equal basis. Adopted in 1801, the plan eventually worked out to the advantage of the Presbyterians; it was discontinued in 1852, leaving the Presbyterians stronger in the West and the Congregationalists with a virtual church monopoly in New England. But the plan did much to inspire new Congregational missionary work. In 1826 the American Home Missionary Society was founded; it was active in the South before the Civil War and especially effective there toward the end of that conflict with its "contraband" schools for Negroes, one of which became Hampton Institute.

Meanwhile differences of opinion between theological liberals and conservatives were developing within the church. Strict Calvinists and Trinitarians were opposed by Unitarians, and a famous sermon by William Ellery Channing at Baltimore in 1819 made a division inevitable. The American Unitarian Association was established in 1825. Almost all the older Congregational churches in eastern Massachusetts went Unitarian; only 1 Congregational church was left in Boston. Debate and legal action over property and funds were not finished until about 1840.

In spite of the Unitarian defection Congregationalism continued to grow. It assumed such proportions that a national supervisory body became necessary, and a series of national conventions or councils evidenced the growing denominational consciousness of the widely scattered independent local churches. A national council held at Boston in 1865 was so effective that a regular system of councils was established. Following conferences between the associations into which the churches had grouped themselves, the first of the national councils was called at Oberlin, Ohio, in 1871. Known as the General Council of the Congregational Christian Churches, it met biennially and acted as an overall advisory body for the entire fellowship.

The council of 1913 at Kansas City adopted a declaration on faith, polity, and wider fellowship which has been accepted by many churches as a statement of faith. While it did not in any way modify the independence of the local churches, it did give a new spiritual unity to the church. It read as follows:

Faith.—We believe in God the Father, infinite in wisdom, goodness, and love; and in Jesus Christ, His Son, our Lord and Savior, who for us and our salvation lived and died and rose again and liveth evermore; and in the Holy Spirit, who taketh of the things of Christ and revealeth them to us, renewing, comforting, and inspiring the souls of men. We are united in striving to know the will of God, as taught in the Holy Scriptures, and in our purpose to walk in the ways of the Lord, made known or to be made known to us. We hold it to be the mission of the Church of Christ to proclaim the Gospel to all mankind, exalting the worship of the true God, and laboring for the progress of knowledge, the promotion of justice, the reign of peace, and the realization of human brotherhood. Depending, as did our fathers, upon the continued guidance of the Holy Spirit to lead us into all truth, we work and pray for the transformation of the world into the kingdom of God; and we look with faith for the triumph of righteousness and the life everlasting.

Polity.—We believe in the freedom and responsibility of the individual soul and the right of private judgment. We hold to the autonomy of the local church and its independence of all ecclesiastical control. We cherish the fellowship of the churches united in district, State, and national bodies, for counsel and cooperation in matters of common concern.

The Wider Fellowship.—While affirming the liberty of our churches, and the validity of our ministry, we hold to the unity and catholicity of the Church of Christ, and will unite with all its branches in hearty cooperation; and will earnestly seek, so far as in us lies, that the prayer of our Lord for His disciples may be answered, that they all may be one.

The "wider fellowship" is taken seriously; unity and cooperation across denominational lines have been outstanding characteristics of Congregationalism all through its history. Christian Endeavor, the largest young people's organization in all Protestantism, was founded by a Congregationalist, Francis E. Clark, in 1881; by 1885 it had become an interdenominational organization known all over the world as the United Society of Christian Endeavor. In 1924 the Evangelical Protestant Church of North America was received into the National Council of Congregational Churches as the Evangelical Protestant Conference of Congregational Churches; the 2 mergers with the Christian churches and the Evangelical and Reformed churches, coming comparatively close together, again witness to the widening fellowship and vision of the Congregationalists. Into the most recent merger they brought 47 church-related (not church-*controlled*) colleges, 11 theological seminaries, foreign mission stations in Africa, Mexico, Japan, the Philippines, India, Ceylon, Greece, Lebanon, Syria, Turkey, Korea, and Micronesia, and home missionaries in every state in the Union and Puerto Rico.

Christian Church

The Christian churches, like the Congregational, were born in protest against ecclesiasticism and the denial of individual freedom in the church. There were actually 3 revolts which resulted in the establishment of Christian churches in New England and in the South.

The first came in 1792, when James O'Kelly, a Methodist minister in Virginia, withdrew from that church in protest against the development of the superintendency into an episcopacy, especially insofar as it gave the Methodist bishops absolute power in appointing ministers to their charges. O'Kelly and his followers organized under the name Republican Methodists; this was later changed to "Christian," with the new church insisting that the Bible be taken as the only rule and discipline, and that Christian character be made the only requirement of church membership.

Abner Jones, convinced that "sectarian names and human creeds should be abandoned," left the Vermont Baptists to organize at Lyndon, Vermont, in 1801 the First Christian Church in New England. This was done not so much in objection to Baptist organization or doctrine as from a desire to secure a wider freedom in religious thought and fellowship. Like O'Kelly, Jones insisted that piety and character were to be the sole test of Christian fellowship.

In the Great Awakening which swept Tennessee and Kentucky in 1801 there was a great deal of preaching which either ignored the old emphasis on the doctrines of the various denominations involved or was often in direct contradiction to them. Barton W. Stone, accused of anti-Presbyterian preaching, led a number of Presbyterians out of the Synod of Kentucky to organize a Springfield Presbytery. This presbytery was discontinued as its members gradually came to accept the ideology of James O'Kelly and Abner Jones, and adopted the name "Christians." Stone, an ardent revivalist, was deeply influenced by the preaching of Alexander Campbell and led many of his followers and churches into the fold of the Disciples of Christ. But the large majority of his Christian churches remained with the original Christian body.

The groups under O'Kelly, Jones, and Stone engaged in a long series of conferences which resulted in their union on 6 basic Christian principles:

1. Christ, the only head of the Church.
2. The Bible, sufficient rule of faith and practice.
3. Christian character, the measure of membership.
4. A right, individual interpretation of the Scripture, as a way of life.
5. "Christian," the name taken as worthy of the followers of Christ.
6. Unity, Christians working together to save the world.

No council or other body in the Christian church has ever attempted to draw up any other creed or statement. Their creed is the Bible. Their interpretation of Bible teaching might be called evangelical, but no sincere follower of Christ is barred from their membership because of difference in theological belief. Open Communion is practiced; baptism is considered a duty, but it is not required; immersion is used generally, but any mode may be employed.

The union of the Congregational and Christian churches has been thoroughly democratic, leaving both free to continue their own forms of worship and each with its own polity and doctrine. Adhering strictly to the congregational idea, each local church is at liberty to call itself either Congregational or Christian, and the same choice is found in the self-governing district and state associations into which the churches, are organized.

Evangelical and Reformed Church

The Evangelical and Reformed Church was the product of a union established at Cleveland, Ohio on June 26, 1943, between 2 bodies of Swiss and German background with basic agreements in doctrine, polity, and culture—the Evangelical Synod of North America and the Reformed Church in the United States.

The Evangelical Synod was the younger of the 2 bodies, originating with 6 ministers who met at Gravois Settlement near St. Louis in 1840 to form the Evangelical Union of the West. They were ministers of Lutheran and Reformed churches in the Evangelical United Church of Prussia. Two had been sent to America by the Rhenish Missionary Society and 2 by the Missionary Society of Basel; the other 2 were independent, one coming from Bremen and the other from Strassburg.

The Evangelical Union of the West was a cooperative ministerial association until 1849, when the first permanent organization was established. As the movement spread to the East and Northwest among German-speaking Lutheran and Reformed peoples, headquarters were established at St. Louis and a new name, the German Evangelical

Synod of North America, adopted. A series of amalgamations with 4 other bodies of similar belief and polity—the German Evangelical Church Association of Ohio, the German United Evangelical Synod of the East, the Evangelical Synod of the Northwest, and the United Evangelical Synod of the East—resulted in the formation of the Evangelical Synod of North America, giving it a membership of 281,598 at the time of the merger with the Reformed Church in the United States.

The Reformed Church in the United States had its origin in Switzerland and Germany, and particularly in the flood tide of German immigration to Pennsylvania in the eighteenth century. More than half the Germans in Pennsylvania in 1730 were of the Reformed persuasion; their congregations were widely separated along the frontier; and lacking ministers, they often employed schoolteachers to lead their services. Three of their pastors, Johann Philip Boehm, George Michael Weiss, and Johann Bartholomaeus Rieger, were deeply influenced by Michael Schlatter, who had been sent to America by the Synod (Dutch Reformed) of South and North Holland; with him they organized in 1747 a coetus (synod) in Philadelphia. It was a synod directly responsible to and in part financially supported by the synod in Holland, from which it declared its independence in 1793, taking the name of the German Reformed Church; and in that year it reported 178 congregations and 15,000 communicants. The word "German" was dropped in 1869; from that time on the denomination was called the Reformed Church in the United States.

Reformed Church missionaries went early across the Alleghenies into Ohio and south into North Carolina. An overall synod of the church divided the country into 8 districts or classes in 1819, and an independent Ohio classis was formed in 1824. Franklin College (now Franklin and Marshall) was founded at Lancaster, Pennsylvania, with the support of Benjamin Franklin; a theological seminary was opened at Carlisle and later moved to Lancaster; an academy which later became Marshall College was established in 1836. The Synod of Ohio established a theological school and Heidelberg University at Tiffin, Ohio, in 1850. The mother synod in the East and the Ohio Synod were united in the General Synod in 1836, which functioned until the merger with the Evangelical Synod of North America in 1934.

Difficulties arose in the early years of the last century over the languages used in the Reformed Church; the older Germans preferred the use of German, and the second-generation members demanded English. Inevitably in a church of such mixed membership there were conservatives and liberals in conflict. Some of the churches withdrew and formed a separate synod but returned in 1837 as wiser heads prevailed and compromises were made. New district synods of both German-speaking and English-speaking congregations were created, and 2 Hungarian classes were added in 1924 from the Old Hungarian Reformed Church.

By 1934 the boards of the church were directing a widespread home missions work and foreign missionary work in Japan, China, and Mesopotamia. There were 12 institutions of higher learning, 3 theological seminaries, and 3 orphanages. There were 348,189 members in the Reformed Church at the time of the 1934 merger, largely consecrated in Pennsylvania and Ohio.

Few difficulties were encountered in reconciling the doctrines of the 2 bodies when the union was finally accomplished. Both churches were German Calvinistic; the Reformed Church had been based historically on the Heidelberg Catechism, and the Evangelical Synod on the Heidelberg Catchism, the Augsburg Confession, and Luther's Catechism. These 3 standards of faith were woven into 1 in the new constitution of the Evangelical and Reformed Church in these words:

The Holy Scriptures of the Old and New Testaments are recognized as the Word of God and the ultimate rule of Christian faith and practice.

The doctrinal standards of the Evangelical and Reformed Church are the Heidelberg Catechism, Luther's Catechism, and the Augsburg Confession. They are accepted as an authoritative interpretation of the essential truth taught in the Holy Scriptures.

Wherever these doctrinal standards differ, ministers, members, and congregations, in accordance with the liberty of conscience inherent in the Gospel, are allowed to adhere to the interpretation of one of these confessions. However, in each case the final norm is the Word of God.

Two sacraments—baptism, usually administered to infants, and the Lord's Supper—were accepted; confirmation, generally before the thirteenth or fourteenth years, ordination, consecration, marriage, and burial were considered as rites. Although hymns and forms of worship are provided for general use, a wide freedom of worship is encouraged.

Church polity, when this church joined the Congregational Christians in 1957, was modified Presbyterian; each local church was governed by a consistory or church council elected from its own membership. Local churches formed a synod, of which there were 34, each made up of a pastor and lay delegate from each charge; the synod met twice a year and had jurisdiction over all ministers and congregations, examined, licensed, and ordained all pastors, and elected its own officers—a procedure quite different from that of the Congregational Christian Churches. It led many to wonder whether a union between 2 such different forms of government could possibly work; that wonder or hesitancy is a root cause for the dissension of the few churches that have thus far refused to cooperate in the merger.

The Evangelical and Reformed Church was a thriving church, in 1957-60, when the details of union were being worked out. There were 810,000 members in 1959, in 2,740 churches; 8 colleges, 3 theological schools, 2 academies; foreign missionaries in India, Japan, Hong Kong,

Iraq, Africa, and Honduras; and a widespread home missionary work in the United States among the people of the Ozarks, the American Indians, the Volga Germans, Hungarians, and Japanese.

United Church of Christ

On July 8, 1959, representatives of the Congregational Christian Churches and the Evangelical and Reformed Church adopted, at Oberlin, Ohio, a Statement of Faith for the United Church of Christ, into which they were merging. It reads as follows:

We believe in God, the Eternal Spirit, Father of our Lord Jesus Christ and our Father, and to his deeds we testify:

He calls the worlds into being, creates man in his own image and sets before him the ways of life and death.

He seeks in holy love to save all people from aimlessness and sin.

He judges men and nations by his righteous will declared through prophets and apostles.

In Jesus Christ, the man of Nazareth, our crucified and risen Lord, he has come to us and shared our common lot, conquering sin and death and reconciling the world to himself.

He bestows upon us his Holy Spirit, creating and renewing the Church of Jesus Christ, binding in covenant faithful people of all ages, tongues, and races.

He calls us into his Church to accept the cost and joy of discipleship, to be his servants in the service of men, to proclaim the gospel to all the world and resist the powers of evil, to share in Christ's baptism and eat at his table, to join him in his passion and victory.

He promises to all who trust him forgiveness of sins and fullness of grace, courage in the struggle for justice and peace, his presence in trial and rejoicing, and eternal life in his kingdom which has no end.

Blessing and honor, glory and power be unto him. Amen.

This is "a testimony rather than a test of faith"; it is not intended to set forth doctrinal positions (the doctrines and theological positions of the 3 churches now within the United Church of Christ remain as they were before the union was accomplished), nor to stand as a substitute for the historic creeds, confessions, and covenants of the churches involved. It is not binding, in any creedal or theological sense, upon any local church in the denomination; no congregation is required to subscribe to the statement. But it does stand as a tribute to the faith, charity, and understanding of the merging groups.

Equally impressive is the understanding and cooperation evident in the governmental provisions of the constitution. The United Church of Christ represents a union of Congregationalism and Presbyterianism —"it establishes congregationalism as the rule for the local congregation and presbyterianism as the basis for organization of the connectional life of the churches." (Harold E. Fey.) The constitution is explicit: "The autonomy of the local church is inherent and modifiable only by its own action. Nothing . . . shall destroy or limit the right of each local church to continue to operate *in the way customary to it.*" But beyond the local church, protected as it is, are associations, conferences, and the general synod. Local churches in a geographical area are grouped into associations. The association is concerned with the welfare of the churches within its area; assists needy churches; receives new churches into the United Church of Christ; licenses, ordains, and installs ministers; adopts its own constitution, by-laws, and rules of procedure; and is made up of the ordained ministers and elected lay delegates of the area. The association meets annually, and is related to the general synod through its conference.

Associations are grouped into conferences, again by geographical areas. The voting members of the conference are ordained ministers of the associations in the conference and lay delegates elected from the local churches. The conference acts on requests, counsel, and references from the local churches, associations, general synod, and other bodies. It meets annually, and its main function is one of coordinating the work and witness of the local churches and associations, rendering counsel and advisory service, establishing conference offices, centers, institutions, and other agencies.

The general synod is the top representative body of the church; it meets biennially and is composed of 675 to 725 delegates chosen by the conferences, and of ex officio delegates (the elected officers of the church, members of the executive council, the moderator, and assistant moderators). The conference delegates are clergymen, laymen, and laywomen, in equal numbers; there are also associate delegates, with voice but without vote. The general synod has no power to "invade" local churches, associations, or conferences; it nominates and elects the officers of the church (a president, secretary, director of finance, and treasurer) for 4-year terms, a moderator and 2 assistant moderators who preside over the sessions of the general synod and hold office for 1 year only. (The duties are quite similar to those of a moderator among the Presbyterians).

The major boards, commissions, councils, offices, and "other instrumentalities" of the church are established by the general synod; these include the Board for World Ministeries (foreign missions spread from Europe to Southern Asia and Latin America), made up of 225 ministers, laymen, and laywomen; the Board for Homeland Ministries (home missions), also with 225 ministers, laymen, and laywomen; the Council for Higher Education, composed of the executive heads of the 2 academies, 31 colleges, and 14 schools of theology of the church; the Council for Health and Welfare Services, administered by the heads of 65 church institutions in these fields; the Council for Christian Social Action; Council for Church and Ministry; Council of Lay Life and Work; and the Stewardship Council. Public relations, TV, radio, and visual aids are under the charge of an office of communication. Pension and relief activities are administered by a nonprofit corporation responsible to and reporting annually to the general synod. Two committees (nominating and credentials) are also appointed by the general synod, and the synod is authorized to appoint such other committees as they are necessary.

An executive council of 42 voting members and 12 ex officio members (ministers, laymen, and laywomen) is elected by the general synod to act for the synod in the interims between synod meetings. It determines the salaries of the officers of the church, appoints the editor of *A.D.*, a joint publication of the United Church of Christ and the United Presbyterian Church in the U.S.A., prepares the agenda for all meetings of general synod, and appoints committees not otherwise provided; it also submits to general synod "any recommendation it may deem useful" to the work of the church.

As of 1959, there were 1,419,171 members and 5,500 churches in the Congregational Christian Churches; there were approximately 810,000 members in 2,740 churches in the Evangelical and Reformed Church. While some local churches in both groups declined to enter the merger, there are today 1,895,016 members and 6,635 churches in the United Church of Christ.

The National Church holds membership in the National Council of Churches, the World Council of Churches, and the International Congregational Council.

UNITED HOLY CHURCH
OF AMERICA, INC.

A Pentecostal church organized at Method, North Carolina, in a meeting held by the Rev. Isaac Cheshier in 1886, this body was successively called the Holy Church of North Carolina, the Holy Church of North Carolina and Virginia, and finally (1918) the United Holy Church of America. Its purpose is to establish and maintain holy convocations, assemblies, conventions, conferences, public worship, missionary and school work, orphanages, manual and trade training, and religious resorts, with permanent and temporary dwellings.

Articles of faith contain statements of belief in the Trinity, the record of God's revelation of himself in the Bible, redemption through Christ, justification and instantaneous sanctification following justification, the baptism of the Holy Spirit, divine healing, and the ultimate reign of Christ over the earth. The chief officer is the president; the board of bishops supervises the general work of the church. There are 28,980 members in 470 churches.

UNITY SCHOOL OF CHRISTIANITY

Charles Fillmore, bankrupt and a cripple, and his wife Myrtle, seriously ill with tuberculosis, discovered in 1887 "a mental treatment that is guaranteed to cure every ill that the flesh is heir to." The treatment, or system, is offered today in the Unity School of Christianity as a curative in many areas beyond physical healing. Unity is not a church or denomination, but a nonsectarian religious educational institution devoted to demonstrating that the teaching of Jesus Christ is a practical, seven-day-a-week way of life.

The Fillmores held that "whatever man wants he can have by voicing his desire in the right way into the Universal Mind," and this emphasis upon Mind they found originally in Christian Science. Both studied Christian Science, though neither was ever a part of the movement. They also studied New Thought, Quakerism, Theosophy, Rosicrucianism, Spiritism, and Hinduism; out of their studies came an ideology both old and original, built on ancient truth and concepts but moving in new directions.

Unity teaches that all thought goes back to God, who is "Principle, Law, Being, Mind, Spirit, All Good, omnipotent, omniscient, unchangeable, Creator, Father, Cause and Source of all that is." In the attribute of Mind is found the "meeting ground of man and God." Unity has a Trinity: "The Father is Principle, the Son is that Principle revealed in a creative plan. The Holy Spirit is the executive power of both Father and Son carrying out the creative plan." Jesus Christ is "Spiritual man, . . . the direct offspring of Divine Mind, God's idea of perfect man." Man is a son of God filled with the Christ consciousness. It is through Christ, or the Christ consciousness, that man gains eternal life and salvation, both of which terms have meanings different from those in orthdox Christianity. Salvation here may be said to mean the attainment of that true spiritual body which replaces the physical body when man becomes like Christ. This transformation takes place not in any hereafter but "here in this earth" through a series of reincarnations and regenerations. Man suffers no final death but only changes into increasingly better states until he becomes as Christ. All men will have this experience.

Unity has been described as "a religious philosophy with an 'open end,' seeking to find God's truth in all of life, wherever it may be." It has no strict creed or dogma; it finds good in all religions, and we should keep our minds open to receive that goodness. Each man must do for himself. Others may help, but ultimately it must be a relationship between God and the individual. Knowing and loving God is the key to peace and success: "To them that love God all things work together for good."

Unlike Christian Science, Unity recognizes the reality of matter, the world, sin, and sickness. Sin and sickness are real but may be overcome. Health is natural; sickness is unnatural. Anything that injures the body is to be avoided—such emotions, for instance, as strife, anger, hatred or self-interest, or the use of alcohol or tobacco. But all this is strictly personal, and a matter of individual decision; Unity lays down no laws concerning health but concentrates on spiritual goals, knowing that healthful living habits will follow. Some Unity students are vegetarians in the interests of health; many are not. Unity is personal; there are no social or health "programs" as such, no hospitals or relief agencies.

Solutions are suggested for every human want and illness. The follower is told to repeat over and over certain affirmations, which develop the all-powerful mind and bring to him from the Divine Mind whatever he needs. Mr. Fillmore once wrote a revised version of the twenty-third psalm calculated to help in the area of economic struggle and success:

The Lord is my banker; my credit is good . . . ;
He giveth me the key to His strongbox;
He restoreth my faith in riches;
He guideth me in the paths of prosperity for His name's sake.*

He does, however, stress the importance of giving above receiving and condemns the greed of mere money-getting as sinful and destructive.

The Bible is used constantly in Unity, but it is not considered the sole or final authority in faith and practice; man must be in direct, personal communion with God and not be dependent upon such secondary sources as the Scriptures.

Unity insists that it is not a church. "The true church is a state of consciousness in man." Unity does have annual conferences, a statement of faith, pulpits supplied with ministers who must be approved by Unity headquarters, and rituals for baptism, Communion, weddings, and funerals. Local groups are organized into centers, which are linked to members of the Association of Unity Churches (a separate organization affiliated with Unity School). More than 600 radio and 270 TV stations broadcast 250 Unity programs per week.

The real work of Unity School is done through what is called Silent Unity. A large staff of workers in Unity Village, near Kansas City, is available for consultation day and night, answering telephone calls, telegrams, and letters—an average of 10,000 calls a week. It is a service of counsel, prayer, and affirmation, offering help on every conceivable problem. Each case or call is assigned to one of this staff, who suggests the proper affirmations. The whole staff joins in group prayer and meditation several times a day. All calls and requests are answered. There is no charge for this service, but love offerings are accepted. In 1 year Unity answered 600,000 such calls for help, most

* From *Prosperity*. Used by permission of Unity School of Christianity.

of them coming from members of various Christian churches. No correspondent is ever asked to leave the church to which he belongs. In addition to the services of Silent Unity some 4,000,000 books, booklets, tracts, and magazines are published and undoubtedly used by many who never contact headquarters at all and never in any sense become members of the school.

VEDANTA SOCIETY

The members of the Vedanta Society base their faith and philosophy upon the writings of the Vedas, the scriptures of the Indo-Aryans. This Indian philosophy, explaining the nature and end of all wisdom, harmonizes the findings of modern science, offers a scientific and philosophical basis for religion, and stresses the oneness of all religions as taught in the Upanishads and the Bhagavad Gita. It was first expounded in this country by Swami Vivekananda at the World's Parliament of Religions held in Chicago in 1893; he founded the society in 1894.

There are 12 Vedanta centers, 3 monasteries, and 2 convents in the United States; all belong to and are under the management of the Ramakrishna Math and Mission founded by Swami Vivekananda, with headquarters in Belur Math, near Calcutta. Each center is an independent, self-supporting unit with its own board of trustees made up mostly of American citizens. The Swamis are ordained monks, and come as guest teachers. There are public lectures and classes for instruction which seek not to convert but to enlighten. There are 1,600 members in 13 societies.

VOLUNTEERS OF AMERICA

The Volunteers of America is a religious social welfare organization founded in 1896 by the late Ballington and Maud Booth and incorporated in the same year under the laws of the state of New York; more than 30,000 members were reported in 1973, but this figure hardly tells the whole story of services rendered to hundreds of thousands of people in the principal cities of the United States.

Religious services are offered in missions, Volunteer churches, Sunday schools, companionship leagues, prisons, and on the streets; the organization has its own rituals for baptism, the Lord's Supper, and marriage. Doctrine is evangelical, with strong emphasis on the saving grace of God, the Trinity, the atonement of Christ, regeneration through the Holy Spirit, the necessity of repentance and conversion, immortality, and future rewards and punishments.

The social welfare programs include departments of family welfare, salvage, health camps, day nurseries, hospices for working girls, maternity homes, homes for mothers and children, adoptive placements, clubs and homes for the aged, rehabilitation workshops, family counseling centers, transient men's homes, and boys' and girls' clubs. There is an excellent prison department, assisting discharged and paroled prisoners, men and women in prison, and their families; more than 100,000 prisoners are enrolled in the Volunteer Prison League—a self-help group organized by inmates in various correctional institutions with VOA consultation and guidance. Recent program developments include two score prerelease centers or half-way house facilities. There are also 24 housing projects for low and moderate income families and senior citizens, constructed during the past five years. These facilities provide more than 7,500 units serving nearly 30,000 families and individuals. VOA is also guiding the development and operation of nursing home care and presently operates 10 nursing homes with a 1500-bed capacity.

Operation of the Volunteers is based on a semimilitary organization structure. All officers bear military titles and wear uniforms. The chief governing body is called the Grand Field Council and is composed of those officers bearing the rank of lieutenant major or above. There is a board of 10 members known as the National Executive Board which functions when the Grand Field Council is not in session. The incorporation has a directorate of 9, who are the responsible financial officers and who act as trustees and custodians of all property. Military regulations do not apply in the selection of these top officers; they are chosen by democratic election. The commander in chief is elected for 5 years and is also president of the corporate body. There are 4 administrative regions—Eastern, Western, Midwest and Southern. National officers and staff are located in New York City.

During 1972 nearly 6,000,000 people received material assistance through various departments, exclusive of religious services. There were 9,000,000 meals and 2,000,000 lodgings furnished; in addition, more than 6,500 chldren were cared for in such child service centers as day care centers, foster day care, group homes, summer camps, etc. Nearly 100,000 elderly persons participated in the Sunset Club program; more than 16,000 interviews were held in prisons; 160,000 prisoners attended Volunteer religious services; and 2,000 prisoners were paroled in their custody. Nearly 60,000 men were given job opportunities in the Men's Rehabilitation Centers, and 30,000 unemployed men were aided in securing work in business and industry. Over 30,000,000 articles such as furniture, household appliances, and clothing were distributed free or at nominal cost to low income families and individuals. The annual budget of the Volunteers is in excess of $32 million.

WESLEYAN CHURCH

Until 1968 this was the Wesleyan Methodist Church of America; it represented, at the time of its founding in 1843, a protest against slavery and the Methodist episcopacy which predated by 1 year the historic division of the Methodist Episcopal Church and the Methodist Episcopal Church, South. With the slavery issue settled by the Civil War, other differences of a spiritual or reform nature—entire sanctification and opposition to the liquor traffic—seemed important enough to continue the separate existence of the Wesleyan Methodist Church.

In June of 1968 the Wesleyan Methodist Church merged with the Pilgrim Holiness Church, giving it a membership total of 87,240 in 1,891 churches in the United States and 134,052 worldwide. With this merger, the body became the Wesleyan Church.

The Pilgrim Holiness Church was close in doctrine and polity to the Church of the Nazarene, and thus close to Methodism and in agreement with Wesleyan doctrines. There was no shift or change in doctrinal emphases, when the 2 churches joined. The time-honored teaching of sanctification is still central. Candidates for membership are required, in the Wesleyan Church, to disavow the use, sale, or manufacture of tobacco and alcoholic beverages, and to refrain from membership in secret societies.

An enlarging evangelistic and missionary activity is directed from world headquarters in Marion, Indiana. As of June, 1969, 49 conferences had missionaries at work in Australia, Haiti, Honduras, India, Jamaica, Japan, Mexico, Nepal, New Guinea, Puerto Rico, Taiwan, Sierra Leone, Rhodesia, South Africa, South America, and among the Indians in South Dakota. There are 4 colleges, 2 Bible colleges, 2 academies, and one seminary foundation (associated with Asbury Seminary in Wilmore, Kentucky).

Merger with the Free Methodist Church is under current consideration by both denominations.

HEADQUARTERS OF
DENOMINATIONS

(Addresses of denominational headquarters are given wherever possible; otherwise, the names of chief and preferably permanent officials are listed.)

Adventists:
  Seventh-day Adventists: 6840 Eastern Ave., N. W., Washington, D. C. 20012.
  Advent Christian Church: Rev. Howard Shaw, P. O. Box 23152, Charlotte, NC 28212
  Church of God (Abrahamic Faith): Oregon, IL 61061
  Primitive Advent Christian Church: Sec. Hugh W. Good, Elkview, WV 25071
African Orthodox Church: 122 West 129 St., New York, NY 10027
Amana Church Society: Pres. Charles L. Selzer, Homestead, IA 52236
American Ethical Union: 2 West 64th St., New York, NY 10023
American Evangelical Christian Churches: 192 No. Clark St., Chicago, IL 60601
American Ministerial Assn.: P.O. Box 1252, York, PA 17405
American Rescue Workers: 2827 Frankford Ave., Philadelphia, PA 19134
Anglican Orthodox Church: Bishop James Parker Dees, 315 East Front St., Statesville, NC 28677
Apostolic Christian Church (Nazarean): P. O. Box 5233, Akron, OH 44313
Apostolic Christian Church of America: Elder Roy L. Sauder, 3528 N. Linden Lane, Peoria, IL 61604
Apostolic Faith: Northwest Sixth & Burnside, Portland, OR 92709
Apostolic Overcoming Holy Church of God: Bishop W. T. Phillips, 2212 Tonlours Dr., Mobile, AL 36617
Armenian Churches: Archbishop Hrant Khatchadourian, 138 East 39th St., New York, NY 10016
Assemblies of God, General Council, 1345 Boonville Ave., Springfield, MO 65802
Bahai: 112 Linden Ave., Wilmette, IL 60091
Baptists:
  American Baptist Churches in the U.S.A.: Valley Forge, PA 19481
  Southern Baptist Convention: 460 James Robertson Parkway, Nashville, TN 37209
  National Baptist Convention, U.S.A., Inc.: Rev. T. J. Jemison, Sec., 915 Spain St., Baton Rouge, LA 70872
  National Baptist Convention of America: Rev. Billy H. Wilson, Sec., 2620 S. Marsallis Ave., Dallas, TX 77020
  American Baptist Assn.: P.O. Box 901, Texarkana, AR-TX 75501
  Baptist Bible Fellowship, International: 730 East Kearney, Springfield, MO 65800
  Baptist General Conference: 1233 Central St., Evanston, IL 60201
  Baptist Ministerial Assn.: Box 5353, Evansville, IN 47715

Baptist Missionary Assn. of America: Rev. Ralph Cottrell, P. O. Box 2866, Texarkana, AR 75501

Bethel Ministerial Assn.: 4350 Lincoln Ave., Evansville, IN 47715

Central Baptist Assn.: Duffield RFD 1, Jasper, TN 37347

Conservative Baptist Assn. of America: P.O. Box 66, Wheaton, IL 60187

Duck River (and Kindred) Assns. of Baptists: Elder James F. Patton, Morrison, TN 37357

Free Will Baptists: 1134 Murfreesboro Rd., Nashville, TN 37202

General Baptists: Poplar Bluff, MO 63901

General Assn. of Regular Baptist Churches: 1800 Oakton Blvd., Des Plaines, IL 60018

General Conference of the Evangelical Baptist Church: 1601 East Rose St., Goldsboro, NC 27530

General Six-Principle Baptists: Marjorie DeAngelis, Clerk, Harkney Hill Road, Coventry, RI 02816

National Baptist Evangelical and Soul-Saving Assembly of the U.S.A.: 441 Monroe Ave., Detroit, MI 48207

National Primitive Baptist Convention of the USA.: P. O. Box 2355, Tallahassee, FL 32301

North American Baptist Assn.: 716 Main Street, Little Rock, AR 72201

North American Baptist General Conference: 7308 Madison St., Forest Park, IL 60130

Primitive Baptists: Cayce Pub. Co., S. Second Street, Thornton, AR 71766

Separate Baptists in Christ: Floyd Wilson, Clerk, 59 Greensprings Rd., Indianapolis, IN 46224

Seventh Day Baptists: 510 Watchung Ave, Plainfield, NJ 07061

Seventh Day Baptists (German, 1728): Rev. Crist M. King, Pres., 238 S. Aiken St., Pittsburgh, PA 15206

United Free Will Baptist Church: Kinston College, 1000 University St. Kinston, NC 28501

Bible Protestant Church: 110 Virginia Ave., Audubon, NJ 08106

Bible Way Church, World Wide: 1130 New Jersey Ave., Washington, D.C. 20001

Brethren (Dunkers):

Church of the Brethren: 1451 Dundee Ave., Elgin, IL 60120

Brethren Church (National Fellowship of Brethren Churches): Clyde K. Landrum, Sec., 1108 Chestnut Ave., Winona Lake, IN 46590

Brethren Church (Ashland, Ohio): 524 College Ave., Ashland, OH 44805

Old German Baptist Brethren: Elder M. B. Wagoner, R.D. 4, Delphi, IN 46923

Plymouth Brethren: Paul F. Loizeaux, Correspondent, Mt. Carlem Road, Parkton, MD 21120

River Brethren:

Brethren in Christ: Rev. Owen H. Alderfer, Sec., 26 Leawood Ave., Ashland, OH 44805

United Zion Church: Rev. J. Paul Martin, Sec., 212D, R.D.1, Annville, PA 17003

United Brethren:
  Church of the United Brethren in Christ: 402 United Brethren Building, Huntington, IN 46750
  United Christian Church: Elder Henry C. Heagy, Lebanon R.D.4, Lebanon County, PA 17042
Buddhist Churches of America: 1710 Octavia St., San Francisco, CA 94109
Christadelphians: Edwin A. Zilmer, Sec., 2126 W. 9th St., Waterloo, IA 50702
Christian and Missionary Alliance: 260 West 44th Street, New York, NY 10036
Christian Catholic Church: Dowie Memorial Drive, Zion, IL 60099
Christian Church of North America: P.O. Box 801, Sharon, PA 16146
Christian Church (Disciples of Christ): 222 S. Downey Ave., Indianapolis, IN 46206
Christian Congregation: Rev. Ora Wilbert Eads, Supt., 708 South Bragg St., Monroe, NC 28110
Christian Nation Church: Rev. W. F. Clark, Gen. Sec., 345 Cedar Dr., Loveland, OH 45140
Christian Union: P. O. Box 38, Excelsior Springs, MO 64024
Christ's Sanctified Holy Church: S. Cutting Ave. & East Spencer St., Jennings, LA 70546
Church of Christ (Holiness) U.S.A.: 329 East Monument St., Jackson, MS 39202
Church of Christ, Scientist: 107 Falmouth St., Boston, MA 03100
Church of God (Anderson, Ind.): Box 2420, Anderson, IN 46011
Church of God (Apostolic): St. Peter's Church of God (Apostolic), 11th & Hickory St., Winston Salem, NC 27101
Church of God (Cleveland, Tenn.): Keith St. at 25th., Cleveland, TN 37311
Church of God (Seventh Day, Denver, Colo.): P. O. Box 2370, Denver, CO 80201
Church of God (Seventh Day, Salem, W.Va.): 79 Water St., Salem, WV 26426
Church of God (Tomlinson): 2504 Arrow Wood Drive, Huntsville, AL 35803
(Original) Church of God: 2214 E. 17th St., Chattanooga, TN 37404
Church of God and Saints in Christ: Belleville, Portsmouth, VA 23704
Church of God by Faith: 3220 Haines St., Jacksonville, FL 32206
Church of God in Christ: 938 Mason St., Memphis, TN 38126
Church of God of Prophecy: Bible Place, Cleveland, TN 37311
Church of God in Christ (International): 1331 Quindare Blvd., Kansas City, KS 66104
Worldwide Church of God: Ambassador College, P. O. Box 111, Pasadena, CA 91109
Church of Illumination: Beverly Hall, Clymer Rd., Quakertown, PA 18951
Church of Jesus Christ of Latter-day Saints (Mormons):
  Church of Jesus Christ of Latter-day Saints: 47 E. South Temple St., Salt Lake City, UT 84111

276

Reorganized Church of Jesus Christ of Latter-day Saints: The Auditorium, Independence, MO 64051

Christ of Jesus Christ (Temple Lot): Temple Lot, Independence, Mo 64000

Church of Jesus Christ (Bickertonites): Sixth & Lincoln Sts., Monongahela, PA 15063.

Church of Jesus Christ of Latter-Day Saints (Strangites): Elder Vernon D. Swift, P.O. Box 522, Artesia, NM 88210

Church of Our Lord Jesus Christ of the Apostolic Faith: 112 East 125th St., New York, NY 10035

Church of the Nazarene: 6401 The Paseo, Kansas City, MO 64131

Churches of Christ: B. C. Goodpasture, 1006 Elm Hill Rd., Nashville, TN 37201

Churches of Christ in Christian Union: Circleville Bible College, 459 E. Ohion St., Circleville, OH 43113

Churches of God, Holiness: 170 Ashby St., N.W., Atlanta, GA 30314

Churches of God in North America (General Eldership): 611 S. 17th St., Harrisburg, PA 17105

Churches of the Living God:

Church of the Living God (Christian Workers for Fellowship): Bishop F. C. Scott, 801 N. E. 17th St., Oklahoma City, OK 73105

House of God, Which Is the Church of the Living God: Bishop A. H. White, 6107 Cobbs Creek Pkwy., Philadelphia, PA 19143

Churches of the New Jerusalem:

General Church of the New Jerusalem: Bryn Athyn, PA 19009

General Convention of the New Jerusalem in the U.S.A.: Rev. Richard H. Tafel, 219 Chestnut St., Philadelphia, PA 19106

Congregational Christian Churches (National Assn.): 176 West Wisconsin Ave., Milwaukee, WI 53203

Congregational Holiness Church: Griffin, GA 30223

Conservative Congregational Christian Conference: P. O. Box 171, Hinsdale, IL 60521

Divine Science Church: 1400 Williams St., Denver, CO 80218

Eastern Churches:

Albanian Churches: 54 Burroughs St., Jamaica Plain, MA 02130

American Carpatho-Russian Orthodox Greek Catholic Church: Johnstown, PA 15906

American Holy Orthodox Catholic Apostolic Eastern Church; His Holiness Patriarch Clement, 247 E. 126th St., New York NY 10035

Antiochan Orthodox Archdiocese of Toledo, Ohio and Dependences: 532 Bush St., Toledo, OH 43604

Bulgarian Eastern Orthodox Church: Bishop Znepolsky, 2430 Titan Drive, Akron, OH 44321

Eastern Orthodox Catholic Church in America: 1914 Hwy. 17-92, Fern Park, FL 32730

Greek Archdiocese of North and South America: 10 East 79th. St., New York, NY 10021

277

Holy Apostolic and Catholic Church of the East (Assyrians): 554 Arball Drive, San Francisco, CA 94132

Holy Orthodox Church in America (Eastern Catholic and Apostolic): See House, 321 W. 101st St., New York, NY 10025

Romanian Orthodox Episcopate of America: 2522 Grey Tower Road, RFD 7, Jackson, MI 49201

Russian Orthodox Church of America: 15 East 97th St., New York NY 10029

Russian Orthodox Church Outside Russia: 75 E. 93rd St., New York, NY 10028

Russian Orthodox Greek Catholic Church of America: 59 E. 2nd St., New York, NY 10003

Serbian Eastern Orthodox Church in the USA and Canada: 5701 N. Redwood Dr., Chicago, IL 60656

Syrian Antiochian Orthodox Church: 239 85th. St., Brooklyn, NY 11209

Syrian Orthodox Church of Antioch: 293 Hamilton Place, Hackensack, NJ 07601

Ukranian Orthodox Church of America: 90-34 139th St., Jamaica, NY 11400

Ukranian Orthodox Church in the U.S.A.: P. O. Box 595, South Bound Brook, NJ 08880

Episcopal Church: 815 Second Avenue, New York, NY 10017

Evangelical and Reformed Church: See United Church of Christ

Evangelical Church of North America: 2827 Newton Ave., North, Minneapolis, MN 55411

Evangelical Congregational Church: Bishop P. K. Cressman, 1005 Barberry Road, Wyomissing Park, Reading, PA 19602

Evangelical Covenant Church of America: 5101 N. Francisco Ave, Chicago IL 60625

Evangelical Free Church of America: 1515 E. 66th St., Minneapolis, MN 55423

Federated Churches: National Council of Community Churches, the Ecumenical Center of Ohio: 89 East Wilson Bridge Rd., Worthington, OH 43085

Fire Baptized Holiness Church (Wesleyan): 600 Country Club Drive, Independence, KS 67301

Free Christian Zion Church of Christ: Nashville, AR 71852

Friends:

Friends General Conference: 1520 Race Street, Philadelphia, PA 19102

Friends United Meeting: Lorton G. Heusel, Sec., 101 Quaker Hill Drive, Richmond, IN 47374

Religious Society of Friends (Conservative): Mary S. Autenrieth, Clerk, Iowa Meeting, R.1, Paullina, IA 51046

House of David: P. O. Box 1067, Benton Harbor, MI 49022

Independent Assemblies of God, International: 3840 5th Avenue, San Diego, CA 92103

Independent Christian Churches: North American Christian Convention, 3533 Epley Rd., Cincinnati, OH 45239

Independent Churches: See Federated Churches

Independent Fundamental Churches of America: 1860 Mannheim Rd., P. O. Box 242, Westchester, IL 60153

International Church of the Foursquare Gospel: 1100 Glendale Blvd., Los Angeles, CA 90026

Jehovah's Witnesses: 124 Columbia Heights, Brooklyn, NY 11201

Jewish Congregations: American Jewish Committee, 165 East 56th St., New York, NY 10022

Kodesh Church of Immanuel: 1509 S Street, N.W., Washington, D.C. 20009

Liberal Catholic Church: P. O. Box 185, Miranda, CA 95553

Light of the Way Open Door Church, International: 1391 DeSoto Ave. S.W., Atlanta, GA 30310

Lutherans:

American Lutheran Church: 422 S. 5th St., Minneapolis, MN 55415

Lutheran Church in America: 231 Madison Ave., New York, NY 10016

Church of the Lutheran Brethren in America: Fergus Falls, MN 56537

Evangelical Lutheran Synod: Rev. Alf Merseth, Sec., 106 13th St. So., Norwood, IA 50459

Apostolic Lutheran Church of America: James Johnson, Sec., R. 2, Box 99, L'Anse, MI 49946

Lutheran Church—Missouri Synod: Lutheran Building, 210 N. Broadway, St. Louis, MO 63102

Protestant Conference (Lutheran): Rev. Marcus Albrecht, Sec., Mindoro, WI 54644

Wisconsin Evangelical Lutheran Synod: Rev. Oscar J. Naumann, Pres., 3512 West North Ave., Milwaukee, WI 53208

Mennonites:

Beachy Amish Mennonite Church: Dr. J. C. Wenger, Goshen College Biblical Seminary, Goshen, IN 46526

Church of God in Christ (Mennonite): 420 N. Wedel St., Moundridge, KS 67107

Conservative Mennonite Conference: Daniel Yutzy, Sec., Two Rod Road, Marilla, NY 14102

Evangelical Mennonite Brethren: 5800 14th St., Omaha, NE 68107

Evangelical Mennonite Church, Inc.: 7237 Leo Road, Fort Wayne, IN 46825

General Conference Mennonite Church: 722 Main St., Newton, KS 67114

Hutterian Brethren: Rev. Daniel S. Wipf., Cor., Alexandria, SD 57311

Mennonite Brethren Church of North America: Dr. Frank C. Peters, Chm., Winnipeg, Man., Canada

Mennonite Church: 10600 Higgins Rd., Rosemont, IL 60018

Old Order Amish Mennonite Church: Der Neue Amerikanische Calendar, % Raber's Book Store, Baltic, OH 43804

Old Order (Wisler) Mennonite Church: Henry W. Riehl, Rt. 1, Columbiana, OH 44408

Reformed Mennonite Church: Bishop L. Henry Fisher, 25 Greenfield Road, Lancaster, PA 17602

Unaffiliated Mennonites: Dr. J. C. Wenger, Goshen College Biblical Seminary, Goshen, IN 46526

Methodists:

United Methodist Church: 475 Riverside Drive, New York, NY 10027

African Methodist Episcopal Church: 2295 Seventh Ave., New York, NY 10030

African Methodist Episcopal Zion Church: Rev. R. H. Collins Lee, Gen. Sec., 1328 U Street N.W., Washington, D.C. 20009

The Association of Independent Methodists: Ivan C. Howard, P.O. Box 4274, Jackson, MS 39216

Christian Methodist Episcopal Church: 564 East Frank Ave., Memphis, TN 38106

Congregational Methodist Church: Rev. A. F. O'Connor, Ex. Sec., P.O. Box 555, Florence, MS 39073

First Congregational Methodist Church of the U.S.A.: Decatur, MS 39327

New Congregational Methodist Church: Bishop Joe E. Kelley, 354 9th. St., Jacksonville, FL 32206

Cumberland Methodist Church: Rev. Carl A. Shadrick, Pres., Whitwell, TN 37397

Evangelical Methodist Church: 3036 North Meridian, Wichita, KS 67204

Free Methodist Church of North America: Winona Lake, IN 46590

Fundamental Methodist Church Inc.: Rev. E. J. Ethridge, 2652 Horning, Springfield, MO 65802

Primitive Methodist Church: Rev. Harold K. Hatton, Sec., 408 East Market St., Scranton, PA 18509

Reformed Methodist Union Episcopal Church: Charleston, SC 29407

Reformed Zion Union Apostolic Church: Rev. T. J. Johnson, South Hill, VA 23970

Southern Methodist Church: Rev. Glen S. Comfort, Pres. P.O. Box 132, Orangeburg, SC 29115

Union American Methodist Episcopal Church: Rev. David M. Harmon, 774 Pine St., Camden NJ 08123

Metropolitan Church Assn.: 323 Broad St., Lake Geneva, WI 53147

Missionary Church: 3901 S. Wayne Ave., Ft. Wayne, IN 46807

Moravians:

Moravian Church in America (Unitas Fratrum): 69 West Church Street, Bethlehem, PA 18018

Unity of the Brethren: Stanley F. Mrnustik, Sec., 205 N. Shaw, Caldwell, TX 77836

Muslims: Islamic Center, 2551 Massachusetts Ave., N.W., Washington, D.C. 20008

New Apostolic Church of North America: 3753 N. Troy St., Chicago, IL 60618

Old Catholic Churches:
 American Catholic Church Archdiocese of New York: Most Rev. James
 Francis Lashley, 457 W. 144th St. New York, NY 10031
 American Catholic Church (Syro-Antiochian): St. Peter's Cathedral,
 1811 N.W. 4th Court, Miami, FL 33136
 Old Roman Catholic Church (English Rite): Archbishop Robert Alfred
 Burns, 840 North Oakley Blvd., Chicago, IL 60622
Open Bible Standard Churches Inc.: O. Ralph Isbil, Sec., Bell Ave. at
 Fleur Dr., P.O. Box 1737, Des Moines, IA 50306
Pentecostal Bodies:
 Elim Fellowship: Rev. Carlton Spencer, Pres., Lima, NY 14485
 Emmanuel Holiness Church: J. Robert Hicks, Sec., Rt. 3, Anderson, SC
 29621
 International Pentecostal Assemblies: 892 Berne St., S.E. Atlanta, GA
 30306
 Pentecostal Assemblies of the World: 3040 N. Illinois St., Indianapolis,
 IN 46208
 Pentecostal Church of Christ: Box 263, London, OH 43140
 Pentecostal Church of God of America: 312-316 S. Joplin St. Joplin, MO
 64801
 Pentecostal Fire-Baptized Holiness Church: Toccoa, GA 30577
 Pentecostal Free-Will Baptist Church: Rev. Herbert Carter, Supt., P.O.
 Box 966, Dunn, NC 28334
 Pentecostal Holiness Church: Franklin Springs, GA 30639
 United Pentecostal Church International: 8855 Dunn Road, Hazelwood,
 MO 63042
Pillar of Fire: Zarepath, NJ 08890
Polish National Catholic Church of America: 529 East Locust St., Scranton,
 PA 18505

Presbyterians:
 United Presbyterian Church in the U. S. A.: 510 Witherspoon Bldg.,
 Philadelphia, PA 19107
 Presbyterian Church in the U. S.: 341 Ponce De Leon Ave., N.E., At-
 lanta, GA 30308
 Associate Presbyterian Church of North America: Rev. Paul J. Hindman,
 Clerk, Box 555, Mineola, KS 67865
 Associate Reformed Presbyterian Church: Associate Reformed Presby-
 terian Church Center, Greenville, SC 29601
 Bible Presbyterian Church: Haddon Ave. & Cuthbert Blvd, Collings-
 wood, NJ 08108
 Cumberland Presbyterian Church: Rev. H. Shaw Scates, Clerk, Box
 4149, Memphis TN 42445
 Second Cumberland Presbyterian Church in the U.S.: Rev. Roy Tinsley,
 Clerk, Princeton, KY 42445
 Orthodox Presbyterian Church: 7401 Old York Rd., Philadelphia, PA
 19126

Reformed Presbyterian Church, Evangelical Synod: Rev. Paul R. Gilchrist, Clerk, 107 Hardy Rd., Lookout Mountain, TN 37350

Reformed Presbyterian Church of North America: Rev. Bruce C. Stewart, Clerk, 5139 Argus Dr., Los Angeles, CA 90041

Reformed Bodies:

Reformed Church in America: 475 Riverside Drive, New York, NY 10027

Christian Reformed Church: Rev. William P. Brink, Clerk, 2850 Kalamazoo Ave. S.S., Grand Rapids, MI 49508

Hungarian Reformed Church in America: Bishop D. Abraham, 331 Kirkland Place, Perth Amboy, NJ 08861

Netherlands Reformed Congregations: Rev. W. C. Lamain, Chrmn., 2115 Romance St., N.E., Grand Rapids MI 49500

Protestant Reformed Churches of America: 463 E. 154th Place, South Holland, IL 60473

Reformed Church in the U.S.: Rev. D. W. Treick, Clerk, 1408 S. Lincoln St. Aberdeen, SD 57401

Reformed Episcopal Church: Rev. D. Ellsworth Raudenbush, Sec., 560 Fountain St., Havre de Grace, MD 21078

Roman Catholic Church: U. S. Catholic Conference, 1312 Massachusetts Ave., N.W. Washington, D.C. 20005

Salvation Army: 120-30 West 14th Street, New York, NY 10011

Schwenkenfelder Church: Pennsburg, PA 18073

Social Brethren: Rev. John Bailey, Mod., RFD 2, Simpson, IL 62985

Spiritualists:

International General Assembly of Spiritualists: 1809 East Bayview Blvd., Norfolk, VA 23503

National Spiritual Alliance of the U.S.A.: R.F.D. 1, Keene, NH 03431

National Spiritualist Assn. of Churches: P. O. Box 128, Cassadaga, FL 32706

Theosophy: Theosophical Society of America, 306 West Geneva Road, Wheaton, IL 60187

Triumph the Church and Kingdom of God in Christ: 213 Furrington Ave., S.E., Atlanta, GA 30300

Unitarian Universalist Assn.: 25 Beacon St., Boston, MA 02108

United Church of Christ: 297 Park Avenue South, New York, NY 10010

United Holy Church of America, Inc.: Bishop Thomas E. Talley, 2710 Magnolia St., Portsmouth, VA 28704

Unity School of Christianity: Unity Village, MO 64063

Vedanta Society: 34 West 71st St., New York, NY 10023

Volunteers of America: 340 West 85th Street, New York, NY 10024

Wesleyan Church: D. Wayne Brown, Gen. Sec., P. O. Box 2000, Marion, IN 46952

GLOSSARY OF TERMS

The definitions rendered here depend largely upon six sources: *The Dictionary of Religion and Ethics*, edited by Shailer Mathews and Gerald B. Smith (Macmillan); *Funk and Wagnalls College Standard Dictionary*; *Webster's Dictionary* (Merriam); *The Oxford Dictionary of the Christian Church* (Oxford); *Dictionary of Ecclesiastical Terms*, by J. S. Purvis (Nelson); *Dictionary of Religious Terms*, by Donald T. Kauffman (Revell).

ABSOLUTION: The remission of guilt and penalty for sin by a priest, following confession.

ADOPTION: A legal term appropriated by theology, originating in Paul and signifying the act by which the privileges of a child of God are conferred upon the believer in Christ.

ADVENTIST: A believer in the incarnation of God in Christ, at the time of Christ's birth, or in the Second Coming or Advent.

AFFUSION: The pouring or sprinkling of water in baptism.

ALLAH: In Islam, the name of the Supreme Being or all-powerful God.

ANNUNCIATION: The announcement by the angel Gabriel to the Virgin Mary that she was to be the mother of Christ.

ANOINTING: The act of consecrating by the application of oil, used in consecrating sacred objects or persons, as preparation for death, or in completing the efficacy of baptism.

ANTINOMIANISM: The doctrine that the gospel or the Christian faith does away with the old moral law, so that the Christian is not bound by it.

APOCALYPTIC: Pertaining to or in the nature of a revelation.

APOCRYPHA: A group of books excluded by Protestants from the Bible as not authoritative but worthy of study for their religious and historical value.

APOSTOLIC: Of or pertaining to an apostle or according to the belief or practices of the apostles.

APOSTOLIC SUCCESSION: The doctrine of an unbroken line of succession in the episcopacy from the apostles to the present time, maintained in Greek, Roman, and Anglican churches.

ARMINIAN: The follower of Arminius (1560-1609), a Dutch Protestant theologian. Arminius denied Calvin's doctrine of unconditional predestination, limited atonement, and irresistible grace, and stood for universal salvation for all.

ATHANASIAN: The belief of Athanasius (293-373), who was a defender of the orthodox view of the divinity of Christ. He opposed and won over Arius at the Council of Nicaea; Arius held that Christ was created by but was essentially different from the Father.

ATONEMENT: The reconciliation of the sinner with God through the sufferings of Jesus Christ.

AUTOCEPHALOUS: Ecclesiastically self-controlling, or having jurisdiction as an independent head. "Autocephali" was a term applied to bishops in early Christian times who recognized no ecclesiastical superior.

AUTONOMOUS: Self-governing, or independent.

BAN, THE: A sentence which amounts to excommunication or outlawry by the church upon those guilty of an act or speech forbidden by the church.

BAPTISM: The ceremonial application of water to a person by either sprinkling, immersion, or affusion as a sign of the washing away of sin and of admission into the church as commanded by Christ in Matt. 28:19. Spirit baptism in some sects is a baptism by the Holy Ghost, not with water.

CALVINISTS: Those holding the faith of John Calvin (1509-64).

CANON: The books admitted to the Bible as authentic and authoritative.

CATECHISM: The form or guide of instruction used in instruction of candidates for church membership, preceding baptism. The book containing items for such instruction.

CATHOLIC EPISTLES: The New Testament Epistles (usually James, 1 and 2 Peter, 1 John and Jude, 2 and 3 John) which were addressed to the whole (catholic) church.

CATHOLICOS: An Oriental primate or head of a sect. "Catholikos" was a term assumed by the spiritual head of the Armenian Church and later applied to several prelates under him.

CELIBACY: The state of being unmarried.

CENOBITE: Person in a religious order who lives in a separate cell, but who is also a member of a community of other such persons.

CHALICE: A cup used at Communion services resembling the one used at the original Last Supper.

CHASTITY: The state of refraining from sexual relations in order to obtain religious or moral purity.

CHRISM: An ungent, usually olive oil or balm, used in the Greek and Roman Catholic churches for anointing at baptism, confirmation, ordination, and consecration services, and sometimes for extreme unction. Chrismation is the act of anointing.

CHRISTOCENTRIC: With Christ as the center.

CLASSIS: In some Reformed churches a court made up of ministers and ruling elders with a status between a consistory and a synod, corresponding to the presbytery in Presbyterian churches. It may also mean the district it represents.

COLLECT: Brief prayer asking for specific blessing. Or, generally, in Roman and Anglican liturgies, a prayer read before the Gospel and Epistle are read, to condense or "collect" their teaching.

COMMUNION: The Lord's Supper. "Open" Communion is a sacrament open to all Christians; "closed" Communion is closed to all except those of a particular faith or belief. The word is also used occasionally as a synonym for denomination.

CONFESSION: A statement of the religious beliefs of a religious body, or an admisson of sin upon conversion.

CONFIRMATION: The initiatory rite by which persons are inducted into the church, or the approval of authorites by which the election of bishops is ratified by the church.

CONGREGATIONAL: The church polity which makes the authority of the local congregation supreme within its own area.

CONSECRATE: To set apart as sacred certain persons, animals, places, objects, or times.

CONSISTORY: (1) An ecclesiastical court. The papal (Roman Catholic) consistory is composed of the College of Cardinals, over whom the pope presides, and meets to ratify various measures. (2) The Dutch Reformed consistory corresponds to the Presbyterian session. (3) The French Reformed consistory is similar to the presbytery in Presbyterian polity. (4) The Lutheran consistory (abroad) is appointed by the state. (5) The consistory of the Anglicans has diocesan jurisdiction.

CONSUBSTANTIATION: The theory that, following the words of institution in the Lord's Supper, the substantial body and blood of Christ join sacramentally with the bread and wine (which remains unchanged), the union remaining only until the purpose of the consecration is fulfilled. Applied often to Lutheran doctrine, it is denied by the Lutherans.

CONVERSION: Religiously, a radical spiritual and moral change, commonly attending a change of belief, and involving profoundly altered spirit and conduct—"a change of heart."

COVENANT: Sacred relationship between God and man. The designations "Old Testament" and "New Testament" indicate the Christian concept of the old covenant of works in Judaism being supplanted by the new covenant of grace through the work of Christ.

CREED: A statement of belief including the fundamentals considered necessary to salvation; a creed differs from a confession in that it may be held by Christians and recited in public worship.

DEACON: A minor church officer; its origin is often identified with the appointment of the seven in Acts 6:1-6.

DECALOGUE: The Ten Commandments.

DEISM: School of philosophy and theology teaching God's relation to man as expressed in universal natural law rather than through revelation.

DIOCESE: The territory of a church under the jurisdiction of a bishop.

DOCTRINE: That which is taught as the belief of a church.

DOGMA: Belief authoritatively held by a religious group.

ECCLESIASTICAL: Pertaining to the church or the clergy.

ECUMENICAL OR OECUMENICAL: General, universal, representing the whole Christian church.

ECUMENICAL COUNCILS, THE: The seven early Church councils of Nicaea (I) in 325, Constantinople (I) in 381, Ephesus in 431, Chalcedon in 451, Constantinople (II) in 553, Constantinople (III) in 680, and Nicaea (II) in 787.

ELECTION: Selection of an individual by God for salvation.

ENCYCLICAL: A circular letter sent to local churches, usually a communication from the Pope, but more recently used in a broader sense to report the actions or findings of church conferences.

EPISCOPAL: Having to do with bishops, or governed by bishops.

ESCHATOLOGY: Study of the last things, involving the final coming and triumph of Christ and his Kingdom, and sometimes the resurrection and related topics.

ESOTERIC: A term based on the custom in the Greek Mystery religions to explain advanced doctrines only to the fully initiated.

EUCHARIST: Holy Communion, the Lord's Supper.

EVANGELICAL: A word used to denote primary loyalty to the gospel of Christ in contrast to ecclesiastical or rationalistic types of Christianity; spiritual-mindedness and zeal for Christian living as distinguished from ritualism.

EXCOMMUNICATION: Exclusion from the religious fellowship of the church; can be either permanent or temporary.

EXTREME UNCTION: See unction.

FALL OF MAN: Man's estrangement from God through sin, as symbolized by the disobedience of Adam and Eve.

FASTING: Going without food or certain foods for a specified period.

FOOT WASHING: The practice of washing the feet of fellow church members, sometimes as a ceremonial cleansing from defilement preparatory to worship, sometimes as an ordinance, by Mennonites, Dunkards, the Church of God, and so on.

FREE WILL: Man's power to choose between good and evil without compulsion or necessity.

FUNDAMENTALIST: One who believes in the infallibility of the Bible as inspired by God and that it should be accepted literally—as distinguished from the modernist, who interprets the Bible in accordance with more modern scholarship or scientific knowledge—and who accepts the conservative orthodox position in all manners of doctrine and theology.

FUTURE PUNISHMENT: The punishment inflicted upon sinners *after death*.

GENERAL CONFESSION: A public, congregational confession of sins; among Roman Catholics, a confession in which the individual sums up past sins; among Protestants, a section of the ritual recited in unison by pastor and congregation, modeled on historic Roman Catholic and Anglican forms.

GENERATIONISM: The belief that the soul as well as the body is procreated by the parents of the child, in the act of propagation. Similar to traducianism, but differnt from creationism and preexistence.

GENUFLECTION: The act of bending the knee in worship, or in entering the sanctuary or approaching the altar, as an indication of reverence and humility—a custom dating from the early church, still prevalent in many liturgical churches.

GIFT OF TONGUES: Ecstatic speech induced by religious excitement or emotion.

GLOSSOLALIA: Speaking in tongues—the psychological and religious phenomeon described in the account of Pentecost, in Acts 2.

GRACE: The gift of God to man of the divine favor and inner power necessary to salvation.

HIERARCHY: Government by priests or prelates, as in the Roman Catholic Church.

HOLINESS: A state of moral and spiritual purity and sinlessness, or a title designating persons set apart for religious service.

HOLY ORDERS: The power granted the ecclesiastical leaders of the church (bishops, priests, ministers, elders, deacons, subdeacons, etc.) to direct the spiritual functions of the church.

IMMACULATE CONCEPTION, THE: The dogma that the Virgin Mary was conceived free of original sin.

IMMANENCE: A term describing the presence of God in the world, as opposed to his transcendance.

IMMERSION: Baptism by complete submersion in water.

IMPANATION: The doctrine that the body and blood of Christ are present in one substance in the bread and wine of the Eucharist after consecration, but without transubstantiation; held to be heretical by the Roman Catholic Church.

IMMORTALITY: Life after death, life imperishable.

INCARNATION: God's becoming man in Jesus Christ.

INDULGENCE: In the Roman Catholic Church, a remission "of the temporal punishment due to sins, the guilt of which has already been remitted." Granted only when penance is shown.

INFALLIBILITY: The authority of the Scriptures as incapable of error, or a term applied to the pope of Rome.

INSPIRATION, VERBAL: Signifying the supernatural influence upon the writers of the Scriptures by which divine authority was given their work and which places the Bible beyond error.

JUSTIFICATION: Freeing or being freed from the guilt or penalty of sin and restored to divine favor.

JUDGEMENT, JUDGEMENT DAY: The act of judging by God on the last "judgment day," when rewards and punishments are to be declared.

KISS OF PEACE, OR HOLY KISS: A religious greeting or ceremony, a kiss of welcome.

LAITY: Those members of the church who are not clergy.

LAYING ON OF HANDS: A rite of consecration and affirmation.

LITANY: Form of prayer made up of a series of petitions by the minister or priest, with congregational responses.

LITURGY, LITURGICAL: A liturgy is a prescribed form or collection of forms for public worship; in liturgical churches rite and ceremony are more prominent than the emphasis upon preaching or evangelism.

LOGOS: Christ as the Word, eternally generated from the substance of God the Father; the second Person of the Trinity.

LOVE FEAST: A common devotional meal of the early Christians, culminating in the Eucharist, and sometimes called agape.

MASS, THE: The central worship service of the Roman Catholic Church, consisting of prayers and ceremonies; sometimes the Holy Eucharist as a sacrifice.

MEDIUM: A person through whom supposed messages from the spiritual world are sent, as in Spiritualism.

METROPOLITAN: A bishop in an Eastern church who has provincial as well as diocesan powers.

MINOR ORDER: Orders below those of bishop, priest, deacon, and subdeacon (such as porters, lectors, lay readers, acolytes). Those in minor orders are not ordained, but act under a benediction from the bishop.

MODERNIST: See Fundamentalist.

MONOPHYSITISM: The doctrine that Christ had but one composite divine-human nature.

MONOTHEISM: Belief in one, and only one God, as opposed to polytheism or pantheism.

MYSTICISM: A type of religion which puts the emphasis on an immediate experience of God, a direct and intimate consciousness of divine reality, without the intermediate stages or means often thought essential.

NESTORIAN: Member of a Christian sect named after Nestorius, a fifth-century Syrian patriarch of Constantinople condemned as a heretic; still found in Turkey and Persia.

NICENE: Pertaining to Nicaea, when the Nicene Creed was adopted at the famous council of 325, settling the controversy concerning the persons of the Trinity; properly called the Niceno-Constantinopolitan Creed.

ORDINANCE: A religious rite or ceremony not considered as a sacrament.

ORTHODOXY: Belief in doctrine considered correct and sound, or holding the commonly accepted faith.

PACIFISM: Opposition to all military ideals, preparedness, war, and so on.

PATRIARCH: A bishop of highest rank, standing above metropolitans and ruling patriarchates.

PENANCE: An ecclesiastical punishment inflicted for sin, or a sacrament of the Roman Catholic Church.

PENTECOSTAL: The religious experience of conversion based upon the descent of the Holy Ghost upon the apostles at the biblical Pentecost.

PERFECTION: The complete realization of moral or spiritual possibilities in personal experience.

PIETISM: Specifically, a German Lutheran movement of the seventeenth and eighteenth centuries, in the interests of revival from a stagnant orthodoxy. Generally, a term used to designate those movements in current Christianity emphasizing the personal, spiritual, and practical rather than the institutional, formal, and intellectual aspects of faith.

PLENARY: Full, complete; a plenary council is attended by all its qualified members.

POLITY: A particular form or system of government.

PREDESTINARIAN: A believer in predestinarianism—that all events are predetermined by God and that each person's eternal destiny is fixed by divine decree.

PREMILLENIALISM: Belief that the personal visible return of Christ will precede his reign for a thousand years on earth; postmillenarians believe that the return will come at the end of the millennium.

PRESBYTERY: A church court or assembly having the ecclesiastical or spiritual rule and oversight of a district, or the district itself.

REDEMPTION: God's deliverance of man from sin and death through the sacrificial atonement of Christ.

REGENERATION: A new birth, re-creation, a radical renewal of life, or conversion.

REMISSION OF SIN: Pardon or forgiveness for sin.

REPENTANCE: Turning from a sinful to a godly life.

REPROBATION: Eternal condemnation, the fate of those not included in God's election.

REVELATION: What God makes known to men, as in Scripture.

RITUAL: Religious ceremony or its verbal form.

SABBATARIAN: One who believes that the seventh day should be observed as the Christian Sabbath.

SACERDOTAL: A term denoting a religious system in which everything is valued in relation to the ministrations of the priestly order.

SACRAMENTAL: A religious rite composed of two elements, a physical sign and a spiritual good.

SALVATION: The rescue of man from evil or guilt by God's power, that he may obtain blessedness.

SANCTIFICATION: The work of the Holy Spirit by which the believer is set free from sin and exalted to holiness of life.

SECOND COMING: The second advent of Jesus. *See* PREMILLENNIALISM.

SEE: The local seat from which a bishop, archbishop, or the Pope exercises jurisdiction.

SPEAKING IN TONGUES: *See* GLOSSOLALIA.

SUFFRAGAN BISHOP: An episcopal assistant to a diocesan bishop.

SYNOD: An ecclesiastical council either of regular standing or appointed as needed; in Presbyterian churches a body between the presbyteries and the general assembly.

TOTAL DEPRAVITY: The equivalent of original sin, every human faculty having an innate evil taint.

TONSURED: The shaved head of a person admitted to a monastic order or to holy orders.

TONGUES, GIFT OF: An ecstatic utterance induced by religious excitement.

TRANSCENDENCE: The exaltation of God above the universe and his distinctness from it.

TRANSFIGURATION: Change in form or appearance, such as the transfiguration of Jesus (Mark 9:2-10).

TRANSMUTATION: The change from one nature, substance, or form to another.

TRANSUBSTANTIATION: The doctrine that there is present in the Eucharist after consecration of the elements the substantial body and blood of Christ, with his whole soul and divinity.

TRINE IMMERSION: A form of baptism in which the candidate is immersed three successive times, in the name of the Father, Son, and Holy Ghost.

TRINITARIAN: A believer in the Trinity—that there is a union of Father, Son, and Holy Ghost in one divine nature.

UNCTION: A ceremonial anointing with oil, as in extreme unction in case of death or imminent death. (Extreme unction is now designated as "the anointing of the sick.")

UNIAT: Persons or churches acknowledging the supremacy of the pope but maintaining their own liturgies or rites.

UNITARIAN: The theology which insists upon the unity of God, denying the doctrine of the Trinity.

UNIVERSALISM: The universal fatherhood of God and the final harmony of all souls with God.

UNLEAVENED BREAD: Bread made without yeast, necessary for Jewish Passover, and often used in Christian eucharistic services.

VARUNA: Hinduism's supreme god and creator.

VEADAR: Month in the Jewish calendar which falls between Adar and Nisan on leap years.

VEHICLE: Buddhist term for a way of salvation.

VENERABLE: Anglican title for archdeacon; Catholic title for one who has reached a particular point in the process of beatification; title of honor for one of unusual sanctity, as the Venerable Bede.

VENITE: "Oh come." Latin version of Psalm 95, used frequently at Matins.

VERSICLE: Short statement in a worship service followed by a congregational or choral response.

VESTMENT: Article of clothing worn by religious officiant.

VICAR: Priest or incumbent of a parish; clergyman who serves as the deputy or substitute for another.

VOCATION: Call to serve God, in one's work and life.

VULGATE: Latin version of the Bible translated by Jerome.

WARDEN: Head of an ecclesiastical institution, or official entrusted with the temporal affairs or the protection of property in a parish.

WESTERN CHURCH: Term for Christianity in Europe or America, or for Roman Catholicism as opposed to Eastern Orthodoxy.

WHITSUNDAY: "White Sunday" or Pentecost, Christian festival on the seventh Sunday after Easter.

WORKS: New Testament term for demonstrable activity.

YAHWEH: Jewish name for the Lord.

YESHIVA: Higher Jewish school for rabbinical and talmudic study.

BIBLIOGRAPHY

GENERAL

Included in this listing are titles recommended by scholars and officials within the various denominations, and others added by the editor. They are listed in two classifications: "General," covering the whole field of the church in the United States, and "Denominational," covering the separate bodies.

Beyond this, and not included here, there are treatises, tracts, memorials, disciplines, yearbooks, theological outlines, confessions, and other statements of belief and organization obtainable from the headquarters of the denominations listed on pp. 274-82.

Ahlstrom, Sydney E. *A Religious History of the American People*. New Haven: Yale University Press, 1973.

Bach, Marcus. *Faith and My Friends*. Indianapolis: Bobbs-Merrill, 1951

———. *Report to Protestants*. Indianapolis: Bobbs-Merrill, 1953.

———. *Had You Been Born in Another Faith*. Englewood Cliff, N.J., Prentice-Hall, 1961.

Bainton, R. H. *The Church of Our Fathers*. New York: Charles Scribner's Sons, 1950.

Banks, William L. *The Black Church in the U.S.* Chicago: Moody Press, 1972.

Bates, Ernest Sutherland. *American Faith*. New York: W. W. Norton, 1957.

Brauer, J. C. *Protestantism in America*. Philadelphia: Westminster Press, 1953.

Brown, Robert M. *The Spirit of Protestantism*. New York: Oxford University Press, 1961.

Clark, Elmer T. *The Small Sects in America*. Nashville & New York: Abingdon-Cokesbury Press, 1949.

Cobb, John B. *Varieties of Protestantism*. Philadelphia: Westminister Press, 1960.

Dillenberger, John, and Welch, Claude. *Protestant Christianity*. New York: Charles Scribner's Sons, 1954.

Drummond, A. L. *The Story of American Protestantism*. Boston: Beacon Press, 1950.

Ferm, Vergilius, ed. *The American Church of Protestant Heritage*. New York: Philosophical Library, 1953.

Garrison, W. E. *The March of Faith*. New York: Harper & Brothers, 1933.

Gaustad, Edwin Scott. *Historical Atlas of Religion in America*. New York: Harper & Row, 1962.

———. *A Religious History of America*. New York: Harper & Row, 1964.

Herberg, Will. *Protestant-Catholic-Jew*. New York: Anchor Books, New York, 1955.

Hudson, W. S, *American Protestantism*. Chicago: University of Chicago Press, 1961.

———. *The Great Tradition of American Churches*. New York: Peter Smith, 1963.

———. *Religion in America*. New York: Charles Scribner's Sons, 1965.

———. *The Story of the American Church*. New York: Harper & Brothers, 1958.

Jacquet, Constant H., Jr., ed. *Yearbook of American and Canadian Churches*. (Annual). Nashville: Abingdon Press.

Johnson, D. W., and Cornell, G. W. *Punctured Preconceptions: What North American Christians Think About the Church*. New York: Friendship Press, 1972.

Landis, Benson Y. *Religion in the United States*. New York: Barnes & Noble, 1965.

Latourette, Kenneth S. *Christianity in a Revolutionare Age: the 20th Century Outside Europe*. New York: Harper & Row, 1962.

Mayer, F. E. *The Religious Bodies of America*. St. Louis: Concordia Publishing House, 1954.

Neve, J. L. *Churches and Sects of Christendom*. Blair, Nebr.: Lutheran Publishing House, 1952.

Rosten, Leo. *A Guide to the Religions of America*. St. Louis: Bethany Press, 1963.

Schaff, Philip. *The Creeds of Christendom*. New York: Harper & Brothers, 1919.

Smith, H. Shelton, Handy, Robert T., and Loetscher, Lefferts A. *American Christianity: An Historical Interpretation With Representative Documents*. 2 vols. New York: Charles Schribner's Sons, 1960-1963.

Smith, James W. *Religion in American Life*. 4 vols. Princeton, University Press, 1961.

Spence, Hartzell. *The Story of America's Religions*. Nashville: Abingdon Press, 1962.

Sperry, W. L. *Religion in America*. Boston: Beacon Press, 1963.

Stuber, Stanley I. *How We Got Our Denominations*. New York: Association Press, 1948.

Sweet, W. W. *The American Churches: An Interpretation*. Nashville & New York: Abingdon-Cokesbury Press, 1948.

———. *Religion in the Development of American Culture*. New York: Charles Scribner's Sons, 1952.

———. *The Story of Religions in America*. New York: Harper & Brothers, 1930.

Walker, Williston. *History of the Christian Church*. New York: Charles Scribner's Sons, 1959.

Whalen, William J. *Separated Brethren*. Milwaukee: Bruce Publishing Co., 1957.

Williams, J. Paul. *What Americans Believe and How They Worship*. New York: Harper & Row, 1962.

DENOMINATIONAL

ADVENTISM

Froom, Le Roy E. *The Prophetic Faith of Our Fathers.* 4 Vols. Washington D.C.: Review and Herald Publishing Assn., 1946-54.

Hasel, Gerard F. *Old Testament Theology: Basic Issues in the Current Debate.* Grand Rapids: Eerdmans, 1972.

Herndon, Booton. *The Seventh-day: The Story of the Seventh-day Adventists.* New York: McGraw-Hill Book Co., 1960.

Johnsen, Carsten. *Man-The Invisible.* Norwegian Research Council for Science and the Humanities. Oslo: Universitetsforlaget, 1971.

Maxwell, Arthur S. *Your Friends the Adventists.* Mountain View, Calif.: Pacific Publishing Assn., 1960.

Seventh-day Adventists Answer Questions on Doctrines. Washington D.C.: Review and Herald Publishing Assn., 1957.

Spalding, Arthur W. *Origin and History of Seventh-day Adventists,* 4 Vols. Washington D.C.: Review and Herald Publishing Assn., 1961.

White Ellen G. *The Desire of Ages.* Mountain View, Calif.: Pacific Press Publishing Assn., 1940.

————. *The Great Controversy Between Christ and Satan.* Mountain View, Calif.: Pacific Press Publishing Assn., 1927.

————. *The Ministry of Healing.* Washington, D.C.: Review and Herald Publishing Assn., 1909.

————. *Steps to Christ.* Washington, D.C.: Review And Herald Publishing Assn., 1908.

BAHA'I

Abdul-Bahá. *Some Answered Questions.* Wilmette, Ill.: Baha'i Publishing Trust.

Amato'l-Bahá Ruhiyyih Khanum. *The Priceless Pearl.* Wilmette, Ill.: Baha'i Publishing Trust.

Esselmont, J. E. *Bahaullah and the New Era.* Wilmette, Ill.: Baha'i Publishing Trust, 1971.

Faizi, Gloria. *The Bahai Faith: An Introduction.* Wilmette, Ill.: Baha'i Publishing Trust, 1973.

Hofman, David. *Renewal of Civilization.* Wilmette, Ill.: Baha'i Publishing Trust, 1970.

Nabil. *The Dawn Breakers.* Wilmette, Ill.: Baha'i Publishing Trust.

Shoghi Effenid. *God Passes By.* Wilmette, Ill.: Baha'i Publishing Trust.

Shohgi Effendi. *The World Order of Baha'u'llah.* Wilmette, Ill.: Baha'i Publishing Trust.

Spears, Wm. *Release the Sun.* Wilmette, Ill.: Baha'i Publishing Trust.

BAPTISTS

Armstrong, O. K. and Marjorie. *The Indomitable Baptists.* Garden City, N. Y.: Doubleday & Co., 1967.

Campbell, Alexander. *Christian Baptism with Its Antecedents and Consequences.* Bethany, Va.: A Campbell, 1852.

Cox, Norman W. *Encyclopedia of Southern Baptists.* Nashville: Broadman Press, 1958.

Maring, Norman H., and Winthrop, S. Hudson. *A Baptist Manual of Polity and Practice.* Valley Forge, Pa.: Judson Press, 1963.

Newman, A. H. *History of the Baptist Churches in the United States.* Phildelphia: American Baptists Publication Society, 1913.

Olson, Adolf. *A Centenary History.* (Baptist General Conference of America) Chicago: Baptist Conference Press, 1952.

Pelt, Owen C., and Smith, Ralph Lee. *The Story of the National Baptists.* New York: Vantage Press, 1960.

Ramaker, A. J. *The German Baptists in North America.* Cleveland: German Baptist Publication Society, 1924.

Shelley, Bruce L. *Conservative Baptists: A Story of Twentieth Century Dissent.* Denver: Conservative Baptist Theological Seminary, 1960.

Stealey, S. L. *A Baptist Treasury.* New York: Thomas Y. Crowell, 1958.

Sweet, W. W. *Religion on the American Frontier: The Baptists.* New York: Henry Holt & Co., 1931.

Torbet, R. G. *A History of the Baptists.* Valley Forge, Pa.: Judson Press, 1973.

Tull, James E. *Shapers of Baptist Thought.* Valley Forge, Pa.: Judson Press, 1972.

Vedder, H. C. *A Short History of the Baptists.* Valley Forge, Pa.: Judson Press, 1907.

BRETHREN

Bittenger, Emmert F. *Heritage and Promise.* Elgin, Ill.: Brethren Press. 1970.

Durnbaugh, Donald F. *The Brethren in Colonial America.* Elgin, Ill.: Brethren Press, 1958.

———. *European Origins of the Brethren.* Elgin, Ill.: Brethren Press 1958.

Garber, Ora W. *The Church of the Brethren.* Elgin, Ill.: Brethren Press, 1967.

Sappington, Roger E. *Brethren and Social Policys 1908-1958.* Elgin, Ill.: Brethren Press. 1961.

CHRISTIAN SCIENCE

A Century of Christian Science Healing, Boston: Christian Science Publishing Society, 1966.

Beasley, Norman. *The Cross and the Crown: The History of Christian Science.* New York: Duell, Sloan & Pearce, 1952.

Canham, Erwin D. *Commitment to Freedom: The Story of the Christian Science Monitor.* Boston: Houghton Mifflin, 1958.

———. *Science and Health with Key to the Scriptures.* Boston: Christian Science Board of Directors. Many editions.

Gottschalk, Stephen. *The Emergence of Christian Science in American Religious Life.* Berkeley: University of California Press, 1973.

DeWitt, John. *The Christian Science Way of Life.* Boston: Christian Science Publishing Society, 1971.

Leishman, Thomas. *Why I Am a Christian Scientist.* Camden, N.J. Thomas Nelson, 1958.

Peel, Robert. *Mary Baker Eddy: The Years of Discovery.* New York: Holt, Rinehart & Winston, 1966.

————. *Mary Baker Eddy: The Years of Trial.* New York: Holt, Rinehart & Winston, 1971.

————. *Christian Science: Its Encounter with American Culture.* New York: Holt, Rinehart and Winston, 1958.

CHURCH OF GOD

Brown, C. E. *When the Trumpet Sounded* (History of the Church of God of Anderson, Ind.) Anderson, Ind.: Warner Press, 1951.

Conn, Charles W. *Like a Mighty Army.* Cleveland, Tenn.: Church of God Publishing House, 1955.

Ferguson, C. W. *The New Book of Revelations.* New York: Doubleday, Doran & Co., 1929.

Forney, C. H. *History of the Churches of God.* Harrisburg, Pa.: Christian Publications, Inc., 1914.

Frodsham, S. H. *With Signs Following.* Springfield, Mo.: Gospel Publishing House, 1941.

Riggs, R. M. *The Spirit Himself.* Springfield, Mo.: Gospel Publishing House, 1949.

CHURCH OF THE NAZARENE

Redford, M. E. *The Rise of the Church of the Nazarene.* Kansas City: Nazarene Publishing House, 1951.

CHURCHES OF CHRIST

MacClenny, W. E. *Life of James O'Kelly.* Indianapolis, Ind.: United Christian Missionary Society, 1950.

Stone, B. W. *Biography of Elder Barton Warren Stone.* Cincinnati: Standard Publishing Co., 1847.

West, E. *Search for the Ancient Order.* Indianapolis, Ind.: 1951.

CHURCHES OF THE NEW JERUSALEM (SWEDENBORGIANS)

Barrett, B. F. *The Question, What Are the Doctrines of the New Church? Answered.* Germantown, Pa.: Swedenborg Publication Association, 1909.

Smythe, J. K. *Gist of Swedenborg.* Philadelphia: J. B. Lippincott Co., 1920.

Swedenborg, Emanuel. *Complete Works.* Boston: Houghton Mifflin, 1907.

DISCIPLES OF CHRIST

Beazley, George G. Jr. *The Christian Church (Disciples of Christ): An Interpretative Examination in the Cultural Context.* St. Louis: Bethany Press, 1973.

Campbell, Alexander. *Creative Freedom in Action.* 1832.

Crain, James Andrew. *The Development of Social Ideas Among the Disciples of Christ.* St. Louis: Bethany Press, 1969.

Garrison, W. E., and DeGroot, A. T. *Disciples of Christ, A History*. St. Louis: Bethany Press, 1958.

Garrison, Winifred E. *Heritage and Destiny*. St. Louis: Bethany Press, 1963.

Harrell, David Edwin, Jr. *Quest for a Christian America: The Disciples of Christ and American Society to 1866*. Nashville: The Disciples of Christ Historical Society, 1966.

Humbert, Royal, ed. *A Compend of Alexander Campbell's Theology*. St. Louis: Bethany Press, 1961.

Lair, Loren E. *The Christian Churches and Their Work*. St. Louis: Bethany Press, 1963.

Panel of Scholars. *The Renewal of Church*. St. Louis: Bethany Press, 1963.

Whitley, Oliver R. *The Trumpet Call of Reformation*. St. Louis: Bethany Press, 1963.

EASTERN CHURCHES

Bratsiotis, Panagiotis. *The Greek Orthodox Church*. Notre Dame and London: The University of Notre Dame Press, 1967.

Constantelos, Demetrios J. *The Greek Orthodox Church*. New York: The Seabury Press, 1967.

LeGuillou, M. J. *The Spirit of Eastern Orthodoxy*. New York: Hawthorn Books, 1962.

Meyendorff, John. *The Orthodox Church*. London: Darton, Longman & Todd. New York: Pantheon Books (Random House).

Schmemann, Alexander. *The Historical Road to Eastern Orthodoxy*. New York: Holt, Rinehart and Winston, 1963.

Ware, Timothy. *The Orthodox Church*. Baltimore: Penguin Books, 1963.

Zernov, Nicholas. *Eastern Christendom: A Study of the Origin and Development of the Eastern Orthodox Church*. New York: G. P. Putnam's Sons, 1961.

EPISCOPAL CHURCH

Addison, J. T. *The Episcopal Church in the United States: 1789-1831*. New York: Charles Scribner's Sons, 1951.

Chorley, E. C. *Men and Movements in the American Episcopal Church*. New York: Charles Scribner's Sons, 1946.

Damrosch, Frank, Jr. *The Faith of the Episcopal Church*. New York: Morehouse-Gorham, 1946.

DeMille, George E. *The Episcopal Church Since 1900*. New York: Morehouse-Barlow, 1955.

Manross, W. W. *A History of the American Episcopal Church*. New York: Morehouse-Gorham, 1950.

McConnell, S. D. *History of the American Episcopal Church*. Milwaukee: Morehouse Publishing Co., 1916.

Pittenger, W. Norman. *The Episcopalian Way of Life*. Englewood Cliffs, N.J.: Prentice-Hall, 1957.

Simcox, Carroll E. *Approach to the Episcopal Church*. New York: Morehouse, Barlow, 1961.

Tiffany, C. C. *A History of the Episcopal Church* (American Church History Series) New York: Charles Scribner's Sons, 1895.

Will, Theodore. *The Episcopal Church.* New York: Morehouse-Gorham, 1934.

Wilson, Frank E. *Faith and Practice.* New York: Morehouse-Gorham, 1941.

FRIENDS

Bacon, M. *Quiet Rebels.* New York: Basic Books, 1969.

Barclay, Robert. *Apology for a True Christian Divinity.* 1959.

Boulding, K. E. *Evolutionary Potential of Quakerism.* Pendle Hill pamphlet, 1964.

Brinton, H. *Quaker Education: In Theory and Practice.* Pendle Hill, 1958. Paper. *Friends for 300 Years.* Pendle Hill.

Bronner, Edwin. *American Quakers Today.* Friends World Committee, 1966.

Comfort, W. W. *The Quaker Way: Just Among Friends.* Philadelphia: American Friends Service Committee, 1968. Paper.

Cooper, C. W., ed. *Break the New Ground: Seven Essays by Contemporary Quakers.* Philadelphia: Friends World Committee, 1969.

de Hartog, J. *The Hospital.* New York: Atheneum, 1964.

Jonas, G. *On Doing Good.* New York: Charles Scribner's Sons, 1971.

Loukes, H. *Quarer Contribution.* New York: Macmillan, 1965.

West, J. *Quaker Reader.* New York: Viking Press, 1969.

JEHOVAH'S WITNESSES

Cole, Marley. *Jehovah's Witnesses. The New World Society.* New York: Vantage Press, 1955.

Jehovah's Witnesses in the Divine Purpose. New York: Watch Tower Bible & Tract Society, 1959.

Let God Be True. New York: Watch Tower Bible & Tract Society, 1946.

New World Translation of the Holy Scriptures. New York: Watch Tower Bible & Tract Society, 1961.

The Truth That Leads to Eternal Life. New York: Watch Tower Bible & Tract Society, 1968.

True Peace and Security—From What Source? New York: Watch Tower Bible & Tract Society. 1973.

JEWISH CONGREGATIONS

Agus, Jacob Bernard. *Guidepost in Modern Judaism.* New York: Bloch Publishing Co., 1954.

Bamberger, B. J. *The Story of Judaism.* New York: Union of American Hebrew Congregations, 1957.

Dimont, Max, I. *Jews, God and History.* Garden City, N. Y.: Doubleday, 1972.

Donin, Rabbi Hayim Halevy. *To Be A Jew.* New York: Basic Books, 1973.

Finkelstein, Louis. *The Jews: Their History, Culture and Religion.* New York: Harper & Brothers, 1949.

Friedlander, M. *Jewish Religion*. Shalom.

Gaer, Joseph. *Our Jewish Heritage*. New York: Holt, Rinehart and Winston, 1957.

Glazer, Nathan. *American Judaism*. Chicago: University of Chicago Press, 1957.

Hertzberg, A. *Judaism*. New York: George Braziller, 1961.

Isaacson, Rabbi Benjamin, and Wigoder, Deborah. *The International Jewish Encyclopedia*. Englewood Cliffs, N.J.: Prentice-Hall, 1973.

Jacobs, Louis. *Jewish Thought Today*. New York: Behrman, 1970.

Jewish Encyclopedia. 12 Vols. New York: Keter Publishing Co., 1974.

The Jews: Their Religion and Culture. New York: Shocken, 1970.

Karp, Abraham J. *The Jewish Way of Life*. Englewood Cliffs, N.J.: Prentice-Hall, 1962.

Levinger, Lee J. *A History of the Jews in the United States*. New York: Union of American Hebrew Congregations, 1961.

Millgram, A. E. *Jewish Yearbook*. Jewish Publications, 1971.

Pool, David de Sola. *The American Jew*. New York: Harper & Brothers, 1942.

Roth, Leon. *Judaism: A Protrait*. New York: Viking Press, 1961.

Steinberg, Milton. *Basic Judaism*. New York: Harcourt, Brace & World, 1947.

Wallach, Michael, ed. *Jewish Year Book (Annual)*. New York: Hartmore, 1970.

Wouk, Herman. *This Is My God*. Garden City, N.Y.: Doubleday, 1959.

LATTER-DAY SAINTS (MORMONS)

Anderson, Nels. *Desert Saints: The Morman Frontier in Utah*. Chicago: University of Chicago Press, 1966.

Arrington, L. J. *Great Basin Kingdom: An Economic History of the Latter-day Saints*. Cambridge: Harvard University Press, 1958.

Berrett, W. E. *The Restored Church*. Salt Lake City: Deseret Book Company, 1969.

Brodie, F. M. *No Man Knows My History: The Life of Joseph Smith*. New York: Alfred A. Knopf, 1945.

Hill, M. S., and Allen, J. B., eds. *Mormonism and American Culture*. New York: Harper & Row, 1972.

Hinckley, G. B. *What of the Mormons*. Salt Lake City: Deseret Book Company, 1970.

Howells, R. S. *The Mormon Story*. Salt Lake City: Bookcraft, 1963.

Mullen, Robert. *The Latter-day Saints*. Garden City, N. Y.: Doubleday, 1966.

Nibley, Hugh. *An Approach to the Book of Mormon*. Salt Lake City: Council of the Twelve Apostles of the Church of Jesus Christ of Latter-day Saints, 1957.

O'Dea, Thomas F. *The Mormons*. Chicago: University of Chicago Press, 1957.

Richards, F. D., and Little, J. A. *A Compendium of the Doctrines of the Gospel.* Salt Lake City: Deseret Book Co., 1925.

Richards, Legrande, *Marvelous Work and a Wonder.* Salt Lake City: Deseret Book Co. 1972.

Roberts, B. H. *A Comprehensive History of The Church of Jesus Christ of Latter-day Saints.* Provo: Brigham Young University Press, 1965.

Smith, Joseph. *The Book of Mormon.* Salt Lake City: Deseret Book Co. 1972.

———. *The Doctrine and Covenants.* Salt Lake City: Deseret Book Co. 1971.

———. *The Pearl of Great Price.* Salt Lake City: Deseret Book Co. 1971.

———. *Essential in Church History.* Salt Lake City: Deseret Book Co. 1973.

Talmage, James E. *Articles of Faith.* Salt Lake City: Deseret Book Co. 1971.

West, R. B. *Kingdom of the Saints: The Story of Brigham Young and the Mormons.* New York: Viking Press, 1957.

LUTHERANS

Allbeck, Willard D. *Studies in the Lutheran Confessions.* Philadelphia: Fortress Press, 1968.

Arden, G. Everett. *Augustana Heritage.* Rock Island: Augustana Press, 1963.

Bainton, Roland. *Here I Stand.* Nashville & New York: Abingdon-Cokesbury Press, 1950.

Beck, Victor E. *Why I Am A Lutheran.* New York: Thomas Nelson & Sons, 1956.

Bergendoff, Conrad. *The Church of the Lutheran Reformation.* St. Louis: Concordia Publishing House, 1967.

Bodensieck, Julius, ed. *The Encyclopedia of the Luthern Church.* Philadelphia: Fortress Press, 1965.

Dillenberger, John, ed. *Martin Luther: Selections From His Writings.* Garden City, N.Y.: Doubleday, 1961.

Ebeling, Gerhard. *Luther: An Introduction to His Thought.* Philadelphia: Fortress Press, 1970.

Fendt, E. C., ed. *What Lutherans Are Thinking.* Columbus: Wartburg Press, 1947.

Ferm, Vergilius. *Crisis in American Lutheran Theology.* New York: Century Co., 1927.

Kerr, H. T., ed. *A Compend of Luther's Theology.* Philadelphia: Westminster Press, 1943 (paperback, 1966).

Lowe, Ralph W. *The Lutheran Way of Life.* Englewood Cliffs, N.J.: Prentice-Hall, 1966.

Nelson, E. Clifford. *Lutheranism in North America: 1914-1970.* Minneapolis: Augsburg Publishing House, 1972.

Neve, H. T., and Anderson, B. A., eds. *The Maturing of American Lutheranism.* Minneapolis: Augsburg Pub. House, 1968.

Neve, J. L. *Introduction to the Symbolical Books of the Lutheran Church.* Columbus: Lutheran Book Concern, 1926.

Sasse, Hermann. *Here We Stand,* trans. by T. Tappert. New York: Harper & Brothers, 1938.

Scherer, James A. *Mission and Unity in Lutheranism.* Philadelphia: Fortress Press, 1969.

Schlink, Edmund. *Theology of the Lutheran Confessions.* Philadelphia: Muhlenberg Press, 1961.

Schmidt, John. *The Lutheran Confessions: Their Value and Meaning.* Philadelphia: Muhlenberg Press, 1956.

Swihart, Altman K. *Luther and the Lutheran Church, 1483-1960.* New York: Philosophical Library, 1960.

Tappert, Theodore G., ed. *The Book of Concord: The Confessions of the Evangelical Lutheran Church.* Philadelphia: Muhlenberg Press, 1959.

———. *Lutheran Confessional Theology in America 1840-1880.* (Library of Protestant Thought) New York: Oxford University Press, 1972.

Vajta, Vilmos, ed. *Church in Fellowship. Vol. 1, Pupit and Altar Fellowship Among Lutheran Churches in Europe and North America.* Minneapolis: Augsburg Publishing House, 1963.

Watson, Philip S. *Let God Be God!* Philadelphia: Muhlenberg Press, 1948.

Wentz, Abdel Ross. *A Basic History of Lutheranism in America.* Philadelphia: Fortress Press, 1964.

———. *The Lutheran Church in American History.* Philadelphia: United Lutheran Publication House, 1933.

Wentz, Frederick K. *Lutherans in Concert.* Philadelphia: Fortress Press, 1969.

Wolf, R. C. *Documents of Lutheran Unity in America.* Philadelphia: Fortress Press, 1966.

MENNONITES

Bender, Harold S. *Conrad Grebel, The Founder of the Swiss Brethren.* Scottdale, Pa.: Herald Press, 1971.

———. *The Mennonite Encyclopedia.* 4 vols. Scottdale, Pa.: Herald Press, 1955-59.

van Braght, T. J. *The Bloody Theater or Martyrs Mirror.* Scottdale, Pa.: Herald Press, 1951 (Original Dutch, 1660).

Dyck, Cornelius J., ed. *Introduction to Mennonite History.* Scottdale, Pa.: Herald Press, 1972.

Hershberger, Guy F. *War, Peace and Nonresistance.* Scottdale, Pa.: Herald Press. 1969.

———. *The Recovery of the Anabaptist Vision.* Scottsdale, Pa.: Herald Press, 1957.

Mennonite Confession of Faith. Scottdale, Pa.: Herald Press, 1968.

Smith, C. H. *The Story of the Mennonites.* Newton, Kan.: Mennonite Publication Office, 1957.

METHODISTS

Armstrong, James. *United Methodist Primer.* Nashville: Tidings, 1972.

Asbury, Francis. *Journals and Letters*, ed. by Elmer T. Clark. Nashville and New York: Abingdon-Cokesbury Press, 1958.

Book of Discipline of the United Methodist Church. Nashville: Abingdon Press, 1972.

Bucke, Emory S., ed. *History of American Methodism*. Nashville: Abingdon Press, 1964.

Carter, Henry. *The Methodist Heritage*. Nashville and New York: Abingdon-Cokesbury Press, 1952.

Clark, Elmer; Potts, J. Manning; and Payton, Jacob S. *The Journals and Letters of Francis Asbury*. Nashville: Abingdon Press, 1958.

Colaw, Emerson. *Beliefs of a United Methodist Christian*. Nashville: Tidings, 1972.

Harmon, Nolan B. *Understanding the Methodist Church*. Nashville: Abingdon Press, 1974.

Kennedy, Gerald H. *The Methodist Way of Life*. Englewood Cliffs, N.J.: Prentice-Hall, 1958.

Kirkpatrick, Dow, ed. *The Doctrine of the Church*. (Oxford Institute on Methodist Theological Studies, 1962.) Nashville: Abingdon Press, 1964.

Methodist Church (Membership Manual). Nashville and New York: Abingdon-Cokesbury Press, 1940.

Moore, John M. *The Long Road to Methodist Union*. Nashville and New York: Abingdon-Cokesbury Press, 1943.

Norwood, Frederick A. *The Story of American Methodism*. Nashville: Abingdon Press, 1975.

Stokes, Mack B. *Major United Methodist Beliefs*. Nashville: Abingdon Press, 1972.

Sweet, W. W. *Methodism in American History*. Nashville: Abingdon Press, 1954.

Tigert, John James. *A Constitutional History of American Episcopal Methodism*. Nashville: Publishing House of the M.E. Church, South, 1916. Scan and sample.

Tuell, Jack Marvin. *The Organization of the United Methodist Church*. Nashville: Abingdon, 1972.

Moravians

deSchweinitz, E. A. *The Story of Unitas Fratum*. Bethlehem, Pa.: Moravian Book Shop, 1885.

Hamilton, J. T., and Hamilton, K. G. *History of the Moravian Church*. (The Renewed Unitas Fratum from 1722-1957) Bethlehem, Pa.: Interprovincial Board of Christian Education. 1967.

Schattschneider, A. W. *Through Five Hundred Years*. Interprovincial Board of Christian Education. 1966.

Weinlick, John R. *The Moravian Church Through The Ages*. Bethlehem, Pa.: Interprovisional Board of Christian Education. 1966.

Negro Churches

Frazier, E. Franklin. *The Negro Church in America*. New York: Schocken Books, 1961.

Mays, Benjamin E., and Nicholson, Joseph W. *The Negro's Church.*
(Religion in America Series) New York: Russell, 1969.
——. *The Negro's God as Reflected in His Literature.* New York:
Russell, 1968.
Pelt, O. D., and Smith, Ralph L. *The Story of the National Baptists.*
New York: Vantage Press, 1960.

OLD CATHOLIC CHURCHES

Anson, Peter, *Bishops at Large.* London: Faber & Faber, 1964.
Moss, C. B. *The Old Catholic Movement.* New York: Morehouse, 1964.
Pruter, Fr. Karl. *A History of the Old Catholic Church.* Scottsdale,
Ariz.: St. Willibrord's Press. 1973.

PENTECOSTALISTS

Bennett, Dennis J. *Nine O'clock in the Morning.* Plainfield, N.J.: Logos
International, 1970.
Clark, E. T. *The Small Sects in America.* Nashville and New York:
Abingdon-Cokesbury Press, 1949.
Conn, Charles. *Like a Mighty Army.* Cleveland, Tenn.: Pathway Press,
1955.
Cunningham, Robert C. *Filled With the Spirit.* Springfield, Mo.: Gospel
Publishing House, 1972.
Durasoff, Steve. *Bright Wind of the Spirit.* Englewood Cliffs, N.J.:
Prentice-Hall, 1972.
Frodsham, S. H. *With Signs Following.* Springfield, Mo.: Gospel Pub-
lishing House, 1946.
Gaver, Jessyca Russell. *Pentecostalism.* New York: Universal Publish-
ing and Distribution Corp., 1971.
Gee, Donald. *Concerning Spiritual Gifts.* Springfield, Mo.: Gospel Pub-
lishing House, 1972.
Harper, Michael. *As At the Beginning: The Twentieth Century Pente-
costal Revival.* Plainfield, N.J.: Logos International, 1971.
Harris, Ralph W. *Spoken by the Spirit.* Springfield, Mo.: Gospel Pub-
lishing House, 1973.
Hollenweger, Walter. *The Pentecostals: The Charismatic Movement in
the Churches.* Minneapolis: Augsburg Publishing House, 1972.
Menzies, William W. *Anointed to Serve, The Story of the Assemblies
of God.* Springfield, Mo.: Gospel Publishing House, 1971.
Moon, Elmer Louis. *The Pentecostal Church* (A history of the Pente-
costal Church of God of America, Inc.) New York: Carlton Press,
Inc., 1966.
Nichol, John Thomas. *The Pentecostals.* Plainfield, N.J.: Logos Inter-
national, 1971.
Riggs, R. M. *The Spirit Himself.* Springfield, Mo.: Gospel Publishing
House, 1949.

Sherrill, John. *They Speak With Other Tongues*. Old Tappan, N.J.: Fleming H. Revell, 1964.

Synan, Vinson. *The Holiness-Pentecostal Movement in the United States*. Grand Rapids: Eerdmans Publishing Co., 1972.

———. *The Old-Time Power*. Franklin Springs, Ga., Advocate Press, 1973.

PRESBYTERIANS

Armstrong, Maurice W.; Loetscher, Lefferts A.; and Anderson, Charles A. *The Presbyterian Enterprise*. (Presbyterian Historical Society Publications, 1). Philadelphia: The Westminster Press, 1956.

Briggs, C. A. *American Presbyterianism*. New York: Charles Scribner's Sons, 1885.

Calvin, John. *Institutes of the Christian Religion*. Philadelphia: The Westminster Press, 1960.

Drury, C. M. *Presbyterian Panorama*. Philadelphia: The Westminster Press, 1952.

Gillett, E. H. *History of the Presbyterian Church in the United States of America*. Philadelphia: The Westminster Press, 1864.

Jamison, Wallace N. *The United Presbyterian Story . . . 1858-1958*. Pittsburgh: Geneva Press, 1958.

Loetscher, Lefferts A. *A Brief History of the Presbyterians*. Philadelphia: The Westminster Press, 1958.

———. *The Broadening Church*. Philadelphia: University of Pennsylvania Press, 1954.

Mackay, John A. *The Presbyterian Way of Life*. Englewood Cliffs, N.J.: Prentice-Hall, 1960.

Reed, R. C. *History of the Presbyterian Churches of the World*. Philadelphia: The Westminster Press, 1905.

Slosser, Gaius J., ed. *They Seek A Country. The American Presbyterians*. New York: Macmillan, 1955.

Thompson, Ernest Trice. *Presbyterians in the South*. Richmond: John Knox Press. vol. I, 1963; vols. II & III, 1973.

Thompson, R. E. *A History of the Presbyterian Churches in the United States*. (American Church History Series, Vo. V1). New York: Charles Scribner's Sons, 1895.

Trinterud, Leonard J. *The Forming of an American Tradition*. Philadelphia: The Westminster Press, 1949.

REFORMED BODIES

Berts, H. *The Christian Reformed Church in North America*. Grand Rapids: Eastern Avenue Book Store, 1923.

Boettner, Loraine. *Studies in Theology*. Grand Rapids: Eerdmans Publishing Co., 1941.

Brown, W. D. *History of the Reformed Church in America*. New York: Board of Publication & Bible School Work of the Reformed Church in America, 1928.

Corwin, E. T., *et al. A History of the Reformed Church, Dutch, the Reformed Church, German, and the Moravian Church in the United States.* (American Church History Series, Vol. VIII). New York: Charles Scribner's Sons, 1895.

Hoekema, H. *The Protestant Reformed Churches in America.* Grand Rapids: Eerdman's Publishing Co., 1936.

The Word of God and the Reformed Faith. (American Calvinistic Conference) Grand Rapids: Baker Book House, 1942.

ROMAN CATHOLIC CHURCH

Abbott, Walter M., S.J., ed. *Documents of Vatican II.* New York: American Press, 1966.

Attwater, Donald., ed. *Catholic Dictionary.* New York Macmillan, 1958.

Catholic Almanac. Published annually by Our Sunday Visitor, Huntington, Ind.

Ellis, John Tracy. *American Catholicism.* Garden City, N.Y.: Image Books, 1965.

Greenwood, John., ed. *Handbook of the Catholic Faith.* Garden City, N.Y.: Image Books, 1956.

Hughes, Phillip. *A Popular History of the Catholic Church.* Garden City, N.Y.: Image Books, 1954.

Kung, Hans. *The Church.* New York: Sheed & Ward, 1967.

New Catechism: Catholic Faith for Adults. New York: Herder and Herder, 1967.

New Catholic Encyclopedia. New York: McGraw-Hill Book Co., 1967.

O'Brien, David. *The Renewal of American Catholicism.* New York: Oxford University Press, 1972.

Official Catholic Directory. New York: P. J. Kenedy & Sons (annual).

Welch, Claude. *The Reality of the Church.* New York: Charles Scribner's Sons, 1958.

SPIRITUALISTS

Bach, Marcus. *They Have Found a Faith.* Indianapolis: Boobs-Merrill, 1946.

Braden, Chas. S. *These Also Believe.* New York: Macmillan, 1949.

Graebner, Theodore T. *Spiritism.* St. Louis: Concordia Publishing House, 1919.

Hill, J. A. *Spiritualism: Its History, Phenomena and Doctrine.* New York: Doubleday, Doran & Co., 1919.

Leaf, H. *What Is This Spiritualism?* New York: Doubleday, Doran & Co., 1919.

The Spiritualist Manual. Washington, D. C.: National Spiritualist Assn. of the United States of America, 1944.

UNITARIAN-UNIVERSALIST

Cassara, Ernest. *Hosea Ballou.* Boston: Beacon Press, 1961.

———. *Universalism In America.* Boston: Beacon Press, 1971.

Darling, Edward. *They Cast Long Shadows*. Boston: Beacon Press, 1971.

Marshall, George. *Challenge of a Liberal Faith*. New York: Pyramid Publications, 1971.

Mendlesohn, Jack. *Channing: The Reluctant Radical*. Boston: Little, Brown, 1971.

Parke, David., ed. *The Epic of Unitarianism*. Boston: Beacon Press, 1957.

Robinson, Elmo. *The Story of American Universalism*. New York: Exposition Press, 1970.

Scott, Clinton Lee. *The Universalist Church of America*. Boston: Beacon Press, 1957.

Wilbur, Earl Morse. *A History of Unitarianism*. New York: Cambridge University Press, 1952.

———. *Our Unitarian Heritage*. Boston: Beacon Press, 1925.

Williams, George H. *American Universalism*. Boston: Beacon Press, 1971.

Wright, Conrad. *The Beginnings of Unitarianism in America*. Boston: Beacon Press, 1955.

———. *The Liberal Christians*. Boston: Beacon Press, 1970.

———. *Three Prophets of Religious Liberalism*. Boston: Beacon Press, 1961.

UNITED CHURCH OF CHRIST

Atkins, G. G. *History of American Congregationalism*. Boston: Pilgrim Press, 1942.

Burton, C. E. *Manual of the Congregational and Christian Churches*. Boston: Pilgrim Press, 1936.

Horstman, J. H. E., and Wernecke, H. H. *Through Four Centuries*. St. Louis: Eden Publishing House, 1938.

Horton, Douglas. *The United Church of Christ*. New York: Thomas Nelson & Sons, 1962.

Williams, D. D., and Shinn, R. L. *We Believe: An Interpretation of the United Church Statement of Faith*. New York: United Church Press, 1966.

UNITY SCHOOL OF CHRISTIANITY

Bach, Marcus. *The Unity Way of Life*. Lee's Summit, Mo.: Unity Books, 1972.

Cady, H. Emilie. *Lessons in Truth*. Lee's Summit, Mo.: Unity Books, 1896.

D'Andrade, Hugh. *Herald of the New Age*. New York: Harper & Row, 1974.

Fillmore, Charles R. *The Adventure Called Unity*. Lee's Summit, Mo.: Unity Books, 1971.

———. *Dynamics for Living*. Lee's Summit, Mo.: Unity Books, 1967.

Freeman, J. D. *The Story of Unity*. Lee's Summit, Mo.: Unity Books, 1972.

———. *The Household of Faith*. Lee's Summit, Mo.: Unity Books, 1951.

INDEX

Friends World Committee for
Consultation, 147
Frobisher, Martin, 130
Froelich, S. H., 29
Fundamental Methodist Church,
195
Fundamentalist Fellowship, 49

General Association of Regular
Baptist Churches, 53
General Assembly of the Presby-
terian Church in the Confederate
States of America, 221
General Baptists, 41, 52
General Church of the New Jeru-
salem, 112
General Conference in England
(Swedenborgian), 112
General Conference Mennonite
Church, 180
General Conference of Seventh-
Day Adventists, 20
General Conference of the Evan-
gelical Baptist Church, Inc., 54
General Convention of the New
Jerusalem in the U.S.A., 112
General Council (Lutheran), 167
General Council of Congregational
Churches, 113
General Council of the Congrega-
tional Christian Churches, 261
General Council of the Italian
Pentecostal Assemblies of God,
78
General Six-Principle Baptists, 54
General Synod (Lutheran), 167
German Baptist Brethren, 65
German Baptist Brethren (Dun-
kards), 60
German Baptists, 56
German Evangelical Church As-
sociation of Ohio, 264
German Evangelical Lutheran
Synod of Missouri, Ohio, and
Other States, 175
German Iowa Synod, 167
German Reformed Church, 264
German United Evangelical Synod
of the East, 264
Gibbons, Archbishop, 238
Grace Group, 67
Graves, James Robinson, 54

Great Awakening, the, 220, 262
Great Sobor, the, 126
Greek Archdiocese of North and
South America, 124
Greek (Orthodox) Archdiocese of
North and South America, 124
Gregory of Nazianzus, 216
Gregory the Illuminator, 31
Griswold, Bishop A. V., 132
Gruber, Eberhardt Ludwig, 24
Gul, Archbishop Gerard, 207
Gurney, Joseph John, 144, 149

Hadassah, 160
Hampton Institute, 260
Hands of the Cause, 34
Hanukkah, 158
Hard Shell (Baptist), 57
Harmon, Ellen, 19
Hasidic orthodoxy, 161
Hawaweeny, Bishop Raphael, 123
Hazaad Harishon, 163
Heck, Barbara, 185
Heidelberg Catechism, 231, 232,
265
Helwys, Thomas, 52
Henry VIII, 177
Herford, R. T., 157
Herr, John, 182
Hicks, Elias, 143
Hicksites, 144
Hinayana Buddhism, 74
Hobart, Bishop J. H., 132
Hoffman, George W., 74
Holdeman, John, 179
Holiness Church, 89
Holiness Church of Christ, 105
Holiness Methodist Church, 136
Holy Apostolic and Catholic
Church of the East (Assyrians),
124
Holy Church of North Carolina,
268
Holy Church of North Carolina
and Virginia, 268
Holy Club, the, 183
Holy Eastern Orthodox Greek
Catholic Church, 125
Holy Orthodox Church in Amer-
ica (Eastern Catholic and Apos-
tolic), 125

Holy Synod of the Orthodox
Church in America, 126
Holy Ukranian Autocephalic Or-
thodox Church, 29
Holy Ukranian Autocephalic
Church in Exile, 129
Hooker, Thomas, 259
House of David, 149
House of God, Which is the
Church of the Living God, the
Pillar and Ground of the Truth,
Inc., 111
Howell, Elder James R., 197
Hudson, C. H., 21
Huguenots, 218
Hungarian Reformed Church in
America, 234
Huss, John, 199
Hutchinson, Anne, 259
Hutter, Joseph, 180
Hutteran Brethren, 180

Iakovos, Archbishop, 124
Ignatius, 117, 236
Ignatius of Loyola, 237
Independent African Methodist
Episcopal Church, 195
Independent Assemblies of God
(International) 150
Independent Christian Church of
Gloucester, 254
Independent churches, 151
Independent Episcopal Churches,
23
Independent Fundamental
Churches of America, 152
Independent Fundamental Meth-
odist Church, 195
Inner Light, 146
International Association for Lib-
eral Christianity and Religious
Freedom, 254
International Bible Students, 154
International Church of the Four-
square Gospel, 152
International Council of Christian
Churches, 62, 227
International General Assembly of
Spiritualists, 249
International Humanist and Ethical
Union, 25

International Pentecostal Assem-
blies, 210
International Religious Congress,
252
Islam, 202
Islamic Centers (in U.S.A.), 202
Italian Christian Churches of
North America, 78

Jacob, Henry, 258
Jacobite Apostolic Church, 207
Jacobite Syrian Churches, 207
James, Fannie Brooks, 116
Jarratt, Devereux, 185
Jehovah's Witnesses, 153
Jerome of Prague, 199
Jesuits, 237, 240
Jewish congregations, 157
Jewish Institute of Religion, 160
Job, (Russian Patriarch), 126
John XXIII, Pope, 238
Joint Synod of Wisconsin, 167
Joliet, 237
Jones, Abner, 107
Jones, C. P., 85
Judge, William Q., 251

Kelley Brethren, 70
King David's Spiritual Temple of
Truth Association, 204
King, Samuel, 228
Knorr, Nathan H., 156
Knott, Missal, the 207
Knox, John, 166, 218
Koran, the, 202
Korteniemi, Solomon, 174
Krimmer Mennonite Brethren, 181
Krishnamurti, Jeddu, 251

Laestadius, Lars Levi, 174
Lambeth Quadrilateral on Church
Unity, 132
Landmann, Barbara, 25
Landmark Baptists, 54
Landmarkers, 45
Larger and Shorter Cathechisms
(Presbyterian), 219
Lashley, James Francis Augustine,
206
Laval, Bishop, 237
Law, William, 183
Lawson, R. C., 105

313

DATE DUE

MAR 1 7 1980	MAY 0 9 1990	
MAR 9 1982		
MAR 2 2 1982		
KULL DEC 1 9 1983	Rec'd	
MAY 2 1985		
NOV 1 1988		
MAR 2 9 1989		
APR 1 9 1989		
DEC 0 1 1989		